The State and the Unions

STUDIES IN ECONOMIC HISTORY AND POLICY
THE UNITED STATES IN THE TWENTIETH CENTURY

Edited by
Louis Galambos and Robert Gallman

Other books in the series:

Peter D. McClelland and Alan L. Magdovitz: *Crisis in the making: the political economy of New York State since 1945*
Hugh Rockoff: *Drastic measures: a history of wage and price controls in the United States*
William N. Parker: *Europe, America, and the wider world: essays on the economic history of Western capitalism*
Richard H. K. Vietor: *Energy policy in America since 1945: a study of business–government relations*
Leonard S. Reich: *GE, AT&T, and the making of American industrial research*

The State and the Unions
Labor Relations, Law, and the Organized Labor Movement in America, 1880–1960

CHRISTOPHER L. TOMLINS

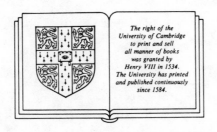

The right of the
University of Cambridge
to print and sell
all manner of books
was granted by
Henry VIII in 1534.
The University has printed
and published continuously
since 1584.

CAMBRIDGE UNIVERSITY PRESS
Cambridge
London   New York   New Rochelle
Melbourne   Sydney

Published by the Press Syndicate of the University of Cambridge
The Pitt Building, Trumpington Street, Cambridge CB2 1RP
32 East 57th Street, New York, NY 10022, USA
10 Stamford Road, Oakleigh, Melbourne 3166, Australia

First published 1985
Reprinted 1986

Printed in the United States of America

Library of Congress Cataloging in Publication Data
Tomlins, Christopher L., 1951–
The state and the unions.
1. Trade-unions – Law and legislation – United
States – History. 2. Labor laws and legislation –
United States – History. 3. Trade-unions – United
States – History. 4. Collective bargaining – United
States – History. I. Title.
KF3389.T6   1985   344.73'018'09   85-414
ISBN 0-521-25840-5   347.3041809
ISBN 0-521-31452-6 (pbk)

FOR GERRY TOMLINS AND
FOR DOUG DOUGLAS

Contents

Editors' preface

Historians of labor and modern labor policy have long agreed that the New Deal decade of the 1930s witnessed a transformation of the legal and political context of the U.S. labor movement. For the most part, scholars have stressed the benefits that accrued to workers and their unions – especially the new industrial organizations – from New Deal legislation, court decisions, and the actions of federal administrative bodies. Christopher L. Tomlins shifts the balance in this bold revisionist study, identifying important long-term costs to labor arising out of the new system created by the National Labor Relations Act of 1935. He shows that the support the unions received from the government came at a high price – too high by his reckoning. Gradually, the National Labor Relations Board restricted the freedom of unions in the interest of the health of the national economy, as perceived by the Board. The Taft-Hartley Act of 1947, he concludes, merely made concrete relationships that had already been fully defined by the NLRB. As Tomlins demonstrates, the innovations of the thirties transformed labor's traditional relationship to the political and legal systems. He describes in detail the manner in which those relationships had developed in the nineteenth and early twentieth centuries and explains why the events of those years warranted labor's suspicion of partisan politics and governmental regulations.

Because the author provides a fresh synthesis of labor–government relations and because he achieves both breadth of analysis and depth of research, we are pleased to add this volume to the growing series of *Studies in Economic History and Policy: The United States in the Twentieth Century*. This is the first volume in the series to deal directly with labor. We hope that there will be many more and that they will strive to meet the standards for research and interpretation set by this pathbreaking institutional history.

Louis Galambos
Professor of History
The Johns Hopkins University

Robert E. Gallman
Kenan Professor of Economics
and History
The University of North Carolina

Preface

Writing in 1926, the economist and labor relations expert William M. Leiserson noted that over the previous twenty-five years an important change had overtaken the study of labor and labor affairs in America. At the turn of the century, students had concentrated their attention on a massive and growing "labor problem" which they saw arising from rapid industrialization and mass immigration. They had identified their task as the discovery of the roots of the problem and the popularization of holistic solutions—the Golden Rule, the Single Tax, socialism. This approach, Leiserson argued, was subsequently found to be wrong-headed. "It was an abstraction, based upon the assumption that employees, owners, employers, and investors could be classified into two more or less mechanical forces, Labor and Capital, between which friction and conflict developed." Students intent on a properly scientific approach had therefore turned away from such simplistic classifications. "Scientific study of labor questions today . . . is directed rather at understanding the nature of the relationship between employers, wage-earners, and the public, and finding the methods by which these labor relations may be organized, administered, and adjusted to the satisfaction of all concerned."[1]

Leiserson was describing the origins of the theory of labor and industrial relations now known as "industrial pluralism." As Leiserson's description indicates, industrial pluralism was predicated on a denial of the proposition that the interests of employers and workers were necessarily incompatible. Pluralists recognized that conflicts of interest arose in the employment relationship, but they saw these as discrete, and hence susceptible to adjustment, rather than as inherent in the nature of employment itself. Assuming that all conflict could be managed, pluralists sought to encourage the development of mechanisms, notably collective bargaining, whereby this could be achieved in practice. The result would be a democracy of industry.

In the forty years after Leiserson broached the topic in 1926, indus-

---

1. William M. Leiserson, "Labor Relations" (unpublished book manuscript), ii-iii, and Chapter One, 12-13. In *Papers of William M. Leiserson* (State Historical Society of Wisconsin, Madison, Wisconsin), Box 52. [Hereinafter referred to as *Leiserson Papers.*]

trial pluralism achieved an extraordinary hegemony over American labor relations theory and practice.[2] George W. Brooks of Cornell University confirmed that ascendancy in 1961 in an address before the fourteenth annual meeting of the Industrial Relations Research Association. Drawing to his audience's attention the "astonishing degree of unanimity" which characterized contemporary discussions of industrial and labor relations, Brooks noted that pluralist assumptions pervaded both the practices of management and unions and the substance and administration of labor relations law and public policy. "Almost all the articulate members of the community," said Brooks, "now accept the same objectives in industrial relations, variously called maturity, industrial stability, responsibility, or statesmanship." So complete was the accord, indeed, that history, like ideology, had finally come to an end, leaving industrial pluralists to bask in the warm glow of a peculiarly whiggish scholarship which celebrated the rapprochement of organized labor and capital by interpreting the major events of American labor history "only in the light of how they contributed to (or delayed)" the fruition of America's unique industrial relations system. "As nearly as I am able to discern," Brooks concluded, "the relevance of labor history to industrial relations is negligible or nonexistent."[3]

Twenty years on, the self-congratulatory complacency which so discouraged George Brooks in 1961 is fast disappearing. The material foundations upon which the hegemonic pluralist consensus was built no longer exist, as "give-back" bargaining and management repudiation of labor contracts attests. As these conditions have altered, so there has appeared alongside conventional labor relations theory the beginnings of a critical analysis of that theory and of the practices and public policies which it informs. Historians and others have rediscovered substance in the conceptual categories of historical materialism and class analysis which the pluralists dismissed.[4] Applying them to the study of labor relations law and practice, they have argued that pluralist accounts of the objects of that discourse misrepresent reality. Industrial democracy, purportedly the keystone of the postwar industrial relations

2. See Katherine Stone, "The Post-War Paradigm in American Labor Law," *Yale Law Journal*, 90, 7 (June 1981), 1509–80.
3. George W. Brooks, "The Relevance of Labor History to Industrial Relations," *Industrial Relations Research Assocation Publications*, 28, Proceedings of the Fourteenth Annual Meeting (Madison, Wisconsin, 1962), 206–13.
4. See, for example, David Montgomery, *Workers' Control in America: Studies in the History of Work, Technology and Labor Struggles* (New York, 1979), and Karl E. Klare, "Labor Law as Ideology: Toward a New Historiography of Collective Bargaining Law," *Industrial Relations Law Journal*, 4 (1981), 450–82.

system, has proven to be highly vulnerable at all times to the pursuit of industrial "stability." The legitimacy of collective bargaining has been conditioned by state institutions on its capacity to be an effective means to higher productivity and efficient capital accumulation.

The contingency which critics find in contemporary labor relations law and practices is hardly a new phenomenon. Rather, as I show in this book, the contingent legitimacy of collective labor action has been a constant theme of the development, over the last hundred years, of a corporate capitalist polity in the United States. It is a theme deeply embedded in that polity's legal and political ideologies.

My analysis, unlike that of some earlier revisionists, is not founded on a conspiratorial model of political and legal decision making, in which all outcomes consciously serve the interests of identifiable business elites.[5] Nicos Poulantzas, Fred Block, and others have in recent years convincingly demonstrated the theoretical inadequacies of such an instrumentalist approach,[6] and the material I present here amply confirms, I think, Block's contention that the actions of "state-managers" – whether nineteenth-century judges or twentieth-century labor relations bureaucrats – owe quite as much to their concern for their own institutional power and prestige as to the lobbying initiatives of businessmen. In particular, there is little evidence that corporate capital, even its liberal wing, engineered federal endorsement of collective bargaining in the 1930s in order to achieve the "incorporation" of the American working class. But rejection of instrumentalist explanations of state action does not entail the further conclusion that the state is in some formalist sense "autonomous" of the prevailing economy. Historically, state institutions have escaped political and ideological constraints arising from private capital's strategic influence over investment, output, and employment only in rather exceptional circumstances.[7] Even then, the very form and structure of the state, and of the law which is the

---

5. See, for example, G. William Domhoff, *The Higher Circle: The Governing Class in America* (New York, 1971); Ronald Radosh and Murray N. Rothbard, editors, *A New History of Leviathan: Essays on the Rise of the Corporate State* (New York, 1972).
6. Nicos Poulantzas, *Political Power and Social Classes* (London, 1973); Fred Block, "The Ruling Class Does Not Rule," *Socialist Revolution*, 33 (1977), 6–28, and "Beyond Relative Autonomy: State Managers as Historical Subjects," in Ralph Miliband and John Saville, editors, *Socialist Register, 1980* (London, 1980), 227–42. See also Theda Skocpol, "Political Response to Capitalist Crisis: Neo-Marxist Theories of the State and the Case of the New Deal," *Politics and Society*, 10, 2 (1980), 155–201.
7. See Charles E. Lindblom, *The Policy-Making Process* (Englewood Cliffs, New Jersey, 1980), and *Politics and Markets* (New York, 1977). In 1976 Poulantzas wrote that in the long run the capitalist state "can only correspond to the political interests of the dominant class or classes." See his "The Capitalist State," *New Left Review*, 95 (1976), 72.

state's language, has continued to exhibit an "essential identity" with the essence of capitalism – the securing of profit through the production and exchange of commodities – sufficient to ensure that even those courses of action consciously chosen and pursued by state managers out of institutional self-interest, or out of idealistic concern for the public interest, courses of action demonstrably damaging to the interests of particular capitalists, will in the long run exhibit an overall bias toward reproduction of the political-economic status quo.[8] Indeed, it is precisely this historic homology of legal form and commodity form underpinning the capitalist state that gives it the capacity to take action which does not necessarily accord with the interests of particular capitalists and yet meet the needs of the greater capitalist system. As Isaac Balbus has put it, "the autonomy of the Law from the preferences of even the most powerful social actors (the members of the capitalist class) is not an obstacle to, but rather a prerequisite for, the capacity of the Law to contribute to the reproduction of the overall conditions that make capitalism possible, and thus its capacity to serve the interests of capital as a *class*."[9] It is with this explanation of the state's "relative autonomy" in mind that I examine the evolution of the relationship between the state and the unions over the last hundred-odd years.

Like Gaul, this book is divided in three parts. Part One addresses the transformation of the American political economy brought about in the post–Civil War epoch by the development of large-scale manufacturing enterprise. It analyzes the reasons for the exclusion of the organized labor movement from the corporate polity which had emerged by 1920, and attributes this both to the desires of corporate managers for unilateral control of the enterprise and to the suspicion which the state had shown toward labor unions since the earliest days of the Republic. Part Two concentrates on the creation of a publicly regulated labor relations system in the 1930s and early 1940s, and on the emergence during this period of industrial pluralism at the forefront of American labor relations theory and practice. Here the focus is on the ideology of New Deal labor relations law, and on the debates occurring within key state institutions, notably the National Labor Relations Board, over the appropriate relationship that should pertain between public and private realms of action in labor relations. Part Three extends analysis of federal labor relations policy into the postwar period, investigating the origins of the Taft-Hartley Act and the extent to which that act represented a modification of the now-dominant pluralist consensus.

8. Isaac Balbus, "Commodity Form and Legal Form: An Essay on the 'Relative Autonomy' of the Law," *Law and Society Review*, 11 (Winter 1977), 571–88.
9. Ibid., 585 [emphasis in original].

Throughout the years of preparation, this study has benefited enormously from the influence of two totally dissimilar yet equally stimulating environments, the History Department of The Johns Hopkins University, where I spent five years training to be a historian and to which I returned briefly as a research fellow in 1981-2, and the Legal Studies Department of La Trobe University, where since 1980 I have tried to apply that training to the social scientific analysis of legal ideologies and institutions. Advisors, colleagues, and friends at both institutions have helped make this a far better book than I could otherwise have hoped.

At Johns Hopkins, Louis Galambos supervised the dissertation upon which this study is based and then helped me make it a book. I owe him far more than a few lines on an acknowledgments page can ever repay. To Rick Rubinson and Mark Kornbluh, too, I owe much. Their consistent interest and encouragement helped counter the loneliness of research and writing. Others at Hopkins – David Harvey, Kenneth Lynn, and Naomi Lamoreaux (now of Brown University) – have always been generous with their time and advice.

To my colleagues at La Trobe I also owe a great deal. Ian Duncanson, Tony Blackshield, and Laura Bennett all helped steer me through the thickets of legal discourse, teaching me what to look for and, equally important, what to ignore. Diane Kirkby of Legal Studies and Eric Jones of Economic History read and commented on major sections of the manuscript. The Legal Studies Department and the School of Social Sciences have supported the project generously and consistently; and Anne Borlase, Janette Gosstray and, especially, Denise Lumsden have coped with every revision with meticulous efficiency and good humor.

I have many people to thank beyond Johns Hopkins and La Trobe. Robert Gallman, Stephen Skowronek, and Steve Fraser all provided detailed criticism of the original manuscript. Howell Harris and David Brody have done their best to prevent my repeating too many of the errors I made there. Morton Horwitz and Bob Gordon, Tony Freyer and Harry Scheiber have, at one time or another, all given me the opportunity to benefit from their considerable experience in the writing of legal history.

Aside from the School of Social Science at La Trobe, I have received generous support from the Research in Legal History Program at the University of Wisconsin–Madison, and from the Harry S Truman Library Institute. Non-material aid was furnished by the staffs of the Georgetown University Archive, the Library of Congress Manuscript Division, the National Archives and Records Service Industrial and Social Branch (particularly Jerry N. Hess), the Harry S Truman Presidential Library, the State Historical Society of Wisconsin and the secretary-treasurer's office, AFL-CIO. Their efforts eased immeasurably the burdens and difficulties of archival research. I wish in particular to express my gratitude to AFL-CIO secretary-treasurer Thomas R. Donahue, and to the AFL-CIO's archivist, Katherine Vogel, for granting me access to AFL records at a time of some inconvenience to them. I also wish to thank the Honorable Robert Taft, Jr., for granting me access to his father's papers.

Ann Tomlins is not paid to be part of any scholarly support apparatus but has nevertheless had to live at firsthand with this book longer than anyone who is. It would have been dedicated to her had circumstances not pressed the claim of others dear to us both.

Notwithstanding the aid of all of the above, errors undoubtedly remain in this book. They are my responsibility alone.

Material which first appeared in my articles, "AFL Unions in the 1930s: Their Performance in Historical Perspective," *Journal of American History*, 65, 4 (March 1979), and "New Directions in American Labor History," *Labour History*, 43 (November 1982), is incorporated here by permission of those journals.

PART I

The legitimacy of the labor union

A huge barbecue was spread to which all presumably were invited. Not quite all, to be sure; inconspicuous persons, those who were at home on the farm or at work in the mills and offices, were overlooked; a good many indeed out of the total number of the American people. But all the important persons, leading bankers and promoters and business men, received invitations. There wasn't room for everybody and these were presumed to represent the whole. It was a splendid feast.

Vernon Louis Parrington, *Main Currents in American Thought*
(New York, 1927), III, 23.

Introduction: "Labor's Ultimatum to the Public"

On a sunny Sunday morning, when the front page had nothing more controversial to announce than the abandonment the day before of the second America's Cup race for want of a breeze, New Yorkers leafing through their *Times* for 18 July 1920 must have been astonished to encounter LABOR'S ULTIMATUM TO THE PUBLIC tucked away inside Section III.[1] Beneath this arresting headline appeared the "defiant" face of Frank Morrison, secretary-treasurer of the American Federation of Labor, and an announcement which the *Times* apparently felt was sufficiently self-condemnatory to warrant no additional comment. "The workers," stated Morrison, "will not concede that the community has any purpose or intention to render justice to the workers should it force itself into participation in industrial relations. On the contrary, its only object . . . is to prevent the workers from taking advantage of natural conditions to better their economic conditions – a right which the community holds sacred when applied to property." For this reason, he continued, the workers would not "surrender to any agency the functions which by right belong to trade unions, and which can be, and have been, successfully solved by themselves through the trade unions."[2]

Morrison's comments were not original to the *Times*. In fact they had been prompted two months previously by a request from one John McDowell, chairman of the Presbyterian Church's Convention Commission on Social Service, for the AFL's opinion of the preliminary draft of a report on social and industrial questions in the United States which the Commission was to present to a church conference in Cleveland.[3] Replying on the Federation's behalf, Morrison had ignored most of the report and concentrated on the conclusions reached in its section on

1. *New York Times* (18 July 1920), III, 3.   2. Ibid.
3. See Frank Morrison to John McDowell (12 May 1920), *Morrison Papers* (William R. Perkins Library, Duke University, Durham, North Carolina).

modern industry, focussing in particular on its premise that "the problem of labor and capital is no longer one which concerns only, or even mainly, these two essential parties to production. As never before it is a community problem . . ." Following closely upon the extraordinary labor unrest of 1919, such an allusion to the pressing "community" interest in the solution of industrial relations problems could hardly have surprised the AFL. Nevertheless, Morrison spent over half of his nineteen-page reply developing a critique of the purposes to be served by "community" intervention and its likely consequences. Nor was this simply a personal opinion. Other union leaders might have been less eager to adopt the same uncompromising position in public, but this was not because they disagreed with it. As one anonymous leader told the *Times,* they simply kept quiet "because the public would misunderstand."[4]

McDowell's report erred, Morrison stated, in assuming the neutrality of the community in industrial relations matters. The community could not be neutral because it was responsible for safeguarding the production of commodities vital to its own welfare. This meant that the community never intervened in industrial disputes "when there were plenty of workers, and in consequence the workers' economic condition was deteriorating and his standard of living was lowered," because such conditions did not threaten the community's interest in low prices and uninterrupted production. The community intervened only when conditions of labor scarcity strengthened the workers' bargaining position and made it more likely that they would attempt to pressure their employers into improving their wages and working conditions, for this threatened to bring disputes which might halt production and curtail altogether the supply of commodities. "[The community]'s concern is not with the wages paid to the workers or the conditions under which they work, but rather with the continuous operation of industry so that its wants may be supplied without interruption. After these wants have been supplied it is a matter of no concern to the community what becomes of the worker."

The behavior of the community in practice, therefore, belied attempts to portray it as a neutral in industrial relations. But Morrison had a more profound point to make. It was not that the capacity of the community to maintain a strict neutrality in labor disputes had unfortunately been compromised by the simple, practical exigencies of specific occasions. Rather, its neutrality was impossible per se. The interests of the community and of the labor movement were structurally and his-

4. In "Labor's Ultimatum," 3. Subsequent quotations are all from this source.

torically antagonistic. This, he declared, was a conclusion reinforced by the experience of workers "in every epoch of the world's history."

Throughout history, workers had occupied "a definite condition of life – a lower order of living than that enjoyed by the prosperous or the well-to-do." To better that condition the workers had to be aroused. "The mind of the [workers] is awakened to a better order, and when thus awakened it is not content with its low estates. Its desires expand. This expansion is naturally reflected in industrial relations. The [workers want] higher wages and better working conditions. The employers deny them. Industry ceases." Immediately the community intervenes to defend industry and to suppress the workers. The press, the pulpit, the army, the courts – all are placed at the disposal of the employers. "The [workers] must be suppressed because industry is necessary to the community. The community is the force which suppresses . . ."

This was indeed a graphic portrayal of the course of events in industrial conflicts. Nevertheless, the community might still justify its interventions on the grounds that, no matter how damaging to the workers its actions might be, their pursuit of their selfish goals was doing even greater damage to the public interest. Before he could establish any alternative view, Morrison had therefore to confront directly the all-important concept of "the community" itself. "Who is the community?" he asked. He was not slow in finding an answer:

> When we read in the daily newspapers that 'the people will not approve of such and so' of plans of the workers to help themselves; when it is said that 'the great American public will not permit this or that to be done'; when we are told that 'the community has rights which must be respected', we know that the class variously referred to as 'the people', 'the great American public' and 'the community' comprise those persons in whose interest the newspapers are published, by whom they are owned and under whose direction the views are given expression. They do not embrace the workers now any more than they have ever done since the beginning of history.

In their pursuit of "a better order," the workers were not challenging the interests of a collective social entity of which they were a part and to whose disinterested good judgment their particular grievances should properly be submitted, for in this sense the community, together with its synonyms – the people, the great American public – was a myth. It did not exist.[5] Rather, the workers were challenging the desires of the "well-

---

5. Morrison returned to this theme in the second half of his commentary in which he addressed the report's contention that "the laborer must realize that he owes his employer an honest day's work in return for a fair wage." Morrison responded:

to-do" whose assertions of community were simply a means to camou-
flage their employment of agencies of state power, over which the
workers had no control, in pursuit of their own interests.[6] "These
views of 'the community' and the motives of 'the community' are
sustained by the experience of the workers throughout the ages and
regardless of the form which 'the community' adopts to accomplish its
particular purpose."

Confronted with state institutions which were always actually or potentially hostile, therefore, workers had no alternative but to protect
their rights and advance their interests through the creation of their
own institutions:

> We are freemen and we shall exercise the powers of freemen in
> maintaining our rights. These rights are embodied in the principles
> of trade unionism. Collective bargaining with equal powers of the
> employers; the right to strike when in our judgment the conditions
> of employment justify such action; the right to take advantage of
> every lawful opportunity to better our condition. We shall resist all
> encroachment upon these rights with all the powers of which we
> are capable. And by our resistance we shall keep clear the road to
> progress.

Morrison's analysis of the threat posed by the state and his conclusion
that trade unionism – the embodiment of workers' rights – was the only
means whereby workers might avoid subordination to their employers
provided the essential foundations for the final step in his argument.
Justice and equality in the relations between employees and employers
could not be achieved through the intervention of state institutions – the
army, the courts, the legislature – for their sole purpose was to suppress

> The worker in this category is classified significantly. He comprises a
> class which is admonished to give an honest day's work to his em-
> ployer and to society. Work is his especial function. Society and the
> employer bids him to do its work and to do it honestly. Now are we to
> assume that this society which is so interested in the laborer that it
> calls upon him to give an honest day's work has no other interest in
> the laborer than to obtain this honest day's work. . . ? What is society?
> Is it something of which the laborer is not a part and for which the
> laborer is working? And this joining of the employer and society?
> Does it mean that the laborer is the only dishonest member of the
> group?

6. Morrison's identification of state power as the expression of particular class interests
    was quite explicit. Having described the community as a mere reflex of the interests
    and desires of those persons "in whose interest the newspapers are published, by
    whom they are owned and under whose direction the views are given expression,"
    Morrison continues "Now let us consider how the community may make effective
    its interest in industrial relations; considering the community as here outlined – the
    State."

workers whether by armed force, judicial decree, or class legislation. Thus alternatives were required. Wholly new methods could be developed (Morrison did not elaborate), but this was unnecessary. "The development of new methods is unnecessary if the trade unions are permitted to function according to their philosophy. All the industrial upheavals of recent years can be traced directly to the denial of the right of the worker to give full exercise to this function."

At the core of Morrison's "ultimatum," then, lay the proposition that "the problem of labor and capital" would be solved permanently only by admitting unions to a position of unconditional equality amid the web of institutions which constituted the political economy of industrial America and allowing them to pursue their goals – "to establish justice for the worker by placing within his reach the means to present his case, to develop his collective power of resistance when justice is denied him," and from this position of collective strength "to harmonize industrial relations through collective bargaining with the full exercise of all the rights which that implies" – uninhibited by coercive state institutions. "There is no question in modern industry which cannot be determined quickly and satisfactorily through the trade union philosophy," Morrison concluded. "On the other hand," he added, "there is no question in modern industry which can be determined quickly and satisfactorily by the community agencies."[7]

In affirming the organized labor movement's claim to a leading role in American industrial society, Morrison's "ultimatum" was addressing the institutional consequences of a half-century of rapid social and economic change. Ever since the Civil War, American society had been beset by a growing political-legal crisis caused by the occurrence of an enormous upsurge in organized industrial and social activity in the midst of a state structure designed for a market economy populated by individual entrepreneur-citizens.[8] In the economy, the growing prominence of the large corporation meant that in many sectors oligopolistic competition and price-fixing had increasingly replaced the atomistic individualism of the free market. In public policy formation, similarly, group organization and group conflict had become decisive. Self-interested organizations such as professional associations had emerged to take control of their particular spheres of activity out of the realm of

7. For a summary of the conclusions reached in contemporary debates over the future of industrial relations conducted outside the organized labor movement, see Gary Dean Best, "President Wilson's Second Industrial Conference, 1919–1920," *Labor History*, 16, 4 (Fall 1975), 505–20.
8. See, for example, Robert Wiebe, *The Search for Order, 1877–1920* (New York, 1967); Samuel P. Hays, *The Response to Industrialism* (Chicago, 1957).

democratic partisan politics. Reform groups were attempting to reorder particular segments of social and political life.[9]

Increasingly, this new politics overshadowed the constitutional mechanisms – courts and partisan legislative politics – upon which the makers of public policy had relied during the nineteenth century.[10] By World War I, as a consequence, the state described in nineteenth-century liberal theory was fast disappearing. Political theorists now argued that the state was constituted out of groups, rather than out of individual citizens, or emphasized that if it still existed as a separate political entity it was only as one such entity, surrounded by many others with which it shared power.[11] Even those theorists who argued that the relationship between the state and the individual citizen was still the only relationship which could endow the exercise of political power with legitimacy now envisaged that relationship as one mediated by a plurality of groups.[12]

In light of the emergence of a polity apparently according manifold contemporary expressions of a common organizational impulse increasing opportunity to influence the course of public life, and with total union membership standing in excess of five million, it is hardly surprising to find American unions in 1920 pressing for acceptance of their social and industrial legitimacy. In the industrial milieu of the postwar period, Robert Zieger has noted "many laborites harbored hopes that . . . with organized labor in a stronger and more influential position than ever before the unions could expand, not only in membership, but in control over industrial processes as well."[13] Morrison's "ultimatum" reflects precisely their desire for freedom from restraints in the

9. See, for example, Glenn Porter, *The Rise of Big Business, 1860–1910* (Arlington Heights, Illinois, 1973); Thomas K. McGraw, "Rethinking the Trust Question," in Thomas K. McGraw, editor, *Regulation in Perspective: Historical Essays* (Cambridge, 1981), 1–55; Samuel P. Hays, *Conservation and the Gospel of Efficiency* (Cambridge, 1959); Jerry Israel, editor, *Building the Organizational Society: Essays on Associational Activities in Modern America* (New York, 1972).

10. Morton Keller, "The Pluralist State: American Economic Regulation in Comparative Perspective, 1900–1930," in McGraw, editor, *Regulation in Perspective*, 56–94; Stephen Skowronek, *Building a New American State: The Expansion of National Administrative Capacities, 1877–1920* (New York, 1982).

11. See, for example, Harold J. Laski, "The Pluralistic State," *The Philosophical Review*, 28 (1919). This question is treated exhaustively by Richard Crockatt, "Pluralism and the Invertebrate State: A Study of American Liberalism, 1900–1925" (unpublished Ph.D. thesis, University of Sussex, 1978).

12. Mary Parker Follett, *The New State: Group Organization the Solution of Popular Government* (New York, 1918); Crockatt, "Pluralism and the Invertebrate State," Chapter 4.

13. Robert H. Zieger, "Herbert Hoover, the Wage-earner, and the 'New Economic System,' 1919–1929," *Business History Review*, 51, 2 (Summer 1977), 180.

"free struggle for life."[14] But in fact, the frontiers of legitimate associational activity within which the new American polity had been developing were carefully drawn and tightly circumscribed. To many, as the reaction of the *New York Times* to Morrison's "ultimatum" indicated, the organized labor movement fell outside them.

14. Walter W. Cook, "Privileges of Labor Unions in the Struggle for Life," *Yale Law Journal*, 27, 6 (April 1918), 779–801.

1

A corporate political economy

It is curious that the mass of the people of this country should fail to recognize their best friends, because corporations have been the only barrier between the despotism of ignorance and the invasion of the rights of property. Doubtless they abuse their privileges at times, but they alone have the ability and the courage to resist attack, and they are doing the work which was done by Jefferson and Madison in the early years of the Republic.

Abram S. Hewitt to R.D. Haislip, 16 June 1898, in Edward C. Kirkland, *Dream and Thought in the Business Community, 1860–1900* (Ithaca, New York, 1956), 127.

In all industrial economies characterized by private ownership of the means of production, advanced forms of business organization, and the use of sophisticated technologies, the web of relationships between employers and employees has been decisively influenced by the organization of significant numbers of workers into labor unions for the protection of their collective interests. In the United States such developments had become commonplace by the second half of the nineteenth century as local organizations of skilled workers began to federate in national trade unions. By 1881 these national unions felt they enjoyed sufficient unity of purpose and community of interest to establish an ad hoc alliance, the Federation of Organized Trades and Labor Unions. By 1886 they had grown strong enough to create a permanent federation of labor organizations, the American Federation of Labor, thereby expressing confidence in their ability to survive and their intention to expand beyond those sectors of the economy where they had first taken hold.

Organization in local and national unions offered the self-conscious industrial worker an opportunity to exercise a greater degree of influence over his immediate economic and political environment through membership in a self-interested group. In this respect, at least, the unions hardly differed from other new associational institutions appearing at the same time. Despite the apparent relevance of these labor movement developments to the general institutional trends characterizing the American political economy, however, organized labor at no time achieved more than a relatively marginal status in the national polity. Explanations for this are not hard to find. First, by the 1890s the pattern of labor relations was being decisively shaped by the center firms of the emerging corporate economy. Their vigor in contesting the terrain over which unions sought control ensured that outside those areas of the economy where unions were already firmly established, collective organization would not be allowed to impinge upon the social relations of production.[1] Second, these same large business corporations were also the central actors in the emergence of the modern American state, dominating its institutional and ideological configuration. By the early twentieth century the American polity had substantially re-arranged itself both politically and culturally around the center corporations, leaving little room for the organized labor movement to establish competing modes of association.[2]

An era of sharp conflicts

For labor and management the last years of the nineteenth century and the first years of the twentieth were an "era of sharp conflicts."[3] Large-scale disputes had already occurred in the 1870s and 1880s on the railroads and also in particular firms, for example the Pullman and Carnegie companies, pioneering the introduction of technological and organizational innovations in the production process and in the man-agement of the enterprise.[4] When union growth resumed after the depression of the 1890s, the "labor problem" assumed general propor-

1. See, generally, Richard T. Edwards, *Contested Terrain: The Transformation of the Workplace in the Twentieth Century* (New York, 1979).
2. See, generally, Alan Trachtenberg, *The Incorporation of America: Culture and Soci-ety in the Gilded Age* (New York, 1982); David Noble, *America by Design: Science, Technology, and the Rise of Corporate Capitalism* (New York, 1979); Gabriel Kolko, *The Triumph of Conservatism* (New York, 1963); Louis P. Galambos, *The Public Image of Big Business in America, 1880–1940: A Quantitative Study in Social Change* (Baltimore, 1975); Thomas K. McGraw, editor, *Regulation in Per-spective: Historical Essays* (Cambridge, 1981).
3. Clarence E. Bonnett, *History of Employers' Associations in the United States* (New York, 1957), 413; P.K. Edwards, *Strikes in the United States, 1881–1974* (New York, 1981), 84–133.
4. Jeremy Brecher, *Strike!* (San Francisco, 1972), 1–52; David Brody, *Steelworkers in America: The Nonunion Era* (Cambridge, 1960), 50–60; Stanley Buder, *Pullman: An Experiment in Industrial Order and Community Planning, 1880–1930* (New York, 1967), 38–74, 131–201; Edwards, *Contested Terrain*, 49–71. See also Harry Braverman, *Labor and Monopoly Capital: The Degradation of Work in the Twenti-eth Century* (New York, 1974).

tions. Conflicts arose in mining, in the steel industry, in meat packing, in metal fabricating plants, in large corporations such as National Cash Register, General Electric, and International Harvester, and on the railroads.

Questions of wages and hours were at the center of the majority of these disputes, but this alone does not explain their occurrence. Between 1897 and 1901 over 27 percent of all strikes were fought over the issue of recognition of unions and their rules. By 1904 the figure was nearer to 40 percent. As this indicates, the question of unionism per se grew in importance relative to wage and hour issues between the late 1890s and early 1900s.[5]

Evidence of employers' desire to contain the influence of unions at the point of production can be found well before the turn of the century. At McCormick Reaper, management in 1886 had introduced innovations with the express intent of undermining the union.[6] Six years later the central issue of the dispute at the Homestead plant of the Carnegie Company, so far as company chairman Henry Clay Frick was concerned, was "whether the Carnegie Company or the Amalgamated Association [of Iron, Steel and Tin Workers] shall have absolute control of our plant."[7] The coal–railroad combination which dominated the anthracite mining industry was similarly obsessed with keeping the United Mine Workers out of its affairs. By 1902 it was seeking the complete elimination of the union, for "there cannot be two masters in the management of business."[8] As Bruno Ramirez has noted, this meant that total control over the miners and mining operations was henceforth to be an exclusive prerogative of management.[9]

Unions were particularly vulnerable to employer pressure in industries affected by the great consolidation movement of 1898–1902. By concentrating control of most of an industry's capacity in one or two centers corporate management could simply switch production from plants where unions were established or growing to non-union plants. The United States Steel Corporation found this tactic particularly effec-

5. Edwards, *Strikes in the United States*, 37. Bruno Ramirez, *When Workers Fight: The Politics of Industrial Relations in the Progressive Era, 1896–1916* (Westport, Connecticut, 1978), 10, 95.
6. Robert Ozanne, *A Century of Labor-Management Relations at International Harvester* (Madison, 1967), 20.
7. In Brody, *Steelworkers in America*, 56. See also Katherine Stone, "The Origins of Job Structures in the Steel Industry," in Richard C. Edwards et al., editors, *Labor Market Segmentation* (Lexington, Massachusetts, 1973), 27–84; Brecher, *Strike!*, 53–63.
8. George F. Baer, president of the Reading Railroad, in Ramirez, *When Workers Fight*, 39.
9. Ibid., 39.

tive in its drive against the Amalgamated Association in the sheet and tin plate industries. Faced with growing union pressure in 1901, the corporation at first appeared unsure of its ability to withstand the union's demands and agreed that the Amalgamated wage scale should prevail in the sheet and tin mills which the union had organized. Emboldened by this success, the union pressed to include non-union mills. But in the meantime the corporation discovered that it had retained control of enough capacity to meet normal demand, enabling it to ignore the union. The Amalgamated was forced into a hopeless general strike in a futile attempt to increase pressure on the corporation. By the end of the strike its position in the sheet and tin mills had been destroyed, and it was confined to the oldest and least efficient plants, some of which were promptly shut down. U.S. Steel recognized that the capacity represented by the non-union mills had provided it with its major weapon. To ensure that it retained that weapon, the corporation "required the union to pledge not to extend, nor even accept, organization in any plant not then under contract." As David Brody has concluded, "It was a settlement from which the union never recovered."[10]

In industries such as bituminous coal, garments, and construction where control of total capacity was divided among a large number of competitors, unions were better able to safeguard their positions, and overall union membership continued to grow. In many instances, however, employers were able to overcome their fragmentation through the creation of "permanently belligerent associations."[11] Between 1900 and 1902, more and more employers turned to these national associations in an effort "to deal with labor matters on a non-union basis."[12]

One such organization was the National Metal Trades Association, formed in 1899. In 1900, acting at the behest of the National Civic Federation, the NMTA concluded a national agreement with the International Association of Machinists covering a large number of metal fabricating firms. This "Murray Hill" agreement was incomplete in coverage with respect both to employers and to conditions of employment; nor, in line with NMTA policy, did it contain any provisions governing wages. The agreement outlawed strikes and provided for the reference of all grievances to a national board of arbitration made up of union and NMTA representatives. It also included a provision granting "freedom for the employer to operate without union restrictions."[13]

10. Brody, *Steelworkers in America*, 62–68.
11. Bonnett, *Employers' Associations*, 443.   12. Ibid., 443.
13. National Labor Relations Board, *Written Trade Agreements in Collective Bargaining* (Washington, 1940), 152.

Provisions limiting working time to fifty-seven hours per week and establishing that an overtime penalty rate would come into effect during specified periods were major gains for the union, but many employers refused unilaterally to implement the shorter workweek when it came due, and when the union protested the NMTA responded by declaring the agreement void. The strike which followed became one of the major national disputes of the early 1900s "and signalled . . . the intensification of the capital-labor struggle in the metal trades sector." The machinists were decisively defeated. The union was crushed in every major metal fabricating enterprise outside its last bastion, Chicago.[14]

At the outset of the 1901 strike, the NMTA had disavowed any intention to interfere with "the proper functions of labor organizations." Observers, however, must have been hard pressed to discover what, in the association's eyes, "a proper function" could possibly be. For instance, it was not regulation of the labor supply or of manning: "the number of apprentices, helpers, and handymen to be employed will be determined solely by the employer." It was not determination of the wages, hours, or conditions of work: "We will not permit employees to place any restriction on the management, methods, or production of our shops, and will require a fair day's work for a fair day's pay." Nor was it even the determination of the appropriate method of payment: "Employees will be paid by the hourly rate, by premium system, piecework or contract, as the employers may elect." The NMTA, in short, was out to eliminate union influence completely. "Since we, as employers, are responsible for the work turned out by our workmen, we must have full discretion to designate the men we consider competent to perform the work and to determine the conditions under which the work will be prosecuted, the question of the competency of the men being determined solely by us . . . We will not admit of any interference with the management of the business."[15]

By 1903 labor–management conflict was widespread. An open shop drive spearheaded by the National Association of Manufacturers had the support of employers throughout industry.[16] In the construction industry, employer associations mobilized to attack unions and their work rules.[17] Elsewhere, the National Founders' Association organized

14. Ramirez, *When Workers Fight*, 106; David Montgomery, *Workers' Control in America: Studies in the History of Work, Technology and Labor Struggles* (Cambridge, England, 1979), 54–57.
15. In Ramirez, *When Workers Fight*, 94–95.
16. Bonnett, *Employers' Associations*, 443–77.
17. Robert A. Christie, *Empire in Wood: A History of the Carpenters' Union* (Ithaca, New York, 1956), 155–67.

pools of strikebreakers.[18] In the meat packing industry, unions of butcher workmen which had appeared in the wake of the industry's late nineteenth-century organizational and technological transformation were broken in the strike of 1904, itself a key battle in the employer campaign against the labor movement's stronghold of Chicago.[19] At National Cash Register, management refused to enter into contracts with unions after 1901 and concentrated instead on undermining the unions' work rules.[20]

Industrial conflict continued throughout the Progressive Era. By 1909 new struggles were spreading through the economy as the sphere of confrontation widened to include the mass of unskilled workers in industries such as clothing and steel. In the clothing trades their strikes brought the establishment of permanent unions. Elsewhere they were less successful, fighting on ground thoroughly under the control of the large corporations. But this did not prevent a constant increment in the level of strike activity, culminating in 1919 in strikes involving over four million workers.

Craft workers, meanwhile, continued to strike in defense of their unions and union-regulated working conditions. Easily the most momentous of these conflicts was the shop crafts' strike against attempts of railroad managers to follow the example of corporate management in other industries and "rationalize" their labor policies. Lasting from 1911 to 1915, this strike became "a major landmark in the history of American syndicalism."[21]

In all some sixteen unions, including the operating brotherhoods not affiliated with the AFL, had members in the railroad industry. Wherever three or more of the AFL unions were active on the lines of a particular carrier, or associated group of carriers, they formed a system federation. Such federations had first appeared on western railroads in the early 1890s, but they had been destroyed in the aftermath of the American Railway Union strike of 1894. In the 1900s, however, the non-operating crafts began to reestablish the federations, in part to defend themselves from attacks similar to those they were experiencing in manufacturing industries, in part to facilitate joint bargaining.[22]

18. Bonnett, *Employers' Associations,* 443–77.
19. David Brody, *The Butcher Workmen: A Study of Unionization* (Cambridge, 1964), 12, 59.
20. Daniel Nelson, "The New Factory System and the Unions: The National Cash Register Dispute of 1901," *Labor History,* 15 (Spring 1974), 163–78.
21. Montgomery, *Workers' Control in America,* 107; Graham Adams Jr., *Age of Industrial Violence, 1910–1915: The Activities of the United States Commission on Industrial Relations* (New York, 1966), 128; Ramirez, *When Workers Fight,* 134.
22. National Labor Relations Board, *Written Trade Agreements,* 152–53.

To the companies the system federations represented "a plan to obtain absolute power over the operations of the carriers and to exert it to
the utmost."[23] They reacted even more strongly when, in the early
months of the strike, the International Association of Machinists voted
to organize a federation of system federations. Such an organization,
managers thought, would be able to dictate the policy not simply of one
railroad but of all railroads. Indeed, such an alliance would become "a
weapon aimed . . . at the heart of practically every manufacturing enterprise in the country," for it would enable the shop craft unions to
extend railroad strikes throughout the manufacturing sector. Confronted by this threat, the board of the Illinois Central Railroad Company decided "that it owed a duty to its stockholders, to its patrons,
and to the country to resist in every legitimate and proper way the
beginning of such a monstrous system."[24] Nothing explains more succinctly the intransigence of the railroads during the shop craft strike. So
far as they were concerned, they were fighting for the survival of every
industrial enterprise in the country.

A culture of control

The immediate cause of the shop craft strike had been the attempts of
railroad managers to reduce their variable costs in response to pressures
on profit levels. This had entailed the reorganization of the work process through the introduction of technological and organizational innovations which in turn provoked resistance at the point of production
from unions active in railroad equipment repair shops. Fundamentally,
therefore, the strike was fought over who should organize and control
the work process. In this regard, the shop craft strike symbolized the
themes of the entire labor–management confrontation. As Bryan
Palmer and many others have shown, during the latter part of the
nineteenth century a "culture of control" built around craft traditions
and, increasingly, unions and union rules, had spread through many
industries regulating the performance of work.[25] It was this culture

23. Julius Krutschnitt, board chairman of Southern Pacific, in Adams, *Age of Industrial
    Violence*, 144.
24. Charles H. Markham, president of Illinois Central, in ibid., 144.
25. Bryan Palmer, *A Culture in Conflict: Skilled Workers and Industrial Capitalism in
    Hamilton, Ontario 1860–1914* (Montreal, 1979), 71–95; Montgomery, *Workers'
    Control in America*, 9–31; David Brody, *Workers in Industrial America: Essays on
    the Twentieth Century Struggle* (New York, 1980), 3–47. See also Andrew Dawson,
    "The Paradox of Dynamic Technological Change and the Labor Aristocracy in the
    United States, 1880–1914," *Labor History*, 20, 3 (Summer 1979), 325–51; David
    M. Gordon et al., *Segmented Work, Divided Workers: The Historical Transforma-
    tion of Labor in the United States* (Cambridge, England, 1982), 100–64.

which employers had to confront if they were to secure control at the point of production for themselves.

The drive for control of the production process mounted by employers in the closing decades of the nineteenth century was rooted in the competitive strategies adopted by America's businesses in the years after the Civil War, and the technological and organizational consequences flowing from them. Prior to the 1840s, the character and organization of American business enterprise was predominantly small-scale. Most firms enjoyed relatively low levels of capitalization, and ownership was typically concentrated within a narrow circle of founding entrepreneurs – a family or partnership. Management responsibilities, too, were handled by the founders. Low levels of capitalization, the small scale of production, the absence from most industries of a detailed division of labor and of a large work-force all rendered the development of a sophisticated managerial bureaucracy unnecessary.[26]

Such firms enjoyed little influence over their competitive environment and relied predominantly on market imperfections for protection from competition. These imperfections, the result of the underdevelopment of transport and communications networks, limited the extent of markets and complemented the technological constraints on manufacturing development which restricted most firms to the production of small quantities of highly differentiated products. But this situation was changed by the transportation and communications revolution which began in the 1840s and 1850s, confronting entrepreneurs for the first time with the necessity of adopting an explicit market strategy. While materially improving a firm's opportunities for expansion by improving its access to raw materials and markets and by accelerating the flow of commercial information, the transportation revolution directly threatened each firm's profits by exposing it to the price-eroding competition of others producing similar products. Entrepreneurs now had to decide whether to continue producing at traditional levels and rely on product differentiation and an inelastic demand curve to render them immune from the competition of rivals, or abandon product differentiation, produce a fairly homogenous product, and seek invulnerability from price competition by maximizing their output and minimizing their unit costs.[27] More and more, entrepreneurs chose low-cost, mass production as the

26. Edwards, *Contested Terrain*, 23–27; Alfred D. Chandler, *The Visible Hand: The Managerial Revolution in American Business* (Cambridge, 1977), 13–78.
27. Naomi R. Lamoreaux, "Industrial Organization and Market Behavior: The Great Merger Movement in American Industry" (unpublished Ph.D. dissertation, The Johns Hopkins University, 1979), 42–98. On the transportation revolution see, generally, George R. Taylor, *The Transportation Revolution, 1815–1860* (New York, 1958); Chandler, *The Visible Hand*, 79–205.

best means to ensure their competitive survival. Product differentiation "was increasingly confined to the most expensive grades of material and to industries not yet amenable to mass production techniques."[28]

This trend had important consequences for the character and organization of production and of the firm.[29] During the initial period of sustained economic growth which began in the quarter-century before the Civil War, capitalists had increasingly taken command of the *coordination* of production, but in most industries they had continued to rely on traditional productive techniques. Thus, expanded output was achieved through increases in the quantity of inputs rather than through altered capital–labor ratios and productivity growth.[30] This reliance on quantitative increases in inputs soon presented the entrepreneurial firm with formidable problems, however, for it was confronted with the problem of maintaining control over rapidly expanding operations without possessing any developed means for so doing. On the railroads the problem became acute in the early 1850s with the completion of the east–west trunk lines. Daniel C. McCallum, general superintendent of the Erie Railroad, argued in 1855 that "any system [of management] which might be applicable to the business and extent of a short road would be found entirely inadequate to the wants of a long one," and expressed his conviction that the secret of the large roads' failures to date lay "in the want of a system perfect in its details, properly adapted and vigilantly enforced . . . "[31]

As the century progressed, the situation was repeated in industry after industry. Firms attempting to increase output massively in order to sustain their competitive positions had to devise managerial strategies to accommodate the effects of the growth of inputs. Intermediate layers of management appeared to supplement the original narrow entrepreneurial group which was now entirely dwarfed by the sheer increase in the

28. Lamoreaux, "Industrial Organization and Market Behavior," 52.
29. Edwards, *Contested Terrain*, 27–42. Thomas K. McGraw argues that when examined for their impact upon consumer welfare, defined as the highest efficiency in allocation of resources possible within a given economic system, the changes here under discussion were extremely beneficial. See McGraw, "Rethinking the Trust Question," in McGraw, editor, *Regulation in Perspective*, 1–55. From the perspective of the distribution of political and economic power both within and outside the enterprise, however, the benefits are less easy to detect (as McGraw also notes). The latter point seems decisive, particularly when one takes into account the necessary relationship between the distribution of political power and the parameters within which maximum allocative efficiency is to be achieved.
30. Gordon et al., *Segmented Work, Divided Workers*, 48–99.
31. In Alfred D. Chandler, *Strategy and Structure: Chapters in the History of the American Industrial Enterprise* (Cambridge, 1962), 21–22.

scale of operations and no longer able to engage in day-to-day supervision of production and marketing. "A hierarchical structure was instituted, with foremen and supervisors to watch over other employees . . . A direct chain of command was created in which those who were delegated power were made responsible to successively higher and more concentrated echelons."[32]

The hierarchical mode of organization enabled firms to expand their capacity, but represented no departure from the philosophy of personal supervision embraced in the small entrepreneurial firms of the early nineteenth century. Rather it "was based on the concept that each boss – whether a foreman, supervisor, or manager – would *re-create* in his shop the situation of the capitalist under entrepreneurial control."[33] Incessant competition and persistent price deflation, however, placed entrepreneurs under continuous pressure not only to improve their firms' ability to handle larger and larger quantities of inputs, but also to introduce technological and organizational innovations aimed at sustained improvements in the *productivity* of labor and capital.[34]

The example of the introduction of the Bessemer converter in the iron and steel industry is instructive. Significantly, the most important figure in the development and application of the Bessemer process in America, Alexander Lyman Holley, was not a technical innovator but a designer of plant equipment, facilities, and layout. His goal was always "to assure a very large and regular ouput," for in plants where a capacity for continuous mass production had been achieved through investment in new capital equipment, the cost of the innovations had to be spread over as large a volume of production as possible in order to keep unit costs low. But as growing capital intensity increased the enterprise's fixed costs relative to its variable costs, the latter became of crucial importance, particularly during periods when total demand was low. Hence the object became "to increase the output of a unit of capital *and of a unit of working expense* . . ." This had wide implications, as Holley himself noted in 1877:

> The fact . . . must not be lost sight of that the adaptation of plant . . . is not the only important condition of large and cheap production; the technical management of American works has become equally improved. Better organization and more readiness, vigilance and technical knowledge on the part of the management have been re-

32. Edwards, *Contested Terrain*, 31.   33. Ibid., 31 [emphasis supplied].
34. McGraw, "Rethinking the Trust Question," 6–24.

quired to run works up to their capacity, as their capacity has become increased by better arrangement and appliances.[35]

To attain the degree of control necessary to achieve these objectives employers had to transcend altogether the traditional mode of enterprise management. The role of the foreman was transformed by innovations centralizing the control and planning of operations in the hands of specialists and staff administrators. Personal supervision was further undermined by the recruitment of an army of supervisors to drive production workers. Systematic techniques were introduced to reduce the authority of workers over the tasks they performed and to modify the performance of specific tasks to fit the patterns arising from the new technology. Eventually, through the introduction of personnel administration, recruitment and training programs, and welfare schemes, management began a wholesale reorganization of the work force, seeking both to enhance its control over the behavior of workers and to ensure the separation of the worker from any competing source of authority.[36]

These innovations were integral to a general process of systematization of management and extension of its sphere of administrative authority to all operations undertaken by an enterprise. Beginning with the attempt to gain intellectual control over a firm's operations through the adoption of more systematic bookkeeping and accounting methods, this extension of the authority of management turned inward to control over the production process and outward to control of the enterprise's access to raw materials, of its competitive position, and, eventually, of its markets.[37] The fight for control at the point of production, in short, had by the end of the nineteenth century become part of a larger process in which the large corporation sought control over its total environment.[38]

35. In Chandler, *The Visible Hand*, 259–60 [Chandler's emphasis]. Arthur Moxham of the Du Pont Company also stressed in 1903 that success required that "we . . . keep *our* capital employed to *the full*." In Chandler, 442 [emphasis Chandler's].
36. Stone, "Job Structures," 37; Bryan Palmer, "Class Conception and Conflict: The Thrust for Efficiency. Managerial Views of Labor and the Working Class Rebellion," *Review of Radical Political Economy*, 7, 2 (1975), 31–49; Dan Clawson, *Bureaucracy and the Labor Process: The Transformation of U.S. Industry, 1860–1920* (New York, 1980), 167–201; Daniel Nelson, *Managers and Workers: Origins of the New Factory System in the United States, 1880–1920* (Madison, 1975), 55–78, 101–21; Gordon et all, *Segmented work, Divided Workers*, 100–62.
37. Chandler, *The Visible Hand*, 115–20, 246, 267–8, 277–9, 484–90, 494.
38. Palmer, "Class Conception and Conflict," 31–49; Trachtenberg, *The Incorporation of America*, 38–69. See, generally, Porter, *The Rise of Big Business*, 85–101; Noble, *America by Design*.

Corporations and the state

The labor movement's "culture of control" was not the only obstacle which corporate enterprise had to surmount in the post–Civil War period. Just as the activities of workers and unions threatened to restrict the corporations' ability to react to competitive developments, so management freedom of action was also subject, though increasingly in a formal sense only, to restraints inherent in the legal and political ideology of the nineteenth century democratic-constitutional state. As long as state institutions could assert that they possessed the power to control the structure of corporations and, through that power, their behavior, corporate managers could not be sure that they enjoyed complete control even of their own enterprises, far less that they could seek to control their enterprises' environment.

By the late 1880s the problem had become a crisis. Suffering from high levels of fixed in total costs and excess capacity, large business enterprises in manufacturing industries began to abandon competition, seeking instead to stabilize markets and prices through cooperative control of capacity, first by employing informal pools, then through trusts. Further price falls and rapidly dwindling markets in the early 1890s added to their sense of urgency. But these innovations were forms of structural change, in theory subject to state control. Before the success of corporate attempts to adapt to a deleterious economic situation could be assured, the tension between the nineteenth-century conception of the proper relationship between the state and corporate entities and the reality of contemporary corporate activity had to be resolved.

The issue was central to the political and legal debates of the succeeding thirty years. But by the mid-1890s it was already clear that the autonomy of the large business corporation was in all essentials assured.[39] This coincided with, and was a necessary precondition of, the consolidation movement of 1898–1902, the most explicit expression to that date of the intent of corporate management in the major manufacturing industries to achieve control of the total environment in which the large enterprise operated.

By the early nineteenth century, the state in America, as in Europe, had come to conceive of itself as the sole legitimate embodiment of the

---

39. Galambos, *The Public Image of Big Business*, 117–87; Charles McCurdy, "The *Knight Sugar* Decision of 1895 and the Modernization of American Corporation Law, 1869–1903," *Business History Review*, 53 (1979), 304–42.

public interest, a perception which grew out of the emergence of the state in both America and Europe as a set of distinctively public institutions.[40] In Europe, this exclusive public sphere had originally been created and filled by absolutism. The democratic-constitutional states which succeeded absolutist rule did not, however, abandon the claim to be "distinctive, 'public,' sovereign concentration[s] of faculties of rule."[41] Rather, through constitutional convention, legislative enactment and judicial decision these states developed frameworks of public and private law, the one to govern interactions among state institutions and to provide safeguards to citizens in their relations with those institutions, the other to create an environment in which individuals might pursue their particular interests through private interactions and offering recourse to the state for adjudication of such disputes as arose. Ideally, coercive power characterized only the "vertical" relationships between the state and private individuals. The "horizontal" relationships of private citizens with each other were to be contractual and power-free, enforceable only through reference to the coercive power of the state in a process of litigation.[42] Autonomous concentrations of power intermediate between the state and the citizenry were unacceptable. "No individual or corporate body [could] engage in activities of rule except as an organ, agent or delegate of the state . . . the state alone assign[ed] and determin[ed] the extent of those activities according to its own rules, backed by its own sanctions."[43]

In North America the form of the nineteenth-century state was more complex. Although the Constitution equipped the nation with a new central government, it simultaneously rendered "the focal point of state activity" ambiguous by carefully creating structured conflicts among that government's key institutions. Equally important, the Constitution settlement embraced federalism, ensuring the survival of eighteenth-century regional governments alongside the central government and thereby further inhibiting the development and extension of central power. While state authority was hardly absent from nineteenth-century America, therefore, it was diffused to an extent unparalleled in Europe.[44]

40. Gianfranco Poggi, *The Development of the Modern State: A Sociological Introduction* (London, 1978), 60–117. See also Donald W. Hanson, *From Kingdom to Commonwealth: The Development of Civic Consciousness in English Political Thought* (Cambridge, 1970).
41. Poggi, *The Development of the Modern State*, 80.
42. Ibid., 92–107.   43. Ibid., 92.
44. Stephen Skowronek, *Building a New American State: The Expansion of National Administrative Capacities* (New York, 1982), 19–35.

The diffusion of state authority was not, however, total. It was mitigated by the existence of "two nationally integrated institutional systems [which] tied together this state's peculiar organizational determinants and established its effective mode of operations."[45] These pivotal institutional structures were the legal system and the party system. Each in its own fashion provided "working rules of behavior" which "coordinated action from the bottom to the top of this radically deconcentrated governmental scheme." As a result, "order, predictability and continuity" could develop in governmental activity despite the existence of a Constitution "designed to produce institutional conflicts and riddled with jurisdictional confusions . . ."[46]

The activities of legal institutions were particularly important in helping to provide the decentered state of the early nineteenth century with an ideology of the "public interest." Nowhere is this more evident than in their regulation of property rights and promotion of economic development. Here, according to pioneering studies, legal institutions used their authority to define, promote, and protect the interests of society at large. Corporations, in particular, were regarded as agents of the public interest, instrumentalities created to encourage private investors to fulfill a public need for a particular service in return for privileges in the shape of subsidies, immunities, and franchises.[47]

More recent debates have deepened our understanding of the relationship between economic development, legal institutions, the corporation, and the ideology of the public interest. Morton Horwitz, for example, has argued that rather than guiding the "release of energy" in a direction which would facilitate widespread participation in economic development, legal institutions systematically structured that release to the disadvantage of the majority of the population, creating in the process a legal system closely attuned to the interests of the commercial bourgeoisie. "In an undeveloped society with little available private capital," he writes, "a policy of encouraging development required that

45. Ibid., 24.   46. Ibid., 24.
47. See, for example, Oscar Handlin and Mary Flug Handlin, *Commonwealth: A Study of the Role of Government in the American Economy: Massachusetts, 1774–1861* (Cambridge, 1947); Louis Hartz, *Economic Policy and Democratic Thought: Pennsylvania, 1776–1860* (Cambridge, 1948); Milton Heath, *Constructive Liberalism: The Role of the State in the Economic Development of Georgia to 1860* (Cambridge, 1954). See also Carter Goodrich, *Government Promotion of American Canals and Railroads, 1800–1890* (New York, 1960); Nathan Miller, *The Enterprise of a Free People: Aspects of Economic Development in New York State During the Canal Period, 1792–1838* (Ithaca, 1962); Harry N. Scheiber, *Ohio Canal Era: A Case Study of Government and the Economy 1820–1861* (Athens, Ohio, 1969).

the legal system provide legal arrangements that guaranteed private investors certainty and predictability of economic consequences."[48]

According to Horwitz, the courts' guarantees initially took the form of rules embracing a view of property as in essence exclusionary and monopolistic. This approach underwrote the traditional status of the corporation as a public body "charged with carrying out public functions" and enjoying exclusionary privileges in return. Eventually it began to be recognized that beyond a certain point, concessions of monopoly to private interests obstructed economic development rather than encouraging it, and "state efforts to encourage economic growth began to diverge from private efforts to preserve existing legal expectations." But although corporations continued to invoke the traditional ideology of property rights in order to claim immunity from competition whenever it was in their interests to do so, they simultaneously sought, and won, new privileges guaranteeing them a favored status as private entrepreneurial entities under the developing regime of competition – the limitation of the liability of investors for corporate debts, constitutional protection of corporate property, and so forth. The result was the decline of the conception of the corporation as a public body and the appearance, by the end of the second decade of the nineteenth century, of a new archetype: "the modern business corporation, organized to pursue private ends for individual gain," its behavior conditioned far more by the circumstances it encountered in the marketplace than by the activities of state institutions.[49]

Horwitz's general thesis has attracted a good deal of criticism. According to Harry Scheiber, for example, the mobilization of law on behalf of commercial interests remained subject to "a competing doctrine . . . [which] gave primacy to what judges regularly termed 'the rights of the public,' " and which was clearly expressed in judicial insistence that there existed an explicit relationship between the promotion of economic activity and its regulation through state police powers.[50] It is important to take this point into account in examining the relationship between the state and the corporation. The challenge to the state's monopoly of legitimate ruling authority which was posed by the proliferation of private business corporations in the 1820s led contemporary legal commentators to stress that in the interests of "the safety and

---

48. Morton J. Horwitz, *The Transformation of American Law, 1780–1860* (Cambridge, 1977), 111.
49. Ibid., 112.
50. Harry N. Scheiber, "Regulation, Property Rights, and Definition of 'The Market': Law and the American Economy," *Journal of Economic History*, 41 (March 1981), 106. See also his "Public Economy Policy and the American Legal System: Historical Perspectives," *Wisconsin Law Review*, 6 (1980), 1159–89.

prosperity of the state," governments should ensure that they retained powers over corporations.[51] In response, state governments began to pursue legislative innovations which would ensure that they remained the repositories of final authority.

Of these, the most important was the power of the legislature to stipulate that it could alter or modify the terms of a charter, or repeal it, a measure which would give a state government "unfettered powers over corporate charters."[52] When in the 1830s the growing volume of applications for corporate status made it impossible for state legislatures any longer to exercise control through careful scrutiny of each proposed charter, leading to the passage of general incorporation laws, provision was made in the new laws for the inclusion of a standard clause of reservation in each charter. In this way the state could ensure that the private business corporation remained subordinate to the public interest.

This situation prevailed in the pre–Civil War period.[53] By 1870, however, the private business corporation had begun to build its commanding position in the American economy. In the thirty years which followed, the rapid growth in industrial and commercial activity touched off by the revolution in transportation and communications brought the decentered state of courts and parties and its claim to a monopoly of legitimate coercive power face to face with the expanding and nationalizing institutions of commercial and industrial capitalism and their competing claims of "private ordering."[54] The prominent Chicago attorney, Emery Storrs, neatly summarized the situation in 1885 while dedicating a new building to house the Chicago Board of Trade: "This Board, directly or indirectly, has settled legal questions

51. James (Chancellor) Kent to John R. Bleecker (7 April 1831), quoted in Horwitz, *The Transformation of American Law*, 138. Lawrence M. Friedman, *A History of American Law* (New York, 1973), 171, describes the popular suspicion of corporations rife during the first half of the nineteenth century.

52. Horwitz, *The Transformation of American Law*, 138.

53. Indeed, the clearest expressions of "unitary" democratic-constitutional ideology in nineteenth century America can be found in the two great constitutional crises of Nullification (1831–32) and the Civil War. On the first, see William W. Freehling, *Prelude to Civil War: The Nullification Controversy in South Carolina, 1816–1836* (New York, 1965). Lincoln's "House Divided" speech, delivered in acceptance of the Illinois Republican senatorial nomination on 16 June 1858, is a classic affirmation of the unitary state. See Don E. Fehrenbacher, *Prelude to Greatness: Lincoln in the 1850s* (Standford, 1962), 70–95.

54. Jonathan Lurie, *The Chicago Board of Trade, 1859–1905: The Dynamics of Self-Regulation* (Urbana, Illinois, 1979), 3–23; Charles W. McCurdy, "Justice Field and the Jurisprudence of Government-Business Relations: Some Parameters of Laissez-faire Constitutionalism," *Journal of American History*, 61, 4 (March, 1975), 970–1005. See also Poggi, *The Development of the Modern State*, 94–5.

of the largest importance to the producing and financial interests of the country. It has demonstrated the fact that those customs which, for the convenience of business, merchants have established among themselves, are stronger than any mere legal technicalities, and that to those customs . . . the law must bend, and if it does not it will break."[55]

Severe strains arising from this confrontation had begun to overtake the legal system by the mid-1870s. In the Midwest, state governments attempted to use their police powers to regulate the growing commercial economy. Illinois, for example, established a Railroad and Warehouse Commission in 1871, with powers to oversee corporation conformity with state laws and to prosecute offenders.[56] These governments also sought to protect local producers by regulating the entry of out-of-state goods into local markets. Their measures quickly attracted opposition from the interests affected, but received some support from the Supreme Court in *Munn v. Illinois* (1877) where the Court asserted that state governments had authority to oversee the activities of railroads, warehouses and grain elevators, and any other private enterprise which had become a "practical monopoly."[57]

Federal endorsement of the authority of state governments, however, was hardly unqualified. The Supreme Court's decision in *Munn* stressed that Congress had authority to occupy the field of interstate commerce altogether, and that exercise of that authority would render further state activity unconstitutional. By 1886, the Court had become less circumspect. "[R]egulation of commerce . . . can only appropriately exist by general laws and principles." If it were to be done at all "it should be done by the Congress of the United States under the commerce clause of the Constitution."[58] Meanwhile, lower federal courts had also been developing a body of doctrine limiting the regulatory potential of state law on the basis of the authority proclaimed by the Supreme Court in *Swift v. Tyson* (1844).[59] Diversity of citizenship enabled out-of-state corporations to elude the jurisdiction of state courts and have their cases heard in federal courts. As a result of *Swift*, the federal courts referred not to state law in deciding such cases but to a federal common law of commerce which they developed themselves. "On the basis of the *Swift* doctrine, federal judges erected a bulwark against the uncertainty

---

55. In Lurie, *The Chicago Board of Trade*, 17.
56. Friedman, *A History of American Law*, 391.   57. 94 U.S. 113.
58. *Wabash, St. L. and P. Ry. Co. v. State of Illinois* (1886), 118 U.S. 557, 7 Sup. Ct. Rep. 4, at 13.
59. 41 U.S. (16 Pet.) 1, 10 L. Ed. 865.

and prejudice of local law . . . [and] used the doctrine to support inter-state business."⁶⁰

To some influential jurists, limitation of the uses to which state governments could put their police powers was a necessary condition of harmony in business–government relations. According to Supreme Court Justice Stephen J. Field, for example, it was the task of the Court to formulate rules which would prevent ill-considered state regulation of commercial activity. Field also criticized assertions that states had unlimited powers over the corporations which they chartered, arguing that here too it was up to the Court to "define the limits of the power of the State . . ."⁶¹ But Field did not seek to deny states the opportunity to exercise their police powers altogether. Instead he sought "a harmonious system in which the public and private sectors pursued appropriate goals within proper spheres of action."⁶² In other words, Field's intent was to accommodate corporations within their own sphere rather than to free them from public accountability; he remained sensitive to the threat which "overwhelming corporate power" posed to "the great interests of the country."⁶³

Field's sensitivity proved all too prescient. The immutable rules to which he looked to designate the appropriate spheres of public and private activity "proved to be incongruent with the rapidly-changing needs of an ever-expanding capitalist society," not because they were unable to contain a proliferation of public regulatory initiatives but rather because they proved incapable of withstanding the accelerating rate of capitalist concentration and attendant social-economic tension which had provoked the states to attempt to reassert their authority in the first place.⁶⁴ Rather than employ his strictures on use of the police power to define even a modest sphere within which positive state action in the public interest would be appropriate, Field's successors invoked them to confine the states' police powers even more narrowly within an iron law of freedom of contract.

---

60. Tony Freyer, "The Federal Courts, Localism, and the National Economy, 1865–1900," *Business History Review*, 53, 3 (1979), 351–2. The Supreme Court had assumed, Oliver Wendell Holmes later explained, that there existed "a transcendental body of law outside of any state but obligatory within it" and determinable by the federal courts. See *Black and White Taxicab and Transfer Co. v. Brown and Yellow Taxicab and Transfer Co.* (1928), 276 U.S. 518, 48 Sup. Ct. Rep. 404, at 409.
61. McCurdy, "Justice Field," 997, 999.   62. Ibid., 995.
63. Stephen J. Field to Don M. Dickinson (30 June 1893), in McCurdy, "The *Knight Sugar* Decision," 341.
64. McCurdy, "Justice Field," 1005.

The erosion of the doctrine of *ultra vires* – that is, the erosion of the potential to control corporate strategy and structure inherent in the states' powers of incorporation – provides the most decisive evidence for the demise of the legal and political ideology of the decentered nineteenth century state. As Lawrence Friedman has written, the doctrine of *ultra vires* was "symbolic of the nature of the early corporation" for "it stood for the doctrine that the corporation was a creature of limited authority."[65] As the incorporating body, a state legislature could impose limits on the sphere within which a corporation could validly act through the constructions which it placed upon the powers outlined in the corporation's charter. Of particular significance in the 1880s, given the growth of excess capacity in industry, was the authority which this gave to a state to oversee the structure of business corporations within its jurisdiction; it meant that formally, at least, a wide range of business activity – alterations in capitalization, mergers in response to market conditions, and so forth – was subject to a state's scrutiny. The doctrine of *ultra vires*, therefore, was potentially a very effective check on corporate strategy and on the process of capital concentration.[66]

Earlier in the nineteenth century, as we have seen, states had used the medium of general incorporation laws to impose various restrictions on corporations in the name of the public interest. Enforcement, however, was another matter. Competition among the states for investment after the Civil War meant that meaningful oversight of corporate operations did not occur. In the late 1880s, however, "state attorneys-general were jolted from their protracted inertia" by the appearance of new concentrations of economic power, such as the oil, sugar, beef, and whiskey trusts. "In no state did corporation laws authorize chartered firms to abdicate control of their franchises; thus the combination of corporate assets through the medium of a trust was clearly *ultra vires* of all the constituent firms." Attorneys general in six states initiated *quo warranto* prosecutions. All were successful.[67]

The outcome of the prosecutions of the late 1880s indicated that the doctrine of *ultra vires* might offer a means to control the growing concentration of corporate power. Almost simultaneously, however, eastern states began to abdicate that authority by passing general incorporation laws of unusual generosity. New Jersey was the first. Its 1889 law allowed corporations domiciled in New Jersey to acquire control of foreign corporations (that is, corporations domiciled in other states).

65. Friedman, *A History of American Law*, 453.
66. McCurdy, "The *Knight Sugar* Decision," 304–42.   67. Ibid., 321, 322.

Other states continued to use *ultra vires* prosecutions to restrain their corporations from alienating control of their own franchises to New Jersey holding companies, and also maintained barriers against the entry of foreign corporations. But this policy had to be followed by most states to be effective, otherwise those which did would subject the products of their local corporations to growing competition from the products of interstate combinations active in backsliding neighboring states – products against which they could not discriminate without falling foul of the federal commerce clause. Given the competition for investment, moreover, state governments attempting to use their authority over corporate charters to resist corporate concentration faced the likelihood of the rolling bankruptcy of the state's industrial base, with predictable results for state revenues. These "federal effects" pointed to the final demise of the states' ability to control corporate structure, and one by one, states followed the example of New Jersey and "sold out the public's interest in corporate structures."[68]

The obvious solution was to shift the responsibility for incorporation, and thus the potential to oversee corporate strategy and structure, to the federal level. Congress, however, would not accept the responsibility. By the end of the nineteenth century ". . . regulation of business activity was no longer to be deemed a proper function of the law of corporate organization."[69] The modern business corporation was no more to be "the mere creature of the legislature"[70] at the federal level than it was at the level of the states. Instead it was accepted as a fact of life – a real entity with the same rights and privileges as any natural person.[71] Antitrust agitation and litigation ensured that both Congress and the Supreme Court would continue to maintain a high profile in the symbolic debates over the aggregation of economic power which oc-

68. Ibid., 338.
69. James Willard Hurst, *The Legitimacy of the Business Corporation in the Laws of the United States, 1780–1970* (Charlottesville, Virginia, 1970), 70.
70. In *Horn Silver Mining Co. v. New York* (1892), 143 U.S. 305, at 312, the Court stated "[a] corporation . . . is the mere creature of the legislature, [and] its rights, privileges and powers are dependent solely upon the terms of its charter." In McCurdy, "The *Knight Sugar* Decision," 307.
71. Ibid., 307. Thomas K. McGraw notes that Louis Brandeis's largely unsuccessful campaign against the big corporations during the Progressive period was premised on his refusal to accept the "naturalness" of these corporate entities. McGraw correctly points out that Brandeis's opposition to the large corporation was premised upon political rather than economic considerations. Indeed, we find in Brandeis's rhetoric the classical imagery of nineteenth century liberalism: "We are confronted in the twentieth century, as we were in the nineteenth century, with an irreconcilable conflict," Brandeis wrote 1911. "Our democracy could not endure half free and half slave. The essence of the trust is a combination of the capitalist, by the capitalist, for the capitalist." See McGraw, "Rethinking the Trust Question," 25–55.

curred throughout the early twentieth century, but judicial interpretation ensured that the antitrust approach remained confined within narrow frontiers. Indeed, by 1920 it appeared to one contemporary observer that "judicial interpretation of the anti-trust laws has had the effect of legalizing almost any degree of concentration of economic power if certain legal formalities are observed."[72] The security of the large business corporation, it appeared, was virtually assured.

Conclusion

The rise of the private business corporation and its successful thrust for control of its economic and political environments had, by the early 1900s, established the basis for an epoch of corporate hegemony in American society and culture. Dominant in the economy and secure in their relationship with the state, America's large corporations were free to exert increasing influence over the form of the emerging organizational society. This alone ensured that any attempts by the organized labor movement to develop its social and industrial influence in competition with business would be accompanied by considerable conflict.

The marginality of the unions in the new polity, however, was in any case assured by the consistent hostility of American legal culture to virtually any form of labor organization. That hostility is conveniently symbolized in the familiar roll-call of early twentieth-century Supreme Court decisions – *Loewe v. Lawlor* (1908), *Adair v. United States* (1908), *Gompers v. Buck's Stove and Range Company* (1911), *Coppage v. Kansas* (1915) – condemning unions as an invasion of entrepreneurial rights and dismissing legislative attempts to endorse them as legitimate bargaining agencies.[73] These, however, constituted merely the tip of an iceberg of judicial antipathy reaching far back into the nineteenth century.

In part, that hostility was an expression of the suspicion of associations intermediate between the individual and the state which, we have seen, was a characteristic of the nineteenth-century legal and political tradition. But this is not a sufficient explanation either of its existence or of its persistence. As their accommodation of the business corpora-

---

72. Myron Watkins, "The Sherman Act: Its Design and Its Effects," *Quarterly Journal of Economics*, 43 (1928–9), 32. See also Morton Keller, "The Pluralist State: American Economic Regulation in Comparative Perspective, 1900–1930," in McGraw, editor, *Regulation in Perspective*, 76.
73. *Loewe v. Lawlor*, 208 U.S. 274; *Adair v. United States*, 208 U.S. 161; *Gompers v. Bucks Stove and Range Company*, 221 U.S. 418; *Coppage v. Kansas*, 236 U.S. 1.

tion indicates, the opposition of legal institutions to private nonmarket regulation, and to the concentration of social, political, and economic power which went with it, had been crumbling since the Civil War. What the courts objected to, seemingly, was not the spread of organizations per se, but the spread of labor organizations in particular.

2

Law, labor, and ideology

[In] these days of huge and powerful corporations, which form in the eyes of the law single persons ... why should the law be such that if two steel workers plan a certain act which the law regards as tortious, they should be subject to fine and imprisonment; but if, let us say, the United States Steel Corporation plans and executes the self-same act, the criminal law should be unable to touch it? Is the danger to the state really greater in the first case than in the second? Why should a combination of individuals to commit an act which the law regards as tortious but not as criminal constitute a crime if the individuals are not incorporated but be free from crime if they are incorporated? Is that justice?

Francis B. Sayre, "Criminal Conspiracy," *Harvard Law Review*, 35 (1921–22), 420.

In June 1888, the president of the recently-formed American Federation of Labor, Samuel Gompers, issued a circular to all local, national, and international unions in the United States stressing the urgent need for a "thorough organization of the entire working class." The circular praised autonomous trade-based unions as "the natural growth of natural laws [which] from the very nature of their being have withstood the test of time and experience." It insisted, however, that success in eliminating "the evils of which we, as a class, so bitterly and justly complain" would not be assured until the unions had matched "the superior forces of united capital" with "a yet higher unity" through "the affiliation of all national and international unions in one grand federation, in which each and all trade organizations would be as distinct as the billows, yet one as the sea."[1]

Three distinct ideas are brought together in Gompers's circular. The first is the idea of craft or trade autonomy; the second, that the union was the expression of a natural law of collective action; the third, that working class unity was achievable only through the harmonious coop-

1. Samuel Gompers to All Local, National, and International Trade Unions (4 June 1888), in *The American Federation of Labor Records: The Samuel Gompers Era*, Microfilm Edition (Microfilming Corporation of America, 1979), reel 1 (The Gabriel Edmonston Papers). [Hereinafter cited as *AFL Records*.]

eration of distinct trade unions in one organized movement, and that in
this unity lay "the germ of the future state."[2] Each of these ideas em-
bodies conclusions arrived at by both American and European workers
during distinct, though partially overlapping, periods of activity: the
period of the preindustrial corporate craft guild, *compagnonnage* or
trade community; the early industrial period of enlightenment republicanism and voluntary association; and the period of rapid industrialization, labor federations, and social democracy. During the nineteenth
century these ideas blended together to form a unique synthesis of
artisanal corporate tradition, republican discourse, and social democratic collectivism. It was this synthesis which provided the AFL with its
founding theory of the labor movement and which sustained its earliest
claims to public legitimacy and to a decisive role in the ordering of the
economy.

Both in their separate manifestations and in their final synthesized
form, these ideas were repugnant to the doctrine and practices at the
center of the American common law tradition. As a result, throughout
the nineteenth century American labor organizations lived in a legal
twilight zone, expressions of an associational impulse growing in society at large, yet differentiated from other expressions of that impulse by
society's law and by their own ideology.

The very axis of society

Of the three components of the AFL's founding theory of unionism, the
structural principle of craft autonomy has attracted widest attention.
Essentially, craft autonomy expressed the conviction that every American worker was a member of a discrete national occupational grouping
of workers to which he was bound by common skills and interests. The
founders of the AFL sought to create a labor movement in which each
of these discrete trades, crafts, or callings had its own governing organization through which the interests of the craft could be expressed and
its practitioners defended. The role of the Federation was to help unrep-
resented crafts form national organizations, and to bind each craft into
the organized labor movement by recognizing each national organization, as it appeared, as the exclusive representative of the particular
group by which it had been organized.[3]

2. Samuel Gompers, "Trade Unions – Their Philosophy," (January 1899), in *AFL
   Records*, reel 110 (Speeches and Writings). See also William Dick, *Labor and Socialism in America: The Gompers Era* (Port Washington, New York, 1972), 21.
3. Dick, *Labor and Socialism*, 24. See also Philip Taft, *The AFL in the Time of
   Gompers* (New York, 1957), xv, 147.

The idea that a trade or calling possessed a particular right to govern its own affairs had accompanied craftsmen migrating to North America in the seventeenth and eighteenth centuries.[4] As a rule colonial craft societies were unable to reproduce the civil statutes through which the guilds had engrafted their authority on Europe and proved too weak to assert much authority in local product markets. Nevertheless, the establishment of the workshop mode of production during the eighteenth century in the commercial-manufacturing ports of the eastern seaboard was accompanied by the proliferation of familiar rituals and associations through which apprentices, journeymen, and masters celebrated the moral community of their trade.[5]

The incipient trade communities of the seaboard cities fragmented in the fifty years after the Revolution as commercial investment in domestic industry transformed the relations of workshop production, bringing about the homogenization of journeymen and smaller masters and dividing them from the new generation of capitalist employers who now controlled productive enterprise.[6] This fragmentation was rendered particularly significant by its occurrence within an ideological context dominated by heated debates over the meaning of the idioms of "liberty" and "independence" so central to republican thought.[7] To many of the revolutionary generation, the liberty and independence which they celebrated had promised the establishment of conditions which would enable free men to contract with one another on a basis of real equality by guaranteeing their economic and social indepen-

4. Samuel McKee, *Labor in Colonial New York, 1664–1776* (New York, 1935), 21–2. See also Richard B. Morris, "Criminal Conspiracy and Early Labor Combinations in New York," *Political Science Quarterly*, 52, 1 (1937), 51–85.
5. Sean Wilentz, "Artisan Republican Festivals and the Rise of Class Conflict in New York City, 1788–1837," in Michael H. Frisch and Daniel J. Walkowitz, *Working Class America: Essays on Labor, Community and American Society* (Urbana, Illinois, 1983), 37–77.
6. Howard B. Rock, *Artisans of the New Republic: The Tradesmen of New York City in the Age of Jefferson* (New York, 1979), 237–57; Alan Dawley, *Class and Community: The Industrial Revolution in Lynn* (Cambridge, 1976), 11–41; David Montgomery, "The Working Classes of the Pre-Industrial American City, 1780–1830," *Labor History*, 9, 1 (Winter 1968). See generally, Sean Wilentz, "Artisan Origins of the American Working Class," *International Labor and Working Class History*, 19 (Spring 1981).
7. Wilentz, "Artisan Republican Festivals," 49–65; John R. Howe, "Republican Thought and the Political Violence of the 1790s," in James M. Banner, Jr., et al, editors, *Understanding the American Experience: Recent Interpretations* (New York, 1973), 259–76; Eric Foner, *Politics and Ideology in the Age of the Civil War* (New York, 1980), 58–9. See, generally, Gordon S. Wood, *The Creation of the American Republic, 1776–1787* (Chapel Hill, 1966); Donald Winch, *Adam Smith's Politics: An Essay in Historiographic Revision* (Cambridge, England, 1978).

dence.[8] For others, however, a revolution fought in behalf of liberty and property necessarily sanctified the liberty of individuals to use their property *productively*, free from the restraints of collective regulation. To the latter, that is, revolutionary liberty stood for liberty of industry – entrepreneurial licence.[9] Republican guarantees of independence and autonomy meant no more than the provision of means whereby individuals might constitute and regulate their own lives and property through the medium of contract. They did not encompass measures to ensure their substantive equality in the bargaining which took place.

To the journeymen, the entrepreneurial interpretation of republicanism was triply unattractive. It was hostile to the traditions of the trade community, for these implied the legitimacy of restraints on individual liberty and property; it justified the production and marketing innovations which were undermining the status of journeymen within their own trades; and ultimately it threatened the revolutionary achievement itself, for as the journeymen conceived it revolutionary society was founded on virtue, and the major foundation of virtue was their own manly independence. Their answer was to recast the central concepts of revolutionary republicanism as explicitly collective phenomena. Drawing the benevolent and regulatory traditions of the trade community into a direct relationship with contemporary republican ideology they set about creating associations which could speak to their immediate needs through collective control of wage rates and of the distribution of labor among masters and simultaneously extoll the central position of American artisans in the post-revolutionary world as "the sinews and muscles of our country . . . The very axis of society."[10]

These activities, according to Richard B. Morris, were "contrary to the spirit of colonial statutes setting criminal penalties for the refusal of workmen in stated occupations to work and [to] the practice of the courts of specifically enforcing contracts of employment."[11] The ascen-

8. Wood, *The Creation of the American Republic*, 409–13. See also the important discussions of republican ideology in Isaac Kramnick, "Republican Revisionism Revisited," *American Historical Review*, 87, 3 (June, 1982), 629–64, and Drew R. McCoy, *The Elusive Republic: Political Economy in Jeffersonian America* (Chapel Hill, 1980).

9. Kramnick, "Republican Revisionism," 629–64; Rock, *Artisans of the New Republic*, 151–82.

10. Rock, *Artisans of the New Republic*, 123–43; Wilentz, "Artisan Republican Festivals," 45–53. For a superb analysis of these developments among New York's craftsmen, see Sean Wilentz, *Chants Democratic: New York City and the Rise of the American Working Class, 1788–1850* (New York, 1984).

11. Richard B. Morris, *Government and Labor in Early America* (New York, 1946), 205.

dancy of the entrepreneurial interpretation of republicanism, moreover, meant that efforts by members of trade societies to regulate the labor supply and set wage rates were also wide open to public condemnation as an assault on the principles of revolutionary liberty. Journeymen's associations, it was claimed, oppressed both the master's liberty of industry and the journeyman's liberty to labor. The doctrine of criminal conspiracy beckoned.

A land of law and liberty

In all, some twenty-two "labor" cases have been recorded as occurring in the years between 1805 and 1842.[12] They fall into three groups, coinciding roughly with periods of manufacturing expansion.[13] The five cases in the first group (1805–15) all involved cordwainers' combinations; the most significant were the Philadelphia (*Commonwealth v. Pullis*, 1805–6) and New York (*People v. Melvin*, 1809–10) cases. The second group (1821–9) is more heterogeneous and not well reported. The third group is concentrated in the mid-1830s. Among these were the important New York cases of *People v. Fisher* (1835) and *The Twenty Journeyman Tailors* (1836). Finally, in 1840–2 came the Massachusetts case, *Commonwealth v. Hunt*, which purported to inaugurate a new approach to journeymen's combinations.

At issue throughout was the status of associations of workers in a republic increasingly dominated by the entrepreneurial interpretation of the meaning of the Revolution. The issue was sharply posed in *Commonwealth v. Pullis*. Here the defendants were charged with conspiracy to raise their wages, an indictment condemned by the defense as an assault on revolutionary freedoms and as an attempt to elevate English common law above the natural and inalienable rights won in 1776. The prosecution, in contrast, based its case on the benefits which would redound to the community from the unlimited extension of manufactures, and decried the threat to the liberty of industry posed by men

12. This figure comprises twenty cases listed by Walter Nelles in his appendix to "Commonwealth v. Hunt," *Columbia Law Review*, 32 (1932), 1166–9, the case of *Commonwealth v. Hunt* (1842), 4 Metcalfe 3, itself, and an unnamed case referred to by Anthony F.C. Wallace in *Rockdale: The Growth of an American Village in the Early Industrial Revolution* (New York, 1978), 364–74. See also Marjorie S. Turner, *The Early American Labor Conspiracy Cases: Their Place in Labor Law: A Reinterpretation* (San Diego, 1967).

13. Nelles, "Commonwealth v. Hunt," 1166–8.

"who have no permanent stake in the city; men who can pack up their all [*sic*] in a knapsack, or carry them in their pockets to New York or Baltimore."[14] Cordwainers were entitled to seek the advancement of their wages in association, but not to make oppression of their employers' liberty of industry, or of other workers' liberty to labor at whatever wages they chose, the price of success. Association could be used to overcome the disadvantage of propertylessness, but it could not be used to threaten property itself.

The prosecution's argument would have left the act of association itself legal but its incidents almost invariably unlawful, because coercive. But Recorder Moses Levy, presiding, was not content with this position and proceeded to bind the prosecution's argument into a classically liberal philosophy of the relationship between the state and civil society which demanded not only that the coercive practices of the cordwainers' combination be outlawed but also its very existence as an entity denounced. Not only had the journeymen's combination injured the public welfare with its interference in the "natural" regulation of wages by supply and demand, it had also threatened the survival of republican government by counterposing its own laws to those of the state. Was Pennsylvania to have "besides our state legislature, a new legislature consisting of journeymen shoemakers" which obeyed its own laws and ignored "the laws of Pennsylvania?" It was not "the spirit of '76" that either masters or journeymen should be allowed to set up a rule contrary to the law of the country. "General and individual liberty was the spirit of '76. It is our first blessing. It has been obtained and will be maintained."[15]

Very similar issues arose again three years later in *People v. Melvin*. The case grew out of a strike called by the New York Cordwainers' Society against a master who gave work to a youth apprenticed to a nonmember. When this limited strike was thwarted by the cooperation of other master shoemakers who took in their associate's orders, the society called a strike against all, an act which "forced [the masters] to turn to the courts for redress."[16] Twenty-five of the journeymen were indicted for "perniciously and deceitfully forming an unlawful club and combination to govern themselves and . . . to extort large sums of money by means thereof."[17]

14. In John R. Commons et al., editors, *A Documentary History of American Industrial Society* (New York, 1958), III, 136. See also, Walter Nelles, "The First American Labor Case," *Yale Law Journal*, 41, 2 (December 1931), 165–201.
15. In Commons et al., editors, *Documentary History*, III, 228–30, 234, 235.
16. Rock, *Artisans of the New Republic*, 276. 17. Ibid., 46–77.

Like the Philadelphia society, the New York Cordwainers' Society was a "tightly disciplined and militant organization."[18] It exerted stringent controls over its own members and also attempted to exert disciplinary controls over nonmembers, for example by fining apprentices who did not join up on completion of their indentures and journeymen from out of town who did not become members upon entry into the community.[19] As in *Commonwealth v. Pullis*, this "oppression" of masters and of nonmembers was the key issue. And again the outcome was condemnation of the society's "coercive" behavior. In this case, however, Mayor Radcliff chose, from the bench, to distinguish the means which the defendants used, and which were the "arbitrary and unlawful" incidents of association, from the fact of their association.[20] Like the prosecutor in *Commonwealth v. Pullis*, that is, the court held that association per se was not controversial; it was the methods of the association which were suspect.

Succeeding conspiracy cases did not follow the lead of *People v. Melvin* away from Levy's doctrine of per se illegality.[21] The issue of whether the fact of association was sufficient by itself to warrant conviction was not, however, raised again unambiguously until 1835. Then, amidst spreading journeyman agitation fueled by a rapid rise in the cost of living, the New York Supreme Court denounced as conspiracies all attempts "to enhance the price of [an] article, or the wages of [a] mechanic, by . . . forced or artificial means."[22] The court allowed that an individual worker might set a price below which he would not work, but it insisted that he had no right to force other workers to maintain the same standard. And if no one individual could possess such a right then obviously no number of individuals could. "All combinations . . . to effect such an object are injurious, not only to the individual particu-

18. Ibid., 276.   19. Ibid., 276, note 33.
20. ". . . the Mayor . . . observed to the defendants, that the novelty of the case, and the general conduct of their body, composed of members useful in the community, inclined the court to believe that they had erred from a mistake of the law, and from supposing that they had rights upon which to found their proceedings. That they had equal rights with all other members of the community was undoubted, and they had also the right to meet and regulate their concerns, and to ask for wages, and to work or refuse; but that the means they used were of a nature too arbitrary and coercive, and which went to deprive their fellow-citizens of rights as precious as any they contended for. That the present object of the court was rather to admonish than to punish . . . it was recommended to them, *so to alter and modify their rules and their conduct as not to incur in the future the penalties of the law.*" In Commons et al., editors, *Documentary History*, III, 385 [emphasis supplied].
21. Turner, *The Early American Labor Conspiracy Cases*, 17–18.
22. In Nelles, "Commonwealth v. Hunt," 1168.

larly oppressed but to the public at large."[23] The court therefore found the combination itself to be a crime at common law.

The full impact of this reaffirmation of Levy's judgment was felt the following year in the case of *The Twenty Journeymen Tailors*. This case arose from a strike to enforce rules on the hiring of journeymen promulgated by the Journeymen Tailors' Society of New York. Following the precedent supplied the previous year, the court charged the jury that any action, however moderate, undertaken pursuant to an agreement not to work for a master who violated the society's rules would fulfill the requirements of a charge of conspiracy to restrain trade and render the society a criminal conspiracy. It was up to the jury, said Judge Edwards, to decide whether "any body of men could raise their crests in this land of law and control others by self-organized combination."[24] The jury agreed that the common law alone should rule and Edwards, handing out heavy fines, affirmed that the ascendancy of the entrepreneurial interpretation of republican ideology had so penetrated the judiciary as to result in an almost classical liberal perception of political economy:

> In this favored land of law and liberty the road to advancement is open to all, and the journeymen may by their skill and industry, and moral worth, soon become master mechanics ... Every American knows that he has no better friend than the laws, and that he needs no artificial combination for his protection.[25]

The case attracted considerable popular attention. Edwards was burned in effigy at a mass meeting in New York. At a similar meeting in Washington he was portrayed as the executioner of liberty rather than its defender.[26] The outcry led the judge in another New York case involving a conspiracy indictment against a journeymen's combination, the *Hudson Shoemakers* case (1836), to charge the jury that although "heretofore, all combinations of this nature have been deemed unlawful" yet it was still up to the jury to say whether the controlling of labor in such a manner tended to injure trade. The jury promptly found for the defendants. Just as partisans of the entrepreneurial spirit had formerly hailed the suppression of journeymen's combinations as a victory against oppressive combinations, so now partisans of the journeymen

23. In ibid., 1168. See also Wilentz, *Chants Democratic*, 284–86.
24. In Commons et al., editors, *Documentary History*, IV, 323.
25. In ibid., 330. See also Wilentz, *Chants Democrtic*, 289–93.
26. Edwin E. Witte, "Early American Labor Cases," *Yale Law Journal*, 35 (1928–36), 827.

could hail a verdict "rescuing the rights of the mechanics from the grasp of tyranny and oppression."[27] As had been the case throughout the period since the turn of the century, a common republican language hid an ever-widening gap in conception.

The decision in *Hudson Shoemakers* left the status of journeymen's combinations clouded in mystery. Popular pressure had forced the New York courts to abandon their unqualified endorsement of Levy's conspiracy doctrine in 1836, but *Hudson Shoemakers* was hardly authoritative assurance that henceforth they would be immune from prosecution. The Panic of 1837, and the depression which followed, weakened the combinations and drastically slowed the rate of strike activity, alleviating the pressure on the courts. Nevertheless, by the early 1840s, the issue of their legal status was once more before a number of courts.

An unreported Delaware conspiracy case cited by Anthony F.C. Wallace indicates that courts in different areas were proceeding toward the same position. In that case the judge reviewed the available English and American precedents and concluded that while a combination to seek unlawful ends or to use or plan to use unlawful means to gain lawful ends was a criminal conspiracy, the mere act of combination "to refuse to work at certain wages, or to combine to request or attempt to persuade an employer to raise wages" was not.[28] This indicates that the means–ends distinction first suggested by Mayor Radcliff in *People v. Melvin* had gained wide currency. It only remained for Chief Justice Lemuel Shaw to adopt this approach in *Commonwealth v. Hunt* for the distinction to become established at the center of nineteenth century American labor law.

Commonwealth v. Hunt replayed all the themes of the preceding forty years of conspiracy cases. The case had begun in 1840 with charges brought by one Jeremiah Horne against the Boston Journeymen Bootmakers' Society, a local journeymen's association organized in 1835. Horne, a member of the society, alleged that it had coerced his employer into discharging him for nonpayment of fines levied against him for breach of the society's rules. The indictment charged that the society was a criminal conspiracy and that its effect was to oppress and impoverish employers and nonconforming workmen.[29]

The trial began before Judge Peter Thacher on 14 October 1840. The prosecution based its case on the society's constitution, which, it argued, proved that the society was indeed a criminal conspiracy, and

---

27. In Nelles, "Commonwealth v. Hunt," 1169.
28. In Wallace, *Rockdale,* 373.   29. Nelles, "Commonwealth v. Hunt," 1133.

on the actions it had taken to the detriment of Horne and his employer. According to the prosecutor, Samuel D. Parker, the society's constitution showed it to be "anti-republican, tyrannical, illegal, despotic."[30] He condemned provisions charging increased initiation fees to late-joining journeymen and requiring journeymen to work at the wage rates established by the society as "despotic, tyrannical [and] illegal," as "[an] invasion of the liberty of the subject," and as a "gross violation of right."[31] By arrogating to the society's governing "Board of Judges" the authority to decide all disputes between employers and journeymen the society was interposing itself between the parties to the dispute and the state. "Laws should settle disputes. By such rules for their selfish objects they take away trial by Jury."[32]

The defense attorney, Robert Rantoul Jr., reiterated the arguments of the earlier conspiracy cases and attacked their indiscriminate application of English common law principles to America. "We might as well be governed by England as to adopt blindly in mass her laws which grow out of her institutions and state of society." The Constitution, he said, contained only such English law as suited the conditions of a free people. "Laws against acts done in restraint of trade belong to that portion of the law of England which we have not adopted. They are repugnant to the Constitution and to the first principles of freedom."[33]

Judge Thacher, however, saw the threat to liberty residing in the spirit of association, not in the common law; his charge to the jury reflected that opinion. "You must judge whether they do not propose, by means of this league, to control all masters, journeymen and apprentices in their art; and to compel the people of the Commonwealth to pay for the boots and shoes whatever price this society shall set."[34] Associations of journeymen, moreover, would beget associations of masters, and together these "new, secret and unknown tribunals" would subject citizens "to varying laws by which their property will be taken from them against their consent, and without trial by jury." If such associations were allowed to become general the consequences would be catastrophic. "All industry and enterprise would be suspended, and all property would become insecure. It would involve in one common, fatal ruin, both laborer and employer, and the rich as well as the poor. It would tend directly to array them against each other, and to convulse the social system to its center. A frightful despot-

---

30. In ibid., 1134, note 21.   31. In ibid., 1134, note 21.
32. In ibid., 1134, note 21.   33. In ibid., 1145.   34. In ibid., 1146.

ism would soon be erected on the ruins of this free and happy commonwealth."[35]

The case went on appeal to the Supreme Judicial Court of Massachusetts. There, Shaw overturned the lower court's decision and pointed the conspiracy doctrine in the direction suggested thirty-three years before in *People v. Melvin;* that is, toward depending on an examination of the objects of journeymen's associations in determining their legal status. The formation of a combination by journeymen was not in itself an unlawful act, he said. Whether a combination was a criminal conspiracy or not depended on its purposes. In this case the prosecution had treated the society's constitution as proof in itself of criminality, and had not specified any illegal purpose. But all that the constitution showed was that the society's purpose was to induce all those engaged in the bootmaking trade to join. This provided no proof of illegality, but only of intent to strengthen the power of the society. Such power might be used for "damaging or pernicious" purposes or for "useful and honorable" ones. But in either event it was the objects of a society, as expressed in its constitution or articulated during a strike, which henceforth would determine its legal status.[36]

By firmly reconciling the common law with the existence of journeymen's associations in this manner, Shaw safeguarded it from further angry attacks. In doing so, however, Shaw surrendered nothing of the common law tradition, for rather than molding the law to the social inevitability of journeymen's associated activity, Shaw successfully molded the legal character of that activity into a form compatible with prevailing common law. He was able to do so because by 1840 it had become clear that such associations were purely voluntary organizations.

At the core of earlier judicial denunciations of combinations as common law conspiracies had been suspicion of their corporative pretensions. As Recorder Levy had put it in *Commonwealth v. Pullis*, the laws of the cordwainers "leave no individual at liberty to join the society or reject it."[37] As such, journeymen's combinations seemed to challenge

35. In ibid., 1146–47.
36. Ibid., 1149–50. See also Turner, *The Early American Labor Conspiracy Cases,* 58–72.
37. In Nelles, "The First American Labor Case," 190. According to Levy, "The apprentice immediately on becoming free and the journeyman who comes here from distant places are all considered members of this institution . . . They leave no individual at liberty to join the society or reject it." Similarly, during the subsequent New York case, *People v. Melvin,* the prosecution alleged that "A journeyman [is] neither free to refuse entering into the society, nor at liberty, having done so, to leave it without incurring ruin or unmerited disgrace . . ." See Arthur Jerome Eddy, *A Treatise on the Law of Combinations* (Chicago, 1901), I, 285. Similarly, David J. Saposs notes that the Pittsburgh society of journeyman cordwainers exercised jurisdiction over non-

the state's monopoly of legitimate coercive authority. Even when their activities were clearly voluntarist, their attempts to attain control of employment and wages through tactics such as the closed shop were still treated as if they were attempts to assert the regulatory privileges of a corporation. Thus it is no surprise to find that in 1840 the Boston *Post's* account of the first hearing in *Commonwealth v. Hunt* highlighted the charge that the Bootmakers' Society's constitution gave the society authority to fine journeymen who refused to join it. "This is levying blackmail with a vengeance," commented the *Post*. But a week later, the *Post* announced that it had been mistaken. No such "obnoxious" provision appeared in the society's constitution after all. The society asserted no inherent authority to regulate the trade as a whole, and made no attempt to exert jurisdiction over any persons other than those who had voluntarily become members. From then on, the *Post's* coverage favored the defense.[38]

The unambiguously voluntary character of the Boston Journeymen Bootmakers' Society was typical of the journeymen's societies formed in the 1820s and 1830s. Their voluntarism reflected both their commitment to the revolutionary principles of liberty and independence, and their attempt at the same time to counterpose freedom of association to the common law tradition's increasingly hegemonic interpretation of liberty as freedom of industry and invidual freedom of contract. Earlier cases had ignored the distinction between the fact of combination and the purpose of combination because questions of purpose had been irrelevant to conspiracy laws designed to combat combinations formed in the manner of trade corporations. But the rise of voluntarism meant that the distinction gained increasing point. If joining had become a matter of choice, then coercion could not be held to inhere in the mere existence of the combination. Now the reasons which men gave for bringing their societies into existence were relevant to the question whether or not such societies were legal.[39]

members, "requiring them to appear at meetings and defend themselves against charges, remitting a fine only on condition that the offender promise to join the society." In John R. Commons et al., *History of Labor in the United States* (New York, 1918), I, 130.

38. Nelles, "Commonwealth v. Hunt," 1140. Marjorie Turner's analysis of the conspiracy cases leads her to conclude that judicial hostility to combinations was the most important factor explaining the outcomes of different cases. See Turner, *The Early American Labor Conspiracy Cases*, 31–57.

39. For a superb analysis of the transition from corporatist to voluntarist ideology and organization amongst European artisans, see William H. Sewell, Jr., *Work and Revolution in France: The Language of Labor from the Old Regime to 1848* (New York, 1980). Sean Wilentz, "Artisan Republican Festivals," provides considerable insight into the similar, if rather more ambiguous, transition occurring among New York artisans.

This transformation gave Shaw a bridge to the common law tradition. In place of a corporative body restraining trade by its very nature he found nothing but a group of free individuals who had agreed to improve their economic welfare by jointly refusing to work for employers of non-confederates. "We cannot perceive that it is criminal for men to agree together to exercise their own acknowledged rights in such a manner as best to subserve their own interest," Shaw stated, and thereby accorded unions recognition insofar as they had become and remained associations of free acting individuals who had contracted with each other to pursue jointly "purposes which each individual could legally seek to obtain without agreement."[40] Herein, however, also lay the unions' major problem, for their legality would not be in doubt only for so long as they did not appear to step back outside the limited space accorded them by the contractualist common law paradigm to which Shaw had just succesfully annexed them. Attempts to justify regulatory activity which invoked authority outside this paradigm – for example, the authority of the union to make and enforce rules as an embodiment of the aggregated free wills of its members – remained illegitimate and open to prosecution as criminal conspiracy.[41]

Voluntarism on trial

For twenty-five years following Shaw's decision in *Commonwealth v. Hunt*, the indictment of workers on conspiracy charges was a rare event.[42] Unions everywhere had been greatly weakened by the depression of the late 1830s, and even though recovery had become general by 1844, further economic fluctuations in the late 1840s and 1850s en-

40. In Nelles, "Commonwealth v. Hunt," 1150. See also Christopher Gustavus Tiedeman, *A Treatise on State and Federal Control of Persons and Property in the United States* (St. Louis, 1900), I, 418. The perspective adopted here resolves the apparent contradiction between Shaw's "pro-labor" opinion in this case and his simultaneous reaffirmation of the "anti-labor" fellow servant rule in *Farwell v. Boston and Worcester Railroad* (1842), 4 Metcalfe 49, the "leading American opinion" on this rule. (See Levy, *The Law of the Commonwealth*, 166–82). Both decisions, of course, were affirmations of freedom of contract.
41. Turner, *The Early American Labor Conspiracy Cases*, 58–72; Benjamin J. Taylor and Fred Witney, *Labor Relations Law* (Englewood Cliffs, New Jersey, 1971), 22; Witte, "Early American Labor Cases," 828–37. Richard B. Morris notes that courts in Southern jurisdictions continued to use criminal conspiracy prosecutions against unions per se long after *Commonwealth v. Hunt*. See his "Labor Militancy in the Old South," *Labor and Nation*, 4, 3 (May–June 1948), 32–6.
42. Witte, "Early American Labor Cases," 829.

sured that there was no general revival of trade union activity until the Civil War era.[43]

As journeymen's combinations continued to evolve during the second half of the nineteenth century, however, the constraints inherent in Shaw's restatement of the conspiracy doctrine became more evident. Originally, the boundaries of combinations had been defined by the commonality of their members as craftsmen within a particular locality. In both geographical and social terms, the intimate contact and face-to-face decision making implied in Shaw's contractual definition of their status as a group was unproblematic. Already in the 1830s, however, some local craft groups were attempting to organize national craft societies or unions in response to "impersonal developments," such as transportation innovations, which were bringing craftsmen in adjacent labor markets into competition with each other.[44] As the transportation and communications revolution of the middle decades of the nineteenth century got under way, the rapid expansion in the scope of labor and product markets forced all workers' organizations to expand beyond their local origins.[45]

As the scope of a combination's activities continued to widen the methods it used had to alter. At first, success in pursuit of collective objectives had depended upon the willingness of individuals to be bound by the decisions and rules arrived at by the group. "Hopefully," writes David Montgomery, "the worker's refusal [to obey any directive from an employer which violated his union's rules] would be supported by the joint action of his shop mates, but if it was not he was honor bound to pack his tool box and walk out alone, rather than break the union's laws."[46] In other words, whether or not the union's rules were enforced depended on the voluntary decisions of individual workers, within self-imposed constraints of "honor," whether or not to obey them. As the scope of their activities grew more extensive, however, the

43. Foner, *Politics and Ideology*, 72–3; Bruce Laurie, *Working People of Philadelphia, 1800–1850* (Philadelphia, 1980), 132, 139, 162–3, 194.
44. Edward Pessen, *Most Uncommon Jacksonians: The Radical Leaders of the Early Labor Movement* (Albany, New York, 1967), 35, 44; John C. Simonds and John T. McEnnis, *The Story of Manual Labor in all Lands and Ages* (Chicago, 1887), 436–7.
45. Lloyd Ulman, *The Rise of the National Trade Union: The Development and Significance of its Structure, Governing Institutions and Economic Policies* (Cambridge, 1955), 23–67.
46. David Montgomery, *Workers' Control in America: Studies in the History of Work, Technology and Labor Struggles* (New York, 1979), 16. Montgomery notes Fred Reid's comment on nineteenth century miners' unionism in Scotland: "The strength of organized labor was held to depend upon the manliness of the individual workman." Fred Reid, "Kier Hardie's Conversion to Socialism," in Asa Briggs and John Saville, editors, *Essays in Labour History, 1886–1923* (London, 1971), 29.

unions began to limit their dependence on the proclivities of individual craftsmen by institutionalizing the enforcement of their rules. "Where a trade was well unionized, a committee in each shop supervised the enforcement in that plant of the rules . . . which the union had adopted for the trade as a whole." They also began adopting rules which regulated the behavior of workers as well as of employers.[47]

The codification of the means of performing the craft in a national union's rules, the replacement of reliance on "honor" by institutionalized union discipline, and the formalization of the boundaries of the craft in a national union's jurisdictional structure all strengthened the union's authority. These innovations, however, also altered permanently the relationship between the union and its members. From being simply a conduit through which the interests of the craftsmen might be defended and their demands represented to the employer and to society at large, the union became an institution which governed the craftsmen and defined their interests. As a result, in the last three decades of the nineteenth century, the craft, its practitioners, and the institution which they had created to help ensure its survival became largely indistinguishable.[48]

Such developments ran increasingly afoul of the political-legal traditions adverted to in *Commonwealth v. Hunt*. In the pre–Civil War years these traditions received most comprehensive expression in middle-class anti-slavery thought rather than in renewed assaults on a weakened labor movement.[49] But many anti-slavery men also condemned labor organizations as inherently coercive and restrictive of the full freedom of the individual worker or employer to use his property in his labor or in his capital as he saw fit. The essence of the revolutionary ideals of liberty and equality, they argued, lay in the freedom to contract, that is in property *in self*. Workers and employers should encounter each other in the marketplace as free individuals, the employer at liberty to define the worker's duties as he saw fit, the worker at liberty to accept or reject these terms.[50]

The growth of stronger unions in the Civil War era brought with it a revival in conspiracy indictments, and the courts lost little time in estab-

---

47. Montgomery, *Workers' Control in America*, 16–17.
48. David Montgomery, *Beyond Equality: Labor and the Radical Republicans, 1862–1872* (New York, 1967), 139–96.
49. As Eric Foner has written, "Only a movement that viewed society as a collection of individuals, that viewed freedom as the property of every man, that believed every individual had the right to seek advancement as a unit in competitive society, could condemn slavery as utterly and completely as, in their own ways, abolitionists and Republicans did." See his *Politics and Ideology*, 23–24.
50. Ibid., 24, 57–76. See, generally, Patrick S. Atiyah, *The Rise and Fall of Freedom of Contract*, (Oxford, 1979), 219–568.

lishing an approach to the doctrine which allowed them considerable scope and flexibility. In *State v. Donaldson* (1867), a case arising from an attempt by a combination to seek the discharge of certain fellow employees considered obnoxious, the judge advised the jury that they should find against the defendants. The combination, he held, threatened the employer's control of his business. For this reason it was highly oppressive:

> In the natural position of things, each man acting as an individual, there would be no coercion; and if a single employee should demand the discharge of a co-employee, the employer would retain his freedom, for he could entertain or repel the requisition without embarrassment to his concerns; but in the presence of a coalition of his employees it would be but a waste of time to pause to prove that in most cases he must submit, under the pain of often the most ruinous losses, to the conditions imposed on his necessities. It is difficult to believe that a right exists in law which we scarcely can conceive can produce, in any posture of affairs, other than injurious results. It is simply the right of workmen, by concept of action, and by taking advantage of their position, to control the business of another. I am unwilling to hold that a right which cannot in any event be advantageous to the employee, and which must be always hurtful to the employer, exists in law. In my opinion, this indictment sufficiently shows that the force of the confederates was brought to bear upon their employer for the purpose of oppression and mischief and that this amounts to a conspiracy.[51]

The court was unable to detect criminality either in the means used or in the ends sought. Nevertheless it convicted the defendants, declaring that sufficient reason existed to indict a combination for conspiracy "where the confederacy, having no lawful aims, tends simply to the oppression of individuals."[52]

The decision in *State v. Donaldson* underscored how tenuous was the legitimacy allowed unions by the decision in *Hunt*. The law treated them simply as associations of individuals. Unions had "no legal status or authority" as collective rule-making entities.[53] Their members were subject to indictment for criminal or civil conspiracy not only when the

51. In Eddy, *Law of Combinations*, I, 315, note 1.
52. In Francis B. Sayre, "Criminal Conspiracy," *Harvard Law Review*, 35 (1922), 407. See generally, Foner, *Politics and Ideology*, 97–127.
53. C.B. Labatt, *Commentaries on the Law of Master and Servant* (New York, 1913), VIII, 8531. Arthur Lenhoff, "A Century of American Unionism," *Boston Law Review*, 22 (1942), 372–4.

means they used or the ends they sought transgressed the law, but also whenever a court decided that their existence in a collective form was "oppressive" to the rights of an employer. Thus, in *Walker v. Cronin* (1871), it was held that an employer's right to freedom of contract included the right to freedom from the interference of a union in obtaining the employment services of workers. In *Old Dominion Steamship Company v. McKenna* (1887), the court decided that combinations interfering with an employer's property, including his freedom to manage or conduct his business, or to interfere with the employment of others were illegal. In *Moore v. Bricklayers' Union* (1890), a combination to compel an employer to conduct his business according to the rules and regulations of his employees' union was held illegal, while in *Barr v. Essex Trades Council* (1894), employers were held to enjoy a general right to protection of their control over the enterprise and of their right to do business against "intimidation and coercion" by unions.[54] In this way, the institutionalized means resorted to by unions to enforce their rules – boycotting, unfair lists, most forms of picketing – were all held to be exercises in the oppression and coercion of employers and conspiracies to interfere in their free contractual relations with their employees.

The courts also cast themselves in the role of protectors of individual employees from coercion by unions. "The capital of the laborer is his labor, together with his skill, and he has the right to employ his talents and his industry as he pleases, free from the dictation of others."[55] Thus, in *Curran v. Galen* (1897), it was held to be an actionable conspiracy for an employer and a labor union to enter into any agreement to limit employment to union members or to dismiss non-union members because "public policy and the interests of society favor the utmost freedom in the citizen to pursue his lawful trade or calling."[56] The court continued:

> [I]f the purpose of an organization or combination of workingmen
> be to hamper or to restrict, that freedom, and through contracts or
> arrangements with employers, to coerce other workingmen to be-
> come members of the organization and to come under its rules and

54. Walker v. Cronin (1871), 107 Mass. 555; *Old Dominion Steamship Company v. McKenna* (1887), 30 Fed. 48; *Moore v. Bricklayers' Union* (1890), 23 Weekly Law Bulletin 48; *Barr v. Essex Trades Council* (1894), 30 Atl. 881 (N.J. Ch. 1894). See also *Casey v. Cincinatti Typographical Union* (1891), 45 Fed. 135; *Thomas v. Cincinnatti* (1894), 62 Fed 803; *Vegelahn v. Guntner* (1896), 44 N.E. 1077; *Curran v. Galen* (1897), 46 N.E. 297; *Hopkins v. Oxley Stave Company* (1897), 83 Fed. 912.
55. Eddy, *Law of Combinations*, 412.
56. In Tiedeman, *Persons and Property*, 452–3.

conditions under the penalty of the loss of their positions, and of deprivation of employment, then that purpose seems clearly unlawful and militates against the spirit of our government and the nature of our institutions.[57]

Because unions could only legitimately exist as voluntary associations, they had of necessity to rely on the free choice of individual citizens whether to become or remain members. Anything else would be "a compulsion, or a fettering, of the individual, glaringly at variance with that freedom in the pursuit of happiness which is believed to be guaranteed to all by the provisions of the fundamental law of the state."[58] Furthermore, the state took a direct interest in such organized compulsions and fetterings, for they constituted challenges not simply to the maintenance of the web of contractual relations through which, according to the nineteenth-century common law tradition, individuals produced and reproduced civil society, but also to the state's monopoly of legitimate coercive power which, in that same tradition, guaranteed the society so produced. As the court in *State v. Stewart* (1887) – "a typical statement of current doctrine" – put it:

> The labor and skill of the workman, be it of high or low degree, the plant of the manufacturer, the equipment of the farmer, the investments of commerce, are all in equal sense property. If men, by overt acts of violence, destroy either, they are guilty of crime. The anathemas of secret organization of men combined for the purpose of controlling the industry of others . . . are quite as dangerous, and generally altogether more effective, than acts of actual violence. And while such conspiracies may give to the individual directly affected by them a private right of action for damages, they at the same time lay a basis for an indictment on the ground that the state itself is directly concerned in the promotion of all legitimate industries and the development of all its resources, and owes the duty of protection to its citizens engaged in the exercise of their callings. The good order, peace, and general prosperity of the state are directly involved in the question.[59]

The major judicial expression of the state's desire to protect its citizens' transactions from interference, and to ensure their good order and general prosperity, was the labor injunction. First appearing in the late 1870s, the labor injunction quickly became a juridical staple, supplementing, though not replacing, civil conspiracy actions for damages and

57. Ibid., 452–53.
58. Ibid., 453. See also Eddy, *Law of Combinations*, 427.
59. 59 Vt 273, 9 Atl. 559; and see Francis B. Sayre, "Labor and the Courts," *Yale Law Journal*, 39 (1929–30), 687.

criminal prosecutions. Initially, labor injunctions took the form of court orders issued on behalf of strike-bound public carriers which had been taken into receivership and were thus under the protection of equity. These "orders in receivership," first used to restrain strikers in 1877, were not issued against named individuals but threatened to punish as contempt of court any interference with the operations of the carrier in question. They reappeared in 1885 and 1886, at which time they were made available to carriers not in receivership as well as those that were, on the grounds that the courts had a general duty to protect any carrier against such interference as would prevent it from fulfilling its obligation to serve the public at all times.[60]

The passage of the Interstate Commerce Act and the Sherman Antitrust Act was interpreted by many inferior courts to express in statutory form the right of equity to intervene in the "public interest" to protect the operations of public carriers. Indeed, in many courts the acts were understood to have brought commerce in general within the ambit of the equity power of federal courts. Thus in 1893, almost simultaneously, two different federal courts held the two different federal statutes equally condemnatory of the obstructive effects of labor unions upon the passage of interstate commerce. On March 25, the Circuit Court for the Eastern District of Louisiana granted an injunction under the Sherman Act against the Workingmen's Amalgamated Council of New Orleans in an action brought by the district attorney and arising out of the general strike of 1892. "The evil, as well as the unlawfulness, of the act of the defendants, consists in this," said the court, "that, until certain demands of theirs were complied with, they endeavored to prevent, and did prevent, everybody from moving the commerce of the country."[61] In an Ohio circuit court nine days later, Judge William Howard Taft found that strikes were no less reprehensible to the intent of the Interstate Commerce Act. "The apparent import," wrote Felix Frankfurter of this decision forty years later, "is that no interference with interstate commerce is ever justifiable."[62]

The following year, in the celebrated *Debs* case, the Supreme Court confirmed the state's direct interest in maintaining good order in the transactions undertaken by individual citizens and also affirmed that

60. Witte, "Early American Labor Cases," 832–6. See also Donald L. McMurry, "The Legal Ancestry of the Pullman Strike Injunctions," *Industrial and Labor Relations Review*, 14 (1961), 235–56.

61. *U.S. v. Workingmen's Amalgamated Council of New Orleans, et al.* (1893), 54 Fed. 994, at 1000.

62. *Toledo A.A. and N.M. Ry. Company v. Pennsylvania Company, et al.* (1893), 54 Fed. 730; Felix Frankfurter and Nathan Greene, *The Labor Injunction* (New York, 1930), 6–7.

under the commerce clause federal courts had authority to grant relief against activities of labor unions which threatened that good order.[63] The Court, however, did not rest its decision on the specific provisions of either the Interstate Commerce Act or the Sherman Act. Both statutes were cited as evidence of the federal government's concern that interstate commercial transactions should be subject to regulation, but the injunction itself was justified by reference to the traditional principle that equity would protect any property from irreparable injury.[64] In other words, the Court approved the use of injunctions not just for the protection of the property of public carriers but of anyone engaged in commerce. Furthermore, its judgment indicated that the right to do business – that is, the right of business enterprises to unrestricted access to labor and commodity markets – was paramount in its definition of property.[65] By this token "oppression" and "coercion" of employers would be found to have occurred not only when combinations of employees attempted to deprive an employer of his property but also when workers attempted in association to assert their competing property rights against him. In short, despite the recognition which the courts had accorded voluntary associations ever since Shaw's decision in *Hunt*, so great was their stress on the qualifying adjective "voluntary" by the end of the nineteenth century that little significance seemed to attach to the noun.

For the labor movement, the actions of the courts amply confirmed that the law's conceptions of individual self-ownership or independence bore little resemblance to the republican tradition. In its eyes, oppression and coercion were inherent in the capitalist mode of production's commodification of labor. According to their leaders, workers were now so thoroughly oppressed and coerced by the superior economic power of employers that they existed in a condition of permanent wage slavery. If evidence were required it existed in abundance in the deterioration of workingmen's status, not only in their own crafts, but in society and in the republican polity as a whole. The assertion that individual liberty and equality were incidents of the free operation of commerce, therefore, left the labor movement cold. Rather, entrepreneurial freedom was treated as a contradiction of republican principles and an assault on the rights, dignity, and independence – the liberty – of workers.[66]

63. *In Re Debs, et al.* (1895), 158 U.S. 440, 15 Sup. Ct. Rep. 900, at 900, 907.
64. Witte, "Early American Labor Cases," 836. 65. Ibid., 836.
66. Foner, *Politics and Ideology*, 58–9. See also the important article by Linda Schneider, "The Citizen Striker: Workers' Ideology in the Homestead Strike of 1892," *Labor History*, 23, 1 (Winter 1982), 47–66.

As the realization dawned that America would not escape Europe's dark satanic mills and its permanent wage-earning class – that it could not enjoy capitalism without class conflict[67] – workingmen's combinations became tighter and more authoritative, a development which would culminate in the formation of the American Federation of Labor in 1886. Furthermore, while the labor movement's republicanism continued to develop there came a growing interest in the collectivist theories now radiating out from the centers of European social democracy. Accelerating rates of industrialization in the latter half of the nineteenth century had created the conditions in which such ideas seemed ever more relevant to the experiences of American workers, and to the strategy and structure of their organizations.[68]

Marx and Lassalle

Late in 1871, Karl Marx wrote to Fred Bolte of the Cigar Packers' Union urging him to support Friedrich Sorge's campaign to break the links between American labor and reformist politics. His letter is one of the many examples which historians have found of the extensive influence of European social democratic thought on early modern American trade unionism.[69] It is necessary, however, to consider the precise nature of this influence, for in the 1860s and 1870s European social democracy was still developing and had not yet become a coherent or unified body of theory. At this time its development was profoundly affected by the disagreements between two major theorists, Karl Marx and Ferdinand Lassalle.

Lassalle and Marx differed most obviously in their analyses of the state. For Lassalle, the state was a universal attribute of society which reflected the ideas and principles of the class which was dominant at any one particular time. As such, Lassalle believed that the state could "change hands." A new group, for example the working class, could

---

67. Foner, *Politics and Ideology*, 127.
68. Leon Fink, "The Uses of Political Power: Toward a Theory of the Labor Movement in the Era of the Knights of Labor," in Frisch and Walkowitz, editors, *Working Class America*, 104–22, particularly 106–9.
69. See, for example, Daniel Bell, "The Background and Development of Marxian Socialism in the United States," in Donald Drew Egbert and Stowe Persons, editors, *Socialism and American Life* (Princeton, 1952), I, 213–93; Dick, *Labor and Socialism*, 11–12; Stuart B. Kaufman, *Samuel Gompers and the Origins of the AFL* (Westport, Conn., 1973), 22–42, 214–22. See also, Bruce Laurie, *Working People of Philadelphia 1800–1850* (Philadelphia, 1980), 161ff; Susan E. Hirsch, *Roots of the American Working Class: The Industrialization of Crafts in Newark, 1800–1860* (Philadelphia, 1978), 118, 129–31.

challenge the group hitherto dominant, for example the bourgeoisie, by contesting its control of the state. Once successful, it could use the state to establish the sway of its principles, just as the state had been used by the former incumbents to maintain the sway of theirs. For Marx, in contrast, the state did not exist as a disembodied entity to be captured in an electoral contest. For Marx, the state was the mechanism through which the dominant class ruled society and existed only as "the representation of the concrete material interests" of this class. A capitalist state and a workers' state were not examples of the different uses to which the same entity could be put but were completely unrelated phenomena, each specific to the material interests of which it was the representation.[70]

Two distinct theories of working-class action flowed from these different analyses of the state. Lassallean theory emphasized that through independent political organization and the achievement of universal suffrage, the workers could begin to influence and eventually capture the state, all the while using it to turn their ideas and principles into practice. Specifically, the state would be used to initiate the socialization of production through the provision of increasing amounts of state aid to a quasi-syndicalist system of workers' cooperatives which would conduct the business and industry of the nation. Universal suffrage was the key to this program for "If universal suffrage were achieved, then the workers would have the leverage for pressuring the government to provide state-help on a vast scale." Eventually the workers would gain full control of the state. This would guarantee that the cooperatives would become the only form of industrial activity, and would enable the workers to unlock the vast potential of state power to realize their goals.[71]

Trade unions played no part in Lassalle's theory. Indeed, he regarded trade unionism as a snare and a delusion. Economic organization prior to the initiation of the political campaign to wean the state from its capitalist masters was futile; the iron law of wages made the improvement of the workers' material position through trade union action impossible under capitalism. Marx, in contrast, insisted on the fundamental importance of economic organizations of workers. The capitalist state could not in some idealistic sense be separated from capitalism and transferred into the custody of the workers simply through the ballot, for it was rooted in the capitalist mode and relations of production. The ultimate goal in the class struggle, therefore, was not capture of the

---

70. Vernon L. Lidtke, *The Outlawed Party: Social Democracy in Germany, 1878–1890* (Princeton, 1966), 22.
71. Ibid., 24–5.

state as such but the destruction of the capitalist mode and the transformation of the relations of production. Workers should organize politically to oppose the state as an instrument of capitalist domination. But the appearance and growth of organizations representative of the material interests of workers was an essential condition of successful political action. For this reason, and because they would make an important contribution to the workers' attempts to undermine the capitalist mode, Marx stressed the importance of organizing the workers' material strength and its further development through the activity of trade unions.[72]

Considerable tension, personal as well as intellectual, existed between the two theorists,[73] and Marx's letter to Fred Bolte betrays his concern that the infant trade union movement in America would be adversely affected by the spread of Lassallean heresies to the far side of the Atlantic. Not only must the American labor movement shun all alliances with bourgeois reformers, he warned; independent political action must also await the establishment of "a previous organization of the working class developed up to a point and arising precisely from its economic struggles."[74]

Marx need not have worried. By the end of the decade even that most fervent of American Lassalleans, Peter McGuire, had accepted the importance of trade union activity. "We never can storm the citadel of money power, entrenched as it is behind law-customs," McGuire wrote in 1879, "if we have not disciplined our labor hosts in many a preparatory conflict."[75] Yet the story of social democracy's influence on the early modern American labor movement is far more complex than one simply of the triumph of Marxist ideas over Lassallean. Marx's ideas proved more immediately relevant to the form that labor activity in the United States most often took in the 1870s and 1880s, but American Lassalleans retained their mentor's vision of a society in which all economic activity would be organized through and controlled by workers' cooperatives. The major adjustment they made was in Lassalle's insistence on the creation of a system of state-aided cooperatives through political action, arguing that the unions themselves could be the organizational means whereby this goal might be achieved. "[Trade unions] are indispensable under our present system," McGuire wrote in 1878. "It will be their province to form the

72. Robert A. Christie, *Empire in Wood: A History of the Carpenters' Union* (Ithaca, 1956), 32–3; Kaufman, *Samuel Gompers*, 3–21; Dick, *Labor and Socialism*, 9–26.
73. See, for example, David McLellan, *Karl Marx: His Life and Thought* (New York, 1973), 322–3.
74. In Kaufman, *Samuel Gompers*, 10.   75. In Christie, *Empire in Wood*, 35.

intermediary link between the wage system and that of co-operation . . . In the future they will be the germ of trade co-operation. To a great extent through them a system of universal co-operation will be conducted and managed."[76]

In arguing that trade unionism rather than political action could be the means through which the cooperative commonwealth of trades would ultimately be achieved in America, McGuire was acknowledging the importance of the Marxist emphasis on economic organization and trade union action while reflecting also the links which American trade unionism already enjoyed with cooperation. His argument, however, also reproduced the position embraced by organized workers in France during the first half of the nineteenth century. There, as in America, workers had been confronted with the necessity to reconcile their (more potent) corporatist tradition with a revolutionary ideology of liberty which, in its free contractual and individualist implications, had threatened their trades and their lives with a "devastating torrent" of economic competition. As in America, the course they steered was toward voluntary association. "The corporation became an association freely formed by those who labored in a trade, and the rules it proposed became not an assault on freedom of industry but an expression of the associated free wills of the producers . . ." In this way, "claims for collective regulations became compatible with certain interpretations of liberty."[77]

French workers had not stopped here. They had developed their voluntarism into an "idiom of association" which provided a framework for achieving the unity of the whole class through the association together of all workers organized in their different trades:

> If we remain isolated, scattered, we are feeble, we will be easily defeated and will submit to the law of the masters; if we remain divided, cut off from one another, if we do not agree among our-

76. Ibid., 36. In 1909, William M. Leiserson wrote that by 1850–1 the whole trade union movement in New York, Boston and Pittsburgh had become permeated with the idea "that cooperation offered the best mode of protection to workmen and was the ultimate means of solution for the problems of labor." According to Leiserson, "The idea of productive cooperation grew out of the desire for protection against long hours, low wages, sweating and unemployment. Strikes and the law had both failed to protect the workmen. They would therefore eliminate the menaces to their wages by doing away with the employing class. In their own shops they would establish the laws which the legislatures refused to enact. And when a majority of the industries had been thus transformed there would be no need to petition the government for protective laws. It would be compelled to recognize in law the conditions which already existed in fact." *Leiserson Papers*, Box 48, ("Speeches and Articles, 1901–11").

77. Sewell, *Work and Revolution in France*, 206.

selves, we will be obliged to surrender ourselves to the discretion of our bourgeois. There must hence be a bond that unites us, an intelligence that governs us, there must be an *association*.

Association meant an end to social disorder and the promise of true freedom. "Poverty gives birth to crimes, association kills poverty. Let us push on toward association; the people will become moral, the people will be happy."[78]

Fifty years later, Peter McGuire, Samuel Gompers, and other AFL leaders were using precisely the same syndicalist language and concepts to describe the American Federation of Labor's goals, strategies and aspirations. The unions, their rules and their strategies for the control of jobs had a universal significance, they said. They were the means whereby craftsmen would sustain themselves at the point of production. But they were also the means to their ultimate emancipation:

> To educate our class, to prepare it for the changes to come, to establish a system of co-operative industry in place of the wage system, to emancipate the workers from subjugation to the capitalists, these are our ultimate objectives ... We are approaching a great revolution, which, if based on organized action, is destined to assume control of the industries and the government of the nation.[79]

Similarly, just as French workers emphasized the transcendent moral significance of their "idiom of association" – the only means whereby society might be saved "from annihilation in the egoism of isolation, from regression to the state of savagery, from corruption and deterioration of human nature itself" – so too did the leaders of the AFL. The trade unions, they declared, were "the legitimate outgrowth of modern social and industrial conditions ..." They were "born of the necessity of the workers to protect and defend themselves from encroachment, injustice and wrong." As such they were "justified by all laws of natural growth." More than that, however, the trade unions were the saving remnant, "the only hope of our civilization ... the only power whose mission it is to evolve order out of social chaos, to save us from reaction, brutality and perhaps barbarism."[80]

Finally, just as French workers rejected the paternalist state, arguing that the new social order they envisioned was to be "an emanation of

---

78. In ibid., 216.
79. In Christie, *Empire in Wood*, 67. See also Samuel Gompers in the San Francisco *Daily Report* (10 March 1891), in *AFL Records*, reel 24 (Scrapbooks).
80. Sewell, *Work and Revolution in France*, 216; Gompers, "Trade Unions–Their Philosophy."

the order already implicit in the corporate trades," so the leaders of the AFL also avoided involvement in reform politics, embracing instead the prospect of a new social and political order based on the harmonious interaction of workers voluntarily associated in their various trades and callings.[81] Trade unions, said Gompers, were not simply organizations for the defense of their members' immediate interests. Not only were they the sole means whereby American labor as a whole could be defended, they were also the only appropriate institutional mechanism through which the ultimate liberty of American workers could be achieved. The AFL – the "House of Labor" – was the embodiment of the organizational form which the new society would assume as a result of the deliverance of the workers. It was "the germ of a future state which all will hail with glad acclaim."[82]

To its leaders, then, the AFL was quintessentially "*the* form of class organization prescribed by the history of American capitalism."[83] Synthesizing native and foreign working-class ideologies, they counterposed to nineteenth century liberal political and economic theory an alternative which denied that in individualism and competition lay the embodiment of the republican tradition, and which instead asserted that the organization of unions to govern the trades and callings of all American workers and the gathering of those unions together in the "House of Labor" was the only foundation upon which true freedom and democracy in America might be built. "That the trade union is the historic and natural form of working class organization is becoming day by day more evident to the minds of our people," stated the Executive Council of the AFL in 1888, just two years after the creation of the Federation:

> And the conviction is slowly but surely gaining ground that by the organization of the workers upon the basis of their trades and callings and the Federation of the various unions in a grand universal union, with the autonomy of each guaranteed by all, will be found the practical realization of aspiration voiced by our lamented President Abraham Lincoln in the memorable sentence – "The Government of the people, by the people, for the peonle."[84]

81. Sewell, *Work and Revolution in France*, 242. Gompers, "Trade Unions–Their Philosophy." See also Samuel Gompers, "True Trade Unionism," *Labor World and Silver Champion* (4 September 1897), in *AFL Records*, reel 24 (Scrapbooks).
82. Gompers, "Trade Unions–Their Philosophy."
83. Kaufman, *Samuel Gompers*, 215–16 [emphasis supplied].
84. AFL Executive Council, "To the Officials and Delegates of the International Trade Union Congress in London Assembled" (27 October 1888), in *AFL Records*, reel 59 (Files of the President: General Correspondence, 1888–1904).

Conclusion

Writing in the early years of the twentieth century, the labor economist Robert F. Hoxie drew attention to the extent to which the phenomenon of trade unionism contradicted the basic assumptions of a middle-class competitive capitalist legal and social order. Trade unionism, he concluded, took little notice of individual freedom, as defined in contemporary law. It had no regard for the inviolability of contract or property rights, nor for the authority of prevailing morality, nor even for the authority of the courts. "It conflicts with the legal theory upon which our social and industrial system is based and with the established law and order; in many ways it opposes our conventional ethical standards and notions of right and justice."[85]

Unlike some of his contemporaries, Hoxie did not attribute this state of affairs to the wickedness or moral turpitude of trade unionism's adherents. Rather, he pointed to the irreconcilable conflict which existed between the spirit of the law and the ethos of trade unionism:

> As the law in spirit is individualistic, as it makes the freedom and sacredness of individual contract the touchstone of absolute justice, and as the unions are formed to escape the evils of individualism and individual competition and contract, and all the union acts in positive support of these purposes do involve coercion, the law cannot help being in spirit inimical to unionism. Unionism is in its very essence a lawless thing, in its very purpose and spirit a challenge to law.[86]

One of the most important consequences of this conflict, Hoxie sensed, was that, lacking legitimacy within the boundaries of the rule of law, the organized labor movement sought its legitimacy elsewhere, beyond those boundaries, in its own history, traditions and aspirations. He quoted Gompers to this effect:

> There is not a wrong against which we fail to protest or seek to remedy; there is not a right to which any of our fellows are entitled which it is not our duty, mission, work and struggle to maintain. So long as there shall remain a wrong unrighted or a right denied there will be ample work for the labor movement to do.
>
> The aim of our unions is to improve the standard of life; to foster education and instill character, manhood and an independent spirit

85. Robert F. Hoxie, *Trade Unionism in the United States*, 2nd ed. (New York, 1923), 23, 30.
86. Ibid., 238. According to Hoxie, American law "knows no society apart from an aggregation of individuals and no social welfare apart from individual welfare" (217).

among our people . . . The trade union movement, true to its history, its traditions and its aspirations has done, is doing, and will undoubtedly do more in the interest of mankind to humanize the human family than all other agencies combined.[87]

The unions, that is, claimed legitimacy not as a consequence of submission to the rule of law but in their own right as republican institutions participating in a republican polity and making law as such.

The "organizational impulse" alive in American society at large at the turn of the century seemed to offer the unions a context in which their ambitions to achieve a transformation of the individualistic spirit of nineteenth-century political and legal thought and institutions might be fulfilled. But as we have seen, what in fact emerged from the material and ideational conflicts of the years after the Civil War was an accommodation between American legal culture and large-scale corporate capitalism which gave corporations the rights of individuals. The strategy and ideology of the organized labor movement thus remained fundamentally at odds with the approach to the organization and control of economic activity embodied in the political-legal structure of the American polity, leaving the legal status of unions as profoundly uncertain as before. In such circumstances the early years of the twentieth century hardly seemed likely to bring any lessening of the hostility toward unions that had characterized the state during the nineteenth.

87. Samuel Gompers, "Report to the Twenty-Ninth Annual Convention of the American Federation of Labor" (1909), in ibid., 23–24.

3

From conspiracy to collective bargaining

The workers furnish the creative toil and the intelligent service essential to the best development of our material civilization. Their best interests and their highest development form the greatest incentive in the work with which they are associated. Their welfare and progress are inseparably associated with terms and conditions of daily work. It is essential, therefore, that they should have a voice in determining conditions and terms of work and that they should have an opportunity to establish and maintain their ideals and conceptions of what constitutes their protection and welfare . . .

Trade unions represent principles of human welfare. They represent human ideals. They represent opportunities for better life and work for the masses of the people. They are an integral part of the organization of society, and must be recognized both by employers and by political agents who have a conception of democratic principles of statesmanship.

Samuel Gompers, "Justice and Democracy, the Handmaids of Preparedness," *American Federationist*, 23, 3 (March 1916), 176–7.

The climax of the organized labor movement's confrontation with the "individualistic spirit" of the law came in the 1890s and early 1900s; at the same time, that is, as conflicts over control at the point of production entered their most decisive phase. The coincidence is hardly surprising, and more often than not the unions treated the two struggles as one. In part this was a purely practical matter; the interventions of the judiciary played a particularly important role in hampering the efforts of unions in their fights with employers. But it was also much more. No less than exploitative and domineering corporations, tyrannical courts constituted a grave and potentially fatal threat to the republican institutions and ideology with which the organized labor movement identified.

No matter the forum – factory or court room – in which confrontation took place, the result was more often than not defeat for the unions. Political activity to capture the state, or militant syndicalism in fulfillment of the unions' associational ideology, were both canvassed as possible strategies of response. But in the main, the effect of the reverses of the late 1890s and early 1900s was to accelerate and generalize throughout the organized labor movement the adoption of strategies which abandoned all but the immediate economic struggle, and which concentrated on protecting the power of the leading national unions. The associational visions of the 1880s and 1890s, as a consequence, were rendered progressively more remote of attainment. By World War I, the "federation of trades" had reorganized itself around its strongest constituents and had simultaneously accepted the reality and the inevitability of the new corporate political economy. Henceforth, the goal of the organized labor movement was to be not so much to transform that political economy as to seek accommodation for the national unions within it.

A menace to republican institutions

Sustained conflict between the American Federation of Labor and the judiciary began in the early 1890s. In 1893, for example, AFL president Gompers drew to the attention of the Executive Council the protests of the Workingmen's Amalgamated Council of New Orleans against the action of the Circuit Court for the Eastern District of Louisiana in granting an injunction restraining the New Orleans general strike. "It [is] well to know that, under existing laws as interpreted by the courts, free men can be made slaves," the New Orleans Council had commented. "If this be true the sooner the truth becomes generally known the better; for when it becomes known all men who love liberty will unite in securing the repeal of such iniquitous laws."[1] Early the following year, Charles F. Reichers, General Secretary of the United Garment Workers, called on the Executive Council to provide the union with sufficient financial aid to allow it to appeal an injunction against a strike. "If we do not take advantage of the opportunity," Reichers wrote, "a precedent will be established making it possible for employers on the slightest provocation or pretext to enjoin labor unions from following out their natural sources of protection."[2] By April of that year, Gompers was receiving regular legal advice on the courts' evolving definition of conspiracy.[3]

The AFL's initial responses to the judiciary's attacks on the "oppres-

---

1. Samuel Gompers to the AFL Executive Council (10 April 1893), in *AFL Records*, reel 8 (Executive Council Vote Books).
2. Charles F. Reichers to Samuel Gompers (20 January 1894), in *AFL Records*, reel 8 (Executive Council Vote Books).
3. See, for example, George H. Hart to Samuel Gompers (16 April 1894), in *AFL Records*, reel 59 (Files of the President: General Correspondence, 1888–1904).

sive" and "coercive" activities of its affiliates were couched in the same republican language which had defined the whole realm of public discourse in nineteenth-century America. As we have seen, the labor movement had consistently denied that the entrepreneurial interpretation of revolutionary republicanism, which had long since attained decisive influence over nineteenth-century politics and jurisprudence, was the only interpretation available. As Gompers himself put it, "we in America who enjoy absolute political liberty have long ago recognized that without economic freedom accompanied by economic organization, political liberty is but a fantasy and a delusion."[4] Thus, the AFL's leadership answered the courts' assaults on the legitimacy of unions by reaffirming the organized labor movement's own associational tradition.[5] Labor unions, they asserted, were essential to the survival of a truly republican polity in the United States. It was the judiciary which professed to deny this that threatened the survival of the republic, not the unions.

By the late 1890s, AFL leaders were regularly condemning the intervention of the courts in labor disputes as a threat to the republican polity. In November 1897, for example, Gompers wrote to the newly-elected President McKinley to warn that this "new weapon . . . brought into play in the disputes between employer and employed" was "a menace to republican institutions" which threatened to make the judiciary dominant over the legislative and executive branches of government;[6] the following year he denounced the judiciary as "the pliant tools of corporate wealth."[7] At the same time, Gompers placed addi-

---

4. AFL Executive Council, "To the Delegates of the International Labor Congress, Brussels" (4 August 1891), in *AFL Records,* reel 59 (Files of the President: General Correspondence, 1888–1904). See also Linda Schneider, "The Citizen Striker: Workers' Ideology in the Homestead Strike of 1892," *Labor History,* 23, 1 (Winter 1982), 47–66.
5. "Organization is a natural condition of man. It is the order of nature's law. The fish which swim in shoals, the beasts which travel in herds . . . wherever there is an aggregation of species, there is the best result obtained." Samuel Gompers, in the San Francisco *Daily Report* (10 March 1891), in *AFL Records,* reel 24 (Scrapbooks).
6. Samuel Gompers to President McKinley (18 November 1897) in *AFL Records,* reel 8 (Executive Council Vote Books).
7. Samuel Gompers, "The American Federation of Labor Political Action" (June 1898), in *AFL Records,* reel 110 (Speeches and Writings). The same month, Gompers warned the Executive Council that an indictment of eleven District of Columbia union members for criminal conspiracy in restraint of trade under the Sherman Act, if sustained, "will greatly embarrass and ultimately destroy all labor organizations in the country. The case not only involves the legality of the boycott but the right of labor organizations to compel their members to observe those rules necessary for maintenance of the bodies to which they belong. It therefore involves the rights of organization and this trial is therefore of national interest." Samuel Gompers to the AFL Executive Council (20 June 1898), in *AFL Records,* reel 8 (Executive Council Vote Books).

tional emphasis on the central role of unions in the maintenance of republican institutions. The union, Gompers argued, was not only "a determining factor in all social functions; a main artery of the pulse of trade, of commerce, of society," it was also "the embodiment of democracy" itself:

> If we hope to maintain the rights and liberties of the people of our day and to hand republican institutions down to future generations, purified and unbroken, we must keep abreast of the economic and social factors in our lives, we must organize the forces of labor, and those organizations must be the much despised, but ever progressive and successful trade unions.[8]

In this way, Gompers sought so completely to identify unions as republican institutions as to turn any attack on the organized labor movement into an attack on republicanism itself. Unions, he argued, had a particular mission in the polity which none but they could or should perform:

> The toilers of our country look to [the unions] to devise the ways and means by which a more thorough organization of wage-earners may be accomplished, and to save our children in their infancy from being forced into the maelstrom of wage-slavery . . . To protect the workers in their inalienable rights to a higher and better life; to protect them not only as equals before the law, but also in their rights to the product of their labor; to protect their lives, their limbs, their health, their homes, their firesides, their liberties as men, as workers and as citizens; to overcome and conquer prejudice and antagonism; to secure to them the right to life and the opportunity to maintain that life; the right to be full sharers in the abundance which is the result of their brain and brawn, and the civilization of which they are the founders and the mainstay; to this the workers are entitled beyond the cavil of a doubt. With nothing less ought they, nor will they be satisfied.[9]

These, Gompers insisted, were proper goals for a republican polity. The unions were properly the means by which they would be attained.

The following years saw the AFL continually stress the impossibility of realizing its mission as long as the courts were allowed to block its way by enjoining strikes and boycotts. The climax of this campaign came in April 1906 with the promulgation of "Labor's Bill of Grievances." Addressed to Congress, the "Bill of Grievances" accused the

8. Samuel Gompers, "The Trend of Our Time," *Official Programme of the Central Labor Union, Washington D.C.* (25 February 1897), in *AFL Records*, reel 24 (Scrapbooks).
9. Samuel Gompers, "Trade Unions – Their Philosophy," (January 1899), in *AFL Records*, reel 110 (Speeches and Writings); Schneider, "The Citizen Striker," 63–4.

judiciary and other public officials of ignoring legislation passed to protect workers, and of distorting other legislation, particularly commercial
regulations, in order to use it against the organized labor movement. It
requested that these perversions of legislative intent be remedied, that
additional legislation be passed to protect workers from developments in
fields beyond the AFL's capacity to influence directly – immigration, con-
vict labor, the rights of seamen on the high seas – and that relief be
provided from the courts' use of the injunction to "attack and destroy
personal freedom" by restraining unions from acting effectively in those
fields within their capacity on the spurious grounds that employers had
"some property right in the labor of the workmen."[10] Speaking to the
AFL's annual convention later that year, Gompers used the same language to protest the courts' use of injunctions to protect an employer's
"right" to do business from union "interference," and again called on
Congress to provide relief. The injunction, Gompers told his audience,
was an outgrowth of tyrannical old-world prerogative power which was
now threatening to corrupt the Constitution itself. "[T]here is no tendency more dangerous to personal liberty, so destructive of free institutions and a republican form of government as the present misuse and
extension of the equity power through usurpation by the judiciary."[11]

In furtherance of these initiatives, the AFL sponsored the Pearre anti-
injunction bill, a measure which prohibited the use of injunctions in any
case between employers and employees which grew out of a labor dispute
unless necessary to prevent irreparable injury to property. In an attempt
to establish the legality of boycotts, the bill expressly defined property
rights to exclude the right to do business. T.C. Spelling, the Federation's
legislative representative, warned legislators against remaining indifferent to the unions' complaints against the judiciary:

> I should respectfully warn the legislative power . . . not to uphold
> these despots, these imitators of old-world tyranny, in further
> abuses of authority. Human nature can only endure so much. The
> labor class, those against whom the judges have usurped the power
> to enact special legislation, have already endured much. The placing
> of men in office for life and buttressing them beyond the reach of
> the popular will of public opinion is the principle feature of autoc-
> racy borrowed from former systems and grafted onto ours. It
> should be the zealous care of all fair and patriotic men to discour-

---

10. "Labor's Bill of Grievances" (7 April 1906), in *AFL Records*, reel 57 (Circular and
     Neostyle File).
11. Samuel Gompers, "Report to the 1906 (Minneapolis) Convention of the American
     Federation of Labor," quoted by T.C. Spelling in his "Reply to the Report of the
     House Judiciary Committee on the Pearre Bill" (19 February 1907), in *AFL Rec-
     ords*, reel 126 (Reference Materials).

age abuses by them of their extraordinary powers, and no one should, as he values peace and order and the preservation to the other branches of government of constitutional functions, give countenance by word and act to these judicial discriminations in favor of one class against another.[12]

The AFL continued to criticize the judiciary throughout 1907. The situation became acute in early 1908, however, after the Supreme Court of the District of Columbia granted the Buck's Stove and Range Company an injunction prohibiting AFL leaders from encouraging, whether through speeches or writings, a boycott of the company's products, and in particular after the United States Supreme Court's decision in *Loewe v. Lawlor* (the "Danbury Hatters" case) which affirmed that workers engaging in strikes were liable for conspiracy in restraint of trade under the Sherman Act.[13] The AFL Executive Council immediately resolved to ignore the *Buck's Stove* injunction as a violation of freedom of speech and of the press, and called a conference of national union executives to meet on 18 March 1908 to discuss both cases. The conference condemned "the deprivation of [the workers'] rights and liberties involved in the law as interpreted by recent court decisions" and called for the amendment of the Sherman Act to exclude labor organizations from its jurisdiction.[14] At a mass meeting held the following month at the Labor Lyceum in Brooklyn – one of many called to protest the courts' actions – Gompers argued that the judiciary was attempting to exclude labor unions altogether from political, social, and industrial life:

> Industry cannot go back a century . . . Organization, association, is the very essence of our industrial and our commercial life; and to interpret laws of today to apply to conditions of a century or more ago, is to be blind to our life of this, the twentieth century. Men must understand the conditions of the industrial activity of our day.

If the Constitution could not accommodate modern organized industrial society, as the courts seemed to be claiming, then it should be amended. It was, after all, a living institution, not a sacred and unalterable text.[15]

By mid-1908, the AFL leadership had widened the focus of its criticism to include the Republican Party. The Federation's Legislative Committee condemned the Republicans for using their absolute control of

---

12. Ibid.
13. *The Buck's Stove and Range Company v. The American Federation of Labor et al.* (1907), 35 Washington Law Reporter 525; *Loewe v. Lawlor* (1908) 208 U.S. 274.
14. AFL Executive Council, "Circular to Workers" (18 March 1908), in *AFL Records*, reel 57 (Circular and Neostyle File).
15. Samuel Gompers, "Speech at the Labor Lyceum, Brooklyn" (19 April 1908), in *AFL Records*, reel 110 (Speeches and Writings).

the legislative and executive branches of the federal government to block legislation sought by the Federation and its friends, and for refusing relief to workers oppressed by judicial perversions of the law. The committee pointed in particular to the "unscrupulous" actions of House Speaker Cannon, a man "bitterly opposed to labor and its every interest," who had "a set of rules which are the most arbitrary the world has ever seen to back him up and for which the Republican members of the House are responsible." In the House it seemed that "the spirit of representative government and of the Constitution has been entirely swept aside. . ."[16]

The AFL's most vigorous denunciation came in October, shortly before the elections, when the Executive Council released an election circular to all members and simultaneously published it in newpapers throughout the United States as an open letter to the electorate as a whole. Invoking "the immortal Lincoln" as the epitome of democratic process, the AFL argued that, protected by the Republican Party, the judiciary was step by step *"destroying government by law* and substituting therefore a government by Judges . . . It is sought to make of the judges irresponsible despots, and by controlling them using this despotism in the interests of corporate power." The process was already well advanced:

> It is depriving the workers of their rights as citizens by forbidding the exercise of *freedom of speech, freedom of the press, freedom of assembly and the right of petition,* if, in the opinion of the judge, the exercise of these rights may work injury to the business of some corporation or trust. It is applicable to the worker today and will inevitably be made applicable to the businessman at a later period.[17]

This "virus" had attacked not only the judicial branch but was in increasing evidence in the passage of laws enforceable by equity process – such as the Sherman Act – by Congress. "Between this law, enforceable by equity process, and the extension of the use of the writ of injunction, the individual freedom of the worker to combine with others for mutual aid and protection is swept away and his rights as a citizen disregarded and denied." It was also invading the executive branch. The Republicans had nominated William Howard Taft, "the originator and specific champion of discretionary government," for the presidency, while the incumbent spoke out in defense of the courts. If workers were to fulfill their duty to "that form of government for the preservation of which, Lincoln said, 'men died at Gettysburg,' " they should vote against

---

16. Thomas F. Tracey et al., "Special Report of the Legislative Committee (3 June 1908), in *AFL Records,* reel 65 (Files of the President: General Correspondence).
17. AFL Executive Council, "Election Circular" (12 October 1908), in *AFL Records,* reel 69 (Files of the President: General Correspondence) [emphasis in original].

the Republican Taft, against their Republican and Democratic enemies in Congress, and for Democratic candidate William Jennings Bryan.[18]

The urgency of the AFL's rhetoric was genuine enough. The response, however, was disappointing. John B. Lennon wrote Gompers from Chicago after the election to tell him that rank and file fears of the impact which Bryan's election would have on the economy had proven more influential than the Federation's warnings about the fate of republicanism. "They are afraid of the bread and butter question and that appeared bigger to them than the possibility of being deprived of their rights and liberties."[19]

The sequel was not long in coming. Having delayed its decision for several weeks lest it harm the Republicans' chances of victory in the November elections,[20] on 23 December 1908 the Supreme Court of the District of Columbia found Gompers, secretary-treasurer Frank Morrison, and the Federation's second vice-president, John Mitchell, to be in contempt of court for violating the *Buck's Stove* injunction. In what was in many ways the climax to a decade's confrontation between the AFL and the judiciary, Justice Daniel T. Wright denounced the Federation's leaders for their "utter, rampant, insolent defiance" of the law. Their encouragement of the boycott, Wright stated, constituted "unrefined insult, coarse affront, vulgar indignity" to the court, and confronted society with a choice between "the supremacy of law over the rabble or its prostration under the feet of the disordered throng." In words redolent of one hundred years of common law antipathy, Wright pointed to the case as proof of the existence of "a studied, determined, defiant conflict, precipitated in the light of open day, between the decrees of a tribunal ordained by the Government of the Federal Union and of the tribunals of another federation, grown up in the land." Between these two "one or the other must succumb." Wright left no doubt which it would be if the courts had their way. "Those who would unlaw the land are public enemies."[21]

---

18. Ibid. See also Theodore Roosevelt to Philander C. Knox (21 October 1908), an open letter in reply to the Executive Council circular, in *AFL Records*, reel 69 (Files of the President: General Correspondence).

19. John B. Lennon to Gompers (4 November 1908), in *AFL Records*, reel 69 (Files of the President: Miscellaneous Correspondence, 1907–24).

20. Barry F. Helfand, "Labor and the Courts: The Common-Law Doctrine of Criminal Conspiracy and Its Application in the Buck's Stove Case," *Labor History*, 18, 1 (Winter 1977), 100.

21. *The Buck's Stove and Range Company v. The American Federation of Labor* (1908), 36 Washington Law Reporter 822, at 842. Elsewhere in his judgment, Wright continued his assault on the unions:
    the position of the respondents involves questions vital to the preservation of social order, questions which smite the foundations of civil

Accommodation

To Justice Wright's undoubted dismay, American unions survived the antagonism of the courts. The combination of sustained judicial condemnation and employer hostility, however, had contributed to a pronounced fall in their overall rate of growth, beginning soon after the turn of the century. In the six years of recession-free economic growth between 1897 and 1903, union membership had increased rapidly, from 500,000 to 2 million. Over the next six years, however, overall membership did not expand further, but instead fluctuated around the 1903 mark. Growth began again after 1909, but the rate of growth remained slow. Membership did not pass the 2.5 million mark until 1915.[22]

A retarded rate of growth was not the only alteration in the circumstances of the organized labor movement after 1900. The inter- and intra-industrial distribution of AFL membership also changed as union membership fell in the large firms of the center economy and became concentrated instead in the smaller firms on the periphery of oligopolistic industries, and in industries such as construction, bituminous coal mining, and the garment trades where firms were characteristically small and where, as a result, no one employer could control the competitive structure of the industry. Unions also remained strong in the transportation sector where, apart from the established position of the operating brotherhoods, their presence was growing in the railroad shops and amongst employees of the new urban transportation systems.[23]

These alterations in the distribution of the AFL's membership inevitably increased the influence within the Federation of those affiliates — such as the United Brotherhood of Carpenters and Joiners, the International Association of Machinists and the United Mine Workers — in which membership was becoming concentrated. Unsurprisingly, the

government, and upon which the supremacy of law over anarchy and riot verily depend. Are controversies to be determined in tribunals formally constituted by the law of the land for that purpose, or shall each who falls at odds with another take his own furious way? Are causes pending in courts to be decided by courts for litigants; or the view of each distempered litigant imposed upon the courts? Are decrees of court to look for their execution to the supremacy of Law, or tumble in the wake of unsuccessful suitors who overset them and lay about the matter with their own hands, in turbulence proportioned to the frenzy of their disappointment? (841).

22.   Leo Troy, *Trade Union Membership, 1897–1962* (New York, 1965), 1. See also Leo Wolman, *Ebb and Flow in Trade Unionism* (New York, 1936), and *The Growth of American Trade Unions, 1880–1923* (New York, 1924).

23.   Albert A. Blum, "Why Unions Grow," *Labor History*, 9, 1 (Winter 1968), 46–7.

policies and practices of these major unions, in particular their urge to ensure their own organizational security, came to shape the course which the Federation would follow in its attempts to survive in the emerging corporate economy. The result, between 1900 and 1920, was the wholesale transformation of the American labor movement.

Most important was the erosion of occupational unionism, culminating in 1911 in the formal abandonment of craft autonomy as the central structural principle of the AFL. As we have seen, the Federation had originally adopted the principle of craft autonomy in furtherance of its theory that workers in each distinct occupational group should form their own union. In this theory, the occupation or craft defined the union's structure because the union was the institutional means chosen by the workers to reassert their autonomy and property rights through voluntary associated action. Hence, the union was a representation of the craft and existed to protect the craft, controlling jobs and defining and administering rules of work. The AFL was "The House of Labor," reproducing the social division of labor in its structure, and governing the entire labor movement according to that social division.

Between 1886 and the early 1900s the Federation's leadership had implemented this theory by encouraging the formation of national unions on the basis of strict adherence to craft frontiers.[24] The policy, however, proved increasingly unpopular with the rapidly growing United Mine Workers which claimed jurisdiction over all jobs in and around mines regardless of craft and occupation, and at the AFL's 1901 convention at Scranton, Pennsylvania, the UMW secured a guarantee that unions organizing on craft lines would not be permitted to intrude upon and subdivide its jurisdiction.[25]

Craft autonomy also proved unpopular with non-industrial unions facing a rapidly changing division of labor in manufacturing. As the jobs which constituted their jurisdictions changed or disappeared, these unions had also to change if they hoped to survive as institutions. Notwithstanding the principle of adherence to craft frontiers, therefore, the larger affiliates increasingly took it upon themselves to redefine the extent of the job territory which they sought to control, expanding their jurisdictions beyond the boundaries of the original occupation or craft

---

24. Christopher L. Tomlins, "AFL Unions in the 1930s: Their Performance in Historical Perspective," *Journal of American History*, 65, 4 (1979), 1026; Robert A. Christie, *Empire in Wood: A History of the Carpenters' Union* (Ithaca, New York, 1956), 124–25.
25. Philip Taft, *The A.F. of L. in the Time of Gompers* (New York, 1957), 195–8.

by including craftsmen working in the same or related production processes, and even organizing particular strata of production workers outside the skilled nuclei where this could contribute to the union's control of jobs. Such alterations in jurisdictional strategies inevitably meant alterations in union structure, bringing about the amalgamation of related trades and the recruitment of lesser-skilled workers into "craft" unions. By 1915, in fact, only 28 of 133 AFL unions could still be described as pure craft organizations, and of these at least half were cooperating informally with other affiliates across craft lines.[26]

These trends squarely confronted the AFL with the growing irrelevance of its most important structural principle. Consequently, at its Atlanta convention in 1911, the Federation finally ended the decade of controversy which had begun at Scranton, accepted in theory what had already been true for some years in practice, and announced its conversion to the new structural principle of "craft-industrialism":

> The action of the 1911 convention of the AFL marks a significant turning point in its history, one of greater significance than the Scranton [1901] convention which had simply posed the question of jurisdictional policy in an age of technological change. After a decade of running strife the Atlanta convention of the AFL declared soundly for the principle of organizing by the paramount craft in an industry rather than for craft autonomy.[27]

Henceforth, the AFL was formally committed to the development of single organizations containing all the strategic workers of a particular trade or industry. "Craft-industrial" unions, like the Carpenters and the Machinists were no longer to be restricted by rules binding the structure of the organized labor movement to a division of labor which had ceased to conform with industrial reality, and could take steps to safeguard their position wherever technological developments had so weakened the positions of craftsmen as to threaten the union's survival.

The Atlanta declaration did not abandon craft unionism entirely. Rather, it represented an attempt to achieve a balance between the evolving interests of the AFL's major affiliates and the Federation's original quasi-syndicalist commitment to occupational organization as the best means to unite an industrially diverse working class. The major affiliates, however, were no more prepared to allow the Federation's new formulation to hamper their particularistic responses to continuing alterations in the division of labor than they had been the old. Their adaptations continued, eventually taking them far beyond the Atlanta

26. Tomlins, "AFL Unions," 1025–6. 27. Christie, *Empire in Wood*, 135–6.

Declaration and toward multi-industrial organization. Craft-industrialism was left in tatters along the way, creating a vacuum in which the major affiliates enjoyed a considerable degree of freedom to pursue policies designed to protect their self-interests. Increasingly, each union defined for itself, in the company of the Federation's other affiliates, how far its organizing rights and its authority should extend. By the 1920s, the role of the Federation in determining its own structure was more often than not reduced to symbolic ratifications of the results of struggles amongst its affiliates.[28]

Jurisdictional changes were not the only innovations initiated by the major unions to have a decisive impact on the nature of the organized labor movement. In the years after 1900, the larger affiliates undertook the expansion, professionalization and centralization of their administrative and executive capacities. In part the object was greater operational efficiency, improvement of the union's capacity to manage complex benefit and dues structures, and extension of its ability to coordinate local activities in the face of large firms operating in multiple markets.[29] But bureaucratic innovations also increased national union authority over hitherto virtually autonomous locals, curtailing rank and file participation and concentrating power at all levels of the union in a hierarchy of professional officials answerable ultimately to the national office. Thus, at its 1899 convention, the International Association of Machinists voted to increase national office control of the union's administrative apparatus by providing that half of each local business agent's salary should be paid by the national union. National officers were also given authority to refuse payment of strike benefits to any local striking without national authorization.[30] In a more general vein, Lloyd Ulman has concluded that in both local market and national market industries, national union control over matters of policy and local activities – particularly strike activities – steadily increased in the late nineteenth and early twentieth centuries.[31]

Like the jurisdictional changes of the same period, these innovations permanently altered the "associational" character of the unions, and hence of the AFL. The extension of national union control over local strikes, for example, meant a radical diminution in the incidence of the sympathy strikes through which craftsmen in different occupations had

---

28. Ibid., 170–99, 233–48.
29. Ibid., 155–99. See, generally, James R. Green, *The World of the Worker: Labor in Twentieth Century America* (New York, 1980), 32–66.
30. Mark Perlman, *The Machinists: A New Study in American Trade Unionism* (Cambridge, 1961), 24.
31. Lloyd Ulman, *The Rise of the National Trade Union* (Cambridge, 1955), 155–73.

customarily expressed local solidarity and commitment to the spirit of association which united them in their diversity. Striking, henceforth, was to be avoided; or, if unavoidable, was to be employed narrowly in pursuit of the interests of the members of one organization. In individual unions and the AFL as a whole, as a result, the ideology of craft fraternity was markedly eroded.[32]

Centralization and bureaucratization proceeded closely in line with a third major innovation in union strategy: the growing tendency of unions to seek guarantees of institutional stability and security in their relations with employers through the negotiation of formal written "trade agreements" pledging the union to uninterrupted production in return for material concessions to the work force and recognition of the union. Trade agreements, of course, were not entirely twentieth-century innovations. The earliest craft associations had commonly demanded employer agreement to observe written bills of prices, and in industries with a long history of organization the content of these bills had tended to become broader over time and had become subject to bargaining.[33] Nevertheless, well into the latter half of the nineteenth century negotiations leading to formal agreements between contending parties had been exceptional. Union scales were declared unilaterally. Work rules "were not ordinarily negotiated with employers or embodied in a contract."[34]

As we have seen, by the 1890s increasing levels of competition had led many employers to mount assaults on craft control of the labor process in order to facilitate the expansion of production. In response, unions attempted to transcend the informality and restricted geographic ambit of late nineteenth century bargaining by persuading employers to join in the adoption of uniform working rules and wage scales in regional or even national agreements. By 1900, eight national unions were parties to such agreements with employers – the Bottle Blowers, the Flint Glass Workers, the Potters, the Iron and Steel Workers, the Molders, the Longshoremen, the Machinists and the Mine Workers. Unions in the printing trades were also showing an interest in national agreements, while in the building trades the emergence of the large contractor and of employer associations brought attempts on the part of national unions to begin dealings with employers on an extended-area basis.[35]

32. Ibid., 334–41. See, generally, Green, *The World of the Worker,* 32–66.
33. National Labor Relations Board, *Written Trade Agreements in Collective Bargaining* (Washington, 1940), 20.
34. David Montgomery, *Workers' Control in America: Studies in the History of Work, Technology, and Labor Struggles* (Cambridge, England, 1979), 16. See also his *Beyond Equality: Labor and the Radical Republicans, 1862–72* (New York, 1972), 142–5.
35. Ulman, *The Rise of the National Trade Union,* 190–200, 519–35.

The movement toward the national trade agreement was given considerable impetus by the United Mine Workers. Founded in 1890 and centered on the bituminous coal industry, the UMW's initial experience was one of uninterrupted decline. In 1897, however, the union was able to attract considerable support for a major strike, resulting in the formulation of an interstate agreement which established the eight-hour day, created procedures for the joint determination of wage rates throughout the industry, and set up a joint annual interstate conference for purposes of reviewing and reaffirming the accord. The outcome was stabilization of an industry crippled for the previous twenty years by excess capacity, and the rapid growth of the UMW's membership and influence to the point where, by 1900, it had become the leading organization within the AFL.[36]

A corollary of the growing interest in national-level collective bargaining was the AFL's participation in the creation of institutional mechanisms whereby this new model for stability in labor-management relations might be generalized. In 1900, union leaders such as John Mitchell of the UMW, Daniel Keefe of the Longshoremen, and J.W. Sullivan of the Typographers – all with experience of the successful operation of trade agreements – joined with progressive industrialists in launching the National Civic Federation. Inspired by the contemporary proliferation of organizational activity throughout the American polity, the NCF was intended to embody the new pluralism of American society by becoming "a sort of 'people's congress,' a forum gathering 'the best brains of the nation' and dealing freely [with] the great problems of the day which were being handled only by the politicians in Congress and the state legislatures."[37] In practice, however, the NCF almost immediately became preoccupied with the "labor problem," and, fastening on the trade agreement as a solution, it advertised itself as a body where "industrial decisions could be jointly made," where "the large and the largest employers of labor can meet with the representatives of organized labor to discuss their relative interests and try to find a way out where the mutual interests of both may best be conserved."[38]

In part as a consequence of NCF encouragement, some twenty-six national or district bargaining agreements were adopted or renewed in the years between 1898 and 1905.[39] The trend tapered off after the

36. Bruno Ramirez, *When Workers Fight: The Politics of Industrial Relations in the Progressive Era, 1898–1916* (Westport, Connecticut, 1978), 17–64.
37. Ibid., 66.
38. Ibid., 76; Samuel Gompers, Speech to the First Public Meeting of the Civic Federation of New England (27 April 1905), in *AFL Records*, reel 110 (Speeches and Writings). See also Gompers's speech to the National Civic Federation Conference (11–13 December 1913), in *AFL Records*, reel 111 (Speeches and Writings).
39. Ulman, *The Rise of the National Trade Union*, 521.

collapse of the Machinists' Murry Hill agreement in 1901 graphically demonstrated that NCF and union expectations of widespread endorsement of national-level bargaining by employers were unfounded. As Mark Perlman has written, "[t]he open shop campaign, aggressively waged by the [National Metal Trades Association] as well as by many kindred organizations, put all unions on the defensive ... [and] made the Gompers-Mitchell-O'Connell plan of negotiating with top management no more than a dream."[40] Nevertheless, collective bargaining remained the axis of labor–management relations in AFL policy, and although national level agreements failed to develop outside a few industries there slowly evolved in the years after 1900 a model in which national union interventions – prescription of minimum standards, the dispatching of professional negotiators, strike controls, arbitration requirements – increasingly supplemented local union government.[41]

A new theory for the labor movement

Like the parallel moves to transform the AFL's jurisdictional structure and to centralize and professionalize union administration, attempts to increase national union control of bargaining underlined the importance which the major affiliates attached to the protection of their particular institutional interests. Inevitably, their innovations brought a slow but irrevocable transformation in the ideology and practices of the AFL as a whole. In 1897 Gompers had still been pointing to the organization and education of workers through their unions as the means by which labor would accomplish the transformation of prevailing political and social institutions. Through association, he argued, the workers would come to know that "the state is by rights theirs" and would thereupon take over the functions of government "in the interests of all."[42] Even when the Federation embraced collective bargaining in subsequent years, it did so on the basis that collective bargaining was "an entering wedge toward industrial democracy and abolition of the profit system," which would advance industry toward "full labor control."[43] But by the early 1900s these radical connotations of voluntary association were fast disappearing from the Federation's ideology as it redefined its objectives

40. Perlman, *The Machinists*, 28.
41. Ulman, *The Rise of the National Trade Union*, 199–200.
42. Samuel Gompers, Speech to the Chicago Civic Federation Conference on Trusts (1897), in *AFL Records*, reel 110, (Speeches and Writings).
43. Robert F. Hoxie, *Trade Unionism in the United States*, 2nd ed. (New York, 1923), 274–5.

in almost exclusively economic and organizational terms. National unions, as we have seen, progressively curtailed the capacity of their members to engage in sympathy strikes. The Federation underlined its commitment to strict compliance at all times with contractual obligations.[44] Voluntary association and collective bargaining became mechanisms for the improvement of material conditions within the political and industrial framework of the new corporate economy.

The transformation of the Federation in the years after 1900 was further accelerated by the pronounced movement "away from the institutions that had emerged in the democratic revolutions of the eighteenth and nineteenth centuries" which characterized the development of the state after the onset of corporate hegemony. At the local level, writes Barry Karl, "modern industrial organization had centered attention on problems raised by the application of parliamentary methods to complex mechanical and economic systems requiring technical skills and specialized forms of knowledge . . ."[45] This also happened at the national level where reformers favoring a similar professionalization of "the increasingly technical process of government" sought to meet the multifarious demands for governmental services and supports being generated by the continued rapid growth and consolidation of the economy by creating a modest but growing network of "expert" administrative bureaucracies – the Interstate Commerce Commission, the Federal Reserve System, the Federal Trade Commission, the Federal Tariff Commission – operating outside the process of democratic politics."[46]

---

44. Note, for example the following resolution passed at the Boston (1903) convention of the AFL, in *AFL Records,* reel 126 (Reference Materials):

> It is widely and falsely charged by a hostile press and other opponents of organized labor that trade unions are frequently guilty of violating contracts entered into with employers. There have been a few instances in which unions have unwisely violated agreements, but these are exceptions and not the rule, contracts being more frequently violated by the employer, and while we desire to give the strongest possible denial to the general accusations that agreements are not respected by organized labor, we do not wish to condone the exceptions.
> We wish, in the strongest language possible, to express our regret that any organization of workingmen should fail to rigidly adhere to a contract entered into with employers of its members, and we believe it essential to urge upon trade unionists the absolute necessity of holding contracts between them and their employers inviolate.

45. Barry Karl, *Executive Reorganization and Reform in the New Deal: The Genesis of Administrative Management, 1900–1939* (Cambridge, 1963), 216, 218. See also Stephen Skowronek, *Building a New American State: The Expansion of National Administrative Capacities* (New York, 1982), 163–284. See, generally, Jerry Israel, editor, *Building the Organizational Society: Essays on Associational Activities in Modern America* (New York, 1972).

46. Skowronek, *Building a New American State,* 248–84.

Composed of "non-judicial officers" who nevertheless enjoyed extensive authority to dispense administrative law, the appearance of these agencies freed the government from dependence upon the judicial process in matters of public administration, typifying "the belief of the Progressive generation in efficient government by an administrative state."[47] At the same time, however, the new administrative institutions came under pressure to eschew a regulatory mentality and to concentrate instead on servicing the corporate economy; in other words to legitimate, in the name of the public interest, the on-going dissolution of the border between the public sphere and private corporate enterprise.[48]

Against this background, AFL conceptions of politics underwent a fundamental alteration. As the new bureaucratic-administrative state took shape after the turn of the century, the AFL more and more abandoned the diffuse and broad-based politics of a popular movement for the tightly-focussed lobbying strategies of an economic interest group.[49] The state, Gompers now stressed, was no longer even formally amenable to democratic control. "One need but read the history of the toilers," he warned in 1915, "to learn how potent has been the power vested in the constituted authorities of the time to twist laws intended to be of interest to the workers to their very undoing even to the verge of tyranny and enslavement." Political philosophies predicated on state action were thus fraught with danger. Organized labor's best option was to bring pressure to bear on governments to free the labor movement for "*self*-development and associated effort," thus increasing its capacity "to bear the burdens of the struggle for industrial improvement and freedom" in the economic realm — where matters of real moment were open to its direct influence.[50] Through collective bargaining, an

47. Morton Keller, "The Pluralist State: American Economic Regulation in Comparative Perspective, 1900–1930," in Thomas K. McGraw, editor, *Regulation in Perspective: Historical Essays* (Cambridge, 1981), 73.

48. Jonathan O. Lurie, *The Chicago Board of Trade, 1859–1905: The Dynamics of Self-Regulation* (Urbana, Illinois, 1979), 74, 168–212; Ellis W. Hawley, "Three Facets of Hooverian Associationalism: Lumber, Aviation, and Movies, 1921–1930," in McGraw, editor, *Regulation in Perspective*, 98. See, generally, Gabriel Kolko, *The Triumph of Conservatism* (New York, 1963).

49. David Brody, *Workers in Industrial America: Essays on the Twentieth Century Struggle* (New York, 1980), 27–8.

50. Samuel Gompers, *Seventy years of Life and Labor*, 2 vols. (New York, 1925), I, 287; William M. Dick, *Labor and Socialism in America: The Gompers Era* (Port Washington, New York, 1972), 111–36. See also Samuel Gompers, Address to Senator LaFollette's Conference on Political Action (2 December 1922), in *AFL Records*, reel 57 (Circular and Neostyle File); Samuel Gompers, *Labor, the Courts and the Law* (Washington, American Federation of Labor, 1921); George B. Cotkin, "The Spencerian and Comtian Nexus in Gompers' Labor Philosophy: The Impact of Non-Marxian Evolutionary Thought," *Labor History*, 20, 4 (Fall 1979), 510–532.

institution "founded upon the workers' economic power," employers and unions were already creating disciplined mechanisms for bilateral government of industry. Political action to mobilize the state now seemed of much less importance than efforts to extend this actual power to promulgate industrial laws.[51]

In sloughing off its old associational ideology for a redefined voluntarism which drastically downplayed the radical political connotations of associationalism and identified collective bargaining as a means to institutionalize a given distribution of economic power through the promulgation of written agreements, the AFL exhibited its growing commitment to what has been termed a *gesellschaft* model of society and politics; that is, a model "oriented to the precise definition of the rights and duties of the individual [party]," which reduces "the public interest to another, only *sometimes* overriding, private interest," and, most important, which takes "contract and the quid pro quo associated with commercial exchange" as its model for all legal and social relationships.[52] From this perspective, the ideal polity would be one in which varying numbers of legally equivalent institutions established temporary or permanent accommodations with each other through voluntarist action and looked to the state simply for ratification of the bargains. And indeed, by World War I this ideology was manifest in virtually all of the AFL leadership's actions. During the war the AFL participated in the war mobilization machinery as the spokesman of a functional bloc, certifying and coordinating the negotiation of private labor–management accords and representing "labor" in consultations with other peak organizations and with the administration. After the war AFL leaders called on President Wilson's first National Industrial Conference (1919) to endorse the continuation of wartime innovations through the establishment of joint boards of unions and employer associations in every industry to act as forums for collective bargaining and as the ultimate decision-making agencies on "all subjects affecting the progress and well-being of the trade." It was

---

51. Ramirez, *When Workers Fight*, 77. Even at the height of the *Danbury Hatters* and *Buck's Stove* furor in 1908, arguably the most serious political crisis the Federation had faced, Gompers ignored calls for independent political action and instead advised the Executive Council to steer a course which would "accomplish the best results with the least possible danger of any action being taken likely to result injuriously to our fellow workers." His advice resulted in an endorsement of William Jennings Bryan being traded for Bryan's support of the Pearre anti-injunction bill. See Samuel Gompers to the AFL Executive Council (3 March 1908), in *AFL Records*, reel 23 (Files of the Office of the President).

52. See Eugene Kamenka and Alice Erh-Soon Tay, "Beyond Bourgeois Individualism: The Contemporary Crisis in Law and Legal Ideology," in Eugene Kamenka and R.S. Neale, editors, *Feudalism, Capitalism and Beyond* (Canberra, 1975), 137 [emphasis in original].

intended that the Federal government would cooperate with these boards
"but it was not to intervene by law or decree in [their] operation . . ."[53]

Industry's Manifest Duty, the Executive Council's report to the AFL's
annual convention in 1923, attests even more eloquently to the Federation's commitment to a *gesellschaftlich* ideology.[54] Pointing to the enormous potential for growth which industry had demonstrated over the
previous decade, the report decried the "muddling conflict of groups
who find it impossible to come together in cooperation," and advocated
the creation of mechanisms for the institutionalization of cooperation
"in all phases of industry which vitally affect and reflect upon [the]
status [of] workers." Under such a regime, unions could assume a
greater responsibility for fulfilling policies jointly arrived at, and conflict would be left behind:

> It is not the mission of industrial groups to clash and struggle
> against each other. Such struggles are the signs and signals of dawn-
> ing comprehension, the birth pangs of an industrial order attempt-
> ing through painful experience to find itself and to find its proper
> functioning. The true role of industrial groups, however, is to come
> together . . . to find the way forward in collaboration, to give of
> their best for the satisfaction of human needs.[55]

The implications of this transformation in the AFL's ideas, and the
nature of the accommodation which unions might hope to establish
with employers as a result, received considerable attention in the writing of contemporary labor economists. Embracing for the most part the
premises of institutional economics, this new generation of specialists
argued that economic activity was a collective phenomenon. Consequently, they rejected the individualism of classical political economy
and its faith in the market mechanism as a harmonizing agency, and
concentrated instead on specifying the social mechanisms which adjusted and reconciled differing collective interests and thereby made
economic activity possible.[56] Amongst these, the trade agreement and

53. Haggai Hurwitz, "Ideology and Industrial Conflict: President Wilson's First Industrial Conference of October 1919," *Labor History*, 18, 4 (Fall 1977), 516.
54. The report was described by its authors as "a pronouncement of the aims of labor
that shall more nearly express the full implications of trade unionism than has yet
been undertaken." See "Industry's Manifest Duty," in *Report of the Proceedings of
the 43rd Annual Convention of the American Federation of Labor* (Washington,
1923), 31.
55. Ibid., 32.
56. Paul J. McNulty, *The Origins and Developments of Labor Economics: A Chapter in
the History of Social Thought* (Cambridge, 1980), 127–51. See also, Joseph Dorfman et al., *Institutional Economics: Veblen, Commons and Mitchell Reconsidered*
(Berkeley, 1964); John R. Commons, *A Sociological View of Sovereignty* (New
York, 1965).

collective bargaining stood out as institutions of peculiar importance. "[The trade agreement] implies the equal organization of employers [and employees] and the settlement of a wage scale and conditions of work through conferences of representatives," wrote the doyen of the field, John R. Commons, in 1907. "It is a form of constitutional government with its legislative, executive and judicial branches, its common law and statute law, its penalties and sanctions."[57] This approach was taken up and developed further by William M. Leiserson, a student of Commons who would become one of the most important figures in the development of labor relations policy during the New Deal. According to Leiserson, trade agreements were "nothing less than constitutions for the industries which they cover, constitutions which set up organs of government, define and limit them, provide agencies for making, executing and interpreting laws for the industry, and means for their enforcement."[58]

By conceptualizing the trade agreement as a constitution which distributed legislative and executive functions between the parties contesting the determination of the employment relationship, and which established a rule of law to govern their behavior, Leiserson and Commons underscored their conviction that collective bargaining was in essence a science of adjustment.[59] For both, the institutional approach to political economy meant rejection of the facile assumption that a natural harmony existed between capital and labor which underlay late nineteenth-century liberalism's search for holistic solutions to the "labor problem." On the other hand, neither regarded industrial conflict as an inevitable concomitant of the capitalist mode of production. Historically, they both argued, labor–management strife had developed not out of contradictions inherent in the relations of capitalist production, but in the wake of the extension of markets which had been the dominant factor in American economic development since the early nineteenth century.[60] This extension had disrupted the organic mutuality of employers and employees which had characterized handicraft production and had unhappily split these two complementary parts of industry into distinct segments. Through the trade agreement, Leiserson believed, corporate managers – surrogate employers – and employees might reconstitute that self-governing mutuality and thereby reestablish "industry" as an organic whole:

---

57. John R. Commons, *Trade Unionism and Labor Problems* (Boston, 1905), i, vii.
58. William M. Leiserson, "Constitutional Government in American Industries," *American Economic Review*, 12 (Supp.), 1 (1922), 61.
59. John R. Commons, *Legal Foundations of Capitalism* (New York, 1924), 146–7, 306–12; William M. Leiserson, "Labor Relations" (unpublished book manuscript), ii–v and Part One, 1–14, 57–68, in *Leiserson Papers*, Box 52.
60. Leiserson, "Labor Relations," Part One, 88–90.

In labor relations . . . we have had associations of employers and associations of workers each developing codes of ethics of their own . . . [B]ut we have had few common codes that cut across the line of the contract between buyer and seller of labor. The collective contracts between trade unions and employers represent steps in this direction and the constitutions of employee representation plans are further steps. These contracts and constitutions join employers and employees in one organization, governed by the same rules that embody their agreement on what is justice, at least for the time being . . . and [they] gradually solidify into codes and laws that all understand – the combined views of both wage-earners and employers as to what is right and wrong in labor relations.[61]

The clear implication of Leiserson's analysis was that the way forward for American industry lay in "recreating" a supposedly traditional relationship between management and labor in which each, within its appropriate sphere, was recognized as possessed of expertise crucial to the satisfactory performance of the organic whole. Thus the crucial task of industrial relations theory was to specify the appropriate realms of expertise. All labor–management problems, he argued, could be subsumed under one of three classifications – technical problems, personnel problems, or problems of economic control and government. Technical problems were those which arose from any investment decision which influenced the allocation and direction of labor: they were problems of machinery, materials, and production methods – "organizing the working force, subdividing labor, routing work, assembling, etc." These Leiserson dubbed "production problems" and he separated them from "labor relations proper." Their solution lay with management alone in the realm of scientific investigation, rather than in joint determination.[62]

Problems in the next category, personnel problems, were of two sorts: "problems which have to do with the management of the human material" – hiring, selecting, training, transferring, promotion, and discipline – and problems of employee welfare. In neither case, like production problems, were they considered suitable material for joint determination:

What is a safe place to work in, what constitutes proper lighting, sanitation, air space and other personal needs of the employees, these are questions which safety and sanitary engineers, doctors and other scientific persons are best equipped to decide. They are not questions which involve democracy necessarily, or that can best be settled by majority rule. In recent years, too, scientific study has been extended to the methods of hiring, selecting, training, promo-

61. William M. Leiserson, "Contributions of Personnel Management to Improved Labor Relations," (fragment of "Labor Relations"), 35–6. In *Leiserson Papers*, Box 52.
62. Leiserson, "Labor Relations," Part One, 66.

tion; and scientific managers may be able to determine the best methods of handling these employment problems.[63]

In other words, among all the labor–management problems experienced by modern business corporations, problems of economic control and government alone were appropriate for joint determination and adjustment. Such problems involved the resolution of questions arising from "the distribution of the product of industry between employers and wage earners, the proper length of a working day, the reasonableness of the rules and regulations made by the management for the government of the working force, and the right of the wage-earners to a voice in making the rules that govern them." Even these were matters on which the scientist might be better informed than the wage-earner; "but there is no more reason for letting scientists only decide questions of wages, hours, and shop government than there would be to let only such people decide questions of political government and political policy for the nation. Here questions of the representation of the governed and representation of labor in making rules which govern it combine."[64]

Despite its restrictiveness, Leiserson's definition of constitutional government left plenty of the employment relationship subject to joint determination. Details of his own career as a clothing industry arbitrator, moreover, show that in practice Leiserson extended the ambit of trade agreements well beyond wage and hour questions into the realm of work rules and discipline, and even to an individual employer's investment decisions insofar as these directly affected the work and conditions of his employees.[65] Nevertheless, it was plain that for Leiserson the object in advocating joint determination was not to transcend conflicts inherent in capitalist production and corporate organization and ultimately to transform the mode of production itself for, like Commons, Leiserson did not subscribe to the notion that any such inherent conflict might exist or that any such transformation might be necessary. Rather, the object was to obtain the consent of employees to their continued participation in the further development of the capitalist mode.[66]

Leiserson's approach to labor relations, therefore, restricted unions to

---

63. Ibid., 66.   64. Ibid., 66–67.
65. See, for example, William M. Leiserson, "Problems for an Impartial Chairman: From the Docket of an Industrial Judge," *Atlantic Monthly* (September, 1925), 301–10; also his "Constitutional Government in American Industries," 56–79.
66. Leiserson, "Labor Relations," Part Two, 3. See also William M. Leiserson, "The Worker's Reaction to Scientific Management," An Address to the Taylor Society (7 May 1920), in *Leiserson Papers*, Box 48, ("Speeches and Articles"); William M. Leiserson et al., "Should the Worker Participate in Management," *Business Crucible*, 2, 3 (March, 1921), 5–8.

particular areas of enterprise policy which were deemed susceptible to joint determination in the interests of smooth production. Outside these areas, decision making was the sole prerogative of management and its experts. Within them, the unions were acknowledged to be possessed of rights to confront and bargain with management's experts on a particular range of issues. The object of these joint deliberations was to write a rule of law to distribute the product of the going concern and govern the employment relationship, thereby renewing the consent of the employees to managerial direction of the enterprise.[67]

Leiserson's views paralleled those current within the AFL leadership in the postwar period. As Gompers put it in 1921, "The collective bargain stipulates for a definite period what wages shall be paid, the length of the working day, and other working conditions. It also provides a joint body, composed of the freely-elected representatives of both employees and employers, for the adjudication of all disputes that may arise during the life of the industrial treaty. It thus establishes industrial peace which is essential for the orderly production and distribution of wealth."[68] Four years later his successor, William Green, went much further. "The right of the employer to manage his industry, to control it and to receive a fair profit on his investment should be maintained and recognized."[69] What unions sought in return was the establishment between themselves and the employers with which they dealt of "a proper regard for the functional exercise of each *within their recognized spheres of jurisdiction.*"[70] Yet quite apart from the question whether employers were willing to acknowledge that unions had a sphere at all, the capacity of collective bargaining and, in particular, the trade agreement to serve as a vehicle for the establishment of a mutual "proper regard" was compromised, to an important extent, by the unwillingness of many courts to entertain it as a legally meaningful instrument. As long as this remained the case, a union's opportunity to claim any sort of role for itself in industrial government would be severely restricted and the slow development of what was apparently a fragile consensus on the role of unions under corporate capitalism rendered meaningless.

67. Leiserson "Labor Relations." See generally, Michael Burawoy, *Manufacturing Consent: Changes in the Labor Process under Monopoly Capitalism* (Chicago, 1979); Katherine Van Wezel Stone, "The Post-War Paradigm in American Labor Law," *Yale Law Journal*, 90, 7 (June 1981), 1514–15.
68. Samuel Gompers, "Recognition of the Trade Union" (8 December 1921), in *AFL Records*, reel 116 (Speeches and Writings).
69. William Green, Speech to National Civic Federation Round Table Meeting (11 April 1925), in *AFL Records*, reel 57 (Circular and Neostyle File).
70. William Green, Speech before the Harvard Union (20 March 1925), in AFL *Records*, reel 57 (Circular and Neostyle File) [emphasis supplied].

Legal personality and the union

The courts' stance on the trade agreement was really quite straightforward. As voluntary associations, they argued, unions were lacking in legal personality and, therefore, in the capacity to assert property rights. For this reason they had no standing to sue employers to enforce their agreements.[71] Consequently, no contractual weight could attach to the agreement. Individual union members might sue to enforce provisions of the agreement on their own behalf, on the grounds that the collective agreement was a usage the terms of which were understood to apply to their individual employment contracts. But the courts required strict proof that the usage had indeed been adopted in the individual contract, for "a usage, unless enacted deliberately into a rule of law, cannot be enforced; and the fact that it may look in some respects like a contract will make no difference so long as it is considered to be a usage rather than a contract."[72] As summarized in *Hudson v. Cincinnati* (1913), the terms of the trade agreement would normally be treated as having been adopted in an individual worker's contract only if the employee in question had entered the service of the employer during the operation of the trade agreement, had known of and assented to the trade agreement, and had subsequently made no individual agreement which conflicted with any of the provisions of the trade agreement.[73] The role of the union, according to the court, was "to induce employers to establish usages in respect to wages and working conditions which are fair, reasonable, and humane, leaving to its members each to determine for himself whether or

71. C. Lawrence Christenson, "Legally Enforceable Interest in American Labor Union Working Agreements," *Indiana Law Journal*, 9, 2 (November 1933), 73.
72. Ralph F. Fuchs, "Collective Labor Agreements in American Law," *St. Louis Law Review*, 10, 1 (1925), 3. In *Burnetta v. Marceline Coal Company* (1904), 79 SW 136, the court held that the terms of a collective labor agreement had to be adopted expressly even as between employees who were members of a union and an employer who had an agreement with their union covering their terms of employment. In this case, the court held that the union in question could not contract for the plaintiff employee (who was suing to enforce a provision of the collective agreement), that its agreement with the employer did not constitute a memorandum of usage, and that in the absence of an express adoption of the terms of the collective agreement by the parties to the individual contract the ordinary rules of law should govern. In another case, *Langmade v. Olean Brewing Company* (1910), 121 N.Y. Supp. 388, an employee's suit against his employer for overtime pay owed under the terms of a collective agreement negotiated by the union of which he was a member failed when the court ruled that by remaining in employment despite his employer's refusal to pay the overtime rate, the employee had demonstrated that the terms of the collective agreement had not been incorporated in his individual employment contract. See also *Mastell v. Salo* (1919) 215 SW 583.
73. 154 SW 47, at 50. See also Christenson, "Legally Enforceable Interests," 77; Stone, "Post-War Paradigm," 1518–19.

not and for what length of time he will contract in reference to such usages."[74] Membership in the union at the time an agreement was concluded signified nothing. Consent to the trade agreement was a matter of the explicit and continuously reviewable choice of individual workers.

The decision in *Hudson* expressed the commonly accepted view that there were simply no circumstances in which a labor union or its officers could contract its members. Even if unions chose to seek legal personality through federal incorporation it was still doubtful whether their arguments could gain legal sanction. The impossibility of specifically enforcing employment contracts, it was argued, rendered the union's implicit promise to supply labor valueless, for no one could have property in the capacity to labor except the individual laborer. This meant that trade agreements lacked mutuality of obligation and therefore had no legal weight.[75] In short, the individual contract of employment was all that courts would recognize.

This judicial predisposition to deny unions legal capacity to contract, and therefore to dismiss trade agreements as legal nullities, continued to dog proponents of collective bargaining into the 1920s. As the bureaucratization of unions gave them ever more distinctive *organizational* personalities, however, hints of a different approach began to appear. Thus, as early as 1895, arguments were heard in Congress advocating the treatment of unions in law as organizations possessed of the capacity to bind their members. By doing so, it was held, unions could be enlisted as disciplinary agencies in the service of labor–management peace.

The occasion for the airing of these proposals was debate on the Erdman railroad arbitration bill. According to the bill, arbitration would come into operation on the joint request of union and employer. Once an award was made, employees would be required to respect it by refraining from strike action for three months after the award was handed down, and thereafter except on thirty days notice. Critics of the legislation argued that such provisions were unenforcable, given the Thirteenth Amendment's ban on specific enforcement of labor contracts. Proponents pointed out that enforcement could be had through provisions making unions liable for actions of their members and binding union members to accede to the action of the union. As Hepburn of Iowa stated succinctly, "the whole theory of this bill is that the organization is a unit in the matter and that the individuality of its members is merged in the official action of the organization."[76] Once individual workers had joined the union, an act which the bill sought to encour-

---

74. 154 SW 47, at 49.   75. Stone, "Post-War Paradigm," 1518.
76. *Congressional Record*, 53rd Congress, 3rd Session (1895), 2791.

age, their individual contracts would be interpreted as if bound by the terms of the arbitration awards entered by request of the officers of their union on their behalf. The union itself would be required to incorporate and to make provisions in its articles of incorporation for the expulsion of any member failing to comply with the award. Simultaneously, individual union members would also be liable for prosecution for contempt if they breached the agreement, on the grounds that membership in the union was sufficient to make them, individually, parties to the contract – the arbitration award – "negotiated" on their behalf by the union. On both levels of enforcement, the result would be to grant a considerable degree of authority over individual employment contracts to the collective agreement, giving the union an important disciplinary role vis-à-vis its members. As Hepburn repeated, "the members of the association are a unit . . . in the action that they take; and being such they will, under this law, have the same relations to the decree of this court that the individual stockholder of a corporation has when the corporation is a party to the suit."[77]

The Erdman bill attracted considerable criticism during the early House debates. Van Voorhis of New York, for example, argued that it infringed the individual union member's freedom of contract by using the fact of his membership to bind him to accept a collective agreement.[78] Cannon of Illinois was also alarmed at the erosion of the common law position, and argued that contempt proceedings against individuals for violation of a union's promise not to strike were not lawful. Instead, the legislation should make union members liable to pay damages for their individual breaches of contract.[79] The bill was also opposed by the AFL Executive Council which agreed, early in 1897, that it was "inimical to the interests of labor and destructive of labor organizations."[80] Gompers acknowledged that the Federation's stance had deeply dismayed the railroad brotherhoods (Hepburn had told the House of Representatives that the brotherhoods were quite willing to accept the limitation of their members' liberty in return for the material benefits of arbitration[81]) but after fully reexamining the matter he reassured his colleagues that he was "more than ever convinced that the opinion is not only justified but less severe than it should be."[82]

The logic of the Erdman bill depended on the assumption that unions

---

77. Ibid., 2791.   78. Ibid., 2791, 2793.   79. Ibid., 2791, 2792.
80. Samuel Gompers to AFL Executive Council (25 January 1897), in *AFL Records*, reel 8 (Executive Council Vote Books).
81. *Congressional Record,* 53rd Congress, 3rd Session (1895), 2789.
82. Samuel Gompers to AFL Executive Council (18 February 1897), in *AFL Records*, reel 8 (Executive Council Vote Books).

could be treated as legally identifiable institutions distinct from their members, that as such they could make commitments on their members' behalf, and that they could also discipline their members' acceptance of those commitments and be held answerable for their behavior. The bill, in other words, attempted to give the union legal personality – make it a right- and duty-bearing institution – in order that its agreements, and not merely those of individual workers, might be made subject to the law of contract. The AFL (although not the railroad brotherhoods) resisted the passage of such legislation, in part because it considered that it was not in the interests of unions to be made liable for the actions of their members. But its opposition also demonstrated that at this time the AFL's perception of the relationship between union and member did not allow a hard-and-fast distinction to be drawn between them. As Gompers put it in 1897, "to speak of a union as 'the union' meaning something apart from ourselves, is a misnomer. 'Our union' is more to the point. It is as we make it and cannot rise higher than its units."[83]

The same controversy arose again five years later in a public debate between Gompers and Louis Brandeis on the incorporation of unions held in Boston. Opening, Brandeis argued that the incorporation of unions was necessary to guarantee to employers that relief from irresponsible union action would be available to them through civil suit.[84] Incorporation, he claimed, would mean no great alteration in the legal status of unions for "if a union through its constituted agents commits a wrong or is guilty of violence or of illegal oppression, the union, and not merely the individuals who are the direct instruments of the wrong, can be enjoined or made liable for damages to the same extent that the union could be if it were incorporated."[85] Incorporation, however, would ensure that machinery was also available to employers to enforce trade agreements. It was the lack of redress in this area which had most antagonized employers, Brandeis stated, for they felt themselves bound by law, yet confronted by irresponsible trade unions which were not. Courts had had no alternative but to resort to injunctions to restrain activity otherwise unreachable.[86]

In his reply, Gompers dwelt on Brandeis' accusation that unions were irresponsible:

83. Gompers, "The Trend of Our Time."
84. Boston *Globe* (5 December 1902), in *AFL Recoreds,* reel 126 (Reference Materials).
85. Ibid. It is interesting to note Brandeis' argument that "The *Taff Vale Railway* case, decided last year in England . . . created consternation among labor unions there, but it laid down no principle of law new to this country."
86. Ibid.

The idea upon which the entire proposition is predicated is that the trade unions are irresponsible, that they are unfaithful to an obligation or an agreement, that they do not adhere to agreements entered into with employers and hence their employers want this financial responsibility in unions in order that in the event of their violating these agreements then they can be sued in the courts for damages.

Now, as a matter of fact there are few, exceedingly few, of the unions of labor who break agreements, who violate the terms of agreements. In truth, those who violate agreements . . . usually are the employers.[87]

Both Gompers and Brandeis agreed, therefore, that unions were, or at least ought to be, "responsible." But they disagreed over how "responsibility" was to be achieved. Brandeis argued that responsibility had to be forced on unions through their submission to the rule of law. "The unions should . . . take the position squarely that they are amenable to law, prepared to take the consequences if they transgress, and thus show that they are in full sympathy with the spirit of our people, whose political system rests upon the proposition that this is a government of laws and not of men."[88] By resisting this proposition, Brandeis concluded, Gompers and the AFL were exhibiting an "apprehension of the law, apprehension of the courts and apprehension of everyone who sustains the law and the courts" which "we cannot admit."[89] To Gompers, however, responsibility was not something to be created through submission to the rule of law. Indeed, given the labor movement's experiences at the hands of the courts over the previous decade, "you must excuse us . . . if we decline your invitation to step into your parlor."[90] Rather, responsibility was a quality to be demonstrated, by workers and employers, during the course of the bargain which they had concluded. Measured thus, the responsibility of workers and unions had been proven time and time again; there was no need for the courts to intervene.

Gompers's definition of responsibility in collective bargaining gave it an essentially associational character. Responsibility could not be imposed on the organized labor movement through legislation enjoining unions to police the trade agreements they concluded on pain of legal penalty, for, Gompers argued, trade agreements did not come about through the actions of a distinct personality called a "union." The joint bargain was a collective act of the employees involved – a bargain made

87. Ibid.   88. Ibid.   89. Ibid.   90. Ibid.

by all, rather than a bargain made on behalf of all. It was "the expression of the members of the organization themselves in official and regular form – the best expression of the judgment of each and all in order to obtain the best possible conditions for the employment and labor of all."[91] The institutional structure of the union to which Brandeis and others wanted to attribute "personality" – the central office, bureaucracy, and funds – was nothing more than a piece of machinery and should not be held "responsible" for union members' actions.

As in 1897, Gompers's argument was intended to underline, for unions, the deleterious consequences of liability for the uncontrollable actions of union members. As he said of the contemporary *Taff Vale Railway* case, "the union of these men never took any action, never advised, never consented to the action that these men on strike took." It was "mulcted in damages for the individual action of its members unknown to the union as such."[92] Again as in 1897, however, Gompers was also expressing the anti-individualism of the AFL's admittedly fast-fading associational ideology: being neither contracts concluded by individuals acting singly, nor by an individual entity acting on behalf of others, trade agreements, he implied, transcended all contemporary notions of contract. Therefore, they should be treated *sui generis*.[93]

Gompers's analysis fell on deaf ears. Courts encountering trade agreements considered them in light of the common law of contract. For most courts, as we have seen, this led straightforwardly to a decision that the trade agreement was a nullity. In a few instances, however, courts did show an interest in according the trade agreement some significance. But this did not mean that the status for unions and collective bargaining suggested by Gompers' description of the trade agreement as a collective act of the members, whose associated activity both constituted the union and affirmed the bargain, was receiving judicial recognition. Rather, the courts stuck with the common law of contract and followed Hepburn, Brandeis and the *Taff Vale* decision in pointing to the emerging union bureaucracies as potentially responsible contracting parties.[94]

Considerable doctrinal confusion attended these early attempts to attribute legal status to trade agreements. In *Gulla v. Barton* (1914), for example, the New York Supreme Court decided that a trade agreement had legal weight because it was "a contract made by [the employee's]

91. Ibid.   92. Ibid.
93. See Leon Duguit, "Collective Acts as Distinguished from Contracts," *Yale Law Journal*, 27 (1917–18), 753–68.
94. See the discussion by Fuchs, "Collective Labor Agreements," 12–29.

representative for his benefit."[95] This conflated two separate concepts, that of the union as an agent (representative) of its members, and that of the union as a principal which made agreements on its own behalf and from which its members derived benefits. The two approaches had very different implications for the relationship between union and members, and in later decisions the courts began to distinguish more carefully between the two positions. Thus, in *Schlesinger v. Quinto* (1922), the Appellate Division of the New York Supreme Court sustained an injunction restraining a garment manufacturer's association from breaching a trade agreement then in effect between itself and the International Ladies Garment Workers' Union on the grounds that the agreement was a pact between two organizations, each of which had been empowered "through the consent of the members to enter into a binding obligation in their behalf."[96] By accepting that the individual workers had "authorize[d] officials chosen by them through more or less democratic machinery" to make promises on their behalf, that is, the court was able to treat the officers of the union as the agents of its members and thus enjoin the delinquent employer to perform according to the agreement concluded with those officers.

By treating the union as an agent, courts left union agreements open to challenge from disaffected members who could argue that the union had not in fact possessed authority to act on their behalf. This was the position taken the following year in *Piercy v. Louisville and Nashville Railway:*

> Th[e] contention [that plaintiff ought to act like a loyal member of the union; that he is bound by its acts] ignores the fact that such agreements between organizations of employees and their employer are designed primarily for the individual benefit of the members of the organization, and not to place it within the power of the organization to change or modify the contract at its pleasure so as to affect the individual rights of its members theretofore secured by the agreement . . . Their agreements with employers look always to the securing of some right or privilege for their individual members, and the right or privilege so secured by agreement is the individual right of the individual member, and such organization can no more by its arbitrary act deprive that individual member of his right so secured than can any other person. The organization is not the agent of the member for the purpose of waiving any rights he may have, but is only his representative for the limited purpose of securing to him, together with all other members, fair and just wages and good working conditions . . .[97]

95. 149 N.Y. Supp. 952. 96. 194 N.Y. Supp. 401, at 410.
97. 248 SW 1042, at 1045.

This problem could be avoided through the application of the doctrine of third party beneficiary to trade agreement cases.[98] Under this doctrine, courts could interpret trade agreements as contracts made by unions for the benefit of their members. The rights secured by the contract were individual rights of the individual union members and might be enforced directly by the individual worker in a suit against the employer. Crucially, however, the union and not the individual worker was considered to be the contracting party. This recognition of the union's right to contract limited the individual's recourse against agreements made by the union on behalf of the group.[99] A Massachusetts decision, *Donovan v. Travers* (1934), exemplifies this approach:

> The substantial issue is whether the rights of the plaintiffs are fixed by the terms of the agreement between the union and the railroad corporation as it stood when the several plaintiffs entered upon their service, interpreted only in the light then available; or whether as the agreements changed from time to time, the modifications and possible changes in interpretation of terms agreed upon by the union and the railroad corporation modified and affected the individual contracts of those already in the corporation's employ. We think the latter to be the proper position. *The transaction is an agreement between an employer and a labor union designed by the latter to benefit itself and those members who enter the employer's service. If it modified the agreement with the employer, the employee must acquiesce. In no correct sense is the union an agent. It is a principal* . . .[100]

As these cases indicate, by the 1920s, in a variety of jurisdictions and for a variety of reasons,[101] unions were being accepted as organizations

98. Christenson, "Legally Enforceable Interests," 91–108.
99. Ibid., 93. The limited role of the workers in such circumstances was suggested in an early case, *Saulsberry v. Coopers' International Union* (1912), 143 SW 1013. "The union alone was clothed with power to contract for its members, and the contract, if made at all, had to be made by the union. Hence, the wish or will of individual members cannot be considered in determining the rights of the parties to the controversy. if the union had a right, through its representatives, to contract, which is not denied, then the desire of the individual members cannot be taken into consideration at all, and it is immaterial whether they were satisfied or dissatisfied with the proposed arrangement."
100. 188 NE 705, at 708 [emphasis supplied]. See also *Goldman v. Cohen* (1928), 227 N.Y. Supp. 311.
101. See, generally, T. Richard Witmer, "Collective Labor Agreements in the Courts," *Yale Law Journal*, 48 (1938), 195–239. Witmer concluded that despite the growing incidence of cases dealing with the law of the collective bargaining since the turn of the century, "there is no body of doctrine, in any sense of the word, to which reference can be made to predict the outcome of as yet unsettled questions." 238.

with authority and competency to enter into agreements with employers binding on themselves and on their members. Together with the *Coronado* cases, in which the Supreme Court confirmed that incidents of corporate personality might attach to unincorporated unions,[102] these decisions point to the gradual development, particularly after World War I, of a tendency to bestow a de facto legal personality upon unions. This development allowed courts to reconcile trade agreements with the law of contracts by implying the existence of a legal person with rights distinct from the collectivity of employees to which responsibility might attach. Through the employment of doctrines of agency or third party beneficiary, courts could lend contractual authority to the acts of unions, and hence a degree of legitimacy to the union itself.

The attribution of personality and legitimacy to the union might seem a far cry from Justice Wright's denunciations in *Buck's Stove*. Yet the change was in the labor movement far more than in the law. Originally expressions of an associational ideology profoundly antagonistic to the "individualistic spirit of the law," by World War I the national trade unions had come to regard themselves, and to be regarded, as distinct entities, each with its own administrative capacities, each with its own discrete jurisdictional constituency, each pursuing self-interested goals. The labor movement of the 1920s, in short, was a loose and disaggregated combination of individual organizations, not the quasi-syndicalist association of self-governing trades established in 1886. As such, its reconciliation to the prevailing common law tradition was no longer problematic.

The associative state

Developments in the institutional structure and ideology of the labor movement, in labor relations theory and, finally, in the law thus combined in the years after 1900 to show how unions might be accommodated within the corporate political economy. Within the organized labor movement, the rise of powerful national union bureaucracies like the United Brotherhood of Carpenters and Joiners, the International Association of Machinists and the United Mine Workers created a confederacy of self-interested organizations employing collective bargaining to define and preserve a status quo in place of the class movement built on the harmony of trades foreseen by the founders of the AFL. Simul-

102. *United Mine Workers of America v. Coronado Coal Company* (1922), 259 U.S. 344, and *Coronado Coal Company v. United Mine Workers of America* (1925) 268 U.S. 295; Fuchs, "Collective Labor Agreements," 29.

taneously, industrial relations specialists began to develop a body of functionalist theory which stressed the centrality of organization to the adjustment of industrial disputes, while some courts found ways of ascribing to these organizations a de facto personality and hence a capacity to enter into contractual relations with other legal personalities, creating thereby a framework in which unions would be governed by standards articulated in that unchanged rule of law of which they had been so recently and so completely a contradiction.

These developments paralleled wider trends transforming the structure of the postwar political economy. By the early 1920s those seeking to shift policy-making power further away from the "regular agencies of government" – executive, legislative, and judicial – and place it instead in the hands of associational networks located in the private sector, had achieved the ascendancy they had been seeking. For example, "associational activities" lay at the core of Secretary of Commerce Herbert Hoover's plans for the reconstruction of American industry and society. Relying almost completely on nongovernmental mechanisms for ordering of the basic economy, Hoover envisaged the development of "a systematized network of cooperative associations and councils [which] would provide the ordered freedom needed for continued economic and social progress" and which could promote "a societal regulation . . . superior to any that could emerge from legislative debate or governmental bureaucracies."[103] This did not mean that the administrative state which had been appearing piecemeal since 1880 was without a role; "associational activities" were to take place within an administrative framework provided by an "associative state." But that state was to be "tied to . . . the new associational order." Its role was not to be one of regulation of the new order but of cooperation with it, providing guidance and aid in the associational order's further development.[104] Associational activities, that is, meant the thorough interpenetration of private activity and public bureaucratic-administrative capacity. "This, so it was said, was the path to a higher and more efficient form of democracy, one that would allow liberal societies to overcome social fragmentation and realize their ideals without undergoing either socialist revolutions or some kind of statist regimentation."[105]

Proponents of collective bargaining, therefore, appeared comparatively well placed to emphasize the particular advantages which would accrue from finding room for unions in the postwar polity. Only the

103.   Hawley, "Three Facets of Hooverian Associationalism," 99, 100.
104.   Ellis W. Hawley, "Herbert Hoover, the Commerce Secretariat, and the Vision of an 'Associative State'," *Journal of American History*, 61, 1 (1974), 118.
105.   Hawley, "Three Facets of Hooverian Associationalism," 99.

inclusion of organized labor, it was argued, could guarantee that American workers would continue indefinitely to consent to be participants in a capitalist employment relationship.[106]

The argument was not without effect. Responding in particular to the savage labor–management strife of 1919–20, increasing numbers of employers began to accept that "the older view of labor problems as temporary evils calling for specific and permanent correction" was invalid, and that "some kind of employer-employee relations" was inevitable. As a result, industrial relations "achieved a more or less firm pattern in a number of industries."[107] But this had not resulted from any great rush to accept collective bargaining with independent unions as the appropriate mechanism through which industrial relations should operate. Employers could resort to many other institutional forms – shop committees, shop councils, employee representation plans, company unions – just as expressive of their desire to undertake experiments in joint determination.[108] Compared with these, indeed, cooperation with AFL unions, their attention focussed on developing their own carefully husbanded spheres of influence within the "going concern," seemed a highly unattractive proposition. As Professor Henry Seager, secretary to President Wilson's second National Industrial Conference, put it early in 1920:

> The trade or labor union official has little or no concern with the business success of the plant in which the dispute has arisen. His primary concern is for the success of the union which he represents ... he negotiates with the employer not as a partner in the enterprise wishing to increase his share without jeopardizing the success of the business, as an employee representative might do, but as an outsider willing if necessary to tie up the business altogether to secure the larger share he demands for his constituents ... The psychology of collective bargaining through shop committees is predominantly cooperative; that of collective bargaining through trade or labor union officials is predominantly contentious ... Concessions made by the employer to his shop committees are credited to

106. An important essay by Steve Fraser, "Dress Rehearsal for the New Deal: Shop-Floor Insurgents, Political Elites, and Industrial Democracy in the Amalgamated Clothing Workers," in Michael H. Frisch and Daniel J. Walkowitz, editors, *Working Class America: Essays on Labor, Community and American Society* (Urbana, Illinois, 1983), 212–55, discusses these developments within the context of one union. See also David Brody, "On the Failure of U.S. Radical Politics: A Farmer–Labor Analysis," *Industrial Relations*, 22, 3 (Spring 1983), 142–55.

107. McNulty, *The Origins and Development of Labor Economics*, 162.

108. See, generally, Gary Dean Best, "President Wilson's Second Industrial Conference, 1919–1920," *Labor History*, 16, 4 (Fall, 1975), 505–20; Daniel Nelson, "The Company Union Movement, 1900–1937: A Reexamination," *Business History Review*, 56, 3 (Autumn, 1982), 335–57.

him and serve to increase the loyalty of his employees to the business. Concessions made by the employer to a union negotiator are
credited to the organization and serve to strengthen the loyalty of
members not to their employer but to the union.[109]

Despite the growing interest of employers in industrial relations, then,
the El Paso Convention of the AFL still found itself having to note in
1924 that "the bulk of organized employers" had shown no interest in
cooperation with organized labor.[110]

No more forthcoming was any initiative from the new associative
state to bridge the gap. Secretary of Commerce Hoover, it is true, had
returned from Europe in 1919 convinced of the need for worker participation in the "new industrial system" which he hoped to see emerge in
the postwar years. But, like most businessmen, Hoover had little time
for the organizational premises upon which the AFL's model for labor
relations and industrial order was based. Favoring the organization of
workers in ways which conformed to the reorganized labor process of
the large manufacturing corporations, he was critical of the unions'
"arbitrary and anachronistic" structures. Eventually, Hoover hoped,
unions would be altogether replaced by shop councils or other forms of
employee organization which would "represent workers according to
their actual roles in the affairs of the company."[111]

While proponents of constructive collaboration between organized
business and organized labor busily demonstrated *how* matters appropriate for joint action could be determined and *why* joint determination
in these areas might be desirable, therefore, their arguments had mini-
mal impact. Employers, it seemed, could secure workers' consent by a
variety of means – cooperative or coercive – none of which required the
involvement of independent unions. Nor had the architects of the associative state any reason to doubt their effectiveness. "Impressed by the
apparent efficacy of welfare capitalism, proud of the prosperity enjoyed
by wage earners, and aware of the parochialism and lassitude of the
AFL, Hoover muted his earlier insistence on meaningful, democratic
and independent participation by workers in the economic system."[112]
Circumstances would have to change quite profoundly before anyone
could find reason enough to offer the organized labor movement a
substantive role in the corporate political economy.

109. In Best, "Second Industrial Conference," 512.
110. *Report of the Proceedings of the 44th Annual Convention of the American Federa-
      tion of Labor* (Washington, 1924), quoted in William English Walling, *American
      Labor, American Democracy* (New York, 1926), 57.
111. Robert H. Zieger, "Herbert Hoover, the Wage-Earner, and the 'New Economic
      System,' 1919–1929," *Business History Review*, 51, 2 (Summer 1977), 166.
112. Ibid., 162.

Conclusion

Circumstances did change, of course, and drastically too. The disintegration of the economy after 1929 brought in its wake the disintegration of American industry's labor relations policies. By the early 1930s, considerable support was accumulating in Congress, and even in some segments of the business community, for the proposition that collective bargaining through independent unions was, after all, a realistic model for the conduct of labor relations.

Precisely how such a model might be established, however, and what, in institutional terms, it would comprise, were questions which remained to be debated. As that debate developed, there loomed a set of even more difficult questions concerning the role to be played by the state in the creation and regulation of the model. These confronted many of the proponents of collective bargaining – particularly the unions themselves – with a considerable dilemma. On the one hand, the concerted power which employers demonstrated in resisting the unions during the early 1930s brutally reminded them of their own incapacity to extend significantly the ambit of collective bargaining unaided; this experience encouraged them to turn to the state for assistance in overcoming employer opposition. On the other, the unions were well aware that in seeking the state's aid they were of necessity making themselves hostage to a power over which they had historically enjoyed little control. For institutions reared on suspicion of the state, needing its help yet anxious to avoid any disruption to their own *gesellschaftlich* customs, the problem was a knotty one indeed.

PART II

Labor and the liberal state

In respect to your main contention my answer in brief is this: Whether we will it or not, government in every country is going to be forced to play a more important role in every phase of economic life, and for that reason it seems to me more useful to attempt to direct the nature of that role rather than merely to state the truism that government is likely to be influenced by the forces in society that happen to be strongest. Certainly these forces cannot be checked by governmental self-limitation nor do I believe that governmental action in such matters over a decently long period of time serves to check the struggles that labor must carry on by extra-governmental means.

Robert F. Wagner to Roger N. Baldwin (5 April 1935), *American Civil Liberties Union Papers*, vol. 780. Quoted in Cletus E. Daniel, *The ACLU and the Wagner Act: An Inquiry into the Depression-Era Crisis of American Liberalism* (Ithaca, New York, 1980), 103.

Introduction: "Who Bears the Business Risks?"

Early in 1931, William Leiserson put his duties as chairman of the Ohio Commission on Unemployment Insurance, clothing industry labor arbitrator and professor of economics and politics at Antioch College to one side for long enough to pen for the *Survey Graphic Magazine* a pithy assessment of the current state and future prospects of the American economy.[1] "Because the business man's point of view has dominated our American life," Leiserson argued, analyses of the Depression "have tended to be in terms of production." But in fact, recovery of production and alleviation of unemployment depended upon a prior revival of purchasing power and consumer demand. Such a revival could not be achieved by the current policies of the Hoover administration, for Hoover was simply attempting to maintain aggregate national income at levels at or near those reached during the years of prosperity, whereas analysis of "seasonal and cyclical fluctuations" over the previous twenty years demonstrated that reduced consumer demand, and hence loss of business and unemployment, was a consequence not of fluctuations in aggregate income but of fluctuations in the portions of national income paid out as returns to labor and capital. The crucial task for government, then, lay in improving its capacity to stabilize the distribution of national income.[2]

Given that both public and corporate policy already offered returns to capital considerable protection from business fluctuations, Leiserson argued, public policy innovations should concentrate on safeguarding wage-earners' incomes, so that the stability already enjoyed by recipients of dividends, interest payments, and entrepreneur incomes might be more widely shared. "What has been done for the investment and managing classes can be done for the wage-earning classes. If wage payments were stabilized as other incomes have been made steady, consum-

1. William M. Leiserson, "Who Bears the Business Risks?" *Survey Graphic Magazine* (March 1931), 596–600, 622.
2. Ibid., 600, 622.

99

ing power would flow more evenly and regularly to the vast majority of consumers, thus reducing and eliminating many of the business fluctuations both from year to year and within the years." Stabilization of wage-earner incomes, in other words, would not only relieve workers of the burden of their employers' business risks, it would also help insulate the economy from cyclical fluctuations in general.[3]

Leiserson was not alone in attributing the prolongation of the depression to the lack of stability in income distribution. According to Robert F. Wagner, junior senator from New York, "As our business mechanism has become infinitely more intricate it has become impossible to coordinate its various activities." In particular, "Wages to labor have been so poorly coordinated with returns to capital that recurrent failures of consumer demand have led to cyclical depressions and widespread unemployment . . ."[4]

Adopting the same explanation of the causes of the depression, Wagner was drawn in the same general direction as Leiserson in seeking to alleviate them. Both sought the establishment of planning schemes to coordinate production and prevent further fluctuations in the general distribution of income. Both argued that on the specific question of stabilizing returns to labor, nothing could be more effective than innovations in public policy to encourage collective bargaining between employers and independent unions.

As we have seen, advocates of collective organization and bargaining had met with little success during the 1920s, the majority of employers continuing to rely on belligerent industrial relations strategies predicated on the maintenance of unilateral control of all aspects of enterprise policy through coercion.[5] Even the self-conscious majority of "progressive" firms which had begun to experiment with "employee representation" plans designed to supplement centralized personnel administration with structured channels of communication between management and workers envisaged only a limited and tactical alteration in the distribution of social and economic power in industry, and restricted the scope of the plans to plant-level employment relations. But the Depression, the results of the

---

3. Ibid., 622.
4. Robert F. Wagner, statement for Russel Owen of the *New York Times* (19 May 1933), in *The Robert F. Wagner Papers*, 562 GF (General Files) 335 (Georgetown University Library, Washington D.C.). [Hereinafter cited as *Wagner Papers*].
5. "During the deceptively prosperous decade of the 1920s," writes Steve Fraser, "the relative stability of the economic order relegated such programmatic innovations [as collective bargaining] to the periphery of national politics." See his "Dress Rehearsal for the New Deal: Shop-Floor Insurgents, Political Elites, and Industrial Democracy in the Amalgamated Clothing Workers," in Michael H. Frisch and Daniel J. Walkowitz, editors, *Working-Class America: Essays on Labor, Community, and American Society* (Urbana, Illinois, 1983), 241.

1932 and 1934 elections, and the threat, by 1933, of continually escalating tensions in industrial relations all furnished opportunities for proponents of collective bargaining to press the question with renewed vigor.

Concentrating at first on the creation of conciliation, mediation, and arbitration mechanisms to facilitate the generalization of voluntarist organization and bargaining, by early 1934 Wagner and his advisors had begun to call for collective bargaining to be brought fully within the regulatory ambit of the fast-growing administrative state. Their efforts culminated in a series of dramatic legislative and administrative innovations – the National Labor Relations Act and the decisions implementing it taken by the second National Labor Relations Board in the years after 1935 – establishing collective bargaining and the right to organize at the center of the Roosevelt administration's recovery policy.

Success in achieving the passage of legislation establishing collective bargaining despite strong employer opposition obscured the absence of real agreement amongst its proponents as to what collective bargaining comprised and how it should be constituted. To the AFL, for example, collective bargaining remained a fundamentally private activity, one in which the parties – unions and employers – sought results beneficial first and foremost to themselves. The Federation's concern, as its ally, Leiserson, had pointed out in the mid-1920s, was to resolve "problems of economic control and government" – that is, wages, hours, and working conditions – within the particular "going concern." Its ideal was legislation which would facilitate this process through the elimination of company unionism and protection of the rights of independent unions. Wagner's legislation, in contrast, made collective bargaining a matter of public concern, conducted by institutions with statutorily-defined rights and responsibilities within a framework shaped by state agencies. While this represented a major encouragement to collective bargaining, it also represented what was potentially a severe encroachment upon union autonomy.

These differences in perspective notwithstanding, the alliance between the AFL and Congressional liberals remained fully intact during the legislative debates of 1934 and 1935. Insofar as the course being taken in the formulation of the legislation caused the AFL any real concern, the only sign came in its attempts to press amendments which would ensure direct influence for itself over the enforcement of national policy. Nor did Congressional rejection of these amendments alter the Federation's conviction that the Wagner bill would be highly beneficial to organized labor. It was only after the split in the labor movement and the appearance of rival unionism in the shape of the Committee for Industrial Organization (CIO) that the AFL was led to reconsider its earlier unconditional support of the Wagner Act and to develop a sustained critique of the New Deal collective bargaining policy. Only then – with the development of this new situation – did the more deleterious implications of the policy really begin to hit home.

These implications were profound. Specifically, the unions found that in all questions of representation and collective bargaining their status as organizations had undergone a dramatic alteration. During the 1920s, as we have seen, courts had begun to show a tendency to allow that unions, like business corporations, enjoyed the status of legal persons. The passage of the Norris-La Guardia Act in 1932 built on this common law trend by recognizing that unions possessed rights to engage in competitive economic struggle, unchecked (within wide limits) by law, analogous to rights already enjoyed by corporations. In the New Deal model, in contrast, unions were regarded not as entities with rights but as instruments or agents, designated as representatives by employees through the medium of a government-supervised election. Not only that, by making the National Labor Relations Board responsible for determining the dimensions of the unit from which collective bargaining representatives would be elected, the Wagner Act enabled the Board to ignore the AFL's claim to possess exclusive rights to define the structure and extent of labor representation through the exercise of its jurisdictional rules, and to superimpose its own definition. Unsurprisingly, on this fundamental question of political and economic power – the question of who was to establish the dimensions of the agencies through which bargaining would take place – New Deal policy quickly became the subject of almost constant vilification from leading elements of the organized labor movement.

In giving the National Labor Relations Board such power, the proponents of the New Deal collective bargaining policy indicated that the decisive role in constructing the United States's modern industrial relations system belonged to the new liberal bureaucratic-administrative state. During the 1930s, spirited defenses of workers' rights to organize and bargain expressed that state's genuine social beneficence, its sensitivity "to the deprivations suffered by 'discrete and insular minorities.' "[6] Just as significant, however, was its developing commitment to containing those who sought to redress grievances and to achieve a measure of power strictly within the regulatory frameworks established by state institutions. Order and stability, no less than democracy, were goals of labor relations policy. By 1940, indeed, order and stability were fast becoming the only goals.

---

6.   Peter Irons, *The New Deal Lawyers* (Princeton, 1982), 295.

4

The New Deal collective bargaining policy

[The bill] gives no additional power to labor unions. All that it does is to permit workers, if they so desire, to choose their own organizations free from interference, coercion or intimidation of the employer. In other words, it simply makes the worker a free man.

Robert F. Wagner to Dorothy Straus (21 March 1934), in *Wagner Papers*, 694 LA (Labor Files) 715, folder 7.

Robert F. Wagner's concern at the instability of the national economy began to show soon after he entered Congress in 1927. Arguing that persistent unemployment posed a growing threat to the nation's welfare, the senator introduced a resolution requiring the Department of Labor to compute unemployment statistics. Such statistics were needed, he argued, "for the intelligent conduct of business and as a basis for our effort at regulation and stabilization."[1] Other initiatives followed. In January 1930, for example, Wagner announced the introduction in Congress of three bills to mitigate the effects of rising unemployment. These directed the secretary of labor to prepare and publish monthly unemployment figures; created a Federal Employment Stabilization Board to advise the president and plan public works; and established a system of employment exchanges operated by a United States Employment Service in the Department of Labor in conjunction with existing state agencies.[2]

As the Depression deepened, Wagner's plans for the restoration of an orderly economy focussed more and more upon the expansion of the administrative capacity of government to intervene in social and economic affairs. In this he was hardly alone. As Ellis Hawley has put it, "almost every economic group was crying for salvation through politi-

---

1. *Wagner Papers*, 545 SM (Source Material) 452, undated brief outlining Wagner's maiden speech (delivered 5 March 1928) to the Senate. See also *Wagner Papers*, BB (Black Books) 119 Book 1.
2. J. Joseph Huthmacher, *Senator Robert F. Wagner and the Rise of Urban Liberalism* (New York, 1968), 60–61.

cal means, for some sort of rationalization and planning."[3] Considerable differences existed, however, as to "just who was to do the planning and the type and amount of it that would be required."[4] Eventually, the cacophony of conflicting voices resolved itself into three definable strains of opinion which vied with each other for influence over the administration's economic policies. Committed to the associative state of the 1920s, and to the "servicing" role which it envisaged for administrators in economic affairs, pro-business planners proposed the creation of "a semi-cartelized business commonwealth" in which industry would do the planning and the state would enforce the resulting decisions. Advocates of national economic planning reversed this relationship, seeking a much greater role for state planning agencies and a transfer of power away from business. In reaction to both these approaches a third group rejected planning whether by business or the administrative state, and called instead for a return to vigorous enforcement of the antitrust laws and to the ideal of free competition.[5]

Wagner's position was clearly that of the second group. Within that group, however, he was distinguished by his optimism. Many advocates of national planning were economic "stagnationists" who argued that fundamental changes in the organization of economic activity had to be undertaken through government intervention because after a hundred years of growth American capitalism had finally reached a condition of saturation from which it was completely incapable of self-regeneration. Wagner, in contrast, expressed the belief "that what we need is not a new economic order but greater precision and better organization in the existing order." He saw national planning as a step which would complement the existing organization of American capitalism and allow it to continue fulfilling its endless potential.[6]

3. Ellis W. Hawley, *The New Deal and the Problem of Monopoly: A Study in Economic Ambivalence* (Princeton, 1966), 476.
4. Ibid., 476.   5. Ibid., 35–52.
6. Robert F. Wagner,"Speech to the Conference on Unemployment," (Cleveland, 30 December 1930), in *Wagner Papers*, 546 SM 453. See also Huthmacher, *Senator Robert F. Wagner*, 135–7; Robert M. Collins, *The Business Response to Keynes, 1929–64* (New York, 1981), 9–10. Collins writes, "Keynesian analysis raised questions about the constancy of the government's role . . . a spectrum of views quickly developed. At one end were the pump primers, those who believed that a dose of Keynes, especially of heavy deficit spending, would suffice to get the pump of the capitalist economy back into normal operation. To the left of these pump-primers were the compensatory spenders, those who viewed capitalism as capable of only short periods of stability under its own power, with government intervention a recurrent necessity. Furthest to the left were the interventionists or stagnationists, those who saw the existing style of capitalism as completely incapable of regeneration; they believed that only on-going government intervention (and spending deficits) could prevent permanent depression."

Already heavily involved in the formulation of recovery legislation on his own behalf, Wagner's influence over the course of economic policy debates within the administration was considerably enhanced when, in April of 1933, he was deputized by President Roosevelt to oversee the composition of an administration recovery bill. Roosevelt's hand had been forced by Senate approval, on April 6, of an AFL-endorsed thirty hours bill sponsored by Senator Hugo Black.[7] Opposed to the unilateral adjustment of hours and wages which this legislation proposed to implement, Roosevelt's advisors sought instead to create mechanisms facilitating a planned adjustment based on the rationalization of competitive conditions.[8] Under the direction of a new federal agency, the National Recovery Administration, employers would be permitted to combine in trade associations and construct codes of fair competition which would fix production quotas and prices. Each code was also to contain minimum wage and maximum hours provisions. In addition, Section 7(a) of the administration's bill required that each code contain provisions guaranteeing employees the right of organization and collective bargaining. A program of public works completed the picture.[9]

According to Wagner, the bill meant "a changed concept of the duty of the State." By widening "the area of government control through law," the recovery bill would allow the "purposeful planning on a national scale" necessary to restore business prosperity and stimulate employment.[10] Equally important, government commitments to collective bargaining for all employees meant that for the first time the state had recognized its obligation to play a constructive role in managing industrial relations. Indeed, for Wagner this aspect was so fundamental that he made his support of the legislation conditional upon inclusion of Section 7(a).[11] "[T]here can no more be democratic self-government in industry without workers participating therein, than there could be democratic government in politics without workers having the right to vote" he would later write. "That is why the right to bargain collectively is at the bottom of social justice for the

7. Irving Bernstein, *The New Deal Collective Bargaining Policy* (Berkeley, 1950), 29–31. The bill would have barred from interstate commerce any article produced in an establishment where any person was permitted to work for more than six hours per day or five days per week. According to AFL president William Green, the measure would spread work, reduce technological unemployment, and thus alleviate the depression. He warned that the AFL might call general strikes to secure its passage.
8. Hawley, *The New Deal and the Problem of Monopoly*, 21–26.
9. Bernstein, *New Deal Collective Bargaining Policy*, 31–39.
10. Wagner, Statement for Russel Owen; Robert F. Wagner, "Planning in Place of Restraint," *Survey Graphic Magazine*, 22, 8 (August 1933), 396.
11. Huthmacher, *Senator Robert F. Wagner*, 147.

worker as well as the sensible conduct of business affairs. The denial or observance of this right means the difference between despotism and democracy."[12]

It was characteristic of Wagner that he should show such confidence in the capacity of legislative and administrative action to achieve fundamental social change. His earlier political career in the New York State Senate had been built on the enactment of progressive social legislation.[13] When subsequently appointed to the bench of the state's supreme court he had employed the weapons of legal realism to ward off critics. "Our constitutional government is not an impotent one," he declared in the New York rent control case of 1925. "Not so readily can its arms of protection for those for whose benefit it is imposed be bound and made helpless; its scope and vision is wide; its power flexibly adaptable; its aim the protection of human rights."[14]

During the Hoover years, Wagner had found few opportunities to embody such values in action at the national level. "When every dictate of reason and experience was pleading for revised concepts of the function of law and government in modern society," he stated in 1933, "we continued to adhere to the political notions of 1800."[15] In particular, the potential of law to play a constructive role had been limited by the belief that its role was solely to prevent rather than to encourage. But the change of administrations had created new circumstances. It was now appreciated in Washington that "Law should respond sensitively and rapidly to the social and economic problems created by the interpenetration of our modern industry . . ."[16]

Despite losing its thirty hours bill, the AFL shared Wagner's enthusiasm for the administration's recovery legislation. The Federation had lobbied hard for the inclusion of promises of employee organization in the bill, and President Green, who had suggested much of the language of Section 7(a), described it as a "Magna Charta" for labor.[17] According to Daniel Tobin, president of the International Brotherhood of Teamsters, the legislation that went through the Senate was "about as good, or even better, than we expected."[18] Well before the bill received its final approval, the Federation began drafting the principles which would govern labor's participation in the recovery program. These were formally adopted on 6 June, a week prior to passage of the bill

12. In Leon H. Keyserling, "Why the Wagner Act?" in Louis G. Silverberg, editor, *The Wagner Act: After Ten Years* (Washington, 1945), 12–13.
13. Huthmacher, *Senator Robert F. Wagner*, 24–54.   14. In ibid., 49.
15. Wagner, "Planning in Place of Restraint," 396.   16. Ibid., 396.
17. In Bernstein, *New Deal Collective Bargaining Policy*, 38.   18. In ibid., 38.

in the House, by a conference of national and international union leaders.

The principles adopted on 6 June indicate that the Federation's strong endorsement of the recovery legislation owed much to its perception of the bill as a means to gain recognition and legitimation for industrial self-regulation based upon union-employer cooperation. According to the the AFL, "the agencies through which the labor provisions of the codes of fair competition should be negotiated, put into operation and regulated are the trade associations for the employers and the national trade unions for the employees."[19] Where industries were unorganized "existing national trade unions and trade associations should be afforded every opportunity to bring suitable organizations into being." Similarly, where industries were only partially organized "existing national trade unions and trade associations concerned shall be recognized and accepted by the Administrator as representative respectively of the employees and employers of those industries for purposes of quickly establishing the labor provisions of the codes of fair competition." Representation and code formulation, in other words, were matters for the peak organizations already in place on each side of industry. These would function in their own right as regulators of both organized and previously unorganized areas of industry. Code administration, likewise, was also a matter for them:

> To expedite and facilitate the process of establishing the labor provisions of the codes of fair competition, joint labor code boards, equally representative of labor and employers and under the supervision of the Administrator, shall be set up for this purpose by major industries or groups of industries. The members of these joint labor code boards shall consist of properly-chosen representatives of the national trade unions concerned and representatives designated by the trade association concerned.[20]

The AFL response to the opportunities presented by the passage of the National Industrial Recovery Act was based quite specifically on the *gesellschaftlich* bargaining structures it had been attempting to develop since World War I. In 1927 and 1928, for example, discussions between the AFL and the American Bar Association had mooted the formation of a national industrial council, made up of nominees of the AFL, the ABA, the U.S. Chamber of Commerce, and other peak organizations, charged with "the duty of looking into all industrial situa-

---

19. "Administrative Principles of the American Federation of Labor in Dealings under the National Industrial Recovery Act," (8 June 1933), in *AFL Records,* reel 57 (Circular and Neostyle File).
20. Ibid.

tions, with a view to preventing industrial conflict and promoting industrial peace and agreement between responsible organized groups."
The council was to be a permanent body appointed by the president
with the power to subpoena evidence, conduct hearings, and make
public reports and recommendations, although not to issue binding
orders. It was to be "a non-political body in all respects," a perfect
example of the quasi-public regulatory activity by private groups cham-
pioned during the New Era.[21]

Such contacts gave the Federation's leaders some grounds for optimism that organized business might be persuaded to take seriously their
pretensions to joint action under the Recovery Act, and enactment of
7(a) was followed by a wave of union organizing throughout the economy. Established unions such as the United Mine Workers and the
International Ladies Garment Workers quickly recovered the membership they had lost during the 1920s. In hitherto non-unionized industries—automobiles, rubber, electrical manufacturing—the AFL created
"federal labor unions," local unions directly affiliated to the Federation
itself, to serve as the core for what would eventually be new international unions. Neither employers nor Recovery Administration officials,
however, felt that the vague guarantees of Section 7(a) committed them
to countenance a role for independent employee organization and collective bargaining within the recovery program. In the eyes of both
groups the industrial order which the act was designed to procure was
predicated on cooperation among employers, not cooperation between
employers and labor. The act created procedures designed to enhance
stability in labor relations, they argued, because such stability improved
the chances of achieving overall order in industry. But it did not require
employers to bargain with independent unions, only to pledge not to
inhibit the organization of their employees. Many employers simply
required their employees to join company-sponsored representation
plans sanctioned by the Recovery Administration. When the established
unions insisted that the act recognized that they were the exclusive
representatives of all workers, employers and NRA planners quickly
united against them.[22]

The combination of union organizing initiatives and employer intran-

---

21. "Confidential Memoranda of the Results of the Deliberation of the Committee of
the American Bar Association and the American Federation of Labor Dealing with
the Matter of Constructive Federal Legislation for the Disposition of Industrial
Controversy," Enclosure in Matthew Woll to John P. Frey (3 August 1927), in *The
John P. Frey Papers*, Box 15, folder 215 (Library of Congress, Washington D.C.).
[Hereinafter referred to as *Frey Papers*.]
22. James A Gross, *The Making of the National Labor Relations Board: A Study in
Economics, Politics and the Law* (New York, 1974), 10–15.

sigence meant a rapid increase in industrial unrest. By August, the number of man-days lost to strikes per month had risen from 600,000 (the average for the first six months of the year) to 2.4 million.[23] The situation prompted the National Recovery Administration's Labor and Industry Advisory Boards to call jointly for a moratorium on strikes and lockouts for the duration of the recovery program and for the creation of a bipartisan body to mediate disputes arising within the terms of Section 7(a) of the Recovery Act. On 5 August 1933, Roosevelt created the National Labor Board and made Wagner its first chairman.[24]

Essentially, the National Labor Board was a temporary expedient created to deal with a sudden strike wave. Consisting at the outset of seven members, three each appointed to represent the two sides of industry with Wagner as the representative of the "public," it had almost no supporting staff, no presence (initially) outside Washington and no power to enforce its decisions. The limitation of its jurisdiction to "adjust[ing] and settl[ing] differences and controversies that may arise through differing interpretations of the President's Re-employment Agreement" confirmed its temporary character, for once an industry adopted a code it ceased to operate under that agreement.[25] Codified industries, it was anticipated, would develop their own agencies for adjustment and settlement of disputes if they had not already done so.

These circumstances were not immutable and there were many changes in the following months. The Board expanded; it recruited a small but enthusiastic staff; it created regional organizations; and with some major exceptions it gained jurisdiction over disputes in codified industries. But the stringent limitations upon its powers to enforce its decisions remained. This meant that the Board could play at best a symbolic role in the recovery program.

For most of 1933, Wagner placed primary emphasis upon using the National Labor Board as a mediating body, the primary function of which was to prevent disputes developing into strikes. "Strikes should be abandoned as an instrument of first resort," he said in October. "Industry and labor cannot cooperate by means of the strike." Strikes worked against, not for, what Wagner identified as the proper goals of the recovery program. They obstructed the profitable conduct of busi-

---

23. Irving Bernstein, *Turbulent Years: A History of the American Worker* (Boston, 1971), 172–3.

24. Ibid., 172–3. See also *Wagner Papers* 694 LA (Labor Files) 715, folder 5 (5 August 1933).

25. "Announcement of the Labor and Industry Advisory Boards of the National Recovery Administration," (5 August 1933), in *Records of the National Labor Relations Board* (Record Group 25 of the National Archives and Records Service, Washington D.C.). [Hereinafter cited as *RG* 25.]

ness and thus prevented progress toward better standards of living. They kept workers and their employers from enjoying peaceful and cooperative relations. "These ends are hampered by resort to means which carry us backward to the old system of conflict and destruction and which prevent the building of a cooperative order along the lines of the recovery program."[26] Indeed, resort to striking would imperil labor's position. "Labor is clothed with privileges and responsibilities as great as any other group. In return it must adopt the methods most likely to secure the benefits of the recovery program."[27] Government agencies were now available and should be used "for the amicable and constructive settlement of disputes." Failure to resort voluntarily to these agencies would bring sanctions, for "the national concern about the success of the recovery program rises above the narrow interests of any particular group."[28]

By representing mediation as an alternative to strikes, Wagner hoped to convince employers that recognizing a union did not entail automatic acceptance of its demands under threat of strike action.[29] But mediation proved unpopular both outside and within the Board. Outside, those sympathetic to striking workers argued that mediation achieved noth-

---

26. Robert F. Wagner, "Industry and Labor," Speech on NBC Radio (18 October 1933), in *Wagner Papers*, 600 SF (Speech Files) 103, folder 28.
27. Ibid.　28. Ibid.
29. That this was the case was suggested early in the Board's tenure by William Leiserson, who had become its first secretary. An employer wrote to question 7(a)'s requirement that he recognize his employees' union given that, on past experience, the way he would be required to express his recognition would be by signing a closed shop contract establishing the union rate and union rules. His concern grew from his knowledge of the custom in collective bargaining prior to 7(a). Usually, a union would approach an employer, irrespective of whether it had amongst its members a majority of his employees, and press him under threat of a strike to sign a contract bringing the wages and conditions of those of his employees within the union's jurisdiction into line with those established elsewhere as the going union rate or norm. It was this process which the Norris-LaGuardia Act legitimized. In these circumstances, recognition meant acceptance of the further consequences without more ado; the one action entailed the others. Thus, the choice for the employer under prevailing customs of collective bargaining was to recognize the union, which meant automatically accepting the accompanying conditions, or refuse and face the consequences – strikes and boycotts. Most employers interpreted 7(a) in the light of this experience and therefore assumed that it simply reinforced the union side of the confrontation because it required them to recognize unions. Leiserson's reply indicated something different; 7(a) had created a new situation with new rules. Recognition of a union no longer entailed acceptance of the union's demands. All that recognition meant was that the employer acknowledged that his employees had chosen a representative with which he could negotiate to establish mutually acceptable rules and conditions in a discreet process of bargaining, supplemented, if necessary, by NLB mediation of disagreements. See Leiserson to Congressman Louis Ludlow (9 September 1933), in *RG 25*, Box 81 ("NLB General Correspondence").

ing. The only tangible effect of the Board's campaigns against strikes was to deprive workers of the one real weapon they possessed without putting anything in its place. As the socialist and head of the Conference for Progressive Labor Action, A.J. Muste, put it in a letter to Wagner, "The NLB asserts that the strike is against the public interest, against the government. If the workers go back to work, the Board will see to it that they get a square deal. They will be given a chance to vote in an election supervised by the Board so that there can be no question of impartiality, etc. The next thing that happens is that the election is postponed for some time . . . The ardor of the employees tends to cool. Labor spies and company agents can get in their work, intimidation can be practised . . ." Muste condemned "the whole philosophy underlying the procedure," that is, "the philosophy that a government agency can take care of the workers when the workers have been deprived of their one real weapon, namely, the right collectively to cease labor."[30]

William M. Leiserson, who had become the NLB's secretary, also warned Wagner of the deleterious consequences accompanying reliance on mediation. As long as the Board attempted to mediate disputes, Leiserson predicted, it would simply reproduce within itself the conflicts it was supposed to resolve. "Successful mediation can be acomplished only when the parties have a single mediator to deal with, who is impartial and who suggests concessions to be made by both parties." Instead the Board tended to split along predictable lines of interest. Moreover, Leiserson added, the Board was doomed to fail in any case because it was attempting to re-mediate disputes which had been referred to it precisely because they had already proved immune to mediation in the field. What was required was not mediation but arbitration – the issuance of decisions based on the relevant provisions (that is, Section 7) of the National Industrial Recovery Act:

> By way of example I need only to mention the Philadephia Bakers' case, the Tool and Die Makers strike in Detroit and Flint, and the Jamestown Art Metal Company's case. In each of these, mediators have failed because employers insisted they would not recognize unions of employees or strikers' committees. When the cases came before the Board, therefore, they should have been handled as matters

---

30. Muste to Wagner (27 December 1933), in *RG 25*, Box 80 ("General Correspondence File"). Mary Van Kleeck, Director of the Department of Industrial Studies, Russell Sage Foundation, also wrote to Wagner to protest attempts by the Roosevelt administration to limit the right to strike. See Van Kleeck to Simon Rifkind (8 August 1933), in *Wagner Papers, 694 LA 715*, folder 5. See also American Civil Liberties Union to FDR (19 September 1933), in *RG 25*, Box 82 ("Policy-NRA"). See, generally, Cletus E. Daniel, *The ACLU and the Wagner Act: An Enquiry into the Depression-Era Crisis of American Liberalism* (Ithaca, New York, 1980).

for arbitration or decision by the Board. A ruling was necessary as to whether Section 7(a) did or did not require recognition of the union or the strikers' committee. Instead, the Board attempted to mediate with the result that the whole matter of collective bargaining versus individual bargaining involved in these cases was left as something to be fought out in industrial conflicts and settled on the basis of relative economic power, as it was before Congress enacted Section 7(a).[31]

Leiserson recommended that the Board reestablish itself as a purely arbitral body to decide questions of policy which might then furnish a sound basis for the activities of a separate staff of mediators.

The unrelenting opposition of employers – their demands, for example, that the Board's modest operation be decentralized and replaced with adjustment boards in each major industry – tended to underline the hopelessness of a policy of mediation. Consequently, the Board slowly moved in the direction Leiserson advocated. This made little difference to the majority of employers, for the Board enjoyed no more authority as an arbitrator than as a mediator; the National Recovery Administration and the Justice Department saw to that.[32] Nonetheless, the adoption of an arbitral approach did promise the establishment of a body of principles which might provide the foundations for a rule of law in collective bargaining where none had formerly existed.

The Board's rulings concentrated on two major areas, the behavior of the parties in the course of collective bargaining, and employee representation. Although aimed primarily at employers, the Board's rulings in the first area were not confined to the policing of employer practices. Both parties, that is, found their behavior subjected to its oversight. Thus, the Board established that the employees' right to collective bargaining imposed a correlative duty on employers to meet and negotiate with employee representatives and to embody the results in written agreements; it also held that collective bargaining involved "a duality of obligation – an obligation on the part of employees to present grievances and demands to the employer before striking [as well as] an obligation on the part of the employer to discuss differences with the representatives of the employees." Elsewhere it condemned the breach of collective agreements by either side and also confirmed that it would not take action on behalf of any employee who had been "proven guilty of violence in the course of a strike."[33]

31. Leiserson to Wagner (19 October 1933), in *Leiserson Papers*, Box 43, ("Wagner").
32. Peter H. Irons, *The New Deal Lawyers* (Princeton, 1982), 208–10.
33. "National Labor Board Principles with Applicable Cases," Memorandum from the Office of the Executive Secretary, National Labor Relations Board (21 August 1934), in *RG 25*, Box 20A ("NLRB, Office of the Executive Secretary").

It was in the area of employee representation that the Board had its most lasting impact, however, for it was here that it developed what was to be the centerpiece of the emerging common law of collective bargaining, the principle of majority rule.

Initially, the NLB had adopted the position that the implementation of the right to organize and choose representatives, protected by Section 7(a), was a matter solely for employees. This was consistent with the Board's original intention to play a purely mediatory part. The Board saw no role for itself until a dispute, for example over attempts by employees to exercise Section 7 rights, was actually underway, at which point it would attempt to adjust the dispute. It did not oversee the exercise of employee rights nor tell employees how they should put them into effect. As Leiserson put it in response to an early enquirer, "Section 7 of the Recovery Act gives the employees the right to organize and choose their own representatives. [In] answer [to] question[s] as to what steps are necessary, we can only say that that is a matter for the employees to decide for themselves. They may call a meeting and elect the representatives in any way they desire."[34]

Throughout its period of office the Board continued to affirm that the exercise of Section 7 rights was a matter for no one but employees. In *Edward G. Budd Manufacturing* (1933), for example, the Board stated, "Both the selection of a form of organization and the designation of representatives, as well as the method of designation, are placed by Section 7(a) within the exclusive control of the workers. The law does not tolerate any impairment of this freedom of self-organization."[35] In practice, however, this position came to be qualified as the Board was slowly forced by employer interference with employee rights to develop its own procedures for the designation of representatives on the employees' behalf.

The procedures developed by the Board centered on the device of an election by secret ballot under government supervision, to be held whenever an employer questioned the authority of an individual or organization to act as the representative of his employees. First used in August 1933 to settle a dispute involving over 10,000 hosiery workers in eastern Pennsylvania, this procedure was formalized by the Board and designated "the Reading Formula."[36] The terms of the formula were that the Board would encourage striking workers to return to work in exchange for management guarantees to negotiate with representatives chosen in a government-supervised election.

34. In *RG 25*, Box 81 ("NLB General Correspondence File K").
35. 1 NLB 58, at 60.
36. *H.W. Anthony Mill* (1933), 1 NLB 1. See also Irons, *New Deal Lawyers*, 206–7.

The Reading Formula, clearly, could be applied successfully only in circumstances where employers accepted the Board's mediation. This was quickly made apparent by the simple refusal of companies to give the guarantees of non-interference in the choice of representatives by their employees upon which the formula was predicated. Such displays of employer intransigence – notably in the *Budd Manufacturing* and *Weirton Steel* (1933) cases – proved fatal to the mediation approach and meant that the Board had to develop an alternative procedure if the right to representation were not to become completely irrelevant. The outcome was an attempt to establish majority rule as a principle to be enforced rather than as an "adjustment" to be negotiated.[37]

This outcome was not uncontested and led to the breakdown of consensus on the Board. While Wagner and the labor members were convinced that majority rule was the only feasible response to the collapse of the Reading Formula, the Board's employer members evinced a desire to compromise with opponents of the Formula by recognizing any employee representatives, including those chosen under company-sponsored employee representation plans, insofar as they could demonstrate that they enjoyed support among a proportion of the work force in question. Walter C. Teagle, for example, took the position that employee representation plans were completely lawful under Section 7: "The clearly stated purpose of the law is to permit employees to organize and bargain collectively with employers through whatever representatives they choose to select. A plan restricting representation to fellow workers, if such a plan is desired by the employees, fulfills the requirements of the law, just as fully as does a union."[38] When the Board majority tried to use its decision in *National Lock Company* to establish majority rule as a principle, Teagle called it "an attempt to interpret the law – something which I believe should only be done on the basis of actual court decisions."[39] Pierre S. Du Pont, newly appointed as an employer member of the Board, also objected and called for the Board to endorse instead the principle of proportional representation.[40] Precisely the same dispute arose in the

---

37. National Labor Board, *Decisions* (Washington, 1934), vii. On February 1, 1934 Roosevelt issued Executive Order 6580, authorizing the NLB to conduct representation elections employing the principle of majority rule. This order, however, was immediately interpreted by the National Recovery Administration to sanction proportional representation. See Irons, ibid., 211.

38. Walter C. Teagle, "Employee Representation and Collective Bargaining," A report by the Chairman of the Industrial Relations Committee, Business Advisory and Planning Council of the Department of Commerce, in *RG 25*, Box 84 ("Wagner: Correspondence, 1933–34").

39. Teagle to Jesse L. Miller, NLB Executive Director (21 February 1934), in *RG 25*, Box 87 ("Office of the General Counsel: Drafts of NLB Decisions, 1934").

40. Du Pont to NLB (19 February 1934), in ibid.

subsequent *Denver Tramway, Houde Engineering,* and *Real Silk Hosiery* cases, and in each the Board's employer members recorded their opposition to majority rule. As Ernest Draper, another new appointee, put it in connection with the *Real Silk* case: "the law states quite clearly that workers may have the privilege [sic] of being represented for purposes of bargaining by representatives of their own choosing. To rule, then, that a minority group must be represented by representatives of the majority – the very representatives whom the minority particularly object to – is to make a ruling that defeats rather than carries out the clear meaning of the law."[41]

The transition from mediation to majority rule early in 1934 was the decisive step in the evolution of federal labor relations policy. From an approach based on attempts simply to adjust disputes over employee representation the Board had moved toward a policy of actively facilitating representation through the extension of existing organizations and the construction of new ones. Clearly, this had important repercussions for the employer. Less obviously, but in the long run more importantly, it also had implications for the theory of representation embraced by the established labor movement, for majority rule meant nothing less than a profound alteration in the conceptual and ideological basis of the argument for collective bargaining.

These implications of majority rule can best be explained in the context of developments in the law of labor agreements during the 1920s. By 1920, as we have seen, courts had begun to show a tendency to treat collective bargaining agreements as enforceable contracts on the grounds either that a union was the agent of its members and concluded agreements on their behalf, or that the union was a principal which contracted on its own behalf in transactions with employers from which its members derived benefits as third parties. The first course was embraced and clarified by Wagner himself while he was serving on the bench of the Supreme Court of New York. In the landmark case of *Schlesinger v. Quinto* (1922), the International Ladies' Garment Workers' Union, and its subsidiary, the Joint Board of Cloakmakers' Unions of New York, sought an injunction to restrain the New York Cloak and Suit Manufacturers' Protective Association from breaching its contract with the union. Wagner granted the injunction, the first occasion on which a union had been allowed equitable protection of a contract. But he did not treat the

---

41. Draper to Miller (30 April 1934), in *RG 25*, Box 85 ("Records of Jesse L. Miller, Executive Director, 1933–34"). Similar exchanges of opinion can be found in connection with other important NLB cases of this period. See for example, the files on *Denver Tramway Corporation* and *Houde Engineering Corporation* in *RG 25*, Box 87 ("Office of the General Counsel: Drafts of NLB Decisions, 1934").

action as one brought by the union to protect its own interests as one of two principals to a contract. Instead he treated it as one brought by the 40,000 individual workers involved in the dispute. So far as the court was concerned, that is, "the action of the union officers was the formal means by which they sought to protect the individual interests of all the union members in a single suit."[42] In a subsequent decision sustaining the injunction, the Appellate Division of the Supreme Court confirmed that Wagner's decision had been based on the inference that a relationship of principal and agent existed between the members of the union and the union itself.[43] That meant that the members of the union were the principals involved in the contract, that they had chosen to authorize the union to act as their agent in representing their views to their employers, and that the action had been brought to vindicate rights which they, (not the union), had gained as a result of the contract.

In attributing an agency function to unions, Wagner's decision necessarily implied that the law had a duty to pay some attention to the question of how unions acquired their representative (agency) status. Unions, it indicated, should be endorsed by the law because of their considerable potential to be means for the vindication of the individual rights and interests of their members. But unions were not legal persons in themselves. Rather, they were constructed out of individual legal persons. Hence, a union's claim to legitimacy could not reside in any organic relationship which it might argue existed between itself and its constituency, but only in the more or less explicit bestowal by members of that constituency of authority upon officers to act upon their behalf. Without that expression of consent by the majority, exhibited in an appropriate form, a union could not expect to gain recognition before the law.

This argument was not generally followed elsewhere. During the course of the decade, courts appeared less and less inclined to spend their time in speculation over how a union might have acquired the capacity to act. Instead they more often chose to uphold trade agreements as enforceable contracts on the grounds that the union was the party principal involved.[44] Courts, that is, would decide cases on the basis that the union contracted with employers on its own behalf, treating its members simply as passive third parties who benefitted from the transaction.

42. C. Lawrence Christenson, "Legally Enforceable Interests in American Labor Union Working Agreements," *Indiana Law Journal,* 9, 2, (November 1933), 90.
43. *Schlesinger v. Quinto* (1922), 194 N.Y. Supp. 401. The original decision can be found at 192 N.Y. Supp. 564.
44. Christenson, "Legally Enforceable Interests," 102–8, particularly 105.

The courts' second track fit the wider corporative trends of the New Era political economy. In the 1920s, traditional political institutions which represented Americans as a mass of individual citizens were being overshadowed by the activities of specialized organizations and associations offering new forms of "virtual" representation to a society organized increasingly on a group basis. Labor arbitrator William Leiserson, for example, clearly thought of unions in this way, describing them as quasi-corporate entities which possessed rights "as sacred and inviolable as the rights of corporations of stockholders."[45] The strategies of AFL leaders, as we have seen, were predicated on a similar understanding of the role and status of unions. In the confidential negotiations during 1927 and 1928 between representatives of the American Federation of Labor and the American Bar Association, for example, participants on both sides routinely interpreted the principals to collective agreements to be organizations (employers and unions) which enjoyed equivalent legal stature and which had their rights and duties spelled out in the agreement, not individuals represented by organizations.[46]

The passage of the Norris-LaGuardia Act in 1932 constituted an acceleration in this trend toward the establishment of labor unions as distinct personalities on a par with (although much less powerful than) corporations. Like Section 7(a) of the National Industrial Recovery Act a year later, the act recognized that individual workers were unable to deal effectively with employers under prevailing conditions of economic organization, and therefore endorsed the organization of employees into independent unions for purposes of collective bargaining. Its main concern, however, was not with the process of organization but with the freedom of these organizations to act. Treating unions as entities with rights and interests of their own, the act concentrated on protecting their freedom to engage in economic conflicts to vindicate those rights. As such, the act could best be described as "a monument to the spirit of complete free enterprise for unions."[47] By defining narrowly the circum-

---

45. William M. Leiserson, "A New Attitude Towards Trade Unionism," *The Standard*, 12, 7 (March, 1926). And see Leiserson to Mabel Hastings Hampstone (9 November 1926), in *Leiserson Papers*, Box 16, ("H general"). See also his "Dealing with Trade Unions," in *Leiserson Papers*, Box 51, ("Speeches and Articles"). This remained Leiserson's position throughout the 1930s. Thus, late in 1935 Leiserson told Harry A. Millis (recently retired as a member of the Board replaced by the Wagner Act) that in his opinion labor organizations amounted to corporations of workers. See Leiserson to Harry A. Millis (18 December 1935) and Millis to Leiserson (21 December 1935), both in *Leiserson Papers*, Box 2, ("American Economic Association").

46. "Confidential Memoranda," in *Frey Papers*, Box 15, folder 215.

47. Charles O. Gregory and Harold A. Katz, *Labor and the Law* (New York, 1979), 197.

stances in which courts might use injunctions to protect employers from union activity it guaranteed to labor unions the freedom to promote their economic interests just as the courts at common law had always accorded that same freedom to business associations. "[The act] recognized the economic interest of associated laboring folk in the employment conditions prevailing in any nonunion unit of an industry, in the competing units of which members of the labor association were established. This interest, in turn, *conceived and evaluated for all practical purposes in accordance with the union's views of its importance and reality,* operated as a complete justification for any harm imposed on such nonunion unit through economic coercion."[48]

In the context of legislative and judicial developments such as these, majority rule was a very distinctive departure. Hitherto, the AFL had claimed for itself the authority to decide, through assignment of jurisdiction, which union represented which workers. It based its assignments on a complex web of considerations; tradition, custom, the "property rights" accumulated by a particular organization in the course of its development as an organic representation of a particular craft, and, particularly since World War I, the distribution of power within the Federation.[49] Now the NLB, through majority rule, was developing a traditional political model for the determination of representation rights. Crucially, furthermore, it was only by following the Board's procedures that organizations could gain the advantages which accompanied federal imprimatur as legitimate collective bargaining representatives.

As long as the Board enjoyed no real authority to enforce its decisions, the possibility of contradictions arising between the "collective" or "property" right of the particular union to occupy its jurisdiction and represent the workers who held the jobs which made up that jurisdiction, and the individual or "civil" right of an employee to choose his own representative, was foreclosed. The AFL could safely and happily endorse majority rule because its effective power to define both the appropriate electorate and the appropriate representative within the organized labor movement for that electorate was not being challenged. Yet without enforcement powers there was little chance that the NLB would be able to bring an end to employer obstruction of collective bargaining with independent unions – the outcome which the AFL so ardently desired and which Wagner saw as the key to recovery and thus, ultimately, to the safety of democratic capitalism. By early 1934, with the NRA's self-regulatory program dominated by business cabals,[50]

48. Ibid., 192 [emphasis supplied]. And see generally 184–99.
49. As noted in Chapter 3.
50. Hawley, *The New Deal and the Problem of Monopoly*, 62–6.

and with the unions impaled upon the horns of continuing mass unemployment and worsening industrial strife, it was becoming increasingly clear that without a labor agency possessed of real powers to act, not only would there be no progress in extending bargaining, the unions would also risk losing all the gains which they had made in the previous nine months. Both Wagner and the AFL, therefore, had an interest in attempting to strengthen the recovery program's labor policies. Consequently, when Wagner turned to the task of formulating legislation which would create a Board with adequate authority to enforce labor representation, the Federation stood four-square behind him.

The labor disputes bill of 1934

Wagner's legislation first saw light of day in February 1934. Drafted by the senator's aide, Leon Keyserling, Senate bill S2926 – "to equalize the bargaining power of employers and employees, to encourage the amicable settlement of disputes . . . to create a National Labor Board and for other purposes" – exemplified the themes of economic justice, positive state action and the vindication of individual rights through law characteristic of Wagner's career. According to the bill's preamble, legislation was needed "to ensure a wise distribution of wealth between management and labor, to maintain a full flow of purchasing power, and to prevent recurrent depressions."[51] The bill's first title declared that structural and organizational changes accompanying the growth of the American economy had destroyed the power of the individual worker to bargain effectively and that inadequate recognition had been given to the right of employees to bargain collectively. This had in turn led to strikes by employees seeking to force employers to accept labor's organizations. Both developments had negative effects on commerce and the general welfare. The solution lay in allowing individuals to organize and bargain collectively without interference, and in creating a tripartite administrative board which would ensure that interference did not take place and which would offer its services as a mediator and arbitrator in those disputes which still occurred. In this way the immediate threat to commerce would be diminished and an administrative mechanism created which in the longer term would help to ensure that the returns from industry would be distributed in a manner that would decrease the likelihood of a recurrence of depression and unrest.[52]

51. National Labor Relations Board, *Legislative History of the National Labor Relations Act, 1935*, 2 vols. (Washington, 1949), 1, 15. [Hereinafter cited as *Leg. Hist.*]
52. *Leg. Hist.*, 1–14; Wagner to John Dewey (14 February 1934), in *Wagner Papers*, 562 GF (General Files) 325, folder 26.

The way to industrial stability, according to the bill, was through the negotiation of binding collective contracts between employers and their employees. Its proponents stressed that this did not mean that workers would be forced, or even encouraged, to join unions.[53] The bill did not endorse the closed shop; in fact Wagner claimed that it made the closed shop more difficult to obtain.[54] As NLB member Francis Haas pointed out, the truly fundamental changes intended by the bill lay in the role and status of the contract, rather than in the position of the union:

> Turning to the future, it is necessary to take a totally different concept of the wage contract. We must abandon the notion that the wage contract concerns only an employer and an employee. It concerns everybody else. The amount of wages that a man is paid and the hours that he works certainly affect him, but they affect every other worker both as worker and as buyer. They affect the employer hiring the worker, but they affect also other employers.[55]

The bill, that is, made collective bargaining an expression of the public interest in the terms of individual contracts of employment.

There were plenty of precedents available to invoke in support of a public policy endorsing collective bargaining. Advocates of S2926 could point to affirmations of collective bargaining emanating from the Industrial Commission of 1902, the Commission on Industrial Relations of 1915, the National War Labor Board and the Railway Labor Board. Collective bargaining had also been endorsed in the Railway Labor Act as well as in the Norris–LaGuardia Act and the National Industrial Recovery Act, and Congress had signified its willingness to accept the legality of unions in the Clayton Act. If doubts still remained, advocates of the bill could also point to the opinion of the Supreme Court, delivered in 1930 in *Texas and New Orleans Railroad Company versus Brotherhood of Railway and Steamship Clerks,* that "the legality of collective action on the part of employees in order to safeguard their proper interests is not to be disputed."[56]

Yet although, as the Court concluded in the *Texas and New Orleans Railroad Company* case, Congress could "seek to make [the] appropriate collective action [of employees] an instrument of peace rather than of strife," there existed among these precedents nothing which could be called an example of active promotion of union organization by the

---

53. See, for example, Dorothy Straus to Wagner (14 March 1934) and Wagner to Straus (21 March 1934), in *Wagner Papers,* 694 LA 715, folder 7.
54. *Leg. Hist.,* 16, 25.   55. Ibid., 146.
56. 281 US 548, 1 CD [Court Decisions Relating to the National Labor Relations Act (published by the National Labor Relations Board)] 26, at 38–9.

state.[57] Unions were assumed to be private organizations, performing no public function, owing no public responsibility and therefore without any right to expect public intervention on their behalf. The Clayton Act, for example, expressed labor relations policy in terms of a status quo. Unions were legal entities but their activities obstructed commerce. Thus, unions had a right to exist, but employers had a right to attack them through resort to the coercive powers which the state made available to prosecute violations of commercial law.[58] The following year, the Supreme Court demonstrated its adherence to much the same position in the course of an opinion declaring unconstitutional a Kansas statute invalidating yellow-dog contracts:

> The Act . . . is intended to deprive employers of part of their liberty of contract, to the corresponding advantage of the employed and the upbuilding of the labor organizations. But no attempt is made, or could reasonably be made, to sustain the purpose to strengthen these voluntary associations of persons, as a legitimate object of the police power. *They are not public institutions, charged by law with public or governmental duties, such as would render the maintenance of their membership a matter of direct concern to the general welfare. If they were, a different question would be presented.*[59]

Nor did the railroad labor legislation of the 1920s alter this approach. Commenting on the Transportation [Esch-Cummins] Act of 1920, the Court held it evident "that Congress deems it of the highest public interest to prevent the interruption of interstate commerce by labor disputes and strikes . . ." However, "The decisions of the Labor Board [created by title III of the Act] are not to be enforced by process." Title III, the Court stated, was simply an attempt by Congress to help private parties solve their differences amicably:

> [T]itle III was not enacted to provide a tribunal to determine what were the legal rights and obligations of railway employers and employees or to enforce or to protect them . . . The Labor Board was created to decide how the parties ought to exercise their legal rights so as to enable them to cooperate in running the railroad. It was to

---

57. The *Texas and New Orleans* ruling itself did nothing more than reiterate the Railroad Labor Act's prohibitions against carrier interference with the right of railroad workers to organize. It did not oblige the railroad to deal with the organization they formed or to cease dealing with company unions which it had formed on their behalf. The decision, in short, left the unions no better off than before. See William H. Harris, *Keeping the Faith: A. Philip Randolph and the Brotherhood of Sleeping Car Porters, 1925–37* (Urbana, Illinois, 1977), 171.
58. Benjamin J. Taylor and Fred Witney, *Labor Relations Law* (New York, 1979), 52–4.
59. *Coppage v. Kansas* (1915) 236 U.S. 1, 35 Sup. Ct. Rep. 240, at 244 [emphasis supplied].

reach a fair compromise between the parties without regard to the legal rights upon which each side might insist in a court of law.[60]

This status quo was reaffirmed in 1926 when Congress repealed the Esch-Cummins Act and passed the Railway Labor Act in its place, for although the new legislation endorsed collective bargaining, it failed to go further and also endorse the sixteen standard railroad labor organizations as the only legitimate representatives of railroad workers, as they had demanded. This meant that company unionism could still prevail within the terms of the Act.[61] The overall effect, according to Federal Transportation Coordinator Joseph B. Eastman, was that, as before, "the settlement of disputes was left to a procedure of conference and negotiation between the railroads and their employees with the aid of a government agency designed solely for mediation purposes."[62]

The supporters of S2926, therefore, were proposing a course qualitatively different from that suggested by previous advocacy of collective bargaining. Their intention was to give unambiguous public support to independent unionism as a means to promote collective bargaining, not in the interest of stabilizing relations between existing organized parties – the rationale of previous legislation – but in vindication of the tangible public interest in the stabilization of the wages, hours and working conditions of the labor force at large. From this flowed the two most important features of the bill; first, its critique of company unionism; and second, its proposal to place authority to determine the appropriate dimensions of a collective bargaining relationships in the hands of the Board.

For many of the bill's supporters, the mere fact that company unionism normally entailed an intolerable degree of interference by employers with the civil rights of their employees was sufficient reason for its condemnation. The leading advocates of the bill, however, placed primary emphasis upon an economic argument.[63] Questions involving wages, hours, and working conditions had to be dealt with on an industry- or nationwide basis if settlements conducive to general economic

60. *Pennsylvania Railroad Co. v. United States Railroad Labor Board et al* (1923), 261 U.S. 72, 43 Sup. Ct. Rep. 278, at 83. See also *Pennsylvania Railroad System v. Pennsylvania R. Co.* (1925), 267 U.S. 203, 45 Sup. Ct. Rep. 307.
61. Robert H. Zieger, *Republicans and Labor, 1919–29* (Lexington, Kentucky, 1969). See also footnote 57, above.
62. Testimony before the Committee on Interstate Commerce, U.S. Senate,*Hearings on S3266, To Amend the Railway Labor Act of 1926*, 73 Congress, 2nd Session (April 1934), 10.
63. In other words, company unionism was not condemned because of the existence of employer interference per se. As Wagner stated, "the bill which I have introduced forbids employers to ... exercise *undue* control over employee organizations." *Leg. Hist.*, 21 [emphasis supplied].

stabilization were to result. Organizations which were limited in extent or influence to one plant or company were thus *necessarily* ineffective when it came to bargaining on these issues. No public policy which endorsed collective bargaining as a means to stabilize labor's share of national income could succeed unless it also simultaneously recognized that company unions were institutionally incapable of contributing to the achievement of that stability.[64]

This argument, however, entailed the further conclusion that the simple proscription of company unions was, by itself, no solution. Once freed from employer domination, employees might still choose a form of organization which suffered from structural defects no less damaging to achievement of the public purpose than company unions.[65] In order to further the goals of the recovery program, therefore, statutory protection of the right of employees to organize was supplemented in S2926 by administrative designation of the dimensions of the group from which representatives would be selected by majority vote to bargain on the group's behalf.

This provision did not pass without comment. Wallace B. Donham of the Harvard Business School, for example, told the Senate Committee on Education and Labor that in his opinion the provision "means State control of trade union organizations, jurisdictions, elections; indeed, the death of trade unionism as we now know it."[66] Union witnesses appearing in support of the bill warned in more general terms that administrative intervention should be kept to the minimum necessary to secure employer participation, leaving labor and industry to work out problems arising in the employment relationship in their own fashion, through their own representatives.[67]

William Leiserson, now with the Petroleum Labor Policy Board, also had definite opinions on this question. His advice to Wagner was that S2926 simply specify that employers bargain with labor organizations through their officers. "Much of the trouble with Section 7(a), in my judgment, has been caused by the over-emphasis on the word 'representative'," he wrote on March 8. "The law gives to the employees the

---

64. "The company union has improved personal relations, group welfare activities, discipline, and the other matters which may be handled on a local basis. But it has failed dismally to standardize or improve wage levels, for the wage question is a general one whose sweep embraces whole industries, or even the Nation." Ibid., 23.

65. Under 7(a), as the NLB had recently reiterated, "Whether representation should be by plant or by department is a matter which concerns primarily the employees themselves . . . It is not for the employer or for this Board to dictate the type of organization which should be established." *Budd Manufacturing Company* (1933), 1 NLB 58, 60.

66. *Leg. Hist.*, 640.   67. Ibid., 202.

right to organize and to bargain collectively. The rest about representatives is incidental to these rights. Therefore I think it is important that the employer should recognize and deal with and make and maintain agreements, not with representatives, but with the labor organizations of his employees through any officers or representatives they may have." Leiserson also wanted to rewrite the collective bargaining sections to follow this logic. "That is to say . . . the statement of the right to organize . . . should be followed by something like this: 'Employers shall recognize and/or deal with labor organizations of their employees and shall exert every reasonable effort to make and maintain agreements with such organizations of their employees concerning wages, hours, and other conditions of employment.' "[68]

Leiserson's suggestions could not have been accommodated without altering the whole thrust of the bill, and thus of the developing federal collective bargaining policy. For Leiserson, as for AFL leaders, the concepts "labor" and "employers" stood for established organizational structures. Collective bargaining occurred between those structures. The process of organization meant the extension of those structures to encompass additional constituencies. Public policy should encourage this extension but should leave the actual process to the parties themselves. In labor's case this meant freeing existing national unions to develop in accordance with their own organizing strategies and with the rules and jurisdictional structures of the organized labor movement. In Wagner's bill, however, "labor" was conceived of not as a set of organizations but as the mass of individual employees which constituted the labor force. Given that the goal was collective bargaining, the first problem was to devise a means whereby the mass might become a series of collectivities appropriate for bargaining. Thus the bill proclaimed the right of individual workers to engage in an act analogous to a political election: to gather in an electoral unit, the dimensions of which were to be decided by an administrative agency created by the bill, and to choose a representative who would confer on their collective behalf with management.

At this time, the major danger of such a federal policy, so far as the unions were concerned, appeared to be that it could result in the creation of a weak and atomized labor movement consisting of thousands of uncoordinated local groups. William Green voiced this concern early in 1934:

> Elections in individual plants supported by the National Labor
> Board should not be confused with real collective bargaining . . .

68. Leiserson to Wagner (8 March 1934), in *Leiserson Papers*, Box 33, ("Perkins").

> We must recognize that over and above the National Industrial
> Recovery Act and the National Labor Board, there is need for
> organizations of workers on a basis at least as wide as the organiza-
> tion of employers in trade associations for code making and code
> enforcement. In the long run we must look to independent orga-
> nizations of workers on a national or international basis for real
> collective bargaining.[69]

The problem which Green outlined seemed easily circumvented.
Nothing, after all, prevented any local group of workers from choosing
an existing national union as their representative. Potentially more serious was the absence of any constraints on that choice. Not until after
the moment of its election could a union claim to be a legitimate representative of any particular collectivity of workers, no matter what its
established or customary or jurisdictional rights might lead it to expect.
Yet even this was no great disadvantage, for as long as the existing
national unions showed sufficient enterprise and unity of purpose they
could continue effectively to control the structure of labor representation by ensuring that there was only one organization available for any
given groups of workers to choose. In the bill, moreover, labor was
granted an important role in the agency which would designate the unit
from which representatives were to be elected, making it relatively easy
for the AFL to maintain control over the structure of labor representation which the legislation was designed to initiate.

Rather than enterprise and unity, however, by early 1934 the established unions were exhibiting considerable ambivalence toward the idea
of extending their organizing campaigns beyond the constituencies they
had lost in the early years of the Depression and into the centers of
American manufacturing might. As Nelson Lichtenstein has recently put
it, "Craft-oriented leaders of the AFL, such as Daniel Tobin, who called
the mass production workers 'rubbish,' saw in their alternating militancy
and resignation an unpredictable quality upon which they thought it
foolish to attempt to build solid trade unions."[70] As a result, AFL leaders
failed to give a concerted national direction to local insurgencies, inviting
both the development of precisely the weak and atomized labor movement they feared, and, in reaction, the appearance of rivals to fill the gap.
As for the influence which they hoped to enjoy over the Board, non-labor
witnesses appearing before the Senate Committee both for and against
the bill argued that the Board should be nonpartisan and independent.

---

69. Statement on Executive Order 6580 (3 February 1934), in *AFL Records*, reel 57
    (Circular and Neostyle file).
70. Nelson N. Lichtenstein, *Labor's War at Home: The CIO in World War II* (Cam-
    bridge, England, 1982), 11.

Nathan L. Miller, general counsel to the U.S. Steel Corporation, felt that "when you clothe the board with any such powers as these the individuals composing it should be selected to represent one interest and one alone, and that is the public interest."[71] Similarly, the economist and industrial relations expert, Sumner Slichter, insisted that the Board be completely independent of the Department of Labor "because the Department of Labor . . . is looked upon as the guardian of the interests of the wage-earners."[72] Effectively, proposals like these meant that the proposed Board would be a nonpartisan expert administrative bureaucracy, in charge of a policy directly affecting the organized labor movement but insulated from its influence.[73]

Political circumstances and the AFL's own vacillation, therefore, were creating a situation in which the bill might become less advantgeous than the Federation had initially imagined. Nevertheless, its support for S2926 was unaffected. The opposition of employers, however, was unrelenting, notwithstanding the assurances of the bill's advocates that it conferred no new powers on labor unions and that its only purpose was to speed recovery. Their reward came on March 25 when the Roosevelt administration indicated its own lack of interest in S2926 by embracing proportional representation – the approach favored by the employer spokesmen on the NLB – rather than majority rule in its struggle to settle labor disputes in the automobile industry. This ensured that what slim chances there had been for the bill's passage would disappear.[74] Undercut by the administration and under pressure from Senate Committee Chairman Walsh, Wagner revised the bill to allow the Board to approve company unions as exclusive representatives and to limit its administrative authority.[75] But neither the administration nor the bill's employer opponents could be convinced of the need for an agency of the sort and of the powers that he proposed. The various amendments and compromises incorporated in an attempt to satisfy different critics had created a legislative mess and the Senate Committee decided to

71. *Leg. Hist.*, 48, 51, 927. See also Gross, *The Making of the National Labor Relations Board*, 66–7.
72. *Leg. Hist.*, 94–5.
73. Ibid, 439. The AFL Executive Council, in contrast, insisted that the Board should be bipartisan and that the labor representatives should be "bona fide labor men selected from those connected with national labor organizations." *Minutes of the AFL Executive Council* (4 May 1934). (AFL-CIO Headquarters, Washington D.C.). [Hereinafter cited as Executive Council *Minutes*.] The Council's stress on "bona fide labor men" appears to be a criticism of earlier Administration appointments of non-unionists, such as Leo Wolman and Mgr. Francis Haas, to the Labor Board.
74. Bernstein, *New Deal Collective Bargining Policy*, 71; Irons, *New Deal Lawyers*, 212–14.
75. Bernstein, *New Deal Collective Bargaining Policy*, 72–3.

rewrite the bill completely. But S2926 was still too controversial and was finally abandoned.

Entr'acte

The demise of S2926 occasioned few regrets in the White House or in the Department of Labor. Neither Roosevelt nor Secretary Perkins had lent the bill any support, preferring, as the events of March 25 showed, a decentralized approach to labor relations based on proportional representation and dispute adjustment administered through code authorities and industry boards.[76] In mid-June, however, the administration found itself suddenly confronted with a massive strike wave in mass production industries without any policy to deal with it. With the National Labor Board crippled by the effects of the automobile labor settlement and the Walsh substitute for S2926 as unacceptable to employers as the original had been, the only option appeared to be hasty resort to a stopgap. Consequently, on June 13, Roosevelt presented Congress with a request for passage of an emergency enabling resolution.

By passing Public Resolution 44, as it became known, Congress gave the president power to establish one or more labor boards for a period of one year, and to authorize them to investigate disputes arising under 7(a) and oversee the election of employee representatives. Two weeks later, Roosevelt issued Executive Order 6763, abolishing the old National Labor Board and creating a new nonpartisan National Labor Relations Board with three members – Lloyd K. Garrison, dean of the University of Wisconsin Law School, who temporarily became chairman; University of Chicago professor of economics and labor arbitrator Harry A. Millis; and Edwin S. Smith, formerly commissioner for labor and industries of the Commonwealth of Massachusetts. Garrison's position was subsequently taken over by the Philadelphia corporation lawyer Francis Biddle. The Board was given authority to hold hearings and make findings of fact concerning violations of 7(a) "whenever it is in the public interest" to do so. It was also given exclusive authority to hold elections. Finally, the new Board was directed to study the performance of existing

---

76. See, for example, AFL president William Green to all state federations of labor (20 February 1934): "The Administration intends that industries shall create their own labor complaints committees and industrial relations boards, and shall handle their own adjustment of labor complaints." See also circulars of 23 and 26 February 1934. All in *AFL Records*, reel 57 (Circular and Neostyle file). Green later recounted the story of months of Administration pressure on the AFL to accept the Steel Labor Relations Board's plan for proportional representation in the steel industry. See AFL Executive Council *Minutes* (4 February 1935).

labor and industrial relations boards, to recommend the establishment, where necessary, of regional and special industry boards, and to act as a board of final review over the activities of all other labor boards.[77] Roosevelt justified his action in issuing the executive order as "in the interests of maintaining orderly industrial relations and justice as between employers, employees and the general public" and as "a great step forward in administrative efficiency." The innovations, he said, would clarify the availability of machinery for "adjusting labor relations" and "the adjustment of grievances."[78] Neither PR 44 nor the executive order, however, extended the Board's powers of enforcement in any significant way. Like its predecessor, the NLRB would have to depend for this upon the resolutely antagonistic Justice Department.

Wagner supported PR 44, despite the considerable political embarassment of so doing, because he thought that it would be a "workable compromise for the present" and "generally helpful."[79] He left a decision whether to introduce a revised version of his bill contingent upon "events during the next six months," and during that period refrained from detailed public comments on labor policy, simply repeating previous assertions of the need for responsibility and discipline in collective bargaining. Undoubtedly the 1934 elections were uppermost in Wagner's mind, for the return of a conservative Congress would have made the introduction of new legislation pointless. But there were other considerations: would the NLRB as presently constituted prove able to divert industrial workers from a repetition of the mass strikes of mid-1934? What would be the advice of the small but increasingly influential cadre of labor relations experts, economists and particularly lawyers which constituted the beginning of a permanent federal labor relations bureaucracy? What would be the strategy adopted by the AFL?

So far as the AFL was concerned, its position in the second half of 1934 was really no different from that which it had occupied in the first half of the year. The Federation was encouraged by the continuing revival of its affiliates' membership,[80] and saw as its first priority the

77. NLRB Press Release (10 July 1934) in *RG 25*, Box 20A ("NLRB: Office of the Executive Secretary: Press Releases").
78. Ibid.
79. Wagner to E.G. Grace, President of Bethlehem Steel (25 June 1934), in *Wagner Papers*, 694 LA 715, folder 9.
80. AFL president William Green to all City Central Labor Unions (19 July 1934), in *AFL Records*, reel 57 (Circular and Neostyle File). The AFL's own membership figures showed that membership of affiliated unions had hit its nadir in the second quarter of 1933 and that since then membership had been increasing steadily. Thus, the AFL's average total membership for the period September 1932 to July 1933 was reported as 2,124,512 while the average for the equivalent period 1933–34 was 2,590,319. See Executive Council *Minutes* (20 April 1933–17 August 1934), passim. See also Christopher L. Tomlins, "AFL Unions in the 1930s: Their Performance in Historical Perspective," *Journal of American History*, 65, 4 (1979), Table 1.

task of ensuring that their interests were respected in any further attempts to stimulate recovery. The National Industrial Recovery Act had recognized the legal status of unions, the Federation argued, and had also acknowledged that they had substantive interests to be considered in implementing the recovery program. It was up to the administration to see that recognition was translated into action.[81] The Federation would support any measure which, like S2926, appeared to add to the administration's ability to do so. Aside from this, its main legislative priorities all lay in using its improving industrial position to the direct advantage of its existing members. Thus, apart from obtaining organizing and bargaining guarantees, its program centered on enactment of the thirty hours bill which it had failed to secure in 1933, and on a further attempt to force the NRA into an explicit avowal of union-employer collaboration, this time by amending the Recovery Act to establish a system of joint boards, on which labor and employers would be equally represented, for the purpose of regulating wages, hours and working conditions throughout industry.[82]

The Federation's legislative program reflected both its self-interest and its unaltered commitment to the *gesellschaft* ideology of the previous twenty years. In pressing the thirty hours bill, for example, the Federation's immediate motive seemed to be to redistribute the costs of recovery away from employed and unionized wage earners and onto the unemployed and employers. In its defense of the legislation, the Federation argued that the limitation of hours would increase employment, but it also stressed that this should not be at the expense of wages because that would mean a reduction of purchasing power.[83] From the AFL's point of view, in other words, none of the cost of increasing employment should be born by its members. Its other legislative proposals – particularly the joint boards scheme, which was a direct revival of the AFL's recommendations to the 1919 Industrial Conference[84] – also confirmed that while the AFL supported public enforcement of employer participation in collective bargaining it did so as a means to keep

81. William Green, "What the National Recovery Act Has Done for Labor," Address on CBS Radio (3 September 1934), in *AFL Records,* reel 57 (Circular and Neostyle File). See also William Green, "Some Insistent Problems in Wages and Hours" (March 1934), in same.

82. AFL Press Release on the thirty hours bill (5 January 1935), in *AFL Records,* reel 57 (Circular and Neostyle File); Sumner Slichter, "The Labor Outlook," draft, for *The Annalist,* in *Frey Papers,* Box 15, folder 203. See also Frey to Slichter, confirming that revision of the Recovery Act was "a trade union objective," in same.

83. AFL statement on the thirty hours bill (undated), in *Wagner Papers,* 694 LA 715, folder 7.

84. See above, Chapter Three, and Haggai Hurvitz, "Ideology and Industrial Conflict: President Wilson's First Industrial Conference of October, 1919," *Labor History,* 18, 4 (Fall, 1977), 509–24.

the state's role in industrial government to a minimum. "The success of the National Industrial Recovery Act depends very largely upon the application to human relations in industry of the principle and policy of mutual agreements determined jointly by the parties concerned under governmental supervision," the Executive Council argued early in 1935. "[W]e believe that if self-government is not developed in industry, it will be necessary to extend political control into this sphere and that such political control will inevitably be of an arbitrary nature."[85]

Economists reacted strongly to the AFL's program. Sumner Slichter, for example, was especially critical of the AFL's purchasing power justification for wage maintenance in the face of a reduction of hours – effectively a wage increase. "Wage increases are not a method of starting revival but of controlling it," he wrote to AFL Metal Trades Department president John P. Frey. "[I]f they come too soon or too fast, they will reduce the volume of spending rather than increase it."[86] Once the thirty hours bill went before the Senate, Slichter attacked it vigorously and called for its rejection. "Although I warmly sympathize with the steady reduction of working hours," he told Frey, "I do not believe that this is the proper time in most industries to impose such a reduction."[87] Slichter was rather less restrained in correspondence he was engaging in with Wagner on the same subject. "I can conceive of no worse blow to the progress of recovery at the present time than the imposition of a heavy increase in costs upon business," he wrote. "The bill provides no way by which employers can meet the larger pay rolls it imposes upon them." The bill would force employers into bankruptcy "because there is no gain in purchasing power until employers pay out more to their men." What was needed was more productivity and a gradual and controlled redistribution of the returns which would result from new production. "We need to encourage more men to enter business now – not force thousands of employers who are already in business and giving work into bankruptcy."[88]

While Slichter disagreed with the thirty hours bill, he warmly endorsed the idea of a new collective bargaining measure. "Conditions vary in different industries. One of the great advantages of collective bargaining is that it permits flexible regulation which takes account of the different conditions in the different industries."[89] He was less circumspect than the AFL, however, in his support for government inter-

---

85. AFL Executive Council, "Statement to President Roosevelt," in AFL Executive Council *Minutes* (7 February 1935).
86. Slichter to Frey (29 December 1934), in *Frey Papers*, Box 15, folder 203.
87. Slichter to Frey (7 February 1935), in ibid.
88. Slichter to Wagner (7 and 15 February 1935), in *Wagner Papers*, 700 LA 717, folder 39.
89. Slichter to Frey (7 February 1935), in *Frey Papers*.

vention. What was required was a labor relations measure which combined strong guarantees of freedom of association with equally strong sanctions to ensure the peaceful adjustment of disputes, "otherwise the improvement in the legal position of the organized labor movement is likely to result in strikes which will be detrimental to labor itself."[90]

Slichter's views on collective bargaining legislation were sharpened by his participation, between November 1934 and March 1935, in an important and influential Twentieth Century Fund study of the role of government in labor relations. During the second half of 1934, the Fund assembled a committee of experts representing the viewpoint of "the general public" (rather than "any group or class interest") who would employ empirical data collected by the Fund's research staff as a solid scientific basis on which to construct "a specific and constructive program for government policy in the field of labor relations."[91] Besides Slichter the group included the ever-active Leiserson, now chairman of the National Mediation Board; William H. Davis, a prominent patent lawyer; the "progressive" employer and member of the now defunct National Labor Board, Henry Dennison; and the sociologist, Robert S. Lynd (Lynd, however, resigned before the end of the year). During its deliberations the committee made contact with Wagner, and once it became clear that his aides were also preparing legislation arrangements were made to exchange drafts.[92]

Slichter explained the general position of the Twentieth Century Fund committee in correspondence with Frey in February 1935. The economic situation required that major advances in wages be deferred until there was a substantial improvement in business and a reduction in unemployment. At the same time, the committee recognized that labor was entitled to the right to bargain collectively through the organization which, in any given instance, was the choice of the majority of employees in an appropriate unit. On behalf of the Twentieth Century Fund, therefore, the comittee would recommend the passage of legislation to reenact Section 7(a), add a majority rule clause, give the Labor Relations Board sufficient power to enforce its decisions, establish a strong Federal Mediation Service for the purpose of assisting the parties in

90. Slichter to Wagner (15 February 1935), in *Wagner Papers*.
91. Special Committee on the Role of Government in Labor Relations, "Revised Draft of Recommendations" (18 January 1935), in *Leiserson Papers*, Boxes 40 and 41, ("Twentieth Century Fund"); Minutes of the First Meeting (25 November 1934), in same.
92. Minutes of the Second Meeting (14 December 1934), in ibid. It is important to note, however, that little exchange of information took place during the drafting period. The Fund group early decided to keep its discussions confidential until the release of its final report. Nor did it see a draft of Wagner's new bill until the middle of February 1935, just five days before it was to be introduced in the Senate.

both organized and unorganized industries in working out agreements, and impose on each side the obligation of giving fifteen days' notice of intended changes in wages, standard working hours, or working conditions. In exchange, Slichter concluded, labor would be expected to agree to postpone drives for general wage changes until there had been a general improvement in business.[93]

For his part, Frey was happy to consider any legislation which might further improve organized labor's bargaining position. But he did not see why the Federation should have to abandon the thirty hours bill to get it, arguing that there could be no increase in consumption whatever the state of collective bargaining unless some of the rapid increase in corporate profits currently under way was immediately diverted into reemployment or higher wages (or both).[94] In Frey's mind, that is, wage/ hour reforms and collective bargaining legislation were complementary rather than alternative strategies; both served the AFL's interests. In Slichter's mind, however, economic stability and not the AFL's interests was uppermost, and he left Frey in no doubt that from this point of view the thirty hours bill should be abandoned. Slichter also knew that on this question Wagner shared his position, so it was no surprise to him when, during February, the Senator finally let it be known that his plans were to oppose the thirty hours bill and concentrate upon a new collective bargaining bill.[95]

The national labor relations act

Wagner's new bill was based on the same general hypotheses as the legislation rejected the previous year. Thus, as in 1934, it sought to promote equality in bargaining power so as to "maintain equilibrium between the rate of wages and the rate of industrial expansion" by outlawing company unions and by protecting employees' rights to collective organization and bargaining.[96] But a number of important

93. Slichter to Frey (13 February 1935) in *Frey Papers*, Box 15, folder 203. See also "Recommendations of the Twentieth Century Fund Committee" (draft of 22 February 1935), in *Leiserson Papers*.
94. Frey to Slichter (6 March 1935), in *Frey Papers*. Slichter did not reply to this letter.
95. RFW to Slichter (21 February 1935), in *Wagner Papers*, 700 LA 717, folder 39.
96. As in 1934, proponents of the legislation argued that company unions should be replaced for reasons of economic stability. Wagner, for example, stated that "the primary evil" of the company union was that "because of its intrinsic composition, it is not well suited to extend its cooperative activities beyond the bounds of a single employer unit." *Leg. Hist.*, 2333. Millis, later to be the second chairman of the NLRB, agreed, asking "how can a limited agency [the company union] function effectively in a wide market situation?" *Leg. Hist.*, 1511, 1454. It was also the position adopted in a petition supporting the bill addressed to Wagner by approxi-

changes had been made. These reflected the practical experience accumulated over the previous nine months by the National Labor Relations Board, and the considerable influence which NLRB staff members such as General Counsel Calvert Magruder, Assistant General Counsel William Gorham Rice, and attorneys Thomas Emerson and Philip Levy had enjoyed in the process of revision which had produced the new bill.[97]

Amongst the priorities which NLRB staffers introduced into the debate over revision of the 1934 legislation, none was more important to them than the establishment of the Board as an independent agency with determinative rather than simply facilitative authority, with a commitment to professional lawyerly standards and procedural precision, and also, of course, with its own powers of enforcement.[98] Insofar as it had been able, indeed, the Board had already begun a movement in this direction on its own initiative. After reviewing the regional structure which it had inherited from the National Labor Board, the NLRB had effectively transformed the existing bipartisan boards into advisory bodies and placed the onus of policy administration, mediation and investigation on a full-time official, the regional director, with a full-time (though in all cases modest) staff. It had also downgraded the national board's role as a mediator and attempted instead to develop precise, quasi-judicial procedures to govern the authorization of elections and hearings.[99] Finally, to cope with the growing workload in the central office brought on by the reforms instituted in its relations with the regions, the Board had increased its staff and in so doing had emphasized the importance of recruiting lawyers. Whenever it was able it had also appointed lawyers to fill the new full-time positions in the field.[100]

The Board's emphasis on professionalism, legal process, and centralized review was intended to enhance its efficiency in 7(a) proceedings and to improve its chances of gaining enforcement through the con-

mately fifty economists and social scientists (among them Rupert R.R. Brooks, Mollie R. Carroll, John R. Commons, Albert T. Helbing, Paul H. Douglas, Selig Perlman, and Joseph Warren Madden) in June 1935. See Francis D. Tyson et al., to Wagner (19 June 1935), in *Wagner Papers*, 700 LA 717, folder 38.

97. Gross, *The Making of the National Labor Relations Board*, 109–48. See also Irons, *New Deal Lawyers*, 226–30.

98. Irons, *New Deal Lawyers*, 215–30.

99. See, for example, "Memorandum on Elections" (31 July 1934), in *RG 25*, Box 20A ("NLRB: Office of the Executive Secretary"); "Statement to the Regional Labor Boards" (19 August 1934), in same; "Secondly Monthly Report to the President" (26 September 1934), in same.

100. Irons, *New Deal Lawyers* 215–25. Millis, "Memorandum to the Board" (21 May 1935), in *RG 25*, Box 328 ("Records of Harry A. Millis").

struction of a record which could stand up to the scrutiny of the courts.[101] Inevitably, however, the relationship between the Board and its "clients" also underwent substantial alteration, and not always in ways perceived by those clients to be in their best interests. For example, C.W. Doyle, president of the Central Labor Council of Seattle, wrote AFL president Green in August 1934 that as a result of the reforms instituted by the new Board "the local Regional Labor Board has practically ceased to function. This dormancy is militating against the best interests of the employees and unless there is some modification immediately, many of those unions recently organized are going to suffer as a consequence."[102] Doyle levelled a similar complaint specifically at the Board's new policy that before an election could be held evidence had to be submitted to Washington so that the Board could determine whether or not it was necessary. "Such a ruling is a fallacy, as those on the ground floor are the best judges as to the advisability of holding an election."[103]

Doyle's complaints illustrate one inescapable consequence of the changes which the NRLB had effected in the administration of federal labor policy: as the Board professionalized and refined its involvement in bargaining representative elections – overseeing, determining, certifying and so forth – the election ceased to be an event that the employees in question could, even formally, define and manage for themselves, as it had been in the NLB's early descriptions of 7(a) rights. Decisions about how the process was to be conducted it seemed, could no longer be left to "those on the ground floor." All the more important, then, was the question of how much influence the new bill would allow the unions over the formulation of the policies now being made at national level.

The NLRB's contribution to the development of Wagner's new bill was not confined to the realms of Board composition and procedure. In its substantive decisions the Board had begun to fill in the outline of the common law of collective bargaining sketched by the NLB; it was upon this foundation that much of the bill, and also interpretations of it once enacted, would be built. The Board had endorsed the NLB's ruling that

---

101. Irons, *New Deal Lawyers*, 215–25. See also Gross, *The Making of the National Labor Relations Board*, 73–108.

102. Doyle to Green (17 August 1934), in *RG 25*, Box 327 ("Chairman Garrison's Records"). See also details of the controversy between the Board and unions in the Indianapolis area over the appointment of G.J. Watson, former secretary of the Indianapolis Regional Labor Board, as Associate Director in the new regional organization created by the NLRB. In *RG 25*, Box 328 ("Records of Harry A. Millis").

103. Doyle to Green, ibid.

the employees' right to bargain collectively imposed a correlative duty on the employer and, again like its predecessor, had found that employers who dominated company unions or who discriminated against union members interfered with that right. It also extended the proscription to instances where employer intimidation of workers could be demonstrated. The Board protected strikers from discharge insofar as their strike resulted from an employer's breach of 7(a), but not otherwise, and, like the NLB, refused protection to any employee who, in its opinion, had "maliciously [or wilfully] inflicted physical injury to person or property in connection with any current labor dispute." The Board also held that unlawful conduct or breach of contract on the part of a union justified a company in refusing to bargain with it.[104]

In the realm of representation matters the NLRB reaffirmed the NLB's principle of majority rule. Like the NLB, furthermore, the Board interpreted the rule in a way which gave it enormous potential authority. According to the NLRB, majority rule had introduced "traditional political forms of representation" into industry.[105] Thereby the concept of collective organization of workers for purposes of collective bargaining had been invested with the public legitimacy which it had hitherto always lacked, justifying the otherwise unjustifiable legal requirement that employers recognize and bargain with the representative chosen. The consequence, of course, was that the bestowal of legitimacy necessarily became a Board monopoly because claims based on anything other than majority rule – tradition, custom, and so forth – received no imprimatur and thus imposed no obligation on the employer to recognize the claimant union. This, combined with the presumptive investment of authority in the Board to establish the dimensions of the majorities for whom it then certified representatives, gave the Board determinative power over the structure of labor representation.[106]

104. Paul M. Herzog to David Riesman, Jr. (2 January 1935), in *RG 25*, Box 90 ("NLRB General Corrspondence File R-Z"); Levy to Magruder (6 April 1935), in *RG 25*, Box 38 ("Washington Office: Legal Division Correspondence: Wagner Bill").
105. Memorandum (17 October 1934), in National Labor Board Case File 12, *Houde Engineering Company*, relating to *Houde Engineering Corporation* (1934), 1 NLRB [old] no. 12.
106. The implications of this issue were fully realized by the participants in the debate over federal labor legislation which took place prior to the introduction of the revised Wagner bill in February 1935. Thus, in December 1934, Sumner Slichter told his colleagues on the Twentieth Century Fund Investigative Committee that giving a government agency discretion to determine the unit appropriate for collective bargaining meant "giving them discretion to determine in a significant number of cases the organization and structure of the American Labor movement." Minutes of the Second Meeting of the Special Committee on the Role of Government in Labor Relations (14 December 1934), in *Leiserson Papers*, Boxes 40 and 41, ("Twentieth Century Fund").

As long as it lacked proper means of enforcement, the Board seemed unwilling to exercise that authority. Despite the urgings of its Legal Division that the success of federal labor policy depended upon reshaping the structure of labor representation,[107] the Board stated cautiously that "wherever possible" it would try "to avoid dictating labour union policies or being drawn into deciding union jurisdictional disputes."[108] But with majority rule and Board control over the determination of bargaining units written into Section 9 of the new bill, and enforcement powers guaranteed, Board representatives foreshadowed a new assertiveness. In his appearance before the Senate Committee, for example, Board Chairman Francis Biddle insisted that determinative power over the structure of labor representation was essential if the legislation were to succeed in establishing an orderly and stable collective bargaining system:

> The necessity for the Board deciding the unit and the difficulties sometimes involved can readily be made clear where the employer runs two factories producing similar products: shall a unit be each factory or shall they be combined into one? Where there are several crafts in the plant shall each be separately represented? To lodge the power of determining this question with the employer would invite unlimited abuse and gerrymandering the unit would defeat the aims of the statute. If the employees themselves could make the decision *without proper consideration of the elements which should constitute the appropriate units* they could in any given instance defeat the practical significance of the majority rule: and, by breaking off into small groups, could make it impossible for the employer to run his plant.

Biddle acknowledged that the Board could also gerrymander units if it chose. Nevertheless, he insisted that "the determination of the unit . . . must be made by an impartial agency which is aware of the industrial relationship existing in various types of industry . . ."[109]

Having carried the day in their insistence that federal legislation could be viable only if the Board were guaranteed "the power to certify or determine representation in any manner it sees fit,"[110] Legal Division attorneys naturally lobbied vigorously against any changes which might dilute this authority. One particular target for their efforts was an amendment to Section 9 which would have provided that controversies over representation of employees for purposes of collective bargaining

107. Gross, *The Making of the National Labor Relations Board*, 98.
108. *Houde Engineering Corportion* (1934), 1 NLRB [old] no. 12.
109. *Leg. Hist.*, 1458–9 [emphasis supplied].
110. Memorandum on the Wagner Bill (6 April 1935), in *RG 25*, Box 38 ("Washington Office: Legal Division Correspondence").

should be considered "representation disputes" involving employees alone rather than "labor disputes" which involved the employer and thus made him a party to the dispute. The amendment was proposed by William H. Davis of the Twentieth Century Fund Committee and strongly endorsed by William Leiserson in a cautionary letter to Wagner:

> Section 9(c) of your bill is so worded as to make a representation dispute among employees come within the definition of a labor dispute as defined in Section 2(9). This, it seems to me, is a mistake and should be changed to make the representation dispute purely disputes among employees only, to which the employer is not a party.
>
> If Section 9(c) of your bill was reworded . . . then the representation disputes would be clearly distinguished from labor disputes between employers and employees; the employer and his attorneys would be kept out of the representation disputes before the Board, and the problem of determining the representative would be made a much more simple one.[111]

Replying for the Legal Division, Philip Levy argued that for the purpose of constructing a defensible record for use in enforcement proceedings it was necessary that the employer be recognized as a party to an election hearing and that he be given the opportunity to present evidence and cross-examine witnesses upon the questions whether an election should be held, what the proper unit should be and what organizations should be placed on the ballot.[112] But as Leiserson and Davis had pointed out, this meant that representation disputes could not be treated, even formally, as disputes occurring among employees, to be resolved by themselves with the aid of a fact-finding agency. Instead they would have to be treated in law as adversary proceedings, with employees exercising their right to representation subject to their employer's right to be consulted and to quasi-judicial rulings emanating from the Board. From Leiserson's point of view, this gave the Board power over the structure of labor representation far beyond the level necessary to ensure the bill's stated objectives.

These disagreements over Section 9 demonstrate the absence of a consensus amongst the legislation's supporters regarding the precise nature of the role which the state was to play in the promotion of collective bargaining. So far as the NLRB's legal staff was concerned, the emphasis in labor relations policy was now squarely upon expanding

---

111. Leiserson to Wagner (9 March 1935), in *Leiserson Papers* Box 43, ("Wagner").
112. Philip Levy, Memorandum on the Davis Amendments (6 April 1935), in *RG 25*, Box 38 ("Washington Office: Legal Division Correspondence: Wagner Bill").

the Board's administrative authority so that the substantive employee rights outlined in the statute could be securely established, and correlative duties imposed upon employers.[113] For the industrial relations experts and labor economists who dominated the Twentieth Century Fund committee's deliberations, by contrast, the priority lay with designing procedures to help organized labor achieve orderly adjustments of its disputes with employers. Although the Fund committee agreed that these procedures should be founded on effective implementation of employees' 7(a) rights, they tied implementation specifically to the peaceful resolution of disputes and the promotion of collective agreements. As Slichter put it, "public policy has two main parts: one is the encouragement of organization and collective bargaining . . . the other is the promotion of industrial peace." In the same vein, Leiserson argued that simply denouncing the sins of employers and creating a powerful new agency to stamp them out was not a realistic approach to industrial relations. The government should concentrate instead on developing procedures that both parties to collective bargaining would be required by law to follow.[114]

Other criticisms of the new bill came from the AFL. Conscious of the role that legislation could play in finally opening up industries "well fortified by company unions," the Federation's leaders were as enthusiastic in their support for the bill as they had been the previous year. As in 1934, however, their enthusiasm was tempered by their concern to ensure both that the extent of federal intervention was restricted to effective guarantees of freedom to organize and bargain collectively, leaving determination of the substance of both processes in the hands of the parties directly concerned, and that the Federation itself was assured of a position from which it could oversee and influence the administration and the enforcement of the legislation. Thus, during the hearings

113. As James A. Gross puts it, "The board wanted Congress to state clearly the obligation of the employer to bargain collectively, endorse and define the principle of majority rule, create a judicial and administrative agency 'wholly independent of any executive branch of the government,' provide for vigorous and prompt enforcement of the board's rulings, grant the board 'the widest scope . . . to permit it to build up a constructive body of labor law,' and apply the legislation to all workers in all industries engaged in interstate commerce." Gross, *The Making of the National Labor Relations Board*, 130.

114. Special Committee on the Role of Government in Labor Relations, Minutes of the Third Meeting (18 January 1935), in *Leiserson Papers*, Boxes 40 and 41. In addition to changes in Section 9, the Fund group also proposed amendments to give employers limited rights to bring suit against employees and employee organizations to discourage them from engaging in disputes, and, most important, to make coercion of employees by anyone, not just by employers, an unfair labor practice. See the "Memorandum of Findings and Recommendations" (20 March 1935), in *Leiserson Papers*.

on S1958, Charlton Ogburn, the AFL's general counsel, introduced amendments modifying the majority rule provision by removing the requirement that labor organizations making a closed shop contract should first have to represent a majority of workers in the designated unit, limiting the Board's powers to investigate disputes over representation to occasions when it was requested to intervene by one or other of the parties involved, and depriving the Board of the exclusive power to instigate proceedings to enforce its orders. Each proposal reflected a specific attempt to safeguard the freedom of the established national unions to formulate their own organizing strategy and a more general concern to ensure that they received recognition as autonomous institutions with established rights. As Ogburn's brief presenting the last and most important amendment stated:

> If the rights of a union of employees have been violated and that violation was found by the NLRB, that union of employees should have the right to apply to the court for an enforcement decree . . . [U]nder this bill, as under the N.R.A., labor itself is not permitted to become even a party to the proceedings brought by the Board. They have no opportunity to argue their views in court.

When enforcement cases were brought into court, in other words, the interests of the organized labor movement would not be represented. "The public" was represented by the Board's lawyers and "capital" was represented in the shape of the defendant and his lawyers. Labor, however, had no voice at all:

> This was true in the Weirton trial. The rights of labor were being adjudicated . . . but labor was not permitted to be represented in the court. The Department of Justice attorneys took the view that they were representing the public. Labor itself, in the adjudication of these principles, should be permitted – through its own spokesmen, sympathetic with its attitude and well versed in all labor's contentions, and partisans, in every sense, of labor – to have representation in the court. *This is the most important amendment which we ask this committee to make.*[115]

115. *Leg. Hist.*, 1533 [emphasis supplied]. The AFL could happily endorse majority rule only so long as it was persuaded that where a union was already established the Board would simply endorse the union's definition of what was an appropriate organizational form for the workers involved. Once it became clear, during 1935, that this was not the case and, crucially, that disaffected unions had no recourse in court [a limitation first suggested by the NLRB's Legal Division—see Levy to Magruder (17 April 1935), in RG 25, Box 38 ("Washington Office: Legal Division Correspondence: Wagner Bill")–and confirmed by the Supreme Court in *AFL et al. v. NLRB* (1940), 308 US 401] the AFL's endorsement became increasingly strained.

None of the AFL's amendments, however, were acted on. The NLRB's oversight of the administration and enforcement of federal policy remained unimpaired.

Witnesses for the AFL also repeated their request that the Board should be tripartite rather than nonpartisan and that it should be in the Department of Labor rather than an independent agency. This too was opposed by the NLRB. "It seems to us," said Francis Biddle, "that if . . . the employees and agents of the National Board and any regional boards set up by it are appointed subject to the approval of the Secretary of Labor and are a part of the Department of Labor, and the Board is subject to the budgetary control of the Department, the machinery cannot be considered either impartial or independent." It would be inconsistent with such impartiality and independence to attach the Board to any department in the executive branch of the government, "particularly to a department whose function, in fact and in the public view, is to look after the interest of labor."[116]

Success in opposing union requests for the opportunity to take action to enforce the act's provisions on their own motion and for direct representation on the Board complemented the NLRB's opposition to the attempts of the Twentieth Century Fund committee to steer federal policy in the direction of facilitating union–employer "adjustment." Avoidance of both these alternative strategies meant that the Board would be left to develop a public policy of collective bargaining and an appropriate labor representation structure largely through the exercise of its own administrative expertise. This course had first been suggested during the debates over S2926 the previous year. Following the passage of Public Resolution 44, the NLRB had begun to devote considerable effort to establishing the foundations of the expert and professional administrative structure required to realize it. By the time the hearings on the revised Wagner bill were concluded, it seemed clear that, formally at least, the new Board would be in a position to exercise wide powers subject to remarkably few constraints.

Who shall control the AFL?

S1958 was reported out of the Senate Committee on Education and Labor on May 2, debated, and passed without alteration on May 16. The House hearings ended on May 20, and the House Committee reported a

116. *Leg. Hist.,* 1461–2.

version of the bill virtually identical to the Senate bill, differing only in that it placed the Board within the Department of Labor. This amendment, and the subsequent "Ramspeck" amendment limiting the Board's discretion in the designation of bargaining units were eliminated from the final version in conference, and the act was signed on July 5.

Despite the rejection of their amendments, AFL leaders continued to express their enthusiasm for the bill. Throughout they interpreted it in light of the contribution it might make to the realization of their ideal – a properly constituted NRA in which self-government in industry could be established through "mutual agreements determined jointly by the parties concerned under governmental supervision."[117] The unprecedented authority the bill gave to a public agency, though perhaps unnerving, seemed a necessary price to pay to overcome employer intransigence. Even when the *Schechter* decision swept the NRA out of existence and the AFL lost the codeterminative framework within which the Wagner bill was supposed to fit, it continued to press for the bill's passage, for the crisis had found the Federation with its own legislative initiatives stalled and thus no alternative policy to pursue. Writing to President Green on 5 June 1935, General Counsel Ogburn advised the Executive Council that the AFL had now to concentrate on self-organization if it were to be in a position to protect the wage and hour gains won under the codes. For this reason, there could be no doubt that enactment of the Wagner bill should be made labor's major legislative objective.[118]

Yet by this time doubts about the legislation's implications for the "autonomous" rights of AFL unions were close to the surface. These mounted rapidly in the second half of 1935 as the AFL was drawn more and more deeply into an internal crisis of gargantuan proportions.

The AFL's crisis was rooted in its year-old inability to generalize organizing campaigns beyond familiar constituencies and, in particular, in its leadership's reluctance to admit the new unions emerging in mass production industries to membership of the Federation as long as they laid claim to jurisdictions partially overlapping those of existing AFL affiliates organized on craft-industrial or multi-industrial lines. Instructed by the Federation's 1934 (San Francisco) convention to charter new national unions in the automobile, cement, aluminum and other mass production industries, and to initiate an organizing campaign in the steel industry, the leadership had instead chosen to procrastinate.

---

117. AFL Executive Council *Minutes* (7 February 1935).
118. Ibid. (6 June 1935). Interestingly, Ogburn's endorsement of the bill was confined to its capacity to meet the Federation's needs in the short-term crisis caused by the *Schechter* decision. For the longer term, Ogburn concentrated on the importance of reviving the NRA.

Eventually, in May 1935, United Mine Workers president John L. Lewis warned his colleagues on the Executive Council that their delay in obeying the convention decision was threatening the very survival of the AFL. "If the Wagner bill is enacted," he concluded, "there is going to be increased organization and if workers are organized in independent unions we are facing the merger of those independent unions in some form of national organization."[119] Six months later, Lewis was busily fulfilling his own prophecy at the head of the breakaway Committee for Industrial Organization.

Lewis's warning was perceived as a threat for his ambitions were well known to his colleagues. According to Metal Trades Department president Frey, Lewis had been planning for years to make a bid to take over the AFL presidency or, failing that, to split the organization. "Being outside of the Executive Council interfered with his plans," Frey told an acquaintance, labor attorney William B. Rubin, in November 1935, "and so some four years ago he began to lay the groundwork which led to enlarging the Council by the San Francisco convention last year and making Lewis a member." Once on the Council, Frey continued, Lewis had realized that he did not enjoy sufficient support to win the presidency and so he began to prepare a split. "During this year he endeavored to build up an organization, and in fact discussed secession with the Presidents of several International Unions."[120]

In Frey's eyes, and in the eyes of the Federation's central bureaucracy, their conflict with Lewis and, subsequently, the CIO was not about whether the Federation should incline toward "craft" or "industrial" unionism so much as about control of the organized power of a growing labor movement. As the report of the Resolutions Committee (of which Frey was secretary) to the 1937 convention put it, "In the natural course of events . . . all organizations have changed their form . . . That has been the history of the development of American trade unionism as symbolized by the American Federation of Labor throughout its existence . . . Today there is no definite line anywhere that marks trade and craft unions apart from industrial unions."[121] Knowledgeable contemporaries took the same line. "The issue of craft versus industrial organization is quite a side issue now [and] . . . could be easily settled by a fair compromise on the basis of the San Francisco resolution of the A.F. of L." wrote William Leiserson in March 1936. "[T]he real issue now is a struggle for power as to who shall control the A.F. of L."[122]

119. Ibid. (7 May 1935).
120. Frey to Rubin (30 November 1935), in *Frey Papers*, Box 6, folder 100.
121. *Frey Papers*, Box 13, folder 188.
122. Leiserson to W. Ellison Chalmers (23 March 1936), in *Leiserson Papers*, Box 8, ("Chalmers").

The nature of the Executive Council's deliberations indicates that throughout 1935, jockeying for power within the Federation was the major preoccupation of its members. Lewis, for example, was quite willing to advertize that his motive in pressing for organization of the mass production industries was primarily to enhance the power of the UMW in the Federation. "The United Mine Workers are suffering because these industries are not organized. If we had a competent organization in the steel industry the path of the mine workers would be much easier. If the seeking of trade union security is selfish then we are selfish because that is what we are seeking."[123] Nor was he any less expert than his colleagues in the somewhat arcane politics of preserving position within the Federation through the protection of abstract jurisdictional claims.[124] Nevertheless, as the split in the labor movement gained organizational definition it became clear that, in the context of the revolution in labor law instituted by the Wagner Act, what was in part an uncomplicated power-struggle amongst ambitious men had momentous implications for the future development of the organized labor movement.

Since World War I, the organizational hegemony of the leading craft-industrial and multi-industrial unions had ensured virtually uncontested acceptance throughout the labor movement of the structural and organizational principle – exclusive jurisdiction – which lay at the heart of their power and of the AFL's ideology. The appearance of new organizations and their alliance with a revived United Mine Workers in the CIO challenged the established unions' hegemony, portending both conflict and structural change within the labor movement. But the conjunction of this internal challenge to the leading unions' self-asserted right to govern the labor movement with the challenge to private ordering in labor relations *in general* delivered by the Wagner Act threatened a much more far-reaching transformation of the organized labor movement, for the emergence of inter-union rivalry meant that the AFL could no longer claim hegemony for its organizational and jurisdictional principles in all dealings between the state and the organized labor movement. It was this threat which accounted for the anxiety, the antagonism, and finally the blazing hostility of the AFL leadership toward both the CIO and the evolving New Deal collective bargaining policy.

As early as May of 1935, Edwin S. Smith of the NLRB aroused critics like Dan Tobin of the Teamsters by calling on the American labor movement to conform itself to "the present realities of industry" and

---

123. AFL Executive Council *Minutes* (12 February 1935).
124. Ibid. (1–7 May 1935).

adopt the industrial union type of organization (which, he claimed, was in any case preferred by most employers).[125] As a result, even as Ogburn was advising Green that it was in the AFL's interest that the bill pass, Wagner had hastily to arrange a meeting with the Executive Council to assure AFL leaders that the powers given to the Board to determine units would not result in the transformation of the organized labor movement or the loss of AFL control over questions of union jurisdiction.[126] The Council's anxieties were reawakened later in the year when Board Chairman Madden told the AFL's 1935 convention that the Board would not consider itself bound to respect the jurisdictional boundaries of AFL unions in making its unit determinations. Matthew Woll replied by warning the delegates to bear in mind that:

> We now have legislation on our books which does not make us the sole factor in determining the form and character of organization that shall hereafter prevail in the labor movement. With all this we are merely playing into the hands of those who would delegate the power of self-organization of wage-earners not into the hands of the Councils of the American Federation of Labor or its Executive Council . . . but to delegate it to government bodies.[127]

After the convention, Dan Tobin wrote to Wagner to protest Madden's remarks. "Has this Board the right to say who shall have jurisdiction over certain work after the American Federation of Labor has rendered decisions on jurisdictional lines at convention after convention?" he asked. Wagner replied that, in his opinion, it did not.[128] On December 12, however, Madden repeated his statement in more explicit language in the *Washington Post*. This prompted Tobin to write to Wagner again, this time to denounce the act. "I hope and trust the law will be declared unconstitutional by the courts," Tobin wrote. "Better to fight the antagonisms of the employers against organizations of labor than to have the power and the machinery and the right of labor to settle its own disputes within itself, destroyed."[129]

125. Edwin S. Smith, "Should Government Foster Organization of Labor?" Address before the Commonwealth Club of California, San Francisco (10 May 1935), in *RG 25*.
126. Bernstein, *The New Deal Collective Bargaining Policy*, 125–6.
127. *Report of the Proceedings of the 55th Annual Convention of the American Federation of Labor* (Washington, D.C., 1935), 529–30.
128. Tobin to Wagner (30 October 1935) and Wagner to Tobin (13 November 1935), in *Wagner Papers*, 700 LA 717, folder 39.
129. Tobin to Wagner (13 December 1935), in *Wagner Papers*. See also Wagner to Tobin (20 December 1935); *Washington Post* (12 December 1935). Seven months before David Lawrence had pointed out that Wagner's bill gave the Board "sweeping powers over the character of the union organizations." See his "Labor's Doubtful Victory," *The United States News*, 3, 20 (20 May 1935). For a similar assessment see William P. Mangold, "On the Labor Front," *New Republic* (17 July 1935).

Within three months, Wharton of the IAM, Tracy of the IBEW, and Frey of the Metal Trades Department had also expressed their suspicion of the Board's use of Section 9 of the act. As Frey would remind the Executive Council a year later, Wharton concluded one meeting held in February of 1936 between the three union leaders and the members of the Board by informing the latter that unless they ceased using the act in ways which infringed on the established unions' rights, "we will endeavour to have the law either amended or repealed because you were not created for the purpose of cutting the ground from underneath the feet of bona fide trade unions."[130]

Just how much of their familiar ground would disappear from beneath the unions' feet would be determined in the conflicts of the next five years. But as the AFL hierarchy had evidently begun to realize, irreversible changes had already taken place. Common law developments and statutory innovations such as the Norris-LaGuardia Act had implicitly or explicitly recognized unions as right- and duty-bearing institutions, the legitimate business of which was to seek advantage for themselves and their members in temporary or permanent bilateral contractual relationships with employers. The Wagner Act, however, foreshadowed a very different approach. Expecting to gain license to pursue privately-defined objectives unhindered, unions instead found themselves vulnerable to regulation by the very agency to which they looked for vindication of their traditional practices. "The Board as a public agency acting in the public interest, not any private person or group, not any employee or group of employees, is chosen as the instrument . . . to remove obstructions to interstate commerce," said the Supreme Court in 1940. "When the Board has made its order, the Board alone is authorized to take proceedings to enforce it . . . No private right of action is contemplated."[131] Collective bargaining was now an area of public rather than private interest. The sanction of the NLRB – the sole administrator of the act and the principal arbiter of the labor relations system inscribed in public policy – had displaced the sanction of the labor movement's customs.

Conclusion

Writing in the *Harvard Law Review* in 1937, Louis Jaffe pointed up the radical disparity which had emerged over the previous forty years be-

130. AFL Executive Council *Minutes* (10 February 1937).
131. *Amalgamated Utility Workers v. Consolidated Edison Company of New York, Inc.* (1940) 309 U.S. 261, 2 CD 156, at 159, 160.

tween the distribution of power described in America's "official" political philosophies and constitutional theories and the reality of contemporary political practice. In "official" theory, according to Jaffe, the only political entity to be accorded recognition was the citizen; the only legitimate group was the territorial collectivity of citizens. "These citizens, all of them equal to each other, if not in interest at least in disinterestedness, are the public. And they are moved by a common desire: to promote the public interest. Together they elect representatives who are assumed to promote this interest and all of whose activities purport to be in furtherance of it. This community is the State. This activitity is the Law."[132] In practice, however, the polity was composed more and more of non-territorial groups, variously defined, each one seeking to enlist state institutions in its quest both for powers of self-government and for powers necessary to maintain its position vis-à-vis other competing groups.

Unlike earlier pluralist theorists, Jaffe did not interpret these developments as the beginnings of a general dissolution of the "single authority of the State." Rather, he saw them more as a "reorganization of governmental forms" which could be accommodated within existing legal-political traditions and which would contribute positively to the stability and effectiveness of American government by "plac[ing] consent on a broader and more realistic basis."[133] Rather than treat groups and government as discrete and unrelated institutional phenomena, in short, Jaffe sought a widened concept of the state into which hitherto private groups might be absorbed and their activities made an essential element in the process of defining, and protecting, the public interest:

> Courts must not strike down lightly legislative plans for group participation in law making and government. The machine must be harnessed and run by those who can best run it; and individual will must find employment and expression. For these ends the legislature may legitimately consider that public administration in some cases is inadequate acting alone and in others a positive and unnecessary embarrassment. In a world imperatively needing organization the risk of granting power in some form is inevitable. The devices here [described] do not violate the genius and tradition of our law; and indeed, if sound political judgment goes into

132. Louis L. Jaffe, "Law Making by Private Groups," *Harvard Law Review*, 51 (1937), 201.
133. Ibid., 210, 220–21.

their making, may reinforce and underscore the democratic pattern of our institutions.[134]

The Wagner Act was an example, par excellence, of the reconstitution of the state which Jaffe was describing. Thus on one hand, its passage meant that collective bargaining was guaranteed to play a major role in the regulation of employment practices in a wide range of industries. This held out the opportunity of participation in determining the direction of the American political economy which organized labor had been seeking since the turn of the century.

Simultaneously, however, the act reconstituted collective bargaining, bringing this hitherto private activity fully within the regulatory ambit of the administrative state. This had major implications for employees and for unions. For employees, it meant that the right to create the institutional structures required for participation in collective bargaining could now be vindicated through public proceedings. The right was to be exercised, however, subject to the state's determination of how the public interest might best be served in the resolution of industrial controversies. As we shall see, this would eventually come to mean in practice that the right to organize and bargain could be maintained only so far as the state conceived it to serve an overriding goal of industrial peace.

For the AFL, the adverse effects of state intervention to create a design for labor relations were more immediate. For the AFL the role of the state was best confined to lending its coercive power, where necessary, to compel adherence and respect for the *gesellschaftlich* private ordering system which its affiliates had painstakingly established over the previous quarter-century to govern their relations with their members, with employers, and with each other. Instead those affiliates found themselves confronted by a set of rules which portrayed them as quasi-public instrumentalities whose function was to bargain within the parameters of a model of labor relations defined by a state agency, and which treated their pre-New Deal emphasis on exclusive jurisdiction and all their other methods of safeguarding their existence as autonomous codeterminative private organizations as potential obstructions to the realization of that model. Such "protection" was no longer needed, advocates of the new model argued. From now on the National Labor Relations Board would provide all the protection necessary for workers' representatives to perform their allotted role.

134. Ibid., 253. According to Peter Irons "By defining 'reform' as 'the use of new forms to redistribute or to create new centers of social power,' Jaffe absorbed political militance into the state-run administrative apparatus." See Irons, *New Deal Lawyers*, 296.

5

A legal discourse

Our conception of the law was this: we were attempting to make the workers free from the domination and control of the employer through the company unions, because in the law it specifically states that the company union must go . . . that our men might decide whether they want to belong to a free and independent union or to no union, that the employer must be deprived of his power and control to compel them to belong to a company union.

When the Board was set up under the Act we thought it had really accomplished all we thought it intended to do. Then the question of bargaining agencies and agreements would be worked out between the men who had been made free. [But] here comes the Board set up to say whether even a contract is valid now. Their decision must be based on this fact, that they find collusion between the unions and the employer. When did it happen that we were in collusion with the employer, when we are trying to get the best [and] highest wages possible, the most reasonable hours of work, the most tolerable conditions of employment? It is so absurd on the face of it, the whole procedure.

William Green, in AFL Executive Council *Minutes* (29 August 1938).

In the four years following the passage of the Wagner Act, trade union membership rose from 3,753,300 to 6,555,500, extending, and in many cases creating, organized labor's presence in the strategic sectors of the economy.[1] Unsurprisingly, this growth took place in an atmosphere of growing controversy over the administration of federal labor relations policy as employers redoubled their efforts to thwart the revolution in labor law begun by the Wagner Act. In the years after 1935, however, important segments of the organized labor movement added their voices to the chorus. By 1938, indeed, the debate over federal policy was dominated by an angry dialog between the NLRB and the AFL.

The basis for the AFL's criticism, as we have seen, lay in that organization's history. Well before 1930, trade unions had come to conceive of themselves as primarily self-interested organizations, each claiming to

1. See Leo Troy, *Trade Union Membership, 1897–1962* (New York, 1965), Appendix 1–27; Christopher L. Tomlins, "AFL Unions in the 1930s: Their Performance in Historical Perspective," *Journal of American History*, 65, 4 (1979), 1021–42.

represent for collective bargaining purposes any employee for whom the union was recognized as the spokesman within the organized labor movement, each attempting to enforce its claims through coercive economic action or, more usually, by promising that the employer would derive benefits from cooperation with the union in the form of improved productivity and labor discipline. Crucially, the union's claim in any particular case was based not on any formal designation of the union as a representative by the workers concerned, but rather on the union's institutional status within the organized labor movement as the rightful claimant to jurisdiction over the workers in question. In this context, when union representatives asserted that workers had a right to organize and bargain collectively what they meant was that workers had a right to participate in the structure of organization and collective bargaining sanctioned by the organized labor movement.

Approaching the implementation of the Wagner Act from this perspective, the AFL leadership looked upon it as an instrument which could reinforce the prevailing structure and philosophy of union organization and collective bargaining by backing it with the coercive authority of the state. But instead the act's administrators held that the right to organize and bargain collectively was an individual civil right created by the act, that the exercise of that right could not to be encumbered by private institutional restraints, and that unions, consequently, could expect to gain recognition as collective bargaining representatives only insofar as they had been designated as representatives by administratively-identifiable groups of workers. To the Board, that is, the rights protected by the Wagner Act were ingredients of public policy, created by the passage of legislation and enforceable only through administrative action in accordance with that legislation. Trade unions could not assert rights independently of the act and its agents, for collective bargaining rights had meaning only in the context of positive legal authority.[2] This meant that while unions were to play a central role in the new system of labor relations which the act instituted, it was the union as the representative of specified groups of employees, as a "collective bargaining agent," which was legitimated in public policy, not the owner of jurisdictional "property" which had emerged over the previous twenty-five years.[3]

2. On this point see Karl Klare, "Labor Law as Ideology: Toward a New Historiography of Collective Bargaining Law," *Industrial Relations Law Journal,* 4 (1981), 470–80.

3. In 1934, William Gorham Rice Jr., then assistant general counsel of the National Labor Relations Board, wrote that "Rights are not conferred upon labor unions [by Section 7(a) of the NIRA] but upon employees. Employees may, of course, be represented by unions in the exercise of these rights." Rice to Connally, U.S. Senator for Texas (11 May 1934), in *RG 25,* Box 80 ("General Correspondence File"). The

As we have already seen, aspects of the legislation which appeared to threaten the authority of the established AFL unions, particularly the exclusive power granted the Board to determine the appropriate bargaining unit, early attracted critical attention from some AFL leaders. In most cases that criticism concentrated upon the opportunities the legislation afforded insurgents within the organized labor movement to undermine the hegemony of the established organizations, rather than on its broader ideological implications. Thus, when the AFL was led to engage in an increasingly bitter conflict with the NLRB in the second half of the 1930s it was motivated primarily by the rise of organized insurgency in the shape of the CIO, and its active solicitation of support from the Board.

Nevertheless, the rise of the CIO and its close relationship with the Board was as much the occasion for confrontation between the AFL and the New Deal collective bargaining policy as the cause, for as the conflict developed its wider aspects gradually emerged. This emergence can best be illustrated through examination of the repeated clashes between the AFL and the NLRB occurring in the course of litigation, and of the arguments of the Federation's officers before Congressional committees. Just as the Wagner Act made the "adversary setting," with its "briefs, oral arguments and cross-examinations,"[4] into a major site for labor's conflicts with management, it also turned those same court rooms and hearing rooms into the main forum for what was to be a decisive confrontation between the AFL and the New Deal state.

The lawyers take charge

The new National Labor Relations Board became operational on 24 August 1935, following the Senate's confirmation of the appointment of its first three members. Their recruitment had not been easy. Of the members of the outgoing Board neither Francis Biddle, its chair-

following year, the chairman of the Senate Committee on Education and Labor, David I. Walsh, told the Senate that "The [Wagner] bill gives no legal sanction or approval to any labor organization whatsoever. It does not mention the name 'trade union' or any other national or local labor organization. It does not mention the name 'American Federation of Labor'." *Congressional Record*, 79, 7 (16 May 1935), 7660. Two years later, Wagner himself confirmed that "Labor has no authority under the act to demand or prevent any election [of representatives for the purpose of collective bargaining]. The board and the board alone has the power to decide whether an election is in the public interest." *New York Times Magazine* (25 July 1937).

4. Jerold S. Auerbach, *Unequal Justice: Lawyers and Social Change in Modern America* (New York, 1976), 218.

man, nor Harry A. Millis had shown any interest in serving on the new Board. Only the third member, Edwin S. Smith, was willing to be reappointed. Consequently Roosevelt had found it necessary to enlist Biddle and Secretary of Labor Frances Perkins in a search for replacements.[5]

As the only willing holdover, Smith, a protégé of Perkins, was an obvious choice. A Harvard B.A. and sometime journalist, Smith had gained considerable knowledge and experience of labor relations first as a research assistant to Mary Van Kleek, the Director of Industrial Studies at the Russell Sage Foundation, and subsequently through his work for "progressive" employers such as Lincoln Filene, for whom Smith had been personnel director and personal assistant, and Henry Dennison. Prior to his appointment to the first NLRB in 1934, in addition, Smith had served as Massachusetts' commissioner for labor and industries.[6]

To join Smith, Biddle and Perkins recommended the appointment of John M. Carmody, a government mediator, and Joseph Warren Madden, a law school professor. Carmody, whose appointment was suggested by Senator Wagner, came to the NLRB from the National Mediation Board, prior to which he had been chairman of the National Bituminous Coal Labor Board. Like Smith, he had considerable practical experience of labor relations in private industry. Carmody, however, was to spend only a short time with the Board, and he resigned in 1936. He was replaced by Donald Wakefield Smith, a Virginia lawyer specializing in industrial relations and labor law cases.[7]

The other new appointee, Joseph Warren Madden, became the Board's chairman. At the time of his appointment Madden was professor of law at the University of Pittsburgh; previously he had been dean of the law school at West Virginia.[8] He had no academic background in labor law or industrial relations but while at Pittsburgh he had developed an interest in the subject and had arbitrated several local disputes.[9] Indeed, Madden had been considered by the first NLRB for appointment to its regional office in Pittsburgh, first in August 1934 as regional director, and then in February 1935 as regional board chairman. Described in 1934 as a man "greatly interested in labor" with a "liberal, fairminded attitude, judicial temperament and common sense" who enjoyed "a good reputation with labor, employers and public," Biddle

5. Gross, *The Making of the National Labor Relations Board: A Study in Economics, Politics and the Law* (New York, 1974), 149–51.
6. Ibid., 75.   7. Ibid., 154.   8. Ibid., 150–1.
9. Ibid., 152. See also R. Gordon Wagenet to Harry A. Millis (29 August 1934), in *RG* 25, Box 328 ("Records of Harry A. Millis").

found him to be "an excellent man."[10] This appointment, too, had Wagner's support.[11]

Aside from the Board members themselves, two other senior staff vacancies were of particular importance. The first was that of general counsel. On the recommendation of Calvert Magruder, the outgoing general counsel of the first NLRB, this position was filled by Charles Fahy. Fahy had become a government lawyer in 1933 after spending twenty years in private practice. Entering the Department of the Interior as first assistant solicitor, he had subsequently been appointed general counsel and then chairman of the Petroleum Administration Board. He joined the NLRB in August 1935.[12] The other key staff appointment was that of Board secretary, the most important administrative office in the NLRB's organization. The first incumbent of this position, Benedict Wolf, had been an early recruit to the developing federal labor relations bureaucracy, becoming executive officer of the National Labor Board in November 1933 after spending several years as an attorney in general practice. In November 1937, Wolf was succeeded as secretary by another lawyer, Nathan Witt, who had come to the NLRB as an attorney in 1934 after working on the general counsel's staff at the Agricultural Adjustment Administration. Prior to becoming secretary, Witt had served for two years as assistant general counsel.[13]

The new Board's first tasks were the reorganization of its Washington office, the adaptation of the regional apparatus of the predecessor NLRB and the appointment of additional personnel. In Washington, three central divisions were created: Legal, Trial Examiner, and Economic Research. The Legal Division, supervised by the general counsel, was divided into two sections. One, under the direction of Associate General Counsel Robert B. Watts, conducted the Board's litigation and advised its regional offices. The other, under Assistant General Counsel Witt, analyzed and reviewed the Board's field hearings and drafted its decisions. Initially employing thirteen attorneys, by June 1936 the Legal Division's complement had grown to twenty-seven. The Trial Examiner Division, responsible to the Board itself through the secretary's office, supplied examiners to preside at field hearings. Initially much of this work was done by Board members and members of its legal staff, and by local pools of examiners set up by the regional offices. Consequently,

10. Francis Biddle to John J. Kane (14 February 1935), in *RG 25*, Box 328 ("Records of Harry A. Millis").
11. AFL Executive Council *Minutes* (29 August 1938).
12. Gross, *The Making of the National Labor Relations Board*, 170.
13. Peter H. Irons, *The New Deal Lawyers* (Princeton, 1982), 236–67.

this division's development was slow. A year after the Board commenced operations it still had only four employees. Finally, the Divsion of Economic Research was established, on Edwin Smith's recommendation, to engage in general studies of wages, conditions and employment in different industries, and to research the commercial data which the Board could use to establish its jurisdiction in particular cases. It also had only four employees after the first year of operations.[14]

In organizing and staffing the central office and in adapting the former Board's regional apparatus, the new Board's priorities were largely dictated by the strategies which its legal staff was developing to establish the constitutionality of the Wagner Act. These strategies hinged upon precisely coordinated litigation, demanding the centralization of authority over the administration of the act in the Board's Washington office.[15] Consequently, the Board developed a set of carefully formulated case-handling procedures requiring regional directors to obtain permission from Washington in all unfair labor practice and representation cases before issuing a formal complaint or beginning an investigation. Authority to proceed was communicated by the secretary's office which was permitted by the Board to grant authorization on its own motion except in cases involving novel circumstances or important points of law. The secretary's office was also responsible for coordination of case-handling amongst regions, for day-to-day instruction of the regions in policy and procedural developments, and for general administrative management of the relationship between the Board and its outlying structure. Finally, the Board opened a second line of communication by appointing a regional attorney, responsible to the general counsel, to each regional office to handle all legal work.[16]

14. RG, Smith Committee Box 27, ("Tables and Drafts"); Box 7, ("Chart"). See also Charles Fahy to Howard W. Smith (9 August 1939), in RG 25 Smith Committee Box 4, ("General Correspondence"). On trial examiners see Memorandum to Regional Directors (22 October 1935), in RG 25, Box 335 ("Reports from Regional Attorneys").

15. Thomas I. Emerson, Gerhard Van Arkel, Charles Wood, Garnet Patterson, "Selection of Test Cases under the National Labor Relations Act," Memorandum to Regional Directors and Attorneys (26 September 1935), in RG 25, Box 38 ("Washington Office: Legal Division Correspondence – Legal Memoranda"). See also Irons, *New Deal Lawyers*, 234–43; Gross, *The Making of the National Labor Relations Board*, 156–71.

16. The Board's procedures are summarized in National Labor Relations Board, *First Annual Report* (Washington, 1936), 21–36. See also RG 25, Smith Committee Box 13, ("Procedure Regarding Issuance of Complaints"); RG 25, Smith Committee Box 21–23, ("Board Minutes"). See also Fahy to all Attorneys and Regional Directors (26 September 1935), in RG 25 Box 38 ("Washington Office: Legal Memoranda"); Benedict Wolf to all Regional Offices (21 September 1935), in RG 25 Box 335 ("Reports from Regional Attorneys"); Gross, *The Making of the National Labor Relations Board*, 158–64; Irons, *New Deal Lawyers*, 239.

The Board's innovations ensured that from the outset its model in both organizational and procedural matters would be one rooted firmly in professional legal practice. This reflected trends which had already been apparent during the tenure of the first NLRB. It also reflected the preferences and professional socialization of the senior staff of the new Board. Madden, of course, was already a lawyer, and Edwin Smith, though without legal training, evinced a considerable and growing interest in legal practice and method.[17] Carmody, the former mediator, was highly critical of the Board's case-handling regulations but, as we have seen, he left early in 1936 and was replaced by an experienced lawyer. Most important was the influence of the general counsel, Fahy, who along with Madden played the major role in creating the structure of the Washington office and drafting the Board's case-handling procedures. "Narrow, legalistic and single-minded" in outlook, Fahy had little interest in abstract political, jurisprudential or sociological debates. He saw law as a craft and the lawyer as a technician trained to manipulate legal materials in order to produce the results appropriate to his professional responsibilities and position.[18] As such, Fahy interpreted his job as NLRB general counsel to be "to enforce a statute through the presentation of carefully selected cases in the courts, with meticulous attention to detail and the formulation of narrowly drawn issues the key to success."[19] His determination to establish the Board on a procedural basis consistent with this aim led him to insist on the centralization of authority and detailed supervision of case-handling which characterized the Board's early structure. This approach would indeed offer the best chance of success in establishing the constitutionality of the Wagner Act. Simultaneously, however, it inscribed a lasting legalism onto the Board's very being.

Under the guidance of its lawyers, therefore, the NLRB committed itself to pursue the objects of the New Deal collective bargaining policy through the employment of a peculiarly legal discourse. The adversary system quickly came to dominate the Board's conception of its role as an agency. The Board's hearings were "trials." Its staff attorneys were advised that their function was to "prove" a case.[20] Little other than formal legal rules and practices played any part in its administrative or investigative procedures. In December 1938, for example, Madden delivered a major speech to the annual meeting of the Association of American Law Schools which purported to outline areas in which the Board planned innovations in administrative process. In the course of

17. Irons, *New Deal Lawyers*, 233–4.   18. Ibid., 235.   19. Ibid., 235.
20. See, for example, Fahy to all Attorneys and Regional Attorneys (2 August 1937), in *RG 25*, Smith Committee Box 11, ("Instructions to Attorneys").

the speech it became clear that what the Board considered to be important innovations were in fact nothing more than changes in its rules governing pleading and the submission of evidence:

> To what extent must the complaint recite in detail the alleged unfair labor practice? Under what circumstances is the respondent entitled to a bill of particulars? To what degree can the Board's attorney amend the complaint during the course of a hearing? If such an amendment is made what notice is the respondent entitled to for the purpose of answering and preparing its defence? To what extent is a variation between pleadings and proof fatal to the validity of the Board's order? To what extent may the Board adopt a differing theory of the case from that alleged in the complaint or pursued by the Board's attorney at the hearing? . . . To what extent can the Board ignore the hearsay rule? Should the Board adhere to the best evidence rule? Is it proper for the Board's trial examiners to permit leading questions on direct examination? May counsel impeach his own witnesses? To what extent and under what circumstances are employers entitled to subpoena the records of a labor organization? To what extent may the trial examiner cut short examination or participate in examination himself?[21]

The Board's commitment to a legal discourse stretched far beyond the design of its own operations. In the realm of policy development, for example, it accorded the professional intercourse of lawyers a role of decisive importance. Addressing the National Lawyers' Guild Conference on labor relations in December 1937, Madden argued that labor law could not develop properly unless lawyers in every city and state devised means of encouraging and sustaining a high level of informed professional criticism and debate. "Lawyers who represent large employers, lawyers who represent small employers, lawyers who represent labor unions of all factions and varieties . . . lawyers who speak for the unorganized, lawyers from the north and south and west, should not only come together in conferences such as this, but should be formed into permanent committees to study constantly the development of labor law through the decisions of the courts and the national and state boards, as well as the new legislation that is constantly being enacted." Only in this way, Madden argued, could the bar give labor law "the best thought and attention" of which it was capable.[22]

21. J. Warren Madden, Remarks at the Thirty-Sixth Annual Meeting of the Association of American Law Schools (30 December 1938), Chicago, in *RG 25*, Smith Committee Box 15, ("Speeches").
22. J. Warren Madden, Speech to the National Lawyers' Guild Conference on Labor Relations (December 17, 1937), Washington, in *RG 25*, Smith Committee Box 15 ("Speeches").

The more occlusive implications of the Board's commitment to legal discourse were masked in its early years by the considerable results which the Board achieved. These appeared ample justification of its strategy. The Board's "master plan" to establish itself through litigation proved a remarkable success, winning the Supreme Court's confirmation of what was one of the broadest grants of power and discretion that Congress had ever entrusted to an administrative agency, and enabling the Board to set about the task of bringing the conduct of labor relations fully within the ambit of the beaucratic-administrative state.[23] In the first four and one half years of operations, up to December 1939, over 25,000 cases involving 5.75 million workers were filed with the Board.[24] The Board settled 2,000 strikes and successfully averted a further 800. It held 2,500 elections (1,700 by consent) in which 1.2 million votes were cast, and issued 887 certifications.[25] Inevitably its activities caused considerable controversy, but the Supreme Court repeatedly reconfirmed the Board's authority, both in broad outline and in detail. As an agency created by Congress to be an expert in its field the Board had, according to the Court, "a public right, vested in it as a public body, charged in the public interest" to exercise extensive discretionary powers in controlling the implementation of national labor relations policy.[26] The Court not only allowed the Board a broad sphere within which to exercise its powers, it also found that the Board possessed the authority to determine the exact dimensions of that sphere for itself.[27] Federal policy did not grant the Board such independence or discretion as to make it completely autonomous for, as the Supreme Court recognized, the courts had a statutory responsibility to review the results of its activities. The Court emphasized, however, that in the interests of

23. *NLRB v. Jones and Laughlin Steel Corporation* (1937), 301 U.S. 1. See also Frank W. McCulloch and Tim Bornstein, *The National Labor Relations Board* (New York, 1974), 125.
24. "General Operations of the Board to December 1, 1939," in *RG 25*, Smith Committee Subject Files Box 21, ("Drafts Returned"). See also Harry A. Millis and Emily C. Brown, *From the Wagner Act to Taft-Hartley: A Study of National Labor Policy and Labor Relations* (Chicago, 1950), 76–80.
25. "General Operations of Board to December 1, 1939."
26. *National Liquorice Company v. NLRB* (1940), 309 U.S. 350, at 364. See also Charles J. Morris, editor, *The Developing Labor Law* (Washington, 1971), 759–62.
27. In *Polish National Alliance v. NLRB* (1944), 332 U.S. 643, 4 CD 535, at 538, the Court stated: "Congress . . . left it to the Board to ascertain whether proscribed practices would in particular situations adversely affect commerce when judged by the full reach of the constitutional powers of Congress." See also *Amalgamated Utility Workers v. Consolidated Edison Company of New York, Inc.* (1940), 309 U.S. 261. In *Consolidated Edison v. NLRB* (1938), 305 U.S. 197, at 222, the Court stated that in determining the boundaries of the authority conferred "we have applied the well-established principle that it is the effect upon interstate commerce, not the source of the injury, which is the criterion."

administrative efficiency, that review power was subject to important limitations. "In the [National Labor Relations] Act, Congress provided, 'the findings of the Board, as to the facts, if supported by evidence, shall be conclusive.' It is of paramount importance that courts not encroach upon this exclusive power of the Board if effect is to be given the intention of Congress to apply an orderly, informed and specialized procedure to the complex administrative problems arising in the solution of industrial disputes."[28] Finally, the Court confirmed that the Wagner Act gave the Board exclusive control of all proceedings, hearings and actions for enforcement undertaken under the Act.[29]

The Board's powers provoked many challenges, most conspicuously from employers. After the passage of the Wagner Act, employers had immediately tied it up in the courts with legal arguments alleging that the Board's power to impose upon them a duty to bargain was an infringement of due process which deprived them of their right to contract with whomever they chose. Once the act was upheld by the Supreme Court, employers shifted their ground to focus on the need for amendments protecting employer rights – such as freedom of speech – threatened by the Board's enforcement of the act's unfair labor practice provisions, imposing specific duties on workers and unions correlative with management rights, and generally preserving managerial freedom from the interference of government.[30] Throughout they cooperated closely with Congressional conservatives opposed both to the grant of such extensive authority to a federal agency, particularly in the field of labor relations, and to the wider assault on legislative and judicial authority which the New Deal's expansion of administrative government entailed.[31] The campaigns of these groups were reinforced by the results of the 1938 elections, and bore fruit early in 1939 when the Labor Committees of both houses of Congress agreed under pressure to consider amendments to "equalize" the National Labor Relations Act and to limit the Board's discretionary authority. An even clearer sign of their ascendancy came with the decision taken by the House of Representatives in July 1939 to create a special investigatory committee dominated by conservatives – the Smith Committee – to examine the overall operations of the NLRB.

28. *NLRB v. Waterman Steamship Corporation* (1940), 309 U.S. 206, at 208.
29. *Amalgamated Utility Workers v. Consolidated Edison Company of New York, Inc.* (1940), 309 U.S. 261; *Consolidated Edison v. NLRB* (1938), 305 U.S. 197. The Board enjoyed considerable success before the courts. In 133 cases heard by circuit courts through June, 1940, the Board had its orders set aside in 27 and enforced in full or with modification in the remainder. In 22 cases heard by the Supreme Court over the same period, Board orders were set aside in two, enforced with modifications in two, and enforced in full in the remainder. See Millis and Brown, *From the Wagner Act to Taft-Hartley*, 49, 84–5.
30. Irons, *New Deal Lawyers*, 243–8. 31. Ibid., 243–89.

These, however, were not the only critics of the new national labor policy. The Board had simultaneously to meet a growing chorus of complaints from representatives of the American Federation of Labor. These complainants alleged that the Board's enforcement of the Wagner Act, which they had presumed would be favorable to the established labor organizations, was in fact intolerant of their aims, objects and methods. According to Frank Fenton, the AFL's director of organization, the Board's members had "substituted a theoretical yardstick for self-organization instead of drawing from the experience and tradition of the trade-union movement." As a result, "many of their decisions are contrary to the historical and voluntary development of trade unions in our country." Instead of at last enabling established organizations to pursue their aims unhindered, as they had been led to expect, the act was apparently to be used to tailor the labor movement to a new style of behavior and to a new organizational structure. Fenton left no doubt that this was the obverse of the AFL's priorities and damaging to the interests of its affiliates and their members. "Experience teaches that you can't fit workers' thinking to fit a system no matter how logical it might appear. Logic is one thing – experience another. Rather than attempt to warp workers' thinking to fit a system, it would be much better to warp the system to satisfy the workers' thought."[32]

Like other AFL critics, Fenton was at times inclined to attribute the Board's actions to its members' "utter ignorance of the trade-union set up that we have been functioning under for practically sixty years."[33] But the controversy between the established unions and the Board was not the product of ignorant or incompetent action on the part of the Board members. Rather, it was inherent in the strategies which the Board had chosen to pursue in implementing the Wagner Act, in the interpretation which it placed on the act, and in the role which the Board saw for private organizations in fulfilling the public purposes embraced by the act.

Inevitably, in committing itself to a professional legal discourse as the appropriate method of implementing the Wagner Act, the Board also committed itself to a particular interpretation of what the act

32. Testimony of Frank P. Fenton, *Hearings Before the Committee on Labor, House of Representatives, Proposed Amendments to the National Labor Relations Act,* 76th Congress, 1st Session (Washington, 1939), 922. [Hereinafter cited as *House Hearings.*]

33. Testimony of Frank P. Fenton, *Hearings Before the Committee on Education and Labor, U.S. Senate, National Labor Relations Act and Proposed Amendments,* 76th Congress, 1st Session (Washington, 1939), 1281. [Hereinafter cited as *Senate Hearings.*]

meant. Thus, to Madden and Fahy, the ultimate meaning of the Wagner Act was that it enabled law and order to penetrate and transform a hitherto closed realm of social and economic life. Prior to its passage, according to Madden, the legal right of employees to organize had been "a fraud and a delusion," amounting to "nothing more than the natural right of revolution, that is the right to develop underground an organization of sufficient strength to come out into the open and demand concessions of power, at the risk of the most extreme penalties if the coup should fail."[34] The Wagner Act had transformed this empty natural right to engage in economic struggle into a right enshrined in positive law, the right to self-organization and collective bargaining. It had made of the old formal right a new freedom to be exercised through legal process.[35]

In bringing legal process to the center of the stage in this way, Madden and Fahy both argued, the Wagner Act had "remove[d] the causes" of much of America's industrial strife.[36] That is, they identified conflict in industry with the absence of a rational-legal means of settling disputes over rights and interests and assumed that by changing the process whereby men sought to vindicate their rights from one based on economic struggle to one based on law, Congress had actually done away with the causes of labor disputes. "The progress of civilization is indicated by the extent to which the state has rendered it unnecessary for one to obtain his rights by undergoing personal hardship," Madden told the AFL's convention in 1935. The achievement of a decisive role for "the legal process of statutory law" in dispute settlement would "solve the question of the freedom of self-organization and collective bargaining" quite painlessly.[37]

Ultimately, therefore, the Board approached the act as the foundation of new rights and as the initiator of new processes for solving disputes over their exercise. To its members, furthermore, the law's potential in

34. J. Warren Madden, Address before the American Political Science Association (29 December 1938), Columbus, Ohio, in *RG 25*, Smith Committee Box 15, ("Speeches").
35. Charles Fahy, Address before the National Association of Manufacturers (9 December 1937), New York, in *RG 25*, Smith Committee Box 15, ("Speeches").
36. Charles Fahy, Address at the Annual Convention of the National Petroleum Association (16 September 1937), Atlantic City, in *RG 25*, Smith Committee Box 15, ("Speeches").
37. J. Warren Madden, Address before the Annual Convention of the American Federation of Labor (10 October 1935), San Francisco; Charles Fahy, Address at the Annual Convention of the National Petroleum Association (16 September 1937), Atlantic City, and before the American Bar Association (13 July 1939), San Francisco, all in *RG 25*, Smith Committee Box 15, ("Speeches").

these fields was unlimited. Any attempt from any quarter to limit the Board's authority constituted an assertion that "there are ... limitations to legal processes," that "in a particular situation the social forces involved may be such that the Government must keep its hands off and let those social forces work themselves out."[38] These were assertions that the Board's members were not prepared to accept.

In denying that the reach of legal process could be susceptible to limitation, the Board was simultaneously denying that there could be any statutory requirement that it found its policies upon respect for the practices traditionally adopted by unions in their attempts to vindicate organizing and bargaining rights through persuasion or coercion of employers. Indeed, from the Board's point of view, as we have just seen, by substituting legal process for economic struggle the Wagner Act had, to an appreciable extent, rendered those traditional practices irrelevant. To the AFL, however, for "the members of the Board ... [to] refuse to take cognizance of labor unions, their structure, and their methods of bargaining," was a direct challenge.[39] This resulted in a situation which left little room for manoeuvre on either side.

Nowhere is the clash between the Board and the prevailing custom and practice of the AFL better illustrated than in the furious controversy which developed during the Board's first five years over its exercise of the power to determine units appropriate for collective bargaining. As we have seen, by granting the authority to determine the unit to the Board, the Wagner Act had already aroused considerable anxiety amongst AFL leaders who were concerned that a government agency should gain such a substantive instrument of control over the structure of labor organization and representation at a time when new organizations were posing a considerable challenge to the jurisdictional hegemony of the established unions. In succeeding years, evidence that the Board was prepared to use that authority to force unions to conform to new theories of organizational and representational legitimacy without regard to the consequences this might have for their existing collective bargaining relationships with employers or for the overall struggle between the AFL and CIO bred outright opposition. By the middle of 1938, or just a year after the Wagner Act was upheld in the Supreme Court, the AFL leadership had decided to embark on a course of all-out war against the NLRB.

38. Testimony of J. Warren Madden, *Hearings Before the Special (Smith) Committee to Investigate the National Labor Relations Board, House of Representatives,* 76th Congress, 3rd Session, 24 (10 May–1 August 1940), 4977–78. [Hereinafter cited as *Smith Committee Hearings.*]
39. Testimony of Joseph Padway (AFL general counsel), *House Hearings,* 765.

Property rights and the AFL

AFL unions began to criticize the NLRB almost as soon as it became apparent that its decisions were likely to have a material effect upon the outcome of their struggles with insurgents. In July 1936, for example, the International Seaman's Union appeared before the Executive Council to enlist its support in protesting a Board decision that the ISU's West Coast affiliate, the Sailor's Union of the Pacific, constituted the proper bargaining representative of West Coast seamen notwithstanding that the SUP had recently been suspended by its parent body. The ISU claimed that its contract with the ship owners named the international union as the principal on the union side and thus gave it exclusive representation rights, foreclosing any "question concerning representation." George Harrison, president of the Brotherhood of Railway Clerks and member of the Executive Council, agreed, and stressed that the Board had no right to interfere. "Under the Wagner Act the Board has the power to determine what shall constitute the unit appropriate for collective bargaining. You have already determined that by your contract. That is your unit."[40]

Prior to mid-1937, criticism tended to confine itself to these sorts of occasional outbursts over particular decisions. In part this reflected the comparatively small number of cases filed with the Board in the eighteen months prior to the Supreme Court's affirmation of the Wagner Act's constitutionality, a period which Board attorney Malcolm Ross likened to a state of "suspended animation" in which the Board waited in limbo for the Court to determine its fate.[41] According to Robert Cowdrill, regional director in Indianapolis, employer propaganda against the act during these months resulted in "lack of understanding of provisions [of the act], lack of confidence in the Board, lack of energy in pressing cases, no organization being done and fear of consequences if cases brought."[42] In part also, the absence of sustained AFL criticism reflected the character of the AFL-CIO confrontation in its early stages. For much of 1936, for example, the energies of the two central bodies were mainly devoted to attempts to win the Amalgamated Association of Iron, Steel and Tin Workers' endorsement of their respective plans to organize the steel industry.[43] Not until after negotiations to repair the split had foundered

40. AFL Executive Council *Minutes* (13 July 1936).
41. See Gross, *The Making of the National Labor Relations Board*, 195–212.
42. Memorandum, "Administrative Suggestions and Questions Submitted by Regional Offices," in *RG 25*, Box 338 ("Assistant General Counsel Witt's Records, 1935–36").
43. On 28 January 1936 the AFL Executive Council authorized Green to begin preparing plans for an organizing campaign for the iron and steel industry. On 2 March Green announced the inauguration of the AFL's campaign in a circular to all union

late in 1936, resulting in the AFL Executive Council's suspension of the CIO unions, did the incidence of jurisdictional and factional struggles both between and within unions attain serious proportions.[44]

Once conflict between AFL and CIO unions had begun to appear during late 1936 and 1937, however, the Board almost immediately found itself placed in an extremely delicate position. Initially it reacted with extreme caution. Although Madden had warned the AFL in 1935 that the Board would not consider itself bound to respect the jurisdictional rights of unions, it decided nevertheless to refrain from intervention in controversies over representation "where such controversies are not merely controversies between two opposing labor organizations for the right to represent the employees in collective bargaining, but are in fact (or also) jurisdictional controversies between unions affiliated with the American Federation of Labor (or with some other higher body) or controversies between leaders within a union."[45] The Board also canvassed the possibility of discouraging the filing of petitions by insurgent groups.[46] Because initially much of the conflict in the labor movement was concentrated *within* AFL unions – this was the case, for example, in the maritime, lumber and longshore industries – the Board's policy meant that it was effectively abstaining from these disputes. In its early bargaining unit decisions, too, the Board was careful to do nothing to disrupt existing patterns of organization, basing its decisions on factors such as the eligibility of workers for membership in the petitioning

presidents and called for the creation of a fund of $750,000 and the furnishing of organizers by all interested organizations. On 6 May the Amalgamated Association of Iron, Steel, and Tin Workers appeared at a meeting of the Executive Council to complain at the lack of progress. On 8 June the AAISTW accepted the CIO's plan for the organization of the steel industry. Green released a statement regretting the inability of the labor movement to unite behind a steel organizing drive, and the following month he began issuing public statements highly critical of the CIO's disruption of labor unity. Green's growing antagonism signified the imminent victory of the pro-suspension forces on the AFL Executive Council, and the CIO unions were duly suspended the following August. See AFL Executive Council *Minutes* (28 January–5 August 1936); Green, circulars and statements (2 March, 3 April, 8 June, 8 July, and 10 July 1936), all in *AFL Records*, reel 57 (Circular and Neostyle File). See also Irving Bernstein, *Turbulent Years: A History of the American Worker, 1933–1941* (Boston, 1969), 635–81.

44. See AFL Executive Council *Minutes* (9–15 February and 19–22 April 1937).
45. Nathan Witt to Lee Pressman, CIO general counsel (10 December 1936), in *RG 25*, Box 338 ("Assistant General Counsel Witt's Records, 1935–36"). See also Witt's draft of an article on the NLRB for the *Americana Annual* (submitted 29 December 1936), in same.
46. NLRB *Minutes* (13 May 1937), in *RG 25*, Smith Committee Box 21–23 ("Board Minutes"). See also Nathan Witt, "Union Responsibility and the Function and Future of the National Labor Relations Board," Address before the New York Women's Trade Union League (2 October 1937), in *RG 25*, Smith Committee Box 15, ("Speeches").

union, the extent to which unions had organized workers in a particular location, their expressed desire to be represented by the union and, in cases where two or more unions sought to organize in cooperation, their jurisdictional claims.

As each side expanded its organizing activities, however, the Board found the contest in the labor movement increasingly difficult to avoid. In February 1937 it attracted renewed criticism from the AFL Executive Council for intervening in disputes within the disintegrating ISU.[47] Four months later, in *Interlake Iron Corporation*, the Board affirmed that an employer's contractual recognition of an AFL union was not determinative of its legitimacy as a representative in the eyes of the Board, and directed that an election be held.[48] While the hearings were still in progress in this case, AFL President Green called Madden to advise the Board not to interfere in situations like this where, according to Green, bargaining was established and working. The act, he said, had been passed "for the purpose of giving to those who were denied the right to organize and bargain collectively an opportunity to select their bargaining agency."[49] Here, however, there had been no such denial. Once it became known that the Board would decide to the contrary, Charlton Ogburn, at that time still AFL general counsel, delivered a further warning:

> I assume that the Board, by ignoring my argument that the evidence before the examiner did not disclose that any union of employees in this plant had voted a request for an election under the National Labor Relations Act, has adopted the policy of taking the initiative in calling an election provided any person . . . requests it, and over the objection of a bona fide union which has been recognized by the employer. This is a policy on the part of the government which labor unions will not find acceptable.[50]

As the volume of representation petitions increased in the months following the *Jones and Laughlin* decision, the Board found itself confronted more and more frequently with the necessity of resolving incompatible representation claims from AFL and CIO unions. The remote possibility that such disputes might be resolvable within the organized labor movement having effectively vanished following the suspension of the CIO unions, the Board had no alternative but to begin intervening routinely in contested cases. At first it confined itself to the cases involving competition between unions affiliated to different federations, justify-

---

47. AFL Executive Council *Minutes* (8 February 1937).
48. 2 NLRB 1036 (26 June 1937).
49. Transcript of telephone conversation, Green-Madden (14 May 1937), in *RG 25*, Informal File R-149, *Interlake Iron Corporation*.
50. Ogburn to Madden, in ibid.

ing its action on the grounds that a common source of authority able to resolve disputes between such unions no longer existed.[51] It also discounted specific private jurisdictional agreements between unions no longer affiliated to the same federation. Such agreements, the Board said, were not a sufficient source of common authority either. In any case they could not control its power to determine units.[52] Eventually the Board would hold that its power was not to be set aside even in disputes between affiliates of the same federation.[53]

The Board's growing assertiveness in inter-union disputes coincided with growing self-confidence within the AFL. By the latter part of 1937, the Executive Council appeared to feel that the Federation had weathered the storm and was well on the way to reconfirming its proper position as the leading organization of American labor.[54] This self-confidence helped to shape the Federation's attitude to the Board. According to the AFL, the Board's statutory function was to act as an auxiliary, providing services to unions (principally that of protection from employers). Conflicts arising from the encroachment of CIO unions on the jurisdictional territories of AFL affiliates were private matters, not amenable to Board resolution and resolvable only through negotiations among the unions themselves. In these circumstances, the Board's claim that its authority to determine the appropriate bargaining unit was unrestricted was, in the AFL's eyes, tantamount to bias in favor of the CIO. Thus, during the hearings in *Federal Knitting Mills* (August 1937), Boris Shishkin wrote Madden that AFL federal labor unions organizing workers in the ladies' knit goods industry considered the NLRB to be a sham and a CIO front. "The local board in Cleveland is fair and impartial," one federal organizer had told Shishkin, "but we of the labor movement in Cleveland are of the united opinion that we should ignore

51. NLRB *Minutes* (13 May 1937), in *RG 25*, Smith Committee Box 21–23, ("Board Minutes"); *Federal Knitting Mills* (August 1937), 3 NLRB 257.
52. See, for example, *The Texas Company, West Tulsa Works* (November 1937), 4 NLRB 182; *Waggoner Refining Company, Inc* (April 1938), 6 NLRB 731.
53. See, for example, *Harbison-Walker Refractories Company* (September 1942), 43 NLRB 936; *Iowa Electric Light and Power Company* (December 1942), 46 NLRB 230; *Montgomery Ward and Company, Inc.* (June 1943), 50 NLRB 163; *W.H. Kistler Stationery Company* (July 1943), 51 NLRB 978; *William Koehl Company* (January 1946), 65 NLRB 190.
54. See, for example, AFL Executive Council *Minutes* (13–16 October 1937; 24 January 1938). By October 1937 the AFL was receiving solid evidence of mounting financial crises and organizing cutbacks among CIO unions. See unsigned memorandum to President Green (25 October 1937), in *William Green Papers*, Microfilm Edition (Ohio Historical Society). [Hereinafter cited as *Green Papers*.] See also the Metal Trades Department-AFL Circulars of 28 July 1937 and 28 October 1937 describing the CIO's dues crisis and assessing the AFL's prospects in competition between the two federations. In *Frey Papers*, Box 6, folders 98 and 104.

any decision on labor issues, any calls for elections or any other matters that pertain to our general welfare when it comes from the National Labor Relations Board."[55] Union leaders on the Executive Council were also becoming more critical of the NLRB's "interference," citing it as grounds for reconsidering their support for the Roosevelt administration's projected fair labor standards legislation. Wharton of the International Association of Machinists, for example, expressed doubt whether administrative regulation and autonomous trade unionism could ever be compatible. While he was "fundamentally in favor of legislation which will not restrict in any respect the right to organize," he was "opposed to legislation that will arbitrarily remove from [an] organization the right to function as a labor organization should function." In particular, Wharton concluded, he was opposed to the creation of administrative bodies that would be permitted by law "to interfere to the extent of nullifying organization."[56]

The following six months saw these occasional outburst of criticism grow into an insistent drumbeat. Much of the AFL's commentary was couched in the terms which Shiskin had reported in August, accusing the NLRB of bias against the AFL and in favor of the CIO. To a degree, the complaint was justified. The special House investigation of the Board which took place in 1939 and 1940 would make it clear that amongst both regional and national officers of the Board there were some who were partial to the CIO.[57] Instances of discrimination sufficient to affect the outcome of an election undoubtedly occurred. But examination of the issues involved in the AFL's dispute with the Board indicates that it arose just as much from the very conception that the Board developed of the statute and of its role as a public agency in enforcing it, as from the subjective biases of Board officers. As the dispute worsened, that is, and as each side – the AFL leadership and the Board – was forced to articulate more and more precisely the basis of its position, it became clear that two very different perceptions of the nature and role of trade unions were clashing.

The Board's decision in *Globe Machinery and Stamping Company* (August 1937) affords an early illustration of the conceptual gulf separating the AFL and the NLRB. In this case, three AFL unions sought to divide the production and maintenance workers employed by the company in question into three distinct units conforming to their jurisidic-

55. Shiskin to Madden (12 August 1937), in *RG 25*, Informal File R-202, *Federal Knitting Mills*.
56. AFL Executive Council *Minutes* (28 August 1937).
57. Gross, *The Reshaping of the National Labor Relations Board: National Labor Policy in Transition, 1937-47* (Albany, New York, 1981), 262.

tions. The United Auto Workers-CIO intervened, claiming one unit containing all the workers in question. The Board held that the factors on which it usually based its unit decisions were so evenly balanced in this case that it was unable to determine the appropriate unit. "In such a case," the Board stated, "the determining factor is the desire of the men themselves."[58] The Board held elections in each of the three units claimed by the AFL to determine whether or not the employees wished to be represented by the AFL union in question or by the UAW. In each case the UAW won a majority and was duly certified as the representative of all production and maintenance workers employed by the company.

The Board's decision in *Globe Machinery* appeared to be an attempt to meet the pressure which had come from the AFL's metal trades affiliates for protection of their jurisdiction amongst skilled workers in manufacturing industries.[59] Certainly this was how the decision was interpreted in CIO circles. In October 1937, Heber Blankenhorn, the Board's "special investigator," reported that the CIO saw in *Globe* and subsequent cases decided on the *Globe* principle a fundamental threat to industrial unionism.[60] To the AFL, however, the *Globe* decision had actually worsened the position of its affiliates, for despite appearances the Board had not committed itself to allow craft groups to vote in conformity with the jurisdictional lines of their unions. According to AFL general counsel Padway, "the Board quite definitely stated that it could have very well denied the A. F. of L. requests on the basis that the plant set-up could function just as well as a single industrial unit, but that it was graciously permitting a vote along craft lines because the evidence was easily balanced."[61]

Padway was much happier with the decision on the same issue in *Allis-Chalmers* three months later, for in this case the Board appeared to commit itself to hold elections among separable craft groups when-

58. 3 NLRB 294 (August 1937), at 300.
59. See, for example, AFL Executive Council *Minutes* (February 10, 1937); Gross, *The Reshaping of the National Labor Relations Board*, 44–5.
60. Blankenhorn to the Board (18 October 1937), in *RG 25*, Smith Committee Box 25, ("La Follette Committee").
61. Padway to Green (29 November 1937), in *Green Papers*. In 1939, the AFL Executive Council offered the following "explanatory comment" on its attitude to the NLRB:

> Under the *Globe* Doctrine the right to vote on the unit depends on the will of the Board. The Board may or may not permit the workers to vote for a unit as it sees fit. The Board has made certain [of this] by injecting the subtle, indefinable phrase "where the considerations are evenly balanced." And who determines what these "considerations" are? And who determines when the considerations are "evenly balanced?" The Board of course.

In *RG 25*, Smith Committee Box 14, ("Report of the AFL Executive Council").

ever requested to do so. "If it is adhered to and becomes an established precedent for all time it is an excellent decision," he wrote Green. "The language is so much more definite and clear than previous decisions wherein the same issues were presented to the Board."[62] Yet the decision was not without its problems. Chief amongst them was that it was not unanimous. Board member Edwin Smith argued that the majority's decision to allow self-determination elections amongst the craft groups was an abdication of the Board's statutory responsibility to determine the unit. "The device of holding such an election . . . is obviously inadequate to throw any light on the problem of what is the most appropriate bargaining unit," Smith stated. The Board's unit determinations should be guided by its paramount duty to assist workers to achieve stable employment under collective bargaining. In situations like this the bargaining power of the employees would plainly be weakened by allowing the balkanization of a plant through the separation of craft-based units. This would "tend to lessen reliance upon peaceful collective bargaining as the means for achieving the workers' economic ends." For Smith, such a result was "plainly contrary to the purpose of the Act."[63]

Although Smith was alone in his opinion, the AFL was perturbed. Padway qualified his praise of the majority decision by pointing out some of the implications for the Federation should Smith's position ever be adopted by the Board:

> The decision does emphasize that our fears and apprehensions respecting the danger of lodging in the Board the power of life and death over A.F. of L. unions are well-founded. The dissenting opinion of Mr. Edwin S. Smith is a propaganda plea for industrial unions in mass production and in large industries and that the rights of craft workers must not only be subordinated but denied, and that crafts have no right to exist in these industries. If Mr. Edwin S. Smith could have induced one member of the Board to have agreed with him, it is apparent . . . what would happen to our organizations. Being unable to exercise the most important function for which labor unions are organized, namely to represent and bargain for those affiliated and entitled to affiliate with the organization, our organizations would disintegrate and die. I am, therefore, more convinced than ever that one of the paramount legislative objects of the A. F. of L. must be to repeal Section 9b dealing

---

62. Padway to Green (29 November 1937), in *Green Papers*.
63. *Allis-Chalmers Manufacturing Company* (20 November 1937), 4 NLRB 159, at 175–6. See also Smith to Witt, memorandum on "Allis-Chalmers Manufacturing Company Decision" (11 October 1937), in *RG 25*, Smith Committee Subject Files Box 11, ("Edwin S. Smith Statistical Analysis").

with the unit rule and substitute for it a clause conforming to the
opinion in the Allis-Chalmers case.[64]

In the months after *Allis-Chalmers,* the Board continued to stress that
the doctrine announced in *Globe* remained the best available guide to
its policy in cases involving contested petitions for units of less than all
of a Company's employees. It also showed, however, that it felt free to
qualify or ignore the precedent whenever, in its judgment, the purposes
of the Wagner Act would not be advanced by its exercise. Thus, in
Fried, Ostermann Company (June 1938), the Board refused to hold an
election to test the claims of the International Glove Workers-AFL that
it and not the Amalgamated Clothing Workers-CIO had the support of
the majority of the employees in the glove department of the company's
Milwaukee plant. The company, said the NLRB, had already recognized the ACW as bargaining agent for the whole plant. It was immaterial that the ACW was unable to show that it had any support among
workers in the glove department and that the glove department was
completely separate from the rest of the plant. In *Admiar Rubber Company* (October 1938), similarly, the Board denied employees of a New
York toy manufacturer the opportunity to change their bargaining representative on the ground that the "orderly functioning of the processes
of collective bargaining" would be disrupted thereby.[65]

The AFL's reactions to the decisions in *Globe* and *Allis-Chalmers* indicates the increasing weight accorded the opinions of officials such as
Metal Trades Department president Frey and senior vice-president Matthew Woll in determining the Federation's attitude toward the Board.[66]
Frey in particular had been calling for amendments to restrict the discretion allowed the Board in bargaining unit determinations virtually since
the act was passed.[67] After *Globe,* Frey's criticisms were taken up by
other members of the AFL bureaucracy and over the following twelve
months the Federation's leadership moved inexorably toward open opposition to the Board. One consequence was that the Federation became
isolated from the Roosevelt administration, an early casualty of the anti-
NLRB campaign being official AFL support for projected fair labor standards legislation. This law, the Federation decided, would "very materially interfere with the free functioning of the trade union movement" by
introducing further measures of administrative discretion into the deter-

64. Padway to Green (29 November 1937), in *Green Papers.*
65. *Fried, Ostermann Company,* 7 NLRB 1075; *Admiar Rubber Company,* 9 NLRB
    407.
66. See, generally, Gross, *The Reshaping of the National Labor Relations Board,* 42–
    84, particularly 64–5.
67. See, for example, AFL Executive Council *Minutes* (10 February 1937).

mination of labor relations issues.[68] A second consequence was that within the Federation the influence of the central bureaucracy – the departments, the offices of the president, and the general counsel – was seen to be increasing relative to that of the affiliates, a development which risked the appearance of splits between the Federation and its member unions. By the beginning of 1939, as we shall see, just such a cleavage had emerged within the top ranks of the AFL, threatening to divide the majority of union leaders who sat on the Executive Council from the officers who headed the permanent bureaucracy.

The AFL's top leadership was thus risking much by committing itself to a campaign against the Board. Yet its utter preoccupation with what appeared, by early 1938, to be a developing assault on the very kernels of the AFL's traditional customs and practices, a preoccupation transcending even the conflict with the CIO which was the occasion for the assault, rendered it oblivious to the dangers of its position.[69] Its intransigence is evidenced in particular in two cases which stand out as symbols of the Board's assault and of what it portended for the AFL, *Consolidated Edison Company* (November 1937) and *Shipowners' Association of the Pacific Coast* (June 1938).[70]

The *Consolidated Edison* case, which grew out of rival organizing drives mounted by the International Brotherhood of Electrical Workers-AFL and the United Electrical Workers-CIO early in 1937, was rooted in a long history of corporate resistance to collective bargaining. Like many other corporations, Consolidated Edison had reacted to the passage of the Recovery Act in 1933 by establishing employee representation plans in each of its plants. At the same time, an independent union known as the Brotherhood of Utility Employees had attempted to take advantage of Section 7(a) of the Recovery Act to mount an organizing drive among Consolidated Edison's employees. The Brotherhood was unable to make any headway and in 1936 it merged with the IBEW,

---

68. AFL Executive Council *Minutes* (28 August, 3 October and 3 December 1937). See also Gross, *The Reshaping of the National Labor Relations Board*, 47, and generally 42–84.

69. See, for example, Speech of Joseph Padway to the Denver convention of the AFL, in *Report of Proceedings of the 57th Annual Convention of the American Federation of Labor*, Denver, 1937 (Washington, D.C., 1937), 250–3. In 1939 Padway told the Senate Committee on Education and Labor that "Organized labor would have preferred to have secured its fundamental rights of self-organization and collective bargaining without legislation," while according to Green the Board had established precedents which could be used "not only to take away much of the gains we have made in the last few years, but also to undermine and destroy many of our affiliates completely." In *Senate Hearings*, 713, 644.

70. *Consolidated Edison Company of New York, Incorporated, et al.*, 4 NLRB 71; *Shipowners Association of the Pacific Coast, et al.*, 7 NLRB 1002.

becoming IBEW local B-752. In March 1937, local B-752 began another organizing drive. Simultaneously, it returned its IBEW charter and affiliated with UE. The company persisted in refusing to bargain with anyone except its own representation plans, and on 5 April the UE local (formerly B-752) indicated to the New York Regional Labor Board that it wished to charge the company with unfair labor practices. Meanwhile, the IBEW also began conferring with the company, and on 16 April it demanded recognition and a contract with the company to cover its members. In the wake of the Supreme Court's decision in *Jones and Laughlin* (12 April), the company withdrew recognition from the employee representation plans, and on 20 April indicated that it would recognize the IBEW as the representative of its members. Three days later the representation plans applied for, and were granted, IBEW local union charters, and over the following two months the company and the IBEW entered into members-only contracts in each of the company's plants. By the end of June, 30,000 of 38,000 Consolidated Edison employees were IBEW members. Virtually none had been at the time the company signified it would recognize the union.[71]

The Board ordered the IBEW's contracts dissolved. Although it would not sustain charges brought by UE that the company had dominated or supported the IBEW, and although it acknowledged that the IBEW's contracts were for its members alone and did not purport to represent the IBEW as the exclusive bargaining representative for all the company's employees, the Board held that in fact Consolidated Edison had deliberately construed the contracts to cover its entire work force and had stated that it would not negotiate with any other organization for coverage of its members during their lifetime. In so doing, the Board argued, the company had in effect "recognized and entered into contracts with the IBEW locals as the exclusive bargaining representatives" of its employees. Moreover, it had done so "at a time when it did not know the size of their membership." Hence the contracts were invalid "notwithstanding that they are in express terms applicable only to members of the IBEW locals."[72]

Dan Tracy, president of the IBEW, immediately charged that the Board had "exercised authority with which it is not vested."[73] The union filed a petition for review of the Board's order, contending that the Board's authority to dissolve contracts extended only to contracts concluded by company-dominated organizations and that the IBEW's

71.　4 NLRB 71. And see *RG 25*, Informal File C-245, *Consolidated Edison*.
72.　4 NLRB 71, at 93–4.
73.　Tracy to F.B. Carlisle, Chairman of the Board of Directors, Consolidated Edison Inc. (10 November 1937), in *RG 25*, Informal File C-245.

contracts were clearly valid because it was a bona fide organization. According to the Board attorneys who were assigned to defend the order, however, this begged the whole question:

> The contract is not valid merely because made by a person able to make a contract. A contract made by a labor organization, or a corporation, or an individual, is invalid if it is the result of violations of a very fundamental statute affecting the rights of persons entitled to belong to labor organizations, or unlawfully depriving employees or other labor organizations of rights guaranteed by the Act . . . Contracts are not *per se* valid, important as they are. They are invalid if the result of unfair labor practices or if contrary to the declared public policy of the United States.[74]

On 14 March 1938 the Second Circuit Court of Appeals upheld the Board's order dissolving the IBEW's contracts.[75] The case then went to the Supreme Court. Here, Fahy repeated the Board's basic argument – that the IBEW's contracts were an incident of the company's unfair labor practices which, if allowed to stand, would have perpetuated those practices.[76] AFL general counsel Padway, for the union, indicated that the AFL saw the matter in a completely different light:

> We see a tendency on the part of the Board to . . . restrict us in the making of contracts or in furthering the processes of organization or in carrying on unionism as we have been accustomed to carrying it on before there was a Labor Relations Act. Now, we did not intend and did not believe when the National Labor Relations Act was passed that it was intended to limit the rights of labor organizations and we did not intend it would deter organization in the field of labor unionism. And yet we find on the part of the board a tendency to restrict us under what it terms to be certain sections of the Act which inhibit certain practices.[77]

The Board, Padway said, was preventing the IBEW from approaching an employer and negotiating to establish unionism in his plant. "Is there a single word or letter in this act that says . . . [a union may not] go to [the employer] and say 'here, we want to sell you unionism, we think you ought to run a union plant.' " That, Padway concluded, "is the way

---

74. "Notes for Argument," in *RG 25*, Informal File C-245.
75. *Consolidated Edison Company v. NLRB* (1938), 95 F2 390. And see correspondence, Fahy to Judges Manton, Swan, and Hind (1 March 1938) and William L. Ransom (attorney for Consolidated Edison) to same (4 March 1938) on the Board's power to order an employer to withdraw its recognition of a union. In *RG 25*, Informal File C-245.
76. "Consolidated Edison v. NLRB, Transcript of Proceedings," in *RG 25*, Informal File C-245.
77. Ibid.

labor unions have organized for years, since 1881, when the American Federation of Labor was organized."[78]

Padway's entire argument on behalf of the AFL was based on the premise that a union enjoyed a right to establish a bargaining relationship with an employer entirely independent of the provisions of public policy and irrespective of whether the union represented a majority, a minority, or indeed any, of the employer's employees. "We believe that we have the right to approach an employer in the same manner as we had the right to approach him prior to the act and endeavor to unionize him."[79] Such a right, it was felt, could not be vacated by any action of the Board. William Green followed a similar line in an address at the Economic Club of Chicago, charging that the Board had illegally assumed the authority "to disregard contracts between employers and employees and to reduce to a useless procedure their voluntary action in negotiating

78. Ibid. The Supreme Court's decision, *Consolidated Edison Company Inc., et al. v. NLRB* (1938), 305 US 197, was handed down on December 5. The decision upheld the Board's findings that the company had committed unfair practices, but, crucially, failed to endorse those aspects of its order relating to the invalidation of the IBEW's contracts. While Fahy pressed the Board's argument that the contracts could not stand because they were the outcome of the company's unfair labor practices, the Court insisted on considering the contracts independently from the unfair labor practices, holding (Chief Justice Hughes in particular) that their substantive provisions were beneficial to employees and would tend to preserve industrial peace. See the "Transcript of Proceedings" in Informal File C-245. In its formal decision the Court held that in invalidating the IBEW's contracts, the Board had improperly refused to make the IBEW a party to its proceedings, thereby denying it due process. "... the [IBEW] and its locals having valuable and beneficial interests in the contracts were entitled to notice and hearing before they could be set aside." 305 US 197, at 233.

   Three days after the Court's decision, attorney Benjamin Goldstein wrote to Green to warn the AFL that despite the Court's apparent endorsement of the AFL's contention that the Board was without authority to abrogate contracts, the Board would undoubtedly treat the decision as a rebuke on a matter of procedure rather than as a limitation of its discretion:

> The Court holds that there is no express authority given to the Board to abrogate contracts. But this holding is limited by the holding that Congress granted implied powers to the Board to make the validity of the contract subject to the necessities of enforcing the Wagner Act. In that respect the opinion is a limitation on the freedom of contract rather than an affirmation thereof. I have no doubt that the Board will proceed at the first opportunity to present a case which will bring these contracts within the scope of its jurisdiction.

See Goldstein to Green (8 December 1938), in *Green Papers*.

   Notwithstanding Goldstein's warning, the Court's decision in *Consolidated Edison v. NLRB* was an important affirmation of the supremacy of the common law of contract over the Board's distinctly anticontractual arguments. This point is developed at greater length in Chapter 6. See also Karl Klare, "Judicial Deradicalization of the Wagner Act and the Origins of Modern Legal Consciousness, 1937–41," *Minnesota Law Review*, 62, 3 (March 1978), 265–339.

79. "Transcript of Proceedings," in *RG 25*, Informal File C-245.

such contracts . . ." In doing so, Green charged, the Board had struck at "the very basis of the collective bargaining technique which the American Federation of Labor has established and practised for more than half a century," a technique which had been developed by Federation unions "through experience, during all the years, as suitable and necessary to the requirements of modern industrial life."[80]

Green and Padway were on dubious ground, of course, in claiming that the Board had acted outside its authority. Under Section 8 of the Wagner Act, the Board had ample authority to modify the traditional collective bargaining practices of American unions. Section 8 prohibited employers from discriminating against employees on the grounds that they were union members, or that they sought to organize unions or bargain collectively. But it also prohibited them from dominating or interfering "with the formation or administration of *any* labor organization" and from entering into an exclusive agreement with *any* organization (whether it was "established, maintained or assisted by any action defined in this Act as an unfair labor practice" or not) which was not the certified representative of the employees in a collective bargaining unit approved by the Board.[81] The primary purpose of these provisions was the disestablishment of company unions. In 1934, however, Isador Polier, executive director of the International Juridical Association, had recommended that exclusive agreements made by independent unions which did not represent a majority of the employees concerned should also be banned on the grounds that such agreements "serve no legitimate need of employees."[82] The Senate Committee's report approving the Wagner bill endorsed this position, and thus prohibited a collective bargaining technique widely used for many years by the established unions. "While today an employer may negotiate [a closed shop] agreement even with a minority union," the report stated, "the bill provides that an employer shall be allowed to make a closed-shop contract only with a labor organization that represents the majority of employees in the appropriate collective bargaining unit covered by such an agreement when made."[83]

The Board concurred. An employer who signed a closed shop contract without proof that the union in question represented the majority of his workers in an appropriate bargaining unit was guilty of improperly assisting a labor organization. Under such circumstances, said the

---

80. William Green, Address before the Economic Club of Chicago (15 December 1938), in *Wagner Papers*, 706 LA 719, folder 60.
81. National Labor Relations Act, 49 Stat. 449, Sec. 8(2) and (3) [emphasis supplied]; *Leg. Hist.*, 2308–11.
82. *Leg. Hist.*, 1053.   83. Ibid., 2311.

Board, it had no alternative "other than to restore the status quo by obliterating the illegal contract."[84]

To the AFL, the Board's policy was as good as an accusation that its affiliates were company unions. Green reacted with great indignation:

> I resent even by implication . . . the classification of [an] American Federation of Labor, independent democratic union as a company union. We define the term "labor organization" so as expressly to exclude "company unions," thus making certain that company unions obtain none of the benefits accorded legitimate labor organizations by the Act. For fifty years before there was any C.I.O. the A. F. of L. was leading the fight against company-controlled, company-dominated unions . . . [only] to have a board, none of them ever having had experience with labor, attempt to classify [an AFL union] that had won a collective-bargaining contract for 30,000 workers as a company union.[85]

It was not up to the Board, Green said, to establish the bona fides of a union or to oversee its collective bargaining tactics. The organized labor movement did that for itself. Its record of opposition to company unions should be sufficient guarantee that the activities of the established unions were in the interest of the employees. Hence they should be protected and encouraged, rather than declared illegal. The Board's function should be simply to protect the established unions in the exercise of their bargaining power.

The Senate debates on S1958, however, had already made it quite clear that the final determination of federal policy would be made with considerations other than the AFL's perception of its historical role uppermost. As the chairman of the Senate Committee on Education and Labor, Senator David Walsh, had noted, the bill's constraints on employer behavior applied to relations with any labor organization whether it was an independent union or not. "Personally," Walsh said, "I feel in any law no distinction ought to be made between company unions and trade unions."[86] Consequently, the Board took no notice of the AFL's claims and in *Consolidated Edison* and nine similar cases

---

84. National Labor Relations Board Memorandum, "Invalidation of Contracts," in *Wagner Papers*, 706 LA 719, folder 66.

85. *Senate Hearings*, 637. Green later reemphasized his concern to protect the right of a union "to bargain collectively for itself," and warned the Senate Committee of the damage that would be done to unions "if this Board is clothed with power to set aside contracts entered into by free, democratic trade-unions, with employers, and made by unions that have developed an organization technique over a period of more than one-half century. They have gone through the hardest lesson of cruel experience," he added, "and have learned much in dealing with their employers." 684.

86. *Congressional Record*, 79, 7 (16 May 1935), 7660.

decided in the year following August 1937, it overturned contracts executed by AFL unions. "[In] each, the A. F. L. had come into the plant at the initial suggestion of the company; in several, there was no proof that the A. F. of L. had a majority legitimately gained or not, either at the time of the hearing or at the time of the execution of the contract. In all these cases the employer climaxed his intent to shut out other unions by signing a closed-shop contract. In each case the Board held that the closed-shop contract violated Section 8(3) of the Act and declared it null and void."[87]

The Board invalidated these contracts because they were based on a model of a collective bargaining and of the role of unions in the employment relationship which the Wagner Act did not embrace. A frank acknowledgment of this divergence appears in a 1939 pamphlet, *Problems of the National Labor Relations Board*, published by the American Association for Economic Freedom. In this pamphlet an anonymous Board member alluded to collective bargaining practices which had long been common among AFL affiliates but which were no longer permissible under the Wagner Act. "It is a well-known fact," he stated, "that much so-called organization of labor in the past has not proceeded on the basis of a prior enrollment of a majority membership . . . before an attempt was made by union officials to negotiate with an employer. It was not uncommon for a labor union to make an agreement with an employer, sometimes even a closed-shop agreement, before more than a minority of the employees had been organized, perhaps before any employee had signified his desire to be so represented and contractually dealt with." The Board member acknowledged that these techniques had been both effective and beneficial for unions and for workers. "Many times employers . . . have by argument, or a threat of strike or boycott, signed agreements with unions which have redounded substantially to the good of their employees. Thereafter the union has proceeded to organize the workers to support the union which had gained them these advantages." He confirmed, however, that under the Wagner Act such techniques were no longer available to the unions.[88] As Louis Boudin put it during his appearance for the CIO before the Supreme Court in the *Consolidated Edison* hearing, recognition and bargaining rights were no longer matters to be negotiated privately between a union and an employer. Under the statute, "representation [of workers] becomes a public matter just like any other public facts in a democracy. Therefore the

---

87. NLRB Memorandum, "Invalidation of Contracts."
88. American Association for Economic Freedom, *Problems of the National Labor Relations Board* (1939), in *Wagner Papers*, 706 LA 719, folder 67.

performance as to representation ... is taken from the status of a private contract."[89]

The Board's doctrine that, under the Wagner Act, questions of representation were facts exclusively for public determination was strongly underlined by the decision in *Shipowners' Association of the Pacific Coast*.[90] This case arose from a series of representation petitions filed with the Board late in 1937 in which the International Longshoremen's and Warehousemen's Union-CIO sought certification as the bargaining representative for all Pacific Coast longshoremen over the opposition of the International Longshoremen's Association-AFL. The Board consolidated the petitions and hearings began in February 1938. The hearings established that since 1909 longshoremen on the Pacific Coast had been organized into local unions affiliated to an autonomous district of the ILA. Between 1916 and 1934 the union's presence in Californian ports, particularly San Francisco and Los Angeles, had been purely formal and viable collective bargaining had been confined to the Puget Sound ports, notably Tacoma. Following the 1934 longshore strike, strong local unions were re-established in the major Californian ports and agreements were concluded between these local unions and regional associations of employers based on Seattle, Portland, San Francisco and Los Angeles, putting into effect the terms of the arbitration award made by the National Longshoremen's Board which President Roosevelt had set up to end the strike. In 1936 the employer associations created a joint Coast Committee and negotiated a single coastwide longshore agreement which came into effect in February 1937. In June 1937 the Pacific Coast District of the ILA held a referendum on affiliation to the CIO. This was approved by a large majority and in August all but the four Puget Sound locals took out charters in the new International Longshoremen's and Warehousemen's Union. The remaining ILA locals, led by the Tacoma local, then called a convention in San Francisco to reconstitute the Pacific Coast District.[91]

The ILWU petitioned the Board to designate it as the representative of the entire coast, while the ILA called for a port-by-port vote, hoping at least to ensure the preservation of its traditional Tacoma base.[92] The ILA also challenged the ILWU's claim to "assume" administration of the coast wide agreement in place of the old Pacific Coast District,

89. "Transcript of Proceedings," in *RG 25*, Informal File C-245.
90. 7 NLRB 1002.   91. Ibid.
92. Ibid.; Lawrence Mallen, president of ILA Local 38–79 (San Francisco) to Board (10 February 1938), and Ray Calkins, secretary-treasurer of ILA Pacific Coast District to Frances Perkins (23 February 1938), both in *RG 25*, Informal File R-638, *Shipowners' Association of the Pacific Coast*.

arguing that the referendum which had brought the ILWU into existence could in no sense constitute legal authority to the ILA's Pacific Coast District leaders to dissolve the ILA and set up a new organization; nor could it affect either "the continuity of the ILA locals or the property rights of such locals, including the rights of ILA members to the benefits of the existing contract with the employers and the right (of the ILA locals) to administer the contract."[93] The Board's trial examiner, however, refused to take any notice of the ILA's arguments:

> Inasmuch as what is involved here from a practical standpoint is a determination of a representative or representatives of the longshoremen for the purpose of negotiating a renewal of the present agreement, rather than the adjudication of present technical rights thereunder, it would seem sufficient to recognize that, however it may have come into existence, the I.L.W.U. is now an established fact, and to confine the issue for the Board's decision to the question of whether it has been authorized to act as an employee agency for purposes of collective bargaining and in what unit or units it has been so authorized.[94]

The Board agreed, and on June 21, 1938 found the entire Pacific Coast to be the appropriate unit. It also simultaneously certified the ILWU as the representative, without bothering to order an election, on the basis of a card count which showed that the ILWU had the support of 9,557 of the 12,860 longshoremen in the unit.[95]

The AFL at once declared its intention to have the unit determination overthrown on the grounds that it disestablished the ILA in ports where it was incontrovertibly in the majority, and filed a petition with the District of Columbia Circuit Court of Appeals under Section 10(f) of the Wagner Act which allowed "a person aggrieved by a final order of the Board" to have the Board's order reviewed.[96] The Board, however, moved for dismissal of the petition by the court on the grounds that Board certifications were not final orders, backed by legal compulsion, but simply findings of fact. As such, it said, certifications were not open to review by the courts except in the course of a proceeding to enforce or review an unfair labor practice order made by the Board as a consequence of an employer's refusal to bargain with the certified representative.[97] Such unfair labor practice orders, of course, were final orders. Acknowledging that, so far as the petitioners were concerned, the Board order was indeed "definite, adversary, binding, final," that it

93. Trial Examiner's informal report (31 March 1938), in *RG 25*, Informal File R-638.
94. Ibid. 95. 7 NLRB 1002. 96. See *RG 25*, Informal File R-638.
97. "Reply Memorandum of Board in Support of Motion to Dismiss" (3 December 1938), in ibid.

"struck at the very roots of [their] union and destroyed its effectiveness," the court nevertheless agreed with the Board that under the terms of the act the union was legally estopped from seeking review of the certification on its own motion.[98]

This case also went to the Supreme Court. Here, as in the lower court, the Board claimed that the union was stopped from seeking review because Section 10 of the act allowed review only of final orders. It supplemented its argument, however, with the further contention that unions per se were in any case estopped because the "aggrieved persons" referred to in Section 10 were exclusively persons "alleged to have engaged in unfair labor practices," that is employers. In other words, only employers had the right to court review of Board decisions under the act.[99] In response, the AFL accused the Board of engaging in deliberate legalistic manipulation of the Wagner Act in order to deprive unions of any opportunity to challenge its authority to regulate their organizing and bargaining strategies:

> The Labor Board . . . although in no way minimizing the dire predicament in which appellants are placed by its action, coldly argues that no court exists to which appellants can turn for a determination as to whether the Board has exceeded its authority . . . The Board resorts to technical refinements of the language of the National Labor Relations Act in support of its position. For an administrative body to take such a stand unfortunately gives substance to the early criticism directed against the increasing power of administrative tribunals as dangerous innovation.[100]

If sustained, Padway argued, the Board's contention would mean that the only way a labor organization adversely affected by a Section 9 determination could obtain review would be by forcing the employer whose employees it claimed to represent to (a) reject the Board's bargaining unit decision and thus (b) subject himself to an unfair labor practice proceeding for refusing to bargain within the terms of the unit specified by the Board, (c) have the Board issue an order against himself and (d) refuse to comply with it, leading to (e) a court proceeding brought by the Board for enforcement of its order against him (or, alternatively, a proceeding brought by himself against the Board for review of the Board's order). At that point, and only at that point, would the union be allowed an opportunity to intervene in the court proceeding for enforcement or review in order to argue that the court should review the original bargaining unit decision.[101]

98.   *AFL et al. v. NLRB* (1939), 103 F2 933.   99.   See *RG* 25, Formal File R-638.
100.   "Brief for Appellants" (4 November 1939), in ibid.   101.   Ibid.

If, however, the Board was correct and review of bargaining unit decisions was not available to labor organizations acting on their own behalf, the AFL brief continued, then the Wagner Act itself should be held unconstitutional. It was unconstitutional because it allowed an administrative agency to exercise judicial powers – specifically the power of final determination over "private property rights."

Unions, Padway argued, were possessed of property rights, specifically "the right to engage in business as a labor organization." In the instant proceeding, and in others, the Board's determination of the appropriate bargaining unit had had an adverse effect upon the property rights being litigated. "Whereas in this case one of the contesting unions failed to obtain certification, that union in effect is 'put out of business.' There is no practical advantage to any working man to affiliate himself with a union that has not the legal right to represent him." The involvement of property rights questions in bargaining unit determinations was easily demonstrated. In this case, the ILA's loss of status as collective bargaining agent had meant "the disruption of membership, the loss of many thousands of dollars in organizational expenditures, strike and welfare benefits . . ." All this showed that far from being a simple acknowledgement of prevailing circumstances, or "finding of fact" as the Board claimed, a bargaining unit determination was in reality a substantive adjudication of private property rights. This was sufficient to distinguish bargaining unit determinations from "administrative determinations of matters of primary public concern or matters in which the state has a direct interest" and made it "an essential requirement of due process that a court of law ultimately pass on such determination."[102]

The confrontation in *Shipowners* between the AFL and the Board over the latter's refusal to allow unions to review its bargaining unit determinations is a prime example of the extreme tensions which emerged after *Jones and Laughlin* between the pre-Wagner system of private ordering and the new model of public disposition of representation rights which the Board was now attempting to implement. As such, it illustrates the fundamental divergence in the conceptions of trade unionism embraced by the Federation and the Board. Just as in *Consolidated Edison*, the AFL's position in *Shipowners'* was that unions were

---

102.   Ibid. The Supreme Court affirmed the decision of the District of Columbia Court of Appeals on 2 January 1940 (308 US 401). The court of appeals had hinted, however, that while the AFL might not, in its opinion, obtain review under the National Labor Relations Act, there was nothing to prevent review being obtained through an independent suit in equity begun in a district court. While pursuing its appeal in the original case before the Supreme Court, the AFL commenced a suit against the Board in March 1939.

"real" organizations which could not be uprooted by administrative fiat. They were principals which negotiated with employers to determine the terms and conditions under which labor would be supplied and which acquired vested interests in the contracts which resulted. The AFL accepted that passage of the Wagner Act had altered the situation by making it "a necessary and vital prerequisite or condition of the proper functioning of any labor organization seeking to represent employees for the purpose of collective bargaining"[103] that it obtain the Board's certification that the group of employees for whom it sought to bargain was an appropriate group. But, the AFL argued, as long as the union could show that it had the support of a majority of the group it had designated, it was "entitled" to be certified so that it might retain its property rights. "Refusal on the part of the [Board] to certify these plaintiffs unlawfully denies the said plaintiffs certain property rights, among which are the right to bargain with the employer . . . on behalf of employees as afore alleged, [and] the right to add strength to their organization . . ."[104]

The Board argued differently. In determining the appropriate unit, the Board was engaged in a purely empirical exercise, a "finding of fact," to which claims of prior rights or vested interest were not relevant. Under the Wagner Act, the status of the trade union was not that of a principal agreeing to supply labor on particular terms which had rights of its own in the contracts it negotiated, but an agent which appeared for the real principals – the workers in the bargaining unit – and which negotiated on their behalf to establish the conditions of their employment. As such, a

103. "Bill of Complaint" of the American Federation of Labor, plaintiff, in Civil Action 5517, *American Federation of Labor et al. v. J. Warren Madden et al.* (filed 20 January 1940 in the District Court of the District of Columbia), 6–7, in *RG 25*, Formal File R-638.

104. "Bill of Complaint" of the American Federation of Labor, plaintiff, in Civil Action 2214, *American Federation of Labor v. J. Warren Madden et al,* (filed 24 March 1939 in the District Court of the District of Columbia), 8, in *RG 25*, Formal File R-638. Civil Actions 2214 and 5517 were both suits in equity begun by the AFL and seeking to compel the Board to withdraw its certification of the ILWU. Hearings in Civil Action 2214 were delayed by mutual consent of the parties until after the Supreme Court's ruling on the decision of the District of Columbia Court of Appeals. Following that decision (308 U.S. 401), Civil Action 2214 was dismissed without prejudice on motion of the plaintiffs (22 January 1940), and 5517 immediately filed in its place with an amended bill of complaint. The Board moved to dismiss the action (21 March 1940), but was overruled by the court (3 June 1940). It then sought leave to appeal that ruling to the District of Columbia Court of Appeals. Leave was granted on 11 December 1940, but by this time the Board had begun reconsidering its original certification of the ILWU as a result of an ILA petition filed on 12 September 1940. Events in this second Board case led eventually to the abandonment of the AFL's suit (as noted in Chapter 6), and the Board's appeal against the district court's ruling was never heard.

union could have no legal right to a particular certification and therefore needed no avenues of redress if it were not granted the certification it sought. The Board's finding of fact was the only basis upon which assertions of union rights might be made, and then only by the union certified as the designated representative of the workers in the unit.

Notice that assertions of private right could not in any way vitiate the Board's authority to determine units and certify representatives was further given in July 1938 when the Board handed down its decision in the *Serrick Corporation* case.[105] In this case the United Auto Workers-CIO sought certification as the bargaining representative of all production and maintenance workers employed in two Muncie, Indiana plants which had just been acquired by the Serrick Corporation. Two AFL unions intervened to propose modifications in the petition, each seeking recognition in accordance with contracts which they had already negotiated with the company. These were the Metal Polishers, which sought recognition as the representative of buffers and polishers, and the International Association of Machinists, which sought recognition as the representative of workers in one plant's tool room.

The Board ruled in favor of the Metal Polishers' claim. The UAW did not contest the validity of the Metal Polishers' contract and in any case it did not admit buffers and polishers to membership. The Board refused, however, to allow the tool room workers organized by the IAM to form a separate unit. It held that because employees with minor supervisory duties were among the IAM members who had originally led the union's organizing drive, the IAM had been guilty of collusion with the employer at the time it concluded the closed shop contract. Hence, unlike the Metal Polishers' contract, the IAM's contract did not preclude a representation hearing.[106]

Having voided the IAM's contract, the Board moved to determine the unit. Significantly, it did not dispute the IAM's contention that the tool room workers represented a distinguishable group. But in this case the Board found that the conduct of the company in "favoring" the IAM had effectively disqualified the tool room employees from exercising the privilege of free choice. Moreover, the Board continued, the organizational structure and methods of the IAM were inherently inappropriate. "[F]or the purpose of the Act, and under the circumstances of the present case, the division of the respondent's employees by the IAM international into two locals for organizational purposes must be deemed artificial."[107]

To the AFL the decision was an unambiguous threat to union auton-

---

105. 8 NLRB 621.   106. Ibid., 635, 639.   107. Ibid., 643.

omy. General Counsel Padway advised the Executive Council that in characterizing the form of organization adopted by the IAM as inappropriate and artificial the *Serrick* decision had set a precedent "which could destroy American Federation of Labor unions."[108] Green later described the decision as "a clear attempt to shape the structural form of our unions . . . to take from national unions the right to determine for themselves and the members of those national unions to determine for themselves a plan of organization which best suits them." In 1935, he stated, he had agreed that the Board should be given the power to determine units only in cases where employees and unions could not determine the unit for themselves. "Neither I, nor anyone else, even contemplated that the power to decide the units carried with it the power to determine the form of organization that the trade union movement in this country must assume."[109]

So great was the AFL leadership's disaffection with the Board by this time that on 19 August immediately prior to a scheduled meeting of the Executive Council, Green visited President Roosevelt to seek his support for moves to amend the Wagner Act in ways which would secure the AFL's interests against further erosion.[110] At the subsequent Council meeting Padway presented recommendations that the Board's powers

108. AFL Executive Council *Minutes* (29 August 1938).
109. *Senate Hearings,* 654, 660. The AFL's criticism became particularly pungent after Board member Donald Wakefield Smith told the Senate Committee on Education and Labor that in his opinion the *Serrick* case was unimportant because it was the only one of its kind. "[It] is apparently not the 'usual practice' of the International Association of Machinists to organize the craft workers in one local and the production workers in another local in the same plant," he said. "[This] is, to my knowledge, the only case which has ever been presented to the Board in which such organizing technique was employed by any A.F. of L. affiliate, or, in fact, by any other labor organization." *Senate Hearings* 1211–2. AFL Director of Organization Frank Fenton quickly contradicted him:

> Take the electrical workers, for instance, they have the limitations, they have the men, they have separate local unions of line men, they have separate local unions of armature winders, and I could go on with the bricklayers, the stone setters, the masons, and so forth. That is the set-up of the American Federation of Labor and it has functioned under that set-up very satisfactorily for years. When we come before the Board these organizations are destroyed . . .

General Counsel Padway had earlier made the same point:

> Take the Molders . . . they have five different branches of classification; the Machinists have two; the electrical workers have two; and [the Board] will say that if the C.I.O. was organizing on a plantwide basis, you must revise your constitution and your rules . . .

See *Senate Hearings,* 1281, 908.
110. AFL Executive Council *Minutes* (22 August 1938). See also Gross, *The Reshaping of the National Labor Relations Board,* 61–2.

over units and over contract invalidation be restricted, that its Section 9 orders be made reviewable in court, and that modifications be introduced in Board structure and procedure to limit its administrative discretion.[111] Such amendments, the Council agreed, "would make the Act more specific respecting the powers of the Board, the manner in which the Act is to be administered and the time and circumstances under which elections are to be held." They were necessary because "the many general provisions now contained in the Act, with the vast discretionary powers vested in the Board, coupled with powers assumed unlawfully by the Board have not resulted in fair administration of the Act. If the fundamental guarantees to workers respecting organization, collective bargaining, mutual aid and protection, etc., are to be preserved to them, the Act cannot stand in its present form . . ."[112] Amendments embodying Padway's proposal were duly drawn up. On 25 January 1939 they were introduced by Senator David Walsh, joining a growing pile of bills for amendment of the Wagner Act.

By August 1938, therefore, the leadership of the AFL felt itself confronted with a developing threat of sufficient moment to warrant the wholesale alteration of the Wagner Act. In the months after *Jones and Laughlin* the Federation's leaders had seen their two basic principles – exclusive jursidiction and union-employer cooperation – vitiated in a series of decisions which held on the one hand that designation of the appropriate structure of labor representation in America was exclusively a public function, and on the other that unions were not principals and had no property rights of their own in their relationships with employers but instead simply existed to negotiate on behalf of

111.　AFL Executive Council *Minutes* (24 August 1938). The particular modifications discussed at this meeting were the separation of prosecuting and judicial functions; the use of judicial rules to govern the introduction of evidence; and the admissibility of employer petitions for elections in situations where two or more unions were making conflicting election claims.

112.　AFL Executive Council to Roosevelt, in AFL Executive Council *Minutes* (31 August 1938). The Council's letter was written in reply to a letter from Roosevelt dismissing the AFL's complaints against the administration of the Wagner Act and rejecting the Federation's demands that Board member Donald Wakefield Smith, then up for reappointment, be replaced (Smith's name was put forward by Roosevelt, but eventually withdrawn when it became clear that the Senate would oppose the nomination). The tone of Roosevelt's letter and of the Council's reply, made it clear that relations between the administration and the AFL had reached their lowest ebb. Roosevelt's letter, for example, asserted that the AFL's accusation that Smith was biased "means nothing, and as a mere expression of opinion does not accord with the opinion of thousands of people who know Mr Smith and have appeared before him in connection with his official duties." The Council, angered at Roosevelt's response, reaffirmed its opposition to the Board in general and Smith in particular.

employees.[113] When the AFL had supported the passage of the Wagner Act in 1935, Padway would later argue in defence of his amendments, it had not expected that this "legislation for the protection of labor's fundamental rights and imposing on employers the duty to recognize such rights," would require it to "[surrender] its philosophy of 'voluntarism,' its right to regulate and conduct its own internal affairs, and to maintain or change its form and structure as it deems wise and proper without governmental intrusion."[114] But instead of protecting the practices which had evolved over the previous thirty-odd years, the Board had denied their relevance and had established new rules which dictated to the unions what their organizing and collective bargaining strategies should be. It was attempting, the Executive Council told President Roosevelt, "to destroy many of our organizations by denying to them the right to be constituted an appropriate unit for collective bargaining in conformity with their historical structure." It was establishing "a principle which organized labor has opposed for over fifty years, namely dictating by governmental decree the form of organization a group of workers shall select."[115]

The defense of public authority

Hearings on all amendments to the Wagner Act, including the bill submitted by the AFL, were held by the House and Senate Labor Committees during April and May of 1939. During these hearings AFL leaders confirmed that their goal was to alter the administration of the Wagner Act so that it would do what, according to the AFL, it had originally been intended to do – legitimize the old private ordering system as expressed, historically, in union structure and union behavior. The Board, they argued, should be denied discretion to refuse skilled workers the opportunity to vote for separate representation, "not to prevent craft group employees, when they so decided, from joining with other workers, but . . . to make definite that the craft employees have a right to vote as a separate unit when they so decide . . . [W]e want to separate the right to select the representative and the right to be constituted as a unit."[116] The Board should be compelled to begin proceedings in

113. See Testimony of General Counsel Padway in *House Hearings*, 764–7, and in *Senate Hearings*, 837.
114. *Senate Hearings*, 710.
115. AFL Executive Council to Roosevelt, in AFL Executive Council *Minutes* (31 August 1938).
116. Testimony of Joseph A. Padway, *House Hearings*, 759.

both representation and complaint cases once they were requested, and unions should be guaranteed an opportunity to seek enforcement of the act in independent actions, because "These proceedings definitely involve the rights of unions and of workers. The idea of granting to the Board the power to say whether you shall have your day in court respecting your rights is not sound in labor relations cases."[117] The Board should be denied the power to intervene in jurisdiction disputes, for "the American Federation of Labor feels that it would be harmful to its affiliates to surrender to a government agency control over the internal affairs of its unions."[118] The Board should be required to respect non-closed shop contracts made by bona fide unions on behalf of minority groups of workers pending final determination of a majority representative, even where it found that the employer had been partial, because "unions have, throughout the years they have been in existence, built up their good will and secured union conditions for workers by representing minorities. In fact, it is the commonest method of educating an employer to deal with unions."[119] Finally, unions should have unrestricted rights to seek review of Board decision which affected their interests.

The most elaborate critique of the AFL's amendments came from the Board itself. By early 1939, the Board's perceptions of the relationship which should pertain between state authority and private power had developed to a point where it could see very little room for compromise with the Federation's attempts to remake the old system. Thus it spoke out against amendments making the holding of craft separation elections mandatory or otherwise adapting the Wagner Act to the fast fading principle of exclusive jurisdiction. Similarly, it refused to countenance amendments requiring the Board to respect private arrangements between unions and employers – such as minority contracts – which might dilute its own authority. It also opposed all attempts to limit the discretion of the Board in implementing the act by giving private parties more extensive rights of recourse or powers to seek enforcement of provisions of the act independent of the Board. "A single agency must have the sole power to decide what cases appear sufficiently important, meritorious and in the public interest to warrant proceedings."[120] If the act were amended to allow independent actions in the courts, the Board's "paramount administrative authority" would be weakened. It would become possible that "the fundamental questions of enforcement of the Act would in substantial measure rest with eleven Circuit Courts

117. Ibid., 781.   118. Ibid., 774.   119. Ibid., 753.
120. National Labor Relations Board, *Report to the House Committee on Labor*, 44, appended to *House Hearings*, 8.

of Appeals, proceeding hit or miss upon the prompting of hundreds of private individuals acting only in their own interest."[121] As General Counsel Fahy observed, "at least since the Interstate Commerce Commission was created in 1887, Congress has recognized that the accomplishment of the objectives of regulatory statutes operating in a restricted field for a public purpose cannot be left to the outcome of private litigation . . ."[122] To allow private parties to seek relief on their own motion would be, therefore, "wholly inconsistent with the nature of the act." The Wagner Act was one "to protect commerce from the consequences of industrial strife." It had nothing to do with private rights:

> [A]s has been clearly held by the courts, as is very clear from the act itself . . . proceedings under the act are for the protection and enforcement of public rights. The relief turns upon the proper way of remedying a violation of the public statute and of restoring conditions growing out of such violation. Relief to employees is thus merely incidental to the remedying of the public wrong.[123]

On similar grounds the Board was completely opposed to amendments granting unions the opportunity to seek court review of its unit determinations. The Board conceded that, as the AFL had argued in *Shipowners,* unions had no means of obtaining redress for injustices, real or imaginary, arising from its decisions. But in justification it repeated its own argument from that case: a Board certification was not an order backed by legal compulsion. Therefore, any injury to a labor organization resulted not from the Board's decision but from the employer's willingnesss to abide by that decision. Once an employer proved willing to bargain with a certified representative, the purposes of the act had been fulfilled. Those purposes would be frustrated if a union could obtain court review of the Board's decision simply on the grounds that it felt its campaign for certification had been defeated because of the nature of the unit decided upon. "The injury is of a type that frequently accrues to individuals from the actions of public officers in the administration of public statutes," the Board remarked. "[I]t arises

121. *Senate Hearings,* 347.   122. *House Hearings,* 545.
123. NLRB, *Report to the House Committee on Labor,* 70. See also *Agwilines, Inc. v. NLRB* (1936), 87 F2 146, where the Fifth Circuit Court of Appeals held that "The Act does not purport to confer, it does not confer, private rights . . . The prohibitions against interference by employers with self-organization of employees were not only unknown, they were obnoxious to the common law . . . [For this reason] the proceeding is not, it cannot be made a private one to enforce a private right. It is a public procedure, looking only to public ends." 150–1. See also *Amalgamated Utility Workers v. Consolidated Edison Company of New York, Inc., et al.* (1940), 309 U.S. 261.

from the Board's refusal to enforce the act in the manner which [the injured] organization desires. The issue is the same as if the Board refused to issue a complaint against an employer on a charge alleging that the employer had refused to bargain with the complaining labor organization."[124] To grant unions recourse in such matters would not advance the purposes which the legislation was designed to serve:

> In order to confer upon labor organizations the privilege of judicial review of Board certifications, collective bargaining is seriously hampered in any case where such review is sought. Conceding the advisability of such review, other factors being equal, we believe that the interest of labor organizations in the outcome of a representation proceeding . . . should yield to the superior interest of the public in the prevention of industrial strife.[125]

As to the unions' argument that the lack of power to review meant that their rights could be infringed with impunity, the Board's answer was simple. Unions, it said, had no inherent rights. So far as the legislation was concerned, their only recognizable status was that of instrumentalities – literally collective bargaining agents – which offered workers the opportunity to engage the expertise necessary to negotiate collective bargaining contracts, much as an employer might engage an accountant. Thus, unions could acquire rights, but only when they were chosen by the employees as representatives. Employees, in contrast, did have an inherent civil right to free association. Nevertheless, the Board argued, the freedom to exercise the right was a new freedom which was subject to the Board's oversight. Hence the right was effectively a new right, established by statute. "The Act is designed to promote the general public interest. In accomplishing its ends it imposes obligations upon certain individuals and *confers* rights upon others."[126]

Criticism of the AFL's amendments was not confined to the Board. Within the labor movement itself, the CIO was vociferously opposed to the Federation's attempts to alter the course of national labor policy. Far more significant than this, however, by early 1939 considerable opposition to the amendments had developed within the AFL leadership itself.

CIO opposition to the AFL's attacks on the NLRB is hardly surprising. Active in industries dominated by a few large corporations with considerable experience in frustrating unionism, the CIO's unions and

---

124. NLRB, *Report to the House Committee on Labor*, 42. See also its *Report to the Senate Committee on Education and Labor*, in *Senate Hearings*, 467–614, at 491.
125. NLRB, *Report to the House Committee on Labor*, 43.
126. NLRB, *Report to the Senate Committee on Education and Labor*, 587 [emphasis supplied].

organizing committees needed all the help they could get in overcoming employer opposition. As we have seen, CIO leaders had early realized the Wagner Act's significance and consistently made the Board a central element of their organizing strategies.[127] The CIO's new unions, further, were not encumbered by elaborate histories of private ordering. Consequently, no CIO witness ever found it necessary to complain that the Board was ignorant of the structure and theory of American trade unionism or that unions had been deprived of their inherent rights. Indeed, on the few occasions when the CIO did criticize the Board it was for its undue deference to such expressions of vested AFL interest.

CIO opposition to the AFL's attacks on the Board was also symptomatic of the general willingness of its leadership to entertain a far greater degree of state intervention in labor relations than was acceptable to the AFL.[128] While representatives of the Federation might argue that "there never was, nor will there ever be, a time that labor organizations will not prefer to settle their disputes and differences by direct negotiations with the employer without resorting to outside agencies,"[129] witnesses from the CIO appeared much readier to trust to the efficacy of government regulation. Thus, Philip Murray could tell the Senate Committee "I just happen to be a fellow representing some steelworkers and would rather leave this problem [of labor relations] in your lap believing that after all that is where it has to be solved."[130] By passing the Wagner Act, Murray told the Committee, Congress had enabled "the administrative forces of the Federal Gov-

127. Indeed, in September 1938 CIO General Counsel Lee Pressman warned that CIO overdependence on the Board was having a negative effect on its organizing activities:

> The number of cases filed with the Board has increased in recent months to the point where the wisdom of resorting to the Act is often questionable because of the length of time which is required for decisions. Unless excellent judgment is exercised in this connection, there is danger that organizing work may be seriously impeded by placing too much reliance upon the Board. All officers and organizers must understand that primary reliance must not be placed upon the Board for organizing work, and that the Board is to be used as an auxiliary weapon only.

Lee Pressman to all CIO Regional Directors, Industrial Union Councils, and Local Industrial Unions (20 September 1938), in *RG 25,* Smith Committee Miscellaneous Box 1.

128. On this point see Stanley H. Vittoz, "The American Industrial Economy and the Political Origins of Federal Labor Policy Between the World Wars" (unpublished Ph.D. dissertation, York University, Canada, 1979). See also Steve Fraser, "Dress Rehearsal for the New Deal: Shop-Floor Insurgents, Political Elites, and Industrial Democracy in the Amalgamated Clothing Workers," in Michael H. Frisch and Daniel J. Walkowitz, *Working-Class America: Essays on Labor, Community and American Society* (Urbana, Illinois, 1983), 212–55; Nelson N. Lichtenstein, *Labor's War at Home: The CIO in World War Two* (Cambridge, England, 1982).

129. Testimony of Joseph A. Padway, *Senate Hearings,* 713.

130. *Senate Hearings,* 4712.

ernment" to extend their authority to encompass the creation within industry of "the most satisfactory collective bargaining arrangements" possible, "the kind of labor relationships that were most adaptable to the methods of industry . . . [and] that would reduce to the minimum the possibility of industrial disturbances during the course of those relationships."[131] In this vein, Murray approvingly repeated Walter Lippmann's dictum to the effect that the road to peace in industry lay through unions "which acquire and are compelled to acknowledge the responsibilities that go with power," while Sidney Hillman emphasized that the government's task was now to see to it that unions and employers "do not abuse their power of organization against the interest of the public at large."[132]

That the CIO should oppose their campaigns against state intervention in labor relations made little difference to AFL leaders. To them, after all, the CIO was largely the creation of the NLRB and completely dependent on continued governmental support for its survival; it was an example of "union development under government patronage."[133] Opposition within the Federation, however, was a very different matter. Unless quickly eliminated it would indicate to outside observers that the AFL's official line might be unrepresentative of the Federation as a whole, discrediting both the line and its spokesmen.

As the AFL leadership's criticism of the NLRB had become less and less restrained during 1938, both individual local unions and state federations of labor had expressed a growing concern that the Federation's hostility toward the Board might provide employer groups and Congressional conservatives with opportunities to do considerable damage to the Wagner Act itself.[134] The Federation's central executive ignored this grass-roots concern, and in November it pushed the AFL's Houston convention into endorsing its plans for amendments along the lines of the program which Padway had presented to the Executive Council the pre-

---

131. Ibid., 4732.
132. Ibid., 4643–4, 3795. See also Ronald Radosh, "The Corporate Ideology of American Labor Leaders From Gompers to Hillman," *Studies on the Left*, 6, 6 (1966).
133. William Green, "Editorial," in the *American Federationist*, 45 (September 1938), 802. See also Elwyn Eagen and Grant L. Patterson to Nathan Witt (29 July 1938), "Report on the Portland Lumber Mills Dispute," in *RG 25*, Smith Committee Box 16, ("Seattle Office"). In their report, Eagen and Patterson underlined the contempt of the Portland locals of the United Brotherhood of Carpenters and Joiners for the rival International Woodworkers of America-CIO as "a 'ward of the N.L.R.B.' [which] would long since have expired had it not been for the maternal protection extended to it by the Board," and as an organization which "does not stand on its own feet and fight its own battles and is not capable of doing so and does not function as a union."
134. See, for example, AFL Executive Council *Minutes* (22 April 1937; 3 May 1938); Gross, *The Reshaping of the National Labor Relations Board*, 63–4.

vious August. These amendments concentrated upon safeguarding craft units and unions' contractual rights, and also called for the imposition on the Board of a statutory timetable for the hearing and decision of cases. In addition, the Houston convention was persuaded to endorse a Resolutions Committee motion "recommending" that the Executive Council consider formulating amendments which would embody two further elements of the Padway program: review of Section 9 determinations and separation of the Board's judicial and investigatory functions.[135]

The Federation could not, however, shrug off the serious opposition which emerged after Walsh introduced its amendments in the Senate in January 1939, for unlike the previous year's outbreaks these divisions were in the upper echelons of the leadership itself. Discontent was focussed on two immediate issues. First, the Walsh bill had been introduced in the Senate without being referred to the Executive Council for its final approval. Second, its provisions extended far beyond those approved at Houston. Not only did the bill include the provision covering court review of bargaining unit determinations which, after it had been referred back at Houston, was not further considered by the Council, it also proposed new amendments never raised at Houston at all. These would enable employers to encourage membership in a bona fide labor union with impunity, allow them to petition for representation elections when faced with competing demands for recognition from rival unions, and narrow the statutory definition of company unions so as to permit greater collusion between unions and employers without rendering them subject to statutory restraint.[136]

The AFL's bill had been prepared by officials of the Federation's central bureaucracy – specifically by its general counsel, Padway, in consultation with a committee consisting of President Green and representatives of the Building Trades, Metal Trades, and Union Label Trades Departments – and was based on the recommendations laid before the Executive Council by Padway at its August meeting in Atlantic City. By February 1939, however, some prominent Council members were no longer willing to go along with the central bureaucracy's vendetta against the New Deal collective bargaining policy. Nor were they prepared any longer to watch the central bureaucracy use the controversies over the Board and the CIO to add further to its powers at the expense of the affiliates.[137] Consequently, at the February meeting of the Council in Miami, Council members sharply protested Green's attempt to by-

135. Gross, *The Reshaping of the National Labor Relations Board*, 64–6.
136. Ibid., 94–95.
137. Note, for example, the attempts to establish central authority over union jurisdictions. See AFL Executive Council *Minutes* (9 August 1939).

pass the Council by having the amendments introduced without further consulting the affiliates.[138] Green agreed to submit the amendments to the affiliates for discussion.[139] Several unions then indicated their opposition to anything more than the amendments protecting craft units and union contracts agreed at the Houston convention.[140]

Prominent amongst these dissenters was the International Association of Machinists, a development which represented a change of stance of considerable importance for that organization. In August 1938, after all, the IAM's president, A.O. Wharton, had effectively endorsed Padway's program by joining with the rest of the Executive Council in condemning the Board's administration of the act and in calling for amendments.[141] Moreover, of the cases to which the AFL's leaders repeatedly referred to substantiate their contentions that amendments were justified, several – including the traumatic *Serrick* decision – directly involved the IAM. That the union should now publicly oppose the AFL's bill was a considerable blow to the plans and the prestige of the central bureaucracy.

The IAM's position was clearly predicated upon two considerations. First, notwithstanding the severe implications which the Wagner Act and its administration had been shown to hold for traditional union practices the legislation offered material advantages to labor unions of far greater degree; these would be needlessly endangered if amendments were pressed at a time when the New Deal was already in retreat before a new and hostile Congress. Second, in pressing its amendments in the name of the Federation the central bureaucracy had taken upon itself authority it should not have. Pointing to the more than one thousand cases the IAM had filed with the Board in the previous three years, Wharton stressed that of the eighty or so which had required formal decision by the Board, "the preponderant majority has been of distinct advantage to us." Because it had made such abundant use of the services of the Board, Wharton continued, the IAM had examined the AFL's amendments very carefully in consultation with other AFL organizations which had frequent resort to the Board to discover what effects they might have on union activity. This examination had confirmed the IAM's original suspicions that to call for amendments at this time would be extremely damaging to the interest of all unions, and

---

138. William M. Leiserson to Selig Perlman (21 February 1939), in *Leiserson Papers* Box 33, ("Perlman").
139. Leiserson to Louis Stark (10 February 1939), in *Leiserson Papers*, Box 38, ("Stark"); Joseph Padway, Memorandum to all affiliates (15 February 1939), in *Leiserson Papers*, Box 56, ("Trade Union Correspondence").
140. Gross, *The Reshaping of the National Labor Relations Board*, 96–8.
141. AFL Executive Council *Minutes* (31 August 1938).

that in formulating the amendments now before the Senate the central bureaucracy had far exceeded the authority vested in it by the Houston convention. "We believe that the amendments modifying the substantive provisions of the Act, defining the rights of the employees and the unfair labor practices of employers, and the amendments widening the powers of the courts are dangerous and not in keeping with the spirit of the resolution of the Houston convention to strengthen the National Labor Relations Act by ensuring fairer administration."[142] Nothing in the Houston resolution implied that any change in provisions defining employee rights or unfair employer practices was necessary, nor had it said anything about expanding the authority of the courts. No such changes were necessary to secure the points which the resolution *had* covered.

The IAM singled out for particular attention those amendments which modified the act's strictures against employer-dominated unions and employer interference with employee organization. "In fifteen cases where we succeeded in securing the disestablishment of company unions," the IAM reported, "the only evidence we could produce to prove our charge of company domination was evidence of the participation of straw bosses in these unions and remarks of favoritism by the employer and other acts of interference and non-financial support. All of the conduct upon which we relied to secure the disestablishment of these company unions, each one of which would block our efforts to organize and bargain collectively, would be legitimate conduct under the A. F. of L. amendments as a result of the deletion from the National Labor Relations Act of the word 'interference' and the word 'encouragement', together with the added liberty granted in the A. F. of L. bill to the employer and his agents, including foremen and straw bosses, to make statements of preference." In a further twenty-three cases, charges of discriminatory discharge had been sustained only because the union had been able to use evidence of anti-union statements by straw bosses and other subordinate officials of the company. Under the AFL bill, those officials "would have the liberty to make such statements without making the employer responsible."

The IAM also objected to the bill's advocacy of a wider role for the courts in review of Board decisions. Recent decisions, it argued, showed that the courts wished to restrict labor's rights under the act and simultaneously expand their own powers over the administrative functioning of the Board. Decisions in respect to the evidence upon which the Board relied to sustain its findings, in particular, showed the courts beginning

142. Arthur O. Wharton to William Green (13 April 1939), in *Leiserson Papers*, Box 56, ("Trade Union Correspondence").

to substitute their own evaluations for those of the Board and arrogating to themselves "the real fact finding powers." If this process continued, and the AFL bill could only encourage it, the courts would eventually take complete control of the evaluation of the evidence upon which the Board's findings were based and thus substitute their opinions for the opinions of the Board. Every case tried before the Board would have to be retried in court, placing unions under tremendous pressure to assign lawyers to cases tried before the Board "since our representatives would themselves not be able to carry the case through to the courts."[143]

Although the only explicit reasons the IAM offered for its critique of the amendments were on the one hand its pragmatic assessment of the relative advantages accruing to the unions under the act as it presently stood, plus on the other hand its antipathy toward the central bureaucracy for asserting powers which it did not have, the terms in which it expressed its opinions indicated a more basic reason. The IAM, it appeared, no longer completely shared the *gesellschaft* ideology of union-employer cooperation and exclusive jurisdiction which motivated the group responsible for drafting the amendments.[144] Where that group continued to stress the need to adapt the act to accommodate the meeting of union with employer as a meeting of principals in which the union's business was to "sell" unionism to the employer on terms acceptable to both, the IAM seemed now to see itself much more in the terms of the Wagner Act – as an organization selected by employees in an exercise of *their* civil rights for the purpose of conducting bargaining on *their* behalf. Certainly these were the terms which the union adopted when criticizing the AFL amendments' relaxation of the act's strictures against employer interference with the choice of employee representatives:

> Just as it would be considered unfair for one business man to have any say in the choice of the lawyer of a rival business man for the purpose of negotiating a contract which would define the rights of each, it is unfair for the employer to interfere with the organization

143. Ibid.
144. See Gross, *The Reshaping of the National Labor Relations Board*, 99, on the ideology of the AFL bureaucracy. Mark Perlman has written of the IAM that it was fundamentally altered in orientation by the thrust of federal policy in the years after 1936. "... the shift was made necessary not only because the CIO was organizing the mass production industries, but also because the NLRB assumed the responsibility and right to determine bargaining units. It was not so much the enthusiasm of CIO organizers ... that rang the death-knell of old-style unionism, as it was the active sponsorship of the right to organize (if necessary by the intervention of the federal government, with the entry of the NLRB into the jurisdiction-granting business)." See his *The Machinists: A New Study in American Trade Unionism* (Cambridge, 1961), 92.

of the workers for the purpose of selecting a common representative who is to negotiate an agreement defining the rights of employees.[145]

The IAM's position in early 1939 was typical of the AFL's leading affiliates. After three years of turmoil, most unions had accommodated themselves to public ordering of the structure of labor representation by the NLRB. They had realized either from the start (as in the case of the CIO) or belatedly (as in the case of most AFL affiliates) that public ordering offered them tangible advantages in their disputes with employers with which the abstract freedoms and rights enshrined in voluntarism could not compare. In this situation, the longer the AFL's central leadership continued to fight against the fact of public ordering the more likely it was to achieve nothing more than its own isolation within the labor movement.[146] Plainly, by 1939, a rough consensus against fundamental alterations to the Wagner Act existed among American unions.

A rough consensus on acceptance of public ordering did not, however, mean a consensus in support of the current administration of the act. The members of the Board, as distinct from the institution itself, remained overwhelmingly unpopular within the AFL. This fact alone muted the affiliates' criticism of the central bureaucracy and enabled the opponents of state intervention within the Federation to continue their campaigns against the Board.[147] As Louis Stark, *New York Times* labor columnist, reported to William Leiserson from the February meeting of the Executive Council in Miami, "Tracy of the Electrical Workers assures me that delays in election cases and complaint cases are simply awful, six months to two years and he cannot find out what is going on . . . From other sources I hear of the cavalier attitude of employees . . . of the laxity of people on the staff. George [Harrison, president of the Railway Clerks] thought that the whole Board would have to be changed."[148] Leiserson in turn passed on to Selig Perlman the news that the Executive Council had endorsed Harrison's proposal that the present Board be dismissed and a new one appointed. "The idea is that the main trouble lies in rotten administration of the Wagner Act and not in the provisions of the Act itself," Leiserson wrote. Significantly, he added that "my own sympathy lies in this direction."[149]

145. Wharton to Green (April 13, 1939), in *Leiserson Papers*, Box 56, ("Trade Union Correspondence").
146. Gross, *The Reshaping of the National Labor Relations Board*, 97–9.
147. Ibid., 76–7, 99–100.
148. Stark to Leiserson (6 February 1939), in *Leiserson Papers*, Box 38, ("Stark").
149. Leiserson to Perlman (21 February 1939), in *Leiserson Papers*, Box 33, ("Perlman").

Leiserson's opinion was of considerable importance, for within three months he was to become the central actor in the next phase of development of the New Deal's collective bargaining policy. In April 1939, after months of AFL pressure, the Roosevelt administration agreed to alter the Board's personnel. Plans to reappoint retiring member Donald Wakefield Smith were abandoned and Roosevelt asked a reluctant Leiserson to leave the National Mediation Board and fill the vacancy. "The President asked me 'shall I get down on my knees or shall I bludgeon you to go over to the NLRB?" Leiserson later recounted. "I answered 'you are the Commander-in-Chief. I have enlisted for the war, and wherever you want to place me I'll go.' "[150]

Conclusion

The AFL leadership's attack upon the National Labor Relations Board was based upon its presumption that unions occupied a space beyond the reach of the New Deal's administrative state. As such it was the final flourish of a decaying voluntarist ideology, a world-view rapidly being abandoned by all save a handful of Federation bureaucrats. By 1939 the new world of trade union legality seemed far more attractive to most AFL unions than the metaphysics which was all that their central executive could offer. Increasingly dogmatic and beleaguered, unpopular with its own members and reviled by the CIO, the AFL leadership could sustain its position only through a more and more explicit alliance with the elements outside the labor movement – the congressional conservatives and employer groups – who were attacking the Wagner Act itself.[151]

Participation in the new world of trade union legality, however, did not mean an end to disputes over Board policy. Although by 1939 the established unions were becoming reconciled, more or less, to exchanging their old property-based claims of union rights for a new legitimacy as organizational expressions of the civil rights of employees, they still sought the entrenched institutional security which the old ideology of union-employer cooperation and exclusive jurisdiction had purported to guarantee. Indeed, having been brought within the regulatory ambit of the administrative state, their desire that this security be publicly underwritten was all the greater. Yet the Board had been reluctant to acknowledge union claims for security under the new regime. Committed

---

150. Leiserson to John R. Commons (11 May 1939), in *Leiserson Papers*, Box 9, ("Commons").
151. Gross, *The Reshaping of the National Labor Relations Board*, 200–25.

to a conception of the act as the protector of individual civil rights, the Board tended to treat attempts by unions to entrench themselves in bargaining relationships as encroachments upon the self-activity of workers.

Leiserson's appointment precipitated a new struggle precisely around this point for Leiserson was, of course, identified with an established tradition in labor relations which afforded the institutionalization of unions a much higher priority in its approach to collective bargaining than that so far exhibited by the Board. This set the stage for a confrontation *within* the Board over the role of collective organization in New Deal policy and its relationship to public authority.

6

Utopians and technocrats

"... [T]he contract undoubtedly is the focal point of our labor law."

John H. Fanning, "The Changing Pattern of Issues in Labor
Relations Cases before the Board," *George Washington Law Review*,
29, 2 (1960), 273.

The conflict between the National Labor Relations Board and the American Federation of Labor which matured in the months after August 1938 was but one element in a general crisis threatening to engulf the agency. Externally, the Board had become the subject of massive and growing pressure not only from the AFL but also from the CIO, from employers and from Congressional conservatives; in the heightened economic and political uncertainty arising from the Roosevelt recession of late 1937 and from the growing threat of war in Europe, all sought to acquire greater influence over its administration of the Wagner Act. Simultaneously, the Board was experiencing considerable internal turmoil and the breakdown of administrative procedures. During 1939, these internal and external crises merged, resulting in the development of open struggles within the Board over the future course of labor relations in the United States.

To a degree, the NLRB's crisis might most appropriately be perceived as a predictable phase in its development as an administrative agency. Some years ago, Marver Bernstein suggested that almost all newly established regulatory agencies find themselves forced to retreat from initially broad-ranging and innovative approaches to the implementation of regulatory legislation by the antagonism of special interest groups and by the breakdown of undeveloped and untested policies, and end up adopting a more cautious and circumspect approach to the problem of regulation.[1] Indeed, precisely this sort of "life-cycle" theory of the regulatory process is suggested by the conclusions of the most recent historian of federal labor relations policy, James A. Gross, who describes the NLRB as an

1. Marver H. Bernstein, *Regulating Business by Independent Commission* (Princeton, 1955).

agency transformed by external pressures from "an expert administrative agency which played the major role in formulation of labor policy" before 1940 into a "conservative, insecure, politically sensitive agency preoccupied with its own survival" thereafter.[2]

In attributing most significant changes in administrative policy to factors external to an agency, however, one runs the risk of underestimating the impact of disagreements among, or choices made by, the regulators themselves.[3] In the case of the New Deal collective bargaining policy, disputes within the discourse of industrial relations were highly significant in determining the precise direction in which the NLRB would take the Wagner Act after 1940.

The appointment of William Leiserson to the NLRB in April 1939 is of particular importance in this regard. As Gross points out, Roosevelt appointed Leiserson "to weaken the demands for amendment to the Wagner Act and to reduce the adverse political pressure on himself and on his administration."[4] But Leiserson was not simply an administration hatchet-man sent in to clean up the Board. Already a key figure in the definition of transportation labor policy, Leiserson had also been a central participant for twenty years in the development of the theory and practice of labor relations in America. As we shall see, such changes in the Board's stance as can be dated from Leiserson's arrival owed as much to his application of theories to which he had long subscribed as to the immediate pressures which occasioned his appointment.

What alterations in the Board's practices can we point to emanating from its attempts to resolve the 1939–40 crisis? According to another recent commentator, Howell Harris, there were none of any importance. Federal labor relations policy "was unchanged in all essentials" when the war came.[5] But a close inspection shows a significant weakening in the Board's commitment to the centrality of public ordering in policy formation and a growing willingness to allow the desires and actions of the organized parties in the field greater influence over its strategy. Inspection also reveals a growing willingness to entrench es-

2. James A. Gross, *The Reshaping of the National Labor Relations Board: National Labor Policy in Transition, 1937–47* (Albany, New York, 1981), 267.
3. Ibid., 261–62. For a critique of this approach, see James Q. Wilson, "The Dead Hand of Regulation," *Public Interest*, (Fall 1971), and "The Politics of Regulation," in James W. McKie, editor, *Social Responsibility and the Business Predicament* (Washington D.C., 1974).
4. Gross, *The Reshaping of the National Labor Relations Board*, 89.
5. Howell John Harris, *The Right to Manage: Industrial Relations Policies of American Business in the 1940s* (Madison, Wisconsin, 1982), 106. Contradicting Gross, Harris states that "The opposition of the business community and of its peak associations, the [National Association of Manufacturers] in particular, to the Wagner Act and the NLRB from 1935 to 1941 was largely ineffective."

tablished collective bargaining relationships, and simultaneously to entertain reductions in the opportunities granted workers to exercise the rights guaranteed them by the act. In practical terms, these changes constituted important steps toward the accommodation of the Wagner Act's statutory innovations to the common law regulation of collective organization and bargaining which had prevailed prior to its passage, steps which were to culminate in the establishment of the ideology of industrial pluralism – together with its most important expression, the constitutive contract – at the center of liberal labor relations law.

Particularly so far as the role of unions is concerned, these revisions add up to a significant change of emphasis in the administration of the New Deal collective bargaining policy. As we have seen, the Board's main objective in its early years had been fulfilment of the act's policy of self-organization and freedom of choice amongst workers, stressing in the process the authority of the administrative state to curb the activities of those unions which asserted a right to indulge in autonomous bilateral activity outside its reach. By 1939, however, policymakers were exhibiting growing concern at the institutional weakness of the organized labor movement, particularly the unions' apparent inability to control autonomous *rank and file* activity. The result was a renewed emphasis on the role which firmly established unions could play as sources of stability and order in labor relations, and a growing tendency to enlarge their role at the expense of the workers.

The advent of the pluralists

By mid-1939, the National Labor Relations Board was deeply embroiled in major conflicts in both its external political and its internal operational realms of activity. The former, as we have seen, was in large part a product of the Board's refusal to tailor its administration of the Wagner Act to vested interests on either side of industry. The following year would see it reach a climax in a series of increasingly strident attempts mounted by disaffected AFL hierarchs, employer spokesmen and Congressional conservatives to transform the root and branch of national labor relations policy through legislative action against the Wagner Act and against the NLRB's appropriations.[6] These external pressures, however, were unsuccessful in achieving concrete alterations in the act, although they did bring about some piecemeal changes in the

---

6. For a detailed description of this campaign against the Board, see Gross, *The Reshaping of the National Labor Relations Board*, 151–225.

Board's approach.[7] It was the internal battles accompanying the second, operational, crisis which were to prove decisive in the fight over the direction of national policy.

The origins of the Board's operational crisis can be found in the rapid growth in the volume of cases filed with the Board following the validation of the Wagner Act in April 1937. By June 1938, over ten thousand new complaint and representation petitions had been received.[8] As a result, there had accrued a backlog of 700,000 pages of unanalyzed complaint case transcript in the Board's Review Division.[9] The situation was no better with respect to representation cases, for although there was no backlog of unanalyzed record in this category, the Board's policy of, in many instances, consolidating complaint and representation cases involving employees of the same employer meant that processing of the representation petition often could not be completed until after the unfair labor practice decision was handed down – often many months or even years after the event.[10]

The rapid expansion of the case load had, of course, necessitated a substantial increase in personnel. In June 1937, the Board had employed 131 staff in its Washington office, of whom only 11 were review attorneys, and 144 in the field. By June 1938, the figures were 332 in Washington, 64 of them review attorneys, and 386 in the field. A year later, 543 persons were employed in the Washington office, 98 of them

7. In June and July 1939, the Board instituted a number of changes which (1) allowed employers to initiate representation proceedings when confronted with conflicting representation claims from rival unions; (2) increased the minimum waiting period between issue of complaint and hearing date from five to ten days; (3) provided that labor organizations with contracts affected by Board proceedings should be made parties to such proceedings in every instance; (4) enlarged the right of unions to appeal against dismissal of charges by regional directors; (5) reserved to the Board the function of designating trial examiners, rather than, as formerly, leaving that task to the regional director. See *RG 25*, Smith Committee Box 21, ("Board Minutes"), (20 June 1939); AFL Executive Council, *Report to the 59th Annual Convention of the American Federation of Labor* (2 October 1939), in *RG 25*, Smith Committee Box 14, ("Report of the AFL Executive Council"). The major structural change came a year later with the elimination of the Board's Economic Research Division as a result of pressure from the Smith Committee. See Gross *The Reshaping of the National Labor Relations Board*, 220–2.
8. Harry A. Millis and Emily Clark Brown, *From the Wagner Act to Taft-Hartley: A Study of National Labor Policy and Labor Relations* (Chicago, 1950), 77; James A. Gross, *The Making of the National Labor Relations Board: A Study in Economics, Politics and the Law* (Albany, New York, 1974), 237–8.
9. Legal Survey Committee to Charles Fahy, "Procedural Report" (7 November 1939), in *RG 25*, Smith Committee Box 25, ("Review Section").
10. Thomas I. Emerson to Charles Fahy (19 February 1940), in *RG 25*, Smith Committee Box 19, ("Attorney-General's Committee on Administrative Procedure"). See also Witt to all Regional Directors, "Consolidation of C and R Cases" (20 November 1939), in *RG 25*, Smith Committee Subject Files Box 9, ("Witt–Miscellaneous").

review attorneys, and 403 in the field.[11] But this expansion occurred without any substantial alteration in the Board's organization, structure, or case-handling methods. Designed to facilitate the Board's original litigation-based strategy, these had centralized authority over all significant policy and procedural matters in Washington, and relied on the Board's secretary to coordinate regional and central case-handling. Not surprisingly, by early 1939 the capacity of the unreformed secretary's office to manage case flow had become exhausted.

In its efforts to cope, the secretary's office was led into an increasingly anomalous position vis-à-vis the regions. On the one hand, the secretary, Nathan Witt, pressed the regional offices to cut down on the number of cases being advanced to formal hearing. In "strictest confidence," lest employers found out and began calculatedly flouting the act, Witt told the regional directors that their "most important task by far" was to "avoid the necessity of formal hearings."[12] To this end, "small and unimportant" cases should be adjusted informally, and if this proved impossible pressure should be applied to the petitioner to withdraw the charge. Failing that, the charge should simply be dismissed.[13] Witt, however, offered no advice as to how informal adjustments were to be attempted without involving the regional offices in mediation activities which went beyond the ambit of the statute.[14] Nor did he offer any administrative criteria outlining a clear demarcation of responsibility between the central and regional offices to facilitate the drawing of distinctions between cases to be settled informally and those to be referred for formal proceeding. Instead he circulated the regions with a few unsystematic and impressionistic ideas. For example, Witt advised the regions to concentrate on cases involving large employers, without defining what he meant by "large,"[15] but almost in the same

11. *RG 25*, Smith Committee Box 27, ("Tables and Drafts").
12. Memorandum, Witt to all Regional Directors (8 August 1938), in *RG 25*, Smith Committee Subject Files Box 9, ("Witt–Miscellaneous").
13. Ibid.
14. Ibid. Indeed, two months later Witt and Associate General Counsel Robert Watts circulated another memorandum which imposed a fairly restrictive set of requirements upon all cases going to informal settlement. Settlements achieved prior to the issuance of a complaint had to be in harmony with the act, and withdrawal of the charge had to be conditional upon express performance. Settlements achieved after issue of a complaint had been authorized but while issue was still pending had to be approved by the secretary's office. Settlements achieved after a complaint had been issued had to be approved by the Board. See Witt and Watts to all Regional Directors and Regional Attorneys (13 October 1938), in *RG 25*, Smith Committee Subject Files Box 9, ("Witt–General Exhibits").
15. Witt to all Regional Directors (8 August 1938). Precision was important here if the size of respondent was to be used as a guide in reducing the volume of cases, because, as a 1940 Economic Research Division study showed, most of the Board's

breath added that a case "may involve an employer with relatively few employees and yet be a key case because it is the only non-unionized firm in the industry or because the firm is flouting the law to an extent that its influence is felt throughout the geographic area."[16] Witt also advised, without further elaboration, against the acceptance of "novel" cases which involved further expansion of the Board's jurisdiction or new interpretations of the act.[17]

Witt's ad hoc attempts to solve the case-handling crisis placed the regional directors in an impossible position in their relations with the Board. By making undefined categories of "key" and "novel" cases into administrative sorting devices, Witt placed all the onus for realizing the Board's new policy upon the directors' shoulders while simultaneously jealously guarding an administrative structure in which all significant decisions had to be made by or cleared by the Board's Washington office. The regional directors were also placed in an impossible position vis-à-vis local clients and their own staffs. Good public relations and smooth performance of the Board's overall task required that its regional officers maintain cordial relations with local employers and the local labor movement by processing their petitions with the minimum of arbitrariness and controversy. Yet the Board was now instructing them to put into effect highly selective case-handling policies with nothing but the, at best undeveloped, criteria of the secretary for guidance, and for reasons which they could not divulge even to members of their own staff.[18] While Witt justified his demands, and his growing penchant for secrecy, with dramatic invocations of high policy – as he put it, "we have won battle after battle but the Board feels that the major engagement being fought during this period is no less important than those that have gone before, and indeed may be more vital. If we are to succeed in establishing the great purpose of the Act on a firm basis all of us must work closely and loyally along the lines set forth above"[19] – the regional directors found themselves faced with more and more serious problems of practical administration. Nor were they endeared to a secretary who advised them to use their discretion in dismissing all but the strongest petitions, while simultaneously dispatching special admin-

business came from "large" (that is, firms with larger-than-average asset bases) corporations. Nearly 50 percent of Board cases, for example, came from the 2.3 percent of U.S. corporations with assets valued over one million dollars. See NLRB Division of Economic Research, "Assets of Respondents in Unfair Labor Practice Cases Handled by the NLRB" (25 January 1940), in *RG 25*, Smith Committee Box 25, ("Excerpts from Speeches and Articles"). See also NLRB Division of Economic Research, "The 107 Largest Industrial Corporations and the NLRB" (27 January 1940), in same.

16.   Witt to all Regional Directors.   17.   Ibid.   18.   Ibid.   19.   Ibid.

istrative examiners to investigate union and junior staff complaints that regional directors were discriminating against their cases.[20]

The growing acrimony in the relations between the secretary's office and the regions resulted in two internal investigations of the Board's administrative structure. Both were held in the latter part of 1939, the first by Chief Trial Examiner George Pratt and senior attorney Gerhard Van Arkel and the second by a special committee of regional directors.[21] Each found excessive centralization of administrative functions in the secretary's office and an absence of informed liaison with the regions. Each recommended that the responsibilities of the secretary's office be defined much more narrowly, that its functions be limited to routine administration of the Washington office, and that a new Board division be created to coordinate and supervise regional operations. Both reports also recommended the removal from the secretary of responsibility for the administration of personnel policy and the appointment of a personnel director. Despite the convergence of findings, however, little action was taken by the Board to implement the recommendations arising from the investigations. Consequently the Board's operational crisis continued.[22]

Two factors inhibited resolution of the Board's internal crisis. First, political manoeuvring within the Board inhibited structural change. By early 1939 the politics of the Washington office had become highly factionalized. Secretary Witt was one of the more prominent members of a communist grouping with which Board member Edwin Smith was also identified. Naturally, Smith and Witt cooperated in vociferous opposition to any attempt to undermine the strategic position of the secretary in the Board's structure.[23] Second, and more important, the Board's reluctance to modify its structure underlined its continued commitment to the strategy of administering labor relations policy through formalized assertions of public authority, the strategy which had dictated the creation of its centralized structure in the first place. Advocacy of structural changes to solve the Board's operational crisis thus implied far more than simply the downgrading or dismissal of particular obstrepor-

20. For evidence of the considerable tensions existing between the Board and its regional directors by the end of 1938, see "Minutes of the Conference of Regional Directors" (13 November 1938); Charles N. Feidelson, Chairman, and Elinore M. Herrick, Secretary, Conference of Regional Directors, to the Board (16 November 1938); Herrick to Witt (5 January 1939); Witt to Herrick (10 January 1939), all in *RG 25*, Smith Committee Subject Files Box 17, ("Witt"). See also Herrick to members of the Conference of Regional Directors (15 January 1939), in *RG 25*, Smith Committee Subject Files Box 21, ("Exhibits"); Herrick to Madden (21 February 1939), in *RG 25*, Smith Committee Box 3, ("J. Warren Madden Statement – Gates and Krivonos").
21. See Gross, *The Reshaping of the National Labor Relations Board*, 126–30.
22. Ibid. 130.   23. Ibid., 128, 133–35.

ous individuals imbued with unpopular political philosophies. It implied wholesale alteration of the Board's strategy for conducting labor relations policy and thus a reexamination of its ideology, operational methods, and goals – its regulatory discourse.

The appointment of William M. Leiserson in April 1939 precipitated open struggles at the highest levels within the Board over precisely these issues. First, and most clearly, Leiserson came to the Board with a brief from the president "to clean up the mess" of political factionalism and communist influence at the NLRB. Second, within the federal labor relations establishment Leiserson was already an established critic of the capacity of lawyers and legal method to perform administrative tasks. Finally, Leiserson was identified with a labor relations tradition which predated and to an important extent contradicted the course hitherto embraced by the Board.

Leiserson had been critical of the methods used by the NLRB from the outset. Following the Board's promulgation of its initial organizational procedures and case-handling regulations in September 1935, for example, Leiserson had told his former Antioch colleague, the pioneering industrial sociologist Stanley Mathewson, of his "grave doubts as to whether the National Labor Relations Board will be able to function successfully under the procedure that they have adopted."[24] On becoming a Board member himself, Leiserson discovered to his disgust that nothing other than these purely formal legal rules and regulations, together with amendments periodically released by the Board, existed to guide regional staff in their administration of cases. He was particularly disturbed that despite the Board's emphasis for the past year on minimizing the incidence of formal hearings, no instructions had been provided to educate staff in informal case-handling procedures. Leiserson argued that general instructions outlining administrative procedures and explaining the duties and responsibilities of staff members in all spheres of the Board's operation should immediately be issued. "If we had such a set of regulations," he commented, "the Board would not have to spend half its time trying to untangle balled-up cases."[25]

Leiserson's commission to clean up the Board, and his antipathy toward the reign of lawyers and formal legal procedures in Board administration, both quickly involved him in conflicts with other Board members. Inevitably, these focussed on the secretary's office, for here the two problems coincided with a vengeance. Indeed, the first concrete

24. Leiserson to Stanley Mathewson (27 September 1935), in *Leiserson Papers* Box 27, ("Mathewson").
25. Leiserson to Madden (16 August 1939), in *RG* 25, Smith Committee Box 11, ("Leiserson – Memoranda").

indication of the onset of internal struggle was Leiserson's demand, some three months after he was appointed, that Witt be dismissed. Leiserson insisted that the secretary was not qualified either by training or by experience to administer a large organization, that he showed no understanding of its problems, and that his handling of particular cases made it impossible for Leiserson to have confidence in his ability to perform his duties impartially as between the various parties appearing before the Board.[26] When this attempt to unseat Witt failed, Leiserson promptly refused to have anything to do with any case which he considered to have been mishandled by the secretary's office. Eventually, under pressure from his colleagues and from General Counsel Fahy, Leiserson had to retreat from this position.[27] But his criticisms of Witt's methods continued, and were reinforced by the results of the Pratt-Van Arkel and the regional directors' investigations.

Leiserson also clashed with Madden and Smith in his attempts to introduce new procedure into the actual process of Board decision making. The existing practice, once a hearing had been completed, was for the presiding trial examiner to write an intermediate report containing recommendations which would then be analyzed in the Board's Review Division in light of the record generated by the hearing and in light of any exceptions to the intermediate report filed by the parties concerned. The review attorney would report the results of his or her analysis orally to the Board and this oral report would in most instances furnish the basis for the Board's final decision. Leiserson found the procedure intellectually unintelligible, administratively unworkable (it had helped create the huge backlog of cases in the Review Division) and politically suspect; like the secretary's office, the Review Division was known within the Board for its radical sympathies. He therefore pressed a

26. NLRB *Minutes* (28 July 1939), in *RG 25*, Smith Committee Box 11, ("Leiserson"). See also Leiserson to Madden (20 July 1939), accusing Witt of sloppy work and of generally mishandling cases, and Smith to Leiserson (27 July 1939), demanding substantiation of the charges, in same.

27. See, for example, Fahy to Madden (16 December 1939), reporting on Leiserson's charges of incompetence in the secretary's office, in *RG 25*, Smith Committee Box 11, ("Leiserson"). In answer to Madden's request that he give his opinion as to the duty of a member of the Board to participate in decisions in cases which had been heard under the procedure of the statute and were pending for decision, Fahy stated that:

> it is not consistent with the obligations of a member to refrain from participating in cases for reasons which do not relate to the impropriety of participating because of some personal interest in or connection with the parties, or such other reasons as are recognized as grounds for disqualification. The fact that a member may think that a complaint should not have been authorized or a consolidation was improper does not come within these grounds.

different system upon his colleagues, one in which the record was reviewed and checked before the intermediate report was written. This would enable the Board to base its decision on a written document – the trial examiner's report – and would also prevent the review attorney from performing the final analysis of the case.[28]

Edwin Smith opposed adoption of this procedure at the time the suggestion was made and again criticized it in detail when it was put into operation on a trial basis. "It seems to me that the method . . . is entirely inadequate to the review of the record which the parties at interest have a right to expect from members of the Board," he said. Speaking for Madden as well as for himself, Smith told Leiserson that "the method of oral discussion of the cases by the review attorney and his supervisor with the Board members is an essential part of any adequate judicial consideration of the cases coming before us. The oral report of the review division attorney is based on a minute examination of all the facts in the record, including the Intermediate Report and the exceptions, under careful supervision. As contrasted with an examination of the cases with representatives of the review division, the method which you are pursuing does not meet, I believe, a reasonable test of the discharge of your obligation to decide the cases on all the facts in the record."[29]

Leiserson's attempts to eliminate the Review Division from evaluation of a case in favor of reliance upon the trial examiner complemented his assault on the secretary's office. Both were attempts to increase the Board's case-handling capacity through a decentralization of responsibility away from the two worst bottlenecks in the Board's central organization, and simultaneously to reduce the power of key Board staff members – Witt, obviously, but also Thomas Emerson who headed the Review Division – who strongly opposed decentralization and who were also politically unacceptable to the Roosevelt administration. Both also were attempts to repair relations with the regions damaged by the Board's obsession in its early years with maintaining highly centralized control over how cases were resolved. All this was necessary if the Board were to continue to meet the demands made by an ineluctably increasing case load.

But the implications of Leiserson's conflict with his colleagues were

28. See NLRB *Minutes* (19 July 1939), in *RG 25*, Smith Committee Box 21-23, ("Board Minutes"); Leiserson to Madden and Smith (11 October 1939), in *RG 25*, Smith Committee Box 11, ("Leiserson").
29. See Smith to Leiserson (19 October 1939), replying to Leiserson's memorandum to Smith and Madden (17 October 1939), both in *RG 25*, Smith Committee Box 11, ("Leiserson").

not simply organizational or factional. Leiserson's perception of the role of the Board was different. Where Smith and Madden saw the Board as a maker of law and dispenser of justice, Leiserson thought it should be a dispute-processing mechanism. Thus he could quite happily embrace a case-handling method which evinced a less formal interpretation of the Board's judicial responsibilities because he did not consider it appropriate for the Board to be, or even to appear to be, a judicial forum. As he put it early in 1940, reacting to proposals that the solution to the Board's operational and decision-making problems was to be found in the further formalization of its procedures:

> I do not believe that disputes in the highly complicated and specialized field of labor relations can be handled from a strictly legalistic point of view. The administration [of the Act] has been somewhat handicapped by legal policies which practically compel workers, unions and employers to turn their labor problems over to lawyers in order to get their business before the Board.

> I should prefer to consider the Board as a layman's agency to which workingmen can come and tell their stories in their own way and before which employers can defend themselves in the same informal manner. The Act already provides for sufficient court review to take care of legal technicalities.[30]

Leiserson's critique had broad implications for overall policy. Some of these are revealed in two letters he wrote to his old Wisconsin mentor, John R. Commons, in September 1939 and March 1940.[31] The second of these was Leiserson's widely-publicized commentary upon the Board's attempts to defend its record before the antagonistic Special House Investigatory Committee, created in 1939 under the chairmanship of Howard Smith. In it, Leiserson offered an elaborate critique of the Board's legal discourse and of the problems it had caused in the administration of labor relations policy, and pointed out how that discourse was now crippling the Board's attempts to defend itself before the committee. The first letter, less well-known but in many ways more interesting, tells us much more about the relationship

30. William M. Leiserson, Remarks at a meeting of the Economic Club of Detroit (January 8, 1940), in *RG 25*, Smith Committee Box 11, ("Leiserson"). At least one lawyer endorsed Leiserson's critique. In August, one Joseph S. Graydon, an experienced trial lawyer, wrote to Leiserson to condemn the Board under Madden's chairmanship for adopting less and less intelligible procedures. "It strikes me as exceedingly strange," Graydon commented, "that the epoch-making liberal legislation embodied in the Wagner Act should develop within a few years a technique known only to the inner circle of initiates." Graydon to Leiserson (24 August 1940), in *Leiserson Papers*, Box 15, ("G–general").
31. Leiserson to John R. Commons (9 September 1939, and 27 March 1940), both in *Leiserson Papers*, Box 9, ("Commons").

between Leiserson's own theory of labor relations and that being pursued by the Board.

Leiserson's March 1940 letter echoed the testimony he had given four months previously before the Smith Committee. There was nothing wrong with the Wagner Act itself, he told Commons. The roots of the current crisis were to be found within the Board, in its interpretation of the act and of the administrative process. "The whole trouble and most of the public clamor, I am convinced, stems from two things; one, misconception on the part of the Board and its lawyers as to the basic purpose of the Act; two, poor administration."

First, Leiserson concentrated upon the Board's administrative failings:

> We have 900 employees, half of them scattered to cover all the states of the country. To manage a large, farflung organization of this kind is a job all by itself, requiring technical knowledge of management organization and administration. There is no one here in a responsible position who has any such technical training and knowledge. The result is that we really have no organization to manage our staff at all ... Out of the total of 900 employees just about 38 per cent are lawyers, but the total includes a large clerical staff, messengers, janitors, etc. If we leave these out, something like 60 or 70 per cent of the professional staff is made up of lawyers. We handle about 10,000 cases a year, and this is really a mass production problem. The lawyers who control the administrative work of the Board as well as the legal department have no conception of how to handle the mass production job. Their method is to assign cases to individuals and leave each one to his own devices.

The incompetence of lawyers in matters of administration, reflected in the Board's inability to organize routine case-management, had an even more serious effect which impinged directly on matters of policy-formation; namely, the Board's complete inability to grasp that it was an administrative agency. This, Leiserson said, had direct implications for the Board's attempts to defend itself from the determined efforts of the Smith Committee to alter its structure by separating its "prosecuting" and "judicial" functions, and he criticized both the committee for adopting such a mistaken notion of the Board's statutory role and the Board itself for encouraging the committee in its error:

> As a matter of fact we have neither prosecuting nor judicial powers. We are really a branch of the Congress for investigation and fact-finding purposes similar to the Interstate Commerce Commission or to the Wisconsin Industrial Commission ... Congress imposed no penalties on employers for violating the law. It merely adopted a labor policy for industry engaged in interstate commerce which changed the policy that had been in effect for a century and which

the Supreme Court had surrounded with constitutional sanctions. Congress knew it could not make the old policy a crime or a misdemeanor punishable by fine or imprisonment as it had done in the Railway Labor Act for the transportation industry. Instead it merely created the Board for the purpose of investigating and finding whether employers are pursuing the old practices and if they are the Board is given authority to order them to cease those old practices and to pursue the new practices of collective bargaining with free organization of employees.

The Board and its lawyers can't seem to grasp this idea. Essentially they really agree with the Smith Committee that we do have prosecuting and judicial functions. Therefore their defense before the Smith Committee was that the Board itself is very careful to keep in separate compartments the prosecuting and judicial functions and not to mix the two. I warned them that that kind of defense accepts the premise of the Smith Committee and they are bound to lose. If I thought that we had prosecuting and judicial functions here I would not trust myself to keep them separate, and the evidence before the Smith Committee showed many instance where what was considered prosecuting was mixed with the so-called judicial.

For Leiserson, the Board's managerial failings and the wider controversies over its structure and methods could all be traced to its original decision to adopt a legal methodology to implement the act. Just as the Board's knowledge of labor relations, was "confined to the decisions of courts on labor cases," its knowledge of administrative procedure extended no further than "the decisions of the courts with respect to regulations that involve questions of due process of law." This had caused it to neglect the promulgation of administrative regulations necessary for the effective handling of cases. "The only regulations we have published, for example, are rules of practice for lawyers, and most of the procedures for carrying on the investigations and other work of the Board are not mentioned at all in these regulations."

The problem, Leiserson told Commons, was not peculiar to the NLRB. Legal discourse was threatening "the whole idea of scientific investigation and administrative control as it was thought out and worked out in Wisconsin years ago." Most of the multifarious agencies thrown up by the New Deal over the previous seven years were now dominated by lawyers guided by nothing other than their training in legal method and procedure:

The lawyers seems to have the notion that the only way of arriving at the truth is by two opposing lawyers trying to keep things out of the record and whatever gets in, that is the truth. They have no understanding of the method of investigation that we call economic or social research. This explains the [NLRB's acquiescence in the

Smith Committee's] recommendation that Dave Saposs's economic research division should be abolished. The lawyers identify the investigation with the hearing; they call it the trial. The actual careful investigation that is done before the hearing they consider mere preparation such as a prosecuting attorney would do.[32]

Leiserson predicted that unless the trend was reversed, "it won't be long before we will have an association of practitioners before the Labor Board, to whose members both employers and unions will be forced to go to get the benefits of the Act because no layman could understand the legal practices and procedures." This would result in the appearance of "a new body of technical law just as ill-adapted to dealing with modern problems as the common law and the equity law now are," a development which would seriously threaten "the whole idea of flexible and informed handling of modern economic problems by expert administrative agencies."[33]

Leiserson's portrayal of labor relations policy ever more firmly swaddled in the clothes of a legal discourse preoccupied with technical questions and indifferent toward social scientific investigation received confirmation from a number of sources, but most importantly from General Counsel Fahy. Asked by the Smith Committee to comment on Leiserson's letter after it had been made public by the newspaper columnist David Lawrence, Fahy attacked Leiserson's opinions as totally misconceived. Unfair labor practice proceedings, he insisted, were and should be adversarial in character. Therefore, "procedural due process must be complied with under the laws and the Constitution." Board orders, it was true, had no compulsory effect until approved by a court, but the courts relied upon the findings of fact and gave great weight to the type of remedy applied by the Board, making careful procedures crucial. Consequently, "to indict the Board or its legal staff for following the requirements with respect to procedure contained in the statute itself and required by the Constitution, by affording a trial, is, to me, fantastic."[34]

Fahy's reaction in an earlier draft, even more scathing, gives added substance to Leiserson's accusation that the Board's own intolerance of anything other than legal discourse was making it easy for the conservatives on the Smith Committee to hamstring its performance of administrative and investigative tasks by bifurcating the agency and by depriving it of its only means for accumulating non-legal information and countering business propaganda, the Economic Research Division:

> Sometimes economic research has played an important part as material evidence, but the necessity or desirability in some cases of

32. Leiserson to Commons (27 March 1940).   33. Ibid.
34. In Gross, *The Reshaping of the National Labor Relations Board,* 218.

bringing to bear upon the issues involved economic and social research does not change the character of proceeding in which the
person is accused of violating the law to a mere *ex parte* investigation, as distinct from proceedings adversary in character ... Persons may not be found to have committed unlawful acts by some
[people] called a Board going off by themselves and having a nice
social and economic research party, whatever that is.[35]

Leiserson's March 1940 letter thus confirmed that considerable antipathy to the Board's theoretical approach to labor relations attended
his objections to its administrative practices and some of its personnel.
Leiserson, however had already exhibited this antipathy in his earlier,
September 1939, letter. In this letter, sent in response to Commons'
request for comments upon a manuscript, Leiserson expressed his reservations about the impact which the Board's legal discourse was having
upon the institutions – particularly the unions – which already occupied
the labor relations field.

To Commons, unions were expressions of collective action, analogous to corporations. As such, he argued in his manuscript, unions had
become, like corporations, the recipients of rights and duties granted
from time to time by legislatures. Leiserson agreed. However, he
pointed out that once "legalized" in this way, unions had themselves
commenced "to apportion rights, duties and liberties of wage earners in
the economic field" and that "in many respects ... the rights, duties
and restrictions on individuals brought about by trade union rules have
been more important than the political apportioning of rights." Supreme Court decisions such as *Adair v. United States* (1908) and *Coppage v. Kansas* (1915) had actually reinforced this tendency, for while
they had struck down the attempts of legislatures to grant unions rights
in the fashion Commons was describing, they had also made it clear
that wage earners could use their collective economic strength to enforce the rights and duties apportioned through trade union rules.[36]

---

35. In *RG 25*, Smith Committee Box 11, ("Leiserson"). In this draft Fahy referred to
Leiserson's contentions as "fantastic nonsense." For additional evidence of the tension between lawyers and social scientists at the NLRB see Gross, *The Making of the
National Labor Relations Board*, 174–9, 233–7, and *The Reshaping of the National Labor Relations Board*, 213–18.
36. Leiserson wrote, "So far as labor was concerned the decisions of *Adair v. the United
States* and *Coppage v. Kansas* showed that where wage earners by the economic
strength of their labor organizations could resist the oppressions, they were free to
do so. On the other hand, the employers were free to continue those oppressions if
they could get away with it by breaking the strike. It is only since the N.R.A. and the
Wagner Act came into the picture that the Government has taken the position that it
will protect by law the wage earners who cannot by their own strength overcome the
oppressions of their employers." In Leiserson to Commons (9 September 1939).

Thus, when in 1935 the federal government had "taken the position that it will protect by law the wage earners who cannot by their own strength overcome the oppressions of their employers," the public rule-making bodies which it had set up to put such a policy into effect had found that the field was to some extent occupied by other, non-public, rule-making bodies – the unions – which "are permitted to make laws for the government of their members and the relationships of their members to employers in order that voluntary collective action may be able to work itself out in orderly fashion."

It was crucial to the success of government policy, Leiserson continued, that the newly-created public agencies understand the close analogy which existed between the function which they were to perform and the function which the unions were already performing, and that they learn from the institutions already established in the field. "It seems to me," he stated, "that the rules and regulations of the administrative boards or commissions have a close connection with the rules and regulations or 'laws,' as the trade unions call them, of the labor organizations and similar associations for collective action." Certainly, in circumstances where "the rules of some collective associations conflicted with those of others or with the collective action of the government as a whole" it would be necessary for the administrative agencies established by the government to take responsibility for resolving conflict. But in this, as in their routine operations, they should be guided by the unions' example:

> Where [the administrative agencies] have had sense they have been guided in their regulations by the rules that had been developed or were being developed by the voluntary organizations whose activities they were regulating. Where they have not had sense they have followed the notion that the government appointed them to establish rules that they happened to think were in the public interest. Administration by public agencies works satisfactorily, it seems to me, when the agency finds that the practical rules developed by voluntary associations are the reasonable rules. When they try to impose new rules on their own notions of reasonableness, then they get into trouble.[37]

37. Leiserson here provided a foretaste of his March 1940 letter:
   > one of the complicating factors in dealing with these problems is that the old legal forms must be used to some extent in the administration of these agencies. For example ... the legal concept of giving the parties a hearing in order to provide due process tends in many respects to interfere with a technical and scientific investigation. When the hearing comes, the lawyers' idea of evidence, cross-examination, etc., conflicts with the social science methods of securing information and sifting facts. The lawyers tend to identify the investigation with

Just to make his point completely clear, Leiserson concluded with a reminder that the new agencies were, perforce, making rules not in a vacuum but in an environment already inhabited by rule-making bodies whose authority to make rules had already largely been accepted by the courts. "I think there is some evidence," he said, "that the courts uphold [public] rules as reasonable when they find that the rules have been developed in the ordinary course of operations of the voluntary associations. Otherwise they are inclined to hold the regulations to be arbitrary or capricious."

There can, of course, be little doubt that the NLRB was the source of Leiserson's dissatisfaction with agencies which tried to "impose new rules on their own notions of reasonableness." Consequently, Leiserson's letters offer us considerable insight into the debates over the proper role for unions in labor relations policy which had been taking place within the Board ever since he joined it, and which were reaching their peak at the time his first letter was written. These debates, which focussed on the appropriate bargaining unit, underline that Leiserson's battle with his fellow Board members was indeed much more than an intra-agency power struggle over politics and administrative methods provoked by administration attempts to head off a threatened Congressional coup against an unpopular agency. They canvassed major changes in the Board's theory of labor relations, away from the absolute denial that unions enjoyed private rights and interests which had prevailed in the two years following *Jones and Laughlin* and which had caused the split with the AFL, and toward a more accommodating readiness to be guided by the rules of ordering developed by those unions in their own interests.

The struggle for the bargaining unit

Leiserson's desire that the NLRB change from an agency self-consciously proclaiming its transforming role in the service of the public interest to one which just as self-consciously sought harmony with its existing envi-

the hearing; their idea is that the way to get at the truth is to have a trial by combat of two lawyers fighting for their clients. This is not the social scientists' idea of an investigation that will arrive at the true facts. Having secured the facts by scientific methods, the social administrators will provide a hearing to the parties on those facts, and this is sufficient to meet the test of due process. But the legal concepts that lawyers bring into the picture tend to make the administrative investigation a trial rather than a scientific or technical investigation according to the methods of the social scientists.

ronment became clear soon after he joined the Board. On 21 June 1939, he sent Chairman Madden a memorandum on bargaining unit policy which proposed that in making unit determinations the Board should avoid disrupting bargaining relationships which were established and working.[38] The memorandum quoted at length the decision of the first NLRB in *Omaha and Council Bluffs Street Railway Company* (1934),[39] in which the Board had adopted a restricted definition of its authority over the unit, and suggested that the present Board follow the same approach. In *Omaha* the first Board had stated that "while this Board is vested with broad discretionary powers in election cases, we are limited in ordering elections to cases in which elections would, in our opinion, serve the public interest. On the record ... the company has recognized and continues to recognize the petitioner as a collective bargaining agency ... No other organization is presuming to act as the collective bargaining agency for the employees. It appears, therefore, that the petitioning union is, as a matter of fact, the exclusive collective bargaining representative for all of the employees and that, therefore, an election could not improve their present situation." Such an interpretation would have introduced into Board policy a much more limiting definition of the public interest than had prevailed hitherto, and would have restrained the Board in its exercise of its powers. Not surprisingly, therefore, Leiserson's suggestion was ignored.

Leiserson's proposal ran against the tide of prevailing developments in Board policy. Particularly in the months since its decision in the *Shipowners'* case, the Board had adopted a broad interpretation of its powers over the unit. In *Pittsburgh Plate Glass* (January 1939), for example, the Board certified the Federation of Flat Glass Workers-CIO in a unit comprising all the plants in the company's flat glass division, notwithstanding the desire of a majority of the employees in one of the company's largest plants to maintain their established plant-wide collective bargaining relationship through an independent union.[40] The Board disestablished the independent on the grounds that it was company-dominated. Three weeks later the Board reached an identical decision in another glass industry case, *Libbey Owens Ford Glass Company* (January 1939), again over the opposition of the employees of one plant who desired to maintain an established bargaining relationship, this time through an AFL union.[41] Then, in *Tovrea Packing Company* (May 1939) and *El Paso Electric Company* (June 1939), the Board indicated that it would no longer accept the extent of a union's organization in a

38.   Leiserson to Madden (21 June 1939), in *RG* 25, Smith Committee Box 11, ("Leiserson, Memoranda").
39.   2 NLRB [old] 45.   40.   10 NLRB 1111.   41.   10 NLRB 1470.

plant as determinative of the unit.[42] Such decisions indicated that the Board would deny representation of their own choosing to workers wherever the form of organization proposed was not in accordance with the Board's conception of appropriateness.[43]

Leiserson objected to the Board's use of its authority over the bargaining unit in the glass industry cases to aggregate unorganized and organized plants in single units without allowing the employees involved a chance to determine representatives in accordance with their varied bargaining histories, and in *Chrysler Corporation* (July 1939) and *Briggs Manufacturing* (July 1939) he was successful in persuading Madden to join with him in finding two such multiplant corporationwide units inappropriate.[44] Leiserson and Madden were not, however, a stable decision-making combination. Indeed, in a series of cases considered by the Board in July and August of 1939 involving the status of craft units, it became apparent that the three members of the Board had almost nothing in common when it came to bargaining unit determinations. Each was being guided by a fundamentally different set of assumptions as to what an appropriate unit was and, more important, as

42. *Tovrea Packing Company*, 12 NLRB 1063, and *El Paso Electric Company*, 13 NLRB 213.
43. In its *Third Annual Report* (Washington, 1939), the Board stated that "no question concerning representation exists where [the Board] finds that no unit similar to or within the scope of that which is proposed among the employees named in the petition is appropriate for the purpose of collective bargaining" (164).
44. *Chrysler Corporation*, 13 NLRB 1303, and *Briggs Manufacturing*, 13 NLRB 1326 (both decisions issued on July 13). In a memorandum to Madden and Smith of 14 July 1939, Leiserson underlined his disagreement with the draft decision produced by the Review Division in the *Chrysler* case as follows:
    I disagree with the finding that the 14 plants of the company constitute a single appropriate unit for purposes of collective bargaining. The evidence does not justify any such finding. The existing contracts are specifically membership contracts, and the evidence shows clearly that the company has been bargaining with more than one organization on this basis. It recognized the machinists' organization as the representative of machinists who belonged to it at the same time that it recognized the [United Auto Workers] as the representative of the employees who were members of this organization. It has been carrying on negotiations with the A.F.L.-U.A.W. as well as with the C.I.O.-U.A.W. Under these circumstances it seems to me directly going in the face of the facts to hold that there is any experience, custom or practice to establish the 14 plants of the corporation as one bargaining unit. The finding of a corporation-wide unit seems particularly absurd in view of the fact that collective bargaining has apparently not been practiced at all in the Kokomo plant.
    It would be a "gross impropriety," Leiserson said, to poll the employees of the Kokomo plant in a single unit with the employees of the company's thirteen other plants. See Leiserson to Smith and Madden (14 July 1939), in *RG 25*, Smith Committee Box 11, ("Leiserson–Memoranda").

to what powers the Board enjoyed in determining it. This meant that the Board lacked a stable and hence predictable majority opinion, and therefore that national policy lacked direction.

The differences amongst Board members were revealed clearly in *American Can Company*, decided late in July 1939, a case involving attempts by three AFL craft unions to separate small groups of craftsmen from a previously-established unit of production and maintenance employees.[45] The effect of the Board's decision was further to erode the authority of the two-year-old *Globe* decision, according to which the Board would direct self-determination elections amongst distinguishable groups of workers at its discretion, for it declared that henceforth the Board would not allow severance of such groups from the mass of production workers in cases where collective bargaining relationships had already been established on the wider basis. Some historians have regarded the Board's decision as indicative of a trend in favor of industrial unionism.[46] Neither the policy choices confronting the Board nor the outcome of the case, however, were so simple. Not only was the Board divided in its opinion but the members forming the majority — Leiserson and Smith — were also deeply divided.

Leiserson's carefully-crafted opinion is the key to the dynamics of Board decision-making in this case, for differences of opinion between Smith and Madden meant that his views as to bargaining units were for the first time to be decisive in determining the outcome of a representation case.[47] Unsurprisingly, Leiserson used the occasion to attempt as authoritatively as possible to place the Board on a new track. The purpose of the Wagner Act, he stressed, was to establish collective bargaining. This should be the Board's only criterion in making unit determinations. For this reason the most appropriate unit in any case was the unit which afforded the parties the best opportunity to develop a stable bargaining relationship. Where, as here, the parties had already signed contracts, the contract should define the unit. If the Board used some other criterion, "it would not only be setting aside a provision of a valid contract, but it would be substituting its own preference for the preferences of the employees and the employer as to the appropriateness of a bargaining unit that they have voluntarily agreed in a contract is best for their purposes." The Board, Leiserson stressed, should look "to established custom and practice as embodied in collective bargaining agree-

45. 13 NLRB 1252.
46. See, for example, James O. Morris, *Conflict Within the AFL: A Study of Craft versus Industrial Unionism, 1901–1938* (Ithaca, New York, 1958), 246–7.
47. See Smith to Madden and Emerson (25 July 1939), in *RG 25*, Smith Committee Box 11, ("Leiserson–Memoranda").

ments" when it decided the appropriate unit, "not to theoretical principles that appeal to members of the Board as being fair." Neither in
this case, nor in any other similar case, was the Board authorized "to
split the appropriate unit thus established by collective bargaining and
embodied in a valid, exclusive bargaining contract," for to hold that
arrangements made by the parties and working satisfactorily could be
broken up to accommodate the desires of minority groups for self-
determination, or, alternatively, to satisfy the theoretical principles of
Board members, "would make stability and responsibility in collective
bargaining impossible."[48]

Sympathetic to any decision the practical effect of which was to deter
craft separatism, Smith concurred in Leiserson's conclusion that the
three units petitioned for were not appropriate and should be denied.
But Smith could not accept Leiserson's premises. Thus his concurrence
in the decision took the form of a separate opinion highly critical of
Leiserson's reasoning and of the policy which Leiserson sought to have
the Board adopt. The Board's task, Smith argued, was to find the unit
in every case which would establish collective bargaining on the widest
possible basis. It was not in any sense required to treat units determined
by the parties through their own bargaining and contracts as presumptively appropriate:

> I do not agree . . . that the Board "is not authorized by the Act" to
> find a different bargaining unit from that which has been previously
> embodied in an exclusive bargaining contract. I think the past his-
> tory of collective bargaining in a plant . . . is an important . . . fac-
> tor in the determination of the appropriate bargaining unit. But I
> do not believe that the Board is precluded by anything in the Act
> from finding a different unit to be appropriate.[49]

Madden disagreed with both his colleagues, holding that no change
should be made to the *Globe* doctrine under which groups of workers
petitioning for self-determination elections had been allowed to separate
from already-established plant-wide units whenever they expressed a
desire to do so. The only difference between this and previous cases was
that the incumbent union had secured a contract on the basis of the
industrial unit. Like Smith, Madden denied that this should limit the
Board's authority. "The development of the proper unit for collective
bargaining," Madden believed, "is an evolutionary process." The Board
should accommodate and encourage this evolution by allowing workers
self-determination wherever possible.[50]

48. 13 NLRB 1252, at 1256–57. And see Leiserson to Smith, Madden and Emerson (24
     July 1939), in RG 25, Smith Committee Box 11, ("Leiserson–Memoranda").
49. 13 NLRB 1252, at 1258. 50. Ibid., 1260.

Leiserson's emphasis upon the determinative influence of the contract expressed his conviction that the Board's overriding function was to achieve stability, order and efficiency in collective bargaining, and that the proper way to do that was for the Board simply to lend its imprimatur to whatever working arrangements had been established by the parties concerned. Consequently, he refused all of Smith's attempts to draft a joint opinion in *American Can* which would have preserved the Board's freedom to determine units irrespective of bargaining history or of the contracts produced, stressing instead the guiding force of "custom and practice" and pointing to collective bargaining contracts as the best available evidence of what custom and practice consisted in.[51] Similarly, he told Madden that the *Globe* doctrine should only apply in cases where there was no bargaining history and no contract. "I cannot understand how the Board will accept as binding on it the opinion of a small group of employees who claim that they constitute a craft" he said, but refuse to accept as binding on it "an appropriate unit fixed in an exclusive contract by collective bargaining in which both the employer and the duly-designated representatives have participated and agreed."[52] Smith and Madden, in contrast, were willing to compromise present stability in the interests of achieving an "ideal" structure of labor relations in the future. For Smith the answer lay in industrial unionism, hence his critical concurrence in *American Can*. For Madden it lay in the conditional free choice embodied in *Globe*. Both, however, emphasized the power of the Board to continue adjusting the bargaining structure until the best possible system of labor relations emerged.

The AFL's central hierarchy seized upon the *American Can* decision, and on Leiserson's opinion in particular, as further justification for its campaign against the NLRB. Its amendments to the act launched earlier in the year had, the AFL said, elicited a number of changes in the administration of labor policy, but the Board's discretionary authority and its willingness to abuse it remained substantially unaffected. Joining the list of cases which gave rise to "apprehension and fear of eventual engulfment of craft unions by Board decree," *American Can* was to the AFL a "devastating" demonstration of the Board's antagonism to its affiliates, and consequently proof positive of the continued need for its amendments.[53] But in fact, Leiserson's emphasis upon the centrality of

51. See Smith to Leiserson (25 July 1939), and Smith to Madden and Emerson (same date), in *RG 25*, Smith Committee Box 11, ("Leiserson–Memoranda").
52. Leiserson to Madden, Smith and Emerson (24 July 1939), in *RG 25*, Smith Committee Box 11, ("Leiserson–Memoranda").
53. AFL Executive Council, *Report to the 59th Annual Convention of the American Federation of Labor* (2 October 1939), in *RG 25*, Smith Committee Box 14, ("Report of the AFL Executive Council").

custom to any viable labor policy was itself a warning against "abuse" of discretion by the Board, and was recognized as such by his colleagues. Moreover, Leiserson's opinion advocated the entrenchment of collective bargaining relationships (and, therefore, representatives) once the production of contracts showed that they were working satisfactorily, and thus strongly implied that the Board should look to provide unions with the element of institutional security in collective bargaining which the Board's emphasis on its own unrestricted discretion had hitherto effectively denied them.[54]

Subsequent cases reinforced the distinct impression imparted by *American Can* that Leiserson's appointment had the potential to bring about major alterations in the theory and practice of labor relations policy. In *Milton Bradley Company* (October 1939), for example, Leiserson again insisted that the Board respect institutional arrangements already arrived at in the course of bargaining when determining units. He condemned the Board's invocation of alternative considerations – uniformity of wages, hours, and working conditions, the nature of the production process, equality of bargaining power, feasibility of the unit, bargaining history in the industry, and so forth – as nothing but a spurious empiricism, an attempt to portray the Board as guided in its "fact-finding" exercises by objective principles which were nothing of the sort. No set of administrative categories or legal theories could possibly accommodate the diversity of forms and relations of collective bargaining chosen by organized labor. For the Board to pretend otherwise and on that basis substitute its judgment for the customs and practices of collective bargaining as evidenced by contracts was "dangerous to labor organizations."[55] Leiserson later told his friend, the *New York Times* labor columnist Louis Stark, that his opinion in *Milton Bradley* was the most complete statement of his position on the unit question. "But," he added, "it does not express it fully ... I do not hold that the last contract alone determines the unit but rather that established custom and practice as well as all the contracts that have covered the employees in a particular case are the determining factors."[56]

The extent of Leiserson's commitment to the reproduction of "established custom and practice" was further clarified in *Clyde-Mallory*

---

54. "A bargaining unit established and maintained by contracts," Leiserson wrote, "... may not be changed by the Board." Memorandum re: *Roberts and Manders Stove Company* (19 October 1939), in *RG 25*, Smith Committee Box 11, ("Leiserson").

55. Leiserson to Madden, Smith and Emerson (26 July 1939), in *RG 25*, Smith Committee Box 11, ("Leiserson–Memoranda"); *Milton Bradley Company*, 15 NLRB 938, at 942, 944–8.

56. Leiserson to Louis Stark (26 October 1939), in *Leiserson Papers*, Box 38, ("Stark").

Lines (October 1939), a case which was the subject of extended Board discussion during August 1939.[57] In this case, the International Longshoremen's Association-AFL had successfully persuaded the employer to sign a contract with it in the face of an organizing campaign mounted by the Industrial Union of Marine and Shipbuilding Workers-CIO. Leiserson dissenting, the Board decided that neither the unit covered by the ILA's contract nor the alternative proposed by the IUMSW was appropriate. "The demarcations by which the ILA sought to justify the exclusion of certain categories of ship and pier workers and by which the Industrial Union sought to segregate the ship from the pier workers are arbitrary ones, founded on the fortuitous organizational development of the two labor organizations."[58] The Board found a third unit, conforming to neither of the petitions before it.

Throughout the Board's discussions of the case, Leiserson had repeatedly stressed that the unit was fixed by the ILA's contract.[59] Once it became clear that Smith and Madden had decided to ignore not only the contract but also the IUMSW's alternative description, Leiserson reacted harshly. A bargaining unit legally established by a valid collective agreement "is, for industrial elections, what a congressional district is for political elections." Not only was the Board here proposing to alter the "election district" already established, it was also proposing to create the replacement on a basis "which neither the employer, the employees, nor [either of] their organizations consider appropriate, but which the two Board members consider more effective for collective bargaining." It was, Leiserson concluded, "the units established by Board members on the basis of their own opinions as to appropriateness that seem to me to be arbitrary and fortuitous, whereas those developed in the process of labor organization and collective bargaining are the practical and workable units which form the basis for sound labor relations wherever collective dealing between employees and management prevails."[60]

The extent of the disagreements over the unit which emerged on the Board after Leiserson's appointment rendered the development of a clear line of cases describing bargaining unit policy impossible. No stable majority opinion could exist because the reasoning by which each member reached his respective conclusions differed fundamentally from

57. 15 NLRB 1008. 58. Ibid., 1012.
59. Leiserson to Madden and Emerson (3 August 1939), and Leiserson to Madden and Smith (5 September 1939), both in *RG 25*, Box 11, ("Leiserson–Memoranda").
60. 15 NLRB 1008, at 1017. See also Leiserson to Madden (22 August 1939) concerning the *Buckley Hemlock Mills* case; Leiserson to Madden and Smith (31 August 1939), concerning the *Bendix Products* case, and Leiserson to Smith and Madden (30 November 1939), concerning the *Berkeley Granite Corporation* case.

that of his colleagues. They could not even reach general agreement on major premises.

By the early months of 1940, Board members were finding it necessary to issue elaborate explanations of the extent of their agreement and disagreement with each other to counter the befuddlement growing among Congressional investigators and prospective petitioners alike.[61] Madden, this documentation established, favored units which would give craft or minority groups the opportunity to bargain separately from other employees where they so desired. Smith favored plant-wide, company-wide, or other broad units wherever recognition of any smaller unit would detract from the bargaining strength of all the employees involved. Leiserson favored units established by the scope of exclusive agreements growing out of collective bargaining, or by the history of self-organization among the employees. Unanimity was possible in cases where there was no intervenor and where (a) the unit was stipulated by the parties to the dispute or (b) the proposal was for a unit of a single plant of a company operating over a wide geographic area or (c) the petitioner sought to exclude skilled workers from a production and maintenance unit. Beyond these circumstances, however, problems arose. Madden would dissent wherever an organization seeking a broad unit was opposed by one seeking a smaller unit and the employees in the smaller unit were not given a chance to decide whether they wanted to be included in the broad unit; Smith would dissent wherever the employees in the smaller unit *were* given such an opportunity; and Leiserson would dissent wherever the unit granted departed from that described by a valid collective bargaining contract. Leiserson would also dissent where, in the absence of any bargaining history on a wider basis, preference was nevertheless given to a broad unit over a petition for smaller one, and also where a union was permitted to "enlarge" a unit by adding to it employees not previously covered by the contract without the target group first being polled separately as to their bargaining preferences.

Despite the considerable fluidity imparted by these differing approaches, the major difference of principle which separated Leiserson on the one hand from Smith and Madden on the other was clear. Smith and Madden believed that the Wagner Act gave the Board vast discretionary powers with few limitations implied on their use. Leiserson believed that the act did not authorize the Board to exercise judgment as to the appropriateness of units, but only gave it fact-finding powers to register the units established by the parties.[62] "[I]f the Board pre-

61. See *Leiserson Papers*, Box 29, ("NLRB").
62. Leiserson to Arthur S. Meyer (18 January 1940), in *Leiserson Papers*, Box 26, ("Meyer").

sumes to say that one unit is superior to another it is in effect determining the structure and form of labor organization in the country," he warned. "No responsible officer of either the A. F. of L. or the CIO ever wanted the government to have this authority."[63]

Leiserson's emphasis upon the determinative influence which should be accorded to the parties' custom and practice in unit determinations was simultaneously a critique of the legal positivism implied in the Board's prevailing discourse and an assertion of an alternative set of values expressive of the pluralist industrial relations theory of the 1920s.[64] The passage of the Wagner Act had, of course, greatly altered the environment in which that theory operated, for as Leiserson himself acknowledged, the act provided the only basis upon which unions could be said to enjoy unchallengeable collective bargaining rights.[65] These conditions were not, however, fatal to the pluralist tradition, and as its foremost exponent within the federal labor relations bureaucracy, Leiserson pressed for the Board to repudiate its exercises of discretion and to be guided instead by the decisions of the parties. As he put it in *The Federbush Company, Inc.* (June 1940), the Board was perpetuating a fundamental error in reserving to itself the option of changing units established "by agreement between organizations of employees and their employers."[66] Instead the Board should acknowledge that the behavior of the parties was decisive. "[T]he bargaining unit established by the employees in the exercise of their right of self-organization is binding upon the employer and the Board alike."[67]

Defining the unit through determinable custom and practice in this fashion inevitably greatly increased the opportunities available to labor unions to have their own institutional interests and desires for security of tenure as bargaining representatives readmitted for consideration as matters relevant to Board decision making. This did not mean that

---

63. Ibid. Leiserson was even more emphatic in a first draft of his letter to Meyer:
    I think that every responsible officer of both the A.F. of L. and the C.I.O. would tell you that organized labor would not have approved the Wagner Act if there had been any intimation that the Government Board would have power to decide whether an industrial union should be split up into craft or other smaller units and whether established craft units should be merged into larger plant or industrial units.
    Leiserson Papers, Box 29, ("NLRB").
64. As noted in Chapter Three.
65. Twentieth Century Fund, Committee on Labor and the Government *Minutes of the Eleventh Meeting* (27 January 1939), in *Leiserson Papers*, Box 41, ("Twentieth Century Fund"). The minutes read: "[Leiserson] thought the whole legal situation had been considerably confused by the Labor Relations Act. It had brought fundamental changes in the way courts look at the situation, particularly in respect to the representation of employees, both members and non-members of unions."
66. 24 NLRB 829, at 847.   67. Ibid., 847.

Leiserson's approach satisfied the desires of the AFL hierarchs, for theirs had become an insistence on a blanket endorsement of the principle of craft unionism no matter what the circumstances. In contrast, as events in a number of cases indicated, to be guided by "custom and practice" was not to be guided by transhistorical or immutable principles like "craft separatism" or "exclusive jurisdiction" but by the concrete attributes of the particular situations – by the "fact" which could be "found" through social scientific investigation. In each discrete situation, in other words, any interested party had the opportunity to create the custom and practice by which the Board would be guided, lending the Board's decision-making the degree of plasticity it required.[68]

The significance of a policy of endorsing custom and practice where it had been established, therefore, was not that it meant endorsing a particular institutional or bargaining structure as presumptively appropriate for all units. Rather the significance lay in the act of validation itself. Leiserson's policy was to institutionalize and render secure whatever had been established, to vest the interests on the ground in the service of stability in collective bargaining. If collective bargaining relations had been created, he argued, the Board should preserve them. If they had not, or if a union sought to split a previously appropriate unit or, alternatively, include it in a wider unit, then the unit could be changed as long as it was demonstrated that a majority of the employees in the prevailing unit supported the union's desire for a change in what was customary.

The Board remained in a state of fundamental disagreement over the principles which should guide it on the unit issue throughout the first

---

68. In the first draft of his letter to Arthur Meyer, Leiserson had written:

> [T]he Board must have a guiding principle or a set of guiding principles which are as binding on the Board as on any of the parties that appear before the Board. This principle or set of principles must have as its basis that the working people themselves must be free to organize themselves and to bargain with their employers in any form of bargaining unit that they and their organizations consider most effective ... [T]he job of the Board is to find any established practice, custom, or contract that has already determined the issue in favor of one form or another. If such a determination by the employees has already been made, the Board must consider itself bound by the established practice or custom. If the employees have made no determination by established custom, practice or contract, then I think it is necessary for the Board to permit each self-organized unit of workers to have a separate vote according to the unit around which they have organized.

Leiserson Papers, Box 29, ("NLRB"). Thus, in *Clyde–Mallory Lines*, for example, the record shows both unions jockeying to create their respective forms of organization and then to persuade the Board that their particular form was well-enough established to be considered "customary." See *RG 25*, Informal File R-1329, *Clyde–Mallory Lines*.

fifteen months of Leiserson's term. As we have seen, this did not prevent it from making decisions. It was even able to achieve unanimity on many occasions. Nevertheless, the disagreements were more than sufficient to obstruct the emergence of a clear unit policy.

The obstruction was not destined to last. Both Madden and Smith were close to the ends of their terms of office, and in each case the combined opposition of Congressional critics, of employers and of the AFL was sufficient to ensure that reappointment was impossible. With their departure – Madden in August 1940, Smith a year later – went the insistence that the Board had exclusive authority as a public administrative agency to determine matters of representation. With them also went much of the centralized administrative structure in which had been embodied their commitment to that discourse of public authority.

The triumph of the pluralists

Madden, the first to go, was replaced as NLRB chairman by the University of Chicago economist and former member of the first NLRB, Harry A. Millis, as soon as the 1940 presidential election was out of the way. Millis's appointment, which had the support of Senator Wagner, had been pressed upon Roosevelt by Sidney Hillman, and also by Leiserson who had indicated that he would feel unable to continue at the Board if Madden were reappointed.[69] Leiserson was delighted that the conflict of the previous fifteen months had at last been resolved so decisively in his favor. "Now if the President only appoints Ed Witte next August when Smith's appointment expires, then we would have a real Board," he wrote to Commons a week after Millis's appointment. "You would have all three of the Board members your boys – and you would be sure that the administration of the law was both proper and intelligent."[70]

An immediate consequence of Millis's appointment was the resignation of Leiserson's principal enemies in the internal wars over Board procedure and administration, the secretary, Nathan Witt, and the assistant general counsel in charge of the Review Division, Thomas Emerson. This delighted Leiserson even more. "Both you and I are to be congratulated on having those resignations," he wrote to Millis. "They eliminate a good many headaches that we would otherwise have had."[71]

69. Leiserson to John A. Fitch (9 October 1940), in *Leiserson Papers*, Box 14, ("Fitch").
70. Leiserson to John R. Commons (22 November 1940), in *Leiserson Papers*, Box 9, ("Commons").
71. Leiserson to Harry A. Millis (18 November 1940), in *Leiserson Papers*, Box 26, ("Millis").

General Counsel Fahy had also resigned recently to take up the position of assistant solicitor general of the United States, leaving yet another key position open, and Leiserson and Millis took advantage of the fluid situation to effect a fundamental reorganization of the Board's administrative and procedural structure. First, Associate General Counsel Robert Watts was appointed to fill Fahy's position. Second, the office of secretary was relieved of its extensive responsibilities for managing case-handling and the Board's relations with its regional offices, leaving it with little more to do than manage the routine of the central office. In its place a new division, the Field Division, was created in Washington with full responsibility for coordination with the regions and with complete autonomy in all case-handling matters, including authority to initiate proceedings on its own motion, save only in cases involving new principles or matters of general policy. These innovations comprised a considerable delegation of responsibility from the Board to the Field Division and through it to the regional offices, meeting the recommendations of the internal investigations held by the Board in 1939 which had hitherto been stalled by Smith and Madden. They answered the insistent demands from regional directors for far greater authority and autonomy in the disposition of cases by informal adjustment and in the authorization of formal proceedings.[72]

In addition to these structural changes, Leiserson and Millis put into operation the decision-making procedures which Leiserson had first proposed over a year previously, and over which the Board had been at loggerheads ever since. Henceforth, each Board member would base his decisions in complaint cases on a reading of the trial examiner's report. The report would be prepared in consultation with one of the associate attorneys newly employed in the Board's Trial Examiner Division to assist the trial examiners, and would be accompanied by a memorandum from the attorney. It would be read in conjunction with a second memorandum from one of the Board's review attorneys comparing the trial examiner's report with the record of the hearing and with the briefs and exceptions filed by the parties. Consideration of these documents would enable each member to arrive at a provisional decision, and where they agreed the review attorney would be made responsible for drafting the decision by revising, where necessary, the trial examiner's report. Where the members did not agree, the Board would call a conference, which the review attorney and the trial examiner would attend, to iron out differences. In representation cases, where no inter-

---

72. Millis and Brown, *From the Wagner Act to Taft-Hartley*, 52–56. Gross, *The Reshaping of the National Labor Relations Board*, 229–32.

mediate report was issued, the Board would receive a memorandum from the review attorney commenting on the record, and an informal report from the trial examiner. As in complaint cases, its decision would be arrived at through individual consideration by its members of these documents, and of the briefs and exceptions filed by the parties, together with the results of oral argument if requested by the parties or ordered by the Board, and, where necessary, the results of Board conferences.[73] As Leiserson indicated in a letter to Paul M. Herzog, chairman of the New York State Labor Relations Board and Leiserson's assistant when he had been secretary of the old National Labor Board, the effect of these changes was finally to eliminate the decisive role which had been played by the Review Division in the preparation of Board decisions:

> [T]he Board will no longer rely merely on an oral report of a review attorney as to what is in the record. As a matter of fact, the Board did not read the intermediate reports or briefs or other documents under the former procedure. It depended on the oral statements of the reviewing attorneys for everything and the decisions were made on those oral statements.
>
> The theory on which this was done I never could understand. The theory was that by listening to a review attorney, the Board made its findings on an independent consideration of the record. My view of that was that the Board took the review attorney's interpretation of facts in the record, which often involved conclusions, and disregarded the trial examiner's views although the latter saw and heard the witnesses and was a much more mature and experienced man.[74]

The organizational changes instituted by Leiserson and Millis substantially altered the centralized structure created by Fahy and Madden to facilitate the Board's pursuit of its original litigation-based strategy. In its place they created a decentralized multi-divisional structure in which central departments serviced the regions and in which the Board's major role became one of providing authoritative leadership through the development of policy in key cases. In many ways, these arrangements were far more suitable than the Board's original structure to the "mass production job" to which Leiserson had referred early in 1940, and they reflected the routinization and dispersion of decision-making which that job required.

Structural change, however, could not free the Board from the legal discourse which had suffused its early years. For one thing, its new general counsel was no less committed to the maintenance of "the

73. Leiserson to Paul M. Herzog (7 February 1941), in *Leiserson Papers*, Box 17, ("Herzog"). Millis and Brown, *From the Wagner Act to Taft-Hartley*, 56–7.
74. Leiserson to Herzog (7 February 1941).

highest professional traditions" amongst Board attorneys than his pre-decessor had been.[75] For another, although decentralization helped to spread authority and lessened somewhat the agency's reliance on formal legal procedure, the Smith Committee's decision to bring about the elimination of the Economic Research Division condemned the Board to remain dependant upon exclusively legal tools for its evaluation of cases. Never popular with the Board's lawyers, in the course of the House inquiry the division had become something of a scapegoat, a sop which the Board's lawyers felt could be thrown the committee, if neces-sary, to forestall changes to the act itself.[76] Despite the considerable support shown for the division by Leiserson and by union spokesmen from both federations,[77] and despite attempts to preserve the division under a new name – the Technical Services Division – and with reduced personnel, the Smith Committee was able to persuade the House that the division's activities represented a threat to due process and that it should be dissolved. Ironically, the Board's social scientists found them-selves at their moment of triumph deprived of their only source of systematic non-legal analysis and information.

Just as Madden's departure from the Board allowed the resolution of procedural and administrative conflicts, so it also allowed the resolution of policy conflicts, most importantly the conflict over the unit. Forming a stable majority committed by ideology, temperament and professional training to "realistic industrial relations,"[78] Leiserson and Millis began by revising decisions taken by the Madden Board in two key cases, *Libbey Owens Ford* and *Shipowners' Association of the Pacific Coast*, to bring the unit into conformity with the bargaining that had actually taken place. In its original *Libbey Owens Ford* decision, the Board had designated an employer-wide unit and certified the Federation of Glass, Ceramic and Silica Sand Workers-CIO as the bargaining representative. In doing so it had ignored the complete absence of support for that union in the company's Parkersburg, West Virginia, plant and had dis-

75. Watts to all Attorneys (5 September 1939), in *RG 25*, Smith Committee Box 11, ("Instructions to Attorneys").

76. Gross, *The Reshaping of the National Labor Relations Board*, 214–18.

77. Ibid., 216–17. See also Leiserson to AFL president Green (18 April 1940); Green to Leiserson (25 April 1940); Padway to Leiserson (17 May 1940); David Dubinsky to Leiserson (20 May 1940); E.C. Davison, secretary-treasurer of the IAM, to Madden (22 May 1940); IAM president H.W. Brown to all members of the House of Repre-sentatives (23 September 1940); Railway Labor Executives Association to all mem-bers of the US Senate (25 September 1940); Padway to Wagner (7 October 1940); and Padway to Roosevelt (10 October 1940); all in *Leiserson Papers*, Box 2, ("AFL"), and Box 56, ("Trade Union Correspondence").

78. Gross, *The Reshaping of the National Labor Relations Board*, 242. See also Millis and Brown, *From the Wagner Act to Taft-Hartley*, 236.

missed a petition from the National Flat Glass Workers-AFL which sought to represent the plant as a separate unit. After eighteen months, however, the Federation had been unable to establish any bargaining relationship with the company covering Parkersburg. Meanwhile, in August 1940, the National had renewed its petition.[79] The Board (at that time consisting solely of Smith and Leiserson, Madden's term having expired and no decision on the chairmanship having been taken) sought General Counsel Fahy's advice on whether to allow the petition to proceed, and on 20 September Fahy recommended that the Board hold hearings to review its original unit determination.[80] Comments prepared by regional officials confirmed both that the company had refused to enter into a contract with the Federation covering Parkersburg, and that the Federation had actually made no attempt to organize the plant and was "seemingly content to rely on the decision of the Board in order to obtain collective bargaining."[81] Once Millis had joined the Board, he and Leiserson combined to direct the separation of the Parkersburg plant from the original unit, and ordered an election to determine the representative. Smith, predictably, dissented, and criticized Leiserson for championing unit determination principles which would weaken the bargaining power of employees by "permit[ting] the scope of industrial units to be determined by the desires of the employees in the smallest industrial grouping for which contention is made."[82]

The same conclusion was reached by the Board in the conceptually idential and highly symbolic *Shipowners'* case. In this case the International Longshoremen's and Warehousemen's Union-CIO, certified as the representative of all Pacific coast longshoremen, had been unable to convince employers of its ability to bargain credibly on behalf of the Puget Sound ports controlled by the International Longshoremen's Association-AFL. Consequently, in September 1938 the ILWU had declared that it would not be responsible for the conduct of labor relations in the Puget Sound ports, and agreed to waive its bargaining rights in those ports until such time as it gained majority support there.[83] This meant that although the ILWU remained the coastwide representative,

79. Phillip G. Phillips, regional director NLRB 9th region, to Witt (15 August 1940), in *RG 25*, Informal File R-2164, *Libbey Owens Ford*.
80. Fahy to Beatrice Stern (20 September 1940), in *RG 25*, Informal File R-2164.
81. Phillips to Alexander B. Hawes, chief administrative examiner (27 September 1940), in Informal File R-2164.
82. *Libbey Owens Ford Glass Company* (April 1941), 31 NLRB 243, at 254.
83. Memorandum of Agreement (30 September 1938) between the International Longshoremen's and Warehousemen's Union-CIO and the Waterfront Employers' Association of the Pacific Coast, in *RG 25*, Informal File R-2326, *Shipowners' Association of the Pacific Coast, et al.*

the ILA retained control of the hiring hall, dispatching and other aspects of local labor relations. Then, in August 1940, the ILA sought to bargain on wages and conditions with Puget Sound employers. It was refused on grounds of the ILWU's coastwide certification. The ILA then called a strike. This was held by the coastwide arbitrator to be in violation of the current ILWU coastwide contract. At this point the ILA filed a representation petition with the Board.

As in *Libbey Owens Ford*, Smith and Leiserson could not agree whether to hear the petition, and no movement occurred until after Millis's appointment. Millis and Leiserson then combined to order hearings on the petition, and these duly took place in January 1941. A decision separating the Puget Sounds ports from the coastwide unit was finally issued in June 1941. Again Smith dissented, and went to considerable pains to point out the inconsistencies in Leiserson's position. Having previously held that prior certifications should not be disturbed, Leiserson was nevertheless ready to disturb this one. Having argued that bargaining relationships embodied in contracts should determine the unit, Leiserson was ready to ignore the ILWU's coastwide agreement.[84]

Shipowners' and, to a lesser extent, *Libbey Owens Ford* were exceptional cases which confronted the Board with the necessity of resolving long-running disputes rooted in previous policy decisions. More generally, the unit policy established by the Millis Board followed closely the principles enunciated by Leiserson in the second half of 1939. Rejecting both of the competing models canvassed during the Board's early years – the assertions of unlimited administrative authority upon which Smith and Madden had depended and the unqualified right of craft self-determination for which the AFL's bureaucratic hierarchy had agitated – the Millis Board embraced a dynamic theory of custom and practice which effectively institutionalized bargaining structures wherever they were established and functioning. Where a history of bargaining existed the Board would be guided thereby, particularly when it was embodied in a contract. In the absence of such evidence of appropriate custom or practice the Board would be guided by the desires of the contending parties as reflected in their unit petitions. Board determinations could be adjusted to allow the consolidation of previously distinct units with a common representative, or absorption of new and unorganized (or separately organized) groups where these were first given an opportunity to signify their desires in the matter. Adjustments could also be made to allow separation of an identifiable group from a more inclusive unit. This, however, was contingent upon the agreement of a

84. *Shipowners' Association of the Pacific, et al.* (June 1941), 32 NLRB 668, at 685–91.

majority of the larger unit, or a demonstration by the group seeking
separation that it had been included in the larger unit unwillingly and
had retained its group identity, requirements which halted tendencies
toward institutional fragmentation apparent in the Madden Board's
Globe and *Allis-Chalmers* decisions.[85]

The Millis Board's unit policy thus offered affiliates of both federations a considerable degree of relief from the insecurities engendered by
the Madden Board's earlier conflicts over units. While helping unions to
entrench themselves in stable bargaining relationships with employers,
however, curbs on alterations in the form of representation gave incumbents only partial security of tenure. If unions were to enjoy complete
security in a bargaining relationship for a predictable length of time the
Board had to limit the frequency with which changes of representation
might be made. Here too, the adherents of industrial pluralism who had
succeeded the Madden Board permitted their technocratic respect for
institutional stability and order to overwhelm the act's liberal commitments to freedom of choice.

Thermidor

At any given moment in the history of national labor relations policy
administration after 1935, one of the clearest indications of the extent
to which the Board desired to impose limits on the pursuit of self-determination by employees was the particular status accorded to the contract in collective bargaining policy. That contractual concepts would
have an important role in statutory policy had become likely once the
duty to bargain was inserted in the Wagner bill during the Senate hearings, for as the first NLRB had stated in *Houde Engineering Corporation* (1934), collective bargaining was a means to an end, and "the end
is an agreement."[86] Following this lead the Madden Board had early
established that the Wagner Act contemplated the embodiment of the
terms agreed upon by the parties in a contract binding upon both for a
definite period of time.[87]

In identifying the embodiment of terms and conditions of labor in a
written contract as the goal of the act, however, the Board raised two
absolutely crucial and related questions. First, did the existence of a
contract covering a group of employees preclude their exercise of their
statutory rights to select a new bargaining representative for the life of

85. Millis and Brown, *From the Wagner Act to Taft-Hartley*, 142–3.
86. 1 NLRB [old] no. 12, 39–44.
87. See, for example, *St. Joseph Stockyards Company* (July 1936), 2 NLRB 39.

the contract, or at least for some "reasonable" portion thereof? Second, who were the parties to the contract?

As we have seen, where a union had not been selected in accordance with the provisions of the Wagner Act, the Madden Board quite routinely ignored its demands that the Board respect the collective bargaining relationships which it had established.[88] This constituted a denial that unions could enjoy collective bargaining rights as parties to contracts concluded independently of the act. But even where the union was demanding vindication of collective bargaining rights enjoyed as a consequence of its selection as a bargaining representative its position was no more certain, for just as unions enjoyed no bargaining rights independent of the act so the rights they enjoyed within the framework established by the act were entirely consequential upon their status as agents. They did not enjoy independent legal rights to be vindicated insofar as they had been accorded contractual recognition by an employer. "The position of a national union organization [under the Wagner Act] is considered that of a purely incidental conduit for the free expression of employee will," wrote one commentator in 1942. "Recognition of an independent legal right in the union no longer has the support which it mustered when agreements could be negotiated independent of questions of majority representation."[89] The majority of the employees – identifiable through the administrative processes of the Board – was considered to be the principal in the contractual relationship with the employer, holding rights through the agency of the union. "Thus any exclusive interest claimed by the agent is defeasible at the will of the principal."[90] The union, in short, was no more allowed a vested interest in a contract established in accordance with the act than one established independent of it.

The Madden Board's approach had distinctly anti-contractual implications, for it denied that contracts could inhibit the exercise of statutory rights. This was made clear in *New England Transportation Company* (January 1936), one of the Board's earliest decisions. In this case, the Board was confronted with the contention that the terms of contracts already entered into by the employees petitioning for representation barred them from choosing a new bargaining representative.[91] The

---

88. As noted in Chapter Five.
89. Note, "Change of Bargaining Representative During the Life of a Collective Agreement under the Wagner Act," *Yale Law Journal*, 51 (1942), 471. See also Bertam F. Willcox, "The Triboro Case – Mountain or Molehill?" *Harvard Law Review*, 56 (1943), 576–609.
90. "Change of Bargaining Representative," 472.
91. 1 NLRB 130. On the anticontractual implications of the Wagner Act, see Karl Klare, "Judicial Deradicalization of the Wagner Act and the Origins of Modern Legal Consciousness," *Minnesota Law Review*, 62 (1978), 265–339.

Board's reply was unambiguous. "The whole process of collective bargaining and unrestricted choice of representatives assumes the freedom of the employees to change their representatives while at the same time continuing the existing agreements under which the representative must function."[92] It confirmed this position several months later in *Swayne and Hoyt, Limited* (October 1936), where again it held that no term in an established contract could operate to prevent a redetermination of representatives once a question concerning representation had arisen. Even if the agreement were valid and binding, the Board stated, "it nevertheless is no bar to an election and consequent bargaining by the certified representative of the employees and can in no wise be construed so as to curtail the right of the employees to change their representatives for bargaining."[93] Furthermore, the Board concluded that if a new bargaining representative were chosen by the employees, it would be free to continue the existing agreement, to bargain for its modification, or even to terminate it altogether and seek a completely fresh agreement.

This policy, known as the doctrine of substitution, had been suggested to the Board by principles already developed by the National Mediation Board. Describing these to Madden in August 1936, NLRB attorney Philip Levy pointed out that by granting the right of representation to employees, the National Labor Relations Act, like the Railway Labor Act, had altered the legal status of trade unions. "The trade union's status in the negotiation and consummation of collective agreements is changed from that of a principal agreeing to supply labor at particular terms, to that of agent or representative of the employees . . . whose conditions of employment are the subject of the collective bargain." According to Levy, this meant that the existence of an unexpired agreement could not bar a redetermination of representatives, for the contract existed independently of the incumbent representative and could be assumed by any new representative chosen.[94]

Substitution was to be of considerable importance to the Madden Board throughout its incumbency. Only Edwin Smith held to the theory with complete consistency, however, his colleagues accepting that if the employees' right to change their bargaining representatives were held to be completely unrestricted the status of bargaining relationships established in accordance with the act would be constantly in doubt,[95] and

---

92. 1 NLRB 130, at 139.   93. 2 NLRB 282, at 286.
94. Levy to Madden (17 August 1936), in *RG 25*, Box 338 ("Assistant General Counsel Witt's Records, 1935–36"). See also *New England Transportation*, 1 NLRB 130, at 139, where the NLRB cites the National Mediation Board's *First Annual Report* (1935) in support of its decision.
95. Willcox, "The Triboro Case," 603.

the Madden Board slowly developed policies which imposed some discretionary limits on the exercise of those formal statutory rights. By the
end of 1938 it was well established that once certified a representative
should not be disturbed during its initial year of tenure, and that any
contract negotiated by a certified representative during that period
should preclude the initiation of a representation proceeding for at least
one year.[96] Then, in *National Sugar Refining Company* (January 1939),
the Board held that the extension of an already existing contract for a
further term also barred representation proceedings for at least the first
year of the extended term if the petition were filed after the incumbent
had begun to seek the extension.[97] Smith argued in dissent that if contracts were held to bar representation petitions beyond their first year,
the possibility would arise that the same contract might become a per-
petual bar through serial extensions.[98] But his protest was to no avail,
and by the end of 1941 the Millis Board had succeeded in turning
contract-bar into a major tool for securing incumbent unions. Given
that the purpose of the act was "to attain stabilized labor relations in
industry through collective bargaining," the Board stated in November
of that year, if contracting parties could demonstrate that two-year
contracts were customary in their industries such contracts would be
held to "constitute a bar to an investigation and certification of representatives despite a change of affiliation by a substantial number of
members of the contracting unions to the petitioning union."[99] Recognizing that it was confronted with "weighing and resolving the conflicting interests in maintaining the stability of relationships previously established by collective bargaining contracts as opposed to the right of
the majority of employees to change their collective bargaining representatives at any particular time," the Board found that the act's commitment to stability and order in industry required that the right of
employees to change their representatives be limited. Henceforth, said
the Board, "to hold that such a contract should bar an election . . . is to
insure the industrial stability achieved through a valid collective bargaining agreement . . ."[100]

Smith's opposition to the development of a blanket contract-bar principle reflected his concern that unions in a position to negotiate closed
shop contracts would be enabled thereby to insulate themselves completely from the workings of the act. His apprehension appeared at one

---

96. See, for example, *MGM Studios, and Motion Picture Producers' Association et al.*
    (June 1938), 7 NLRB 662; "Change of Bargaining Representative," 466–9.
97. 10 NLRB 1410. 98. Ibid., 1416.
99. *Owens-Illinois Pacific Coast Company*, 36 NLRB 990, at 990.
100. *Mill B., Incorporated* (April 1942), 40 NLRB 346, at 351.

stage to be shared by Leiserson. Writing while the NLRB was contemplating its *National Sugar* decision and several months before he would himself become a member, Leiserson expressed surprise that the Board should find it necessary to depart from *New England Transportation* and the National Mediation Board precedents upon which that decision had been based, and recommended that it deny contracts the faculty of barring representation proceedings for any period of time. "[U]nder the provisions of the [Railway Labor] Act, the contracts are made between carriers and their employees as the second party, the organization merely acting as representatives for the purpose of negotiating the contract. It seems to me that the same rule is not only applicable to the contracts that prevail in other industries, but under the provisions of [the National Labor Relations] Act no other rule can work out practically and smoothly."[101] Leiserson acknowledged that by permitting unions to seek the inclusion of closed shop clauses in collective bargaining contracts the Wagner Act appeared to allow them the means to establish legal and institutional interests of their own in the contracts. But he argued that the Board should resist pressures to interpret the closed shop provision as readmitting unions as parties to the contract and thus as precluding redeterminations of representatives during the contract's life:

> If the Labor Relations Board permits a closed shop contract to prevent an election when the majority of the employees want to change from one union to another, the Board is in effect denying the employees the right given them by Congress to bargain collectively through representatives of their own choosing. I know that the lawyers think that by authorizing the closed shop under certain conditions Congress itself authorized such a denial of the free choice by the employees. But I consider this a technical legal argument which if it prevails will defeat the fundamental purpose of guaranteeing the right to organize and bargain collectively to the employees. A question of this kind must be settled by what the practices and procedures of collective bargaining and collective labor relations require and not by legal doctrines of agency law. I think the Labor Relations Board would be better advised to ditch its lawyers' advice and to be guided by its labor relations experts.[102]

Once on the Board, however, Leiserson turned out to be susceptible to the legal arguments he had previously criticized. Given an opportunity, in *Ansley Radio Corporation* (December 1939), to join with Smith and establish conclusively that "an otherwise valid agreement of an

101. Leiserson to William Gorham Rice, Jr. (15 December 1938), in *Leiserson Papers*, Box 35, ("Rice").
102. Ibid.

employer with a labor organization to require membership in that organization as a condition of employment becomes inoperative upon a
change in choice of collective bargaining representative by a majority of
the employees within the appropriate collective bargaining unit covered
by the agreement," he refused to participate.[103] Consequently, the point
was left unresolved.[104]

There were two ways in which unions might take advantage of closed
shop clauses to entrench themselves against challengers for the duration
of an agreement, one involving the Board and the other the courts. First,
there was the situation which confronted the Board in *Ansley Radio*.
Here the union in question, the IBEW, had successfully prevailed upon
the employer not to reemploy a number of workers who had agitated for
a change in bargaining representatives by showing that they had not
maintained their membership in the IBEW as required by the contract. In
such situations unions would conventionally argue that even if the dis-
missals were oppressive to the rights of individual employees, as long as it
could be established that the employer's action was in accordance with a
legitimate contract it was beyond the Board's purview.

The *Ansley Radio* situation was clearly illustrated in *Taylor Milling
Corporation*, a case which, according to the AFL, underlined the disruption to collective bargaining relationships which would result from
decisions denying the authority of closed shop clauses.[105] In this case, a
group of employees who had agitated for the replacement of their bargaining representative by a new union had been dismissed by their
employer in accordance with the incumbent's closed shop contract.
Having failed, predictably enough, to obtain redress from the employer
in a grievance proceeding initiated through the incumbent, these employees had then filed a petition with the Board charging the employer
with unfair dismissal. The union in question, the International Brotherhood of Teamsters, argued that the Board had no authority to grant a
hearing on the grounds that "where a contract exist[s] containing provisions for grievances and a member is discharged and the discharge was
not settled to the satisfaction of the worker, that the Board had no

103. 18 NLRB 1028.
104. Smith and Madden agreed that it was illegal for a union to use a closed shop
    proviso to force the discharge of employees supporting a rival as long as they
    remained in compliance with the requirement that they be members in good stand-
    ing of the incumbent. Madden, however, felt that there was no violation of the act
    where, as here, the company had refused to rehire employees who had ceased to be
    members of the incumbent during a layoff. Smith, in contrast, saw this as simply a
    manoeuver to enable the company and the incumbent to conspire to discriminate
    while remaining within the letter of the act. Ibid. 1066–9.
105. See, for example, testimony of Frank P. Fenton, *Senate Hearings*, 1313–14.

jurisdiction and that a worker could seek damages only in a civil court."[106] For the Board to assume jurisdiction would mean compulsory arbitration, directly threatening the authority of independent unions and undermining their ability to achieve the stable collective bargaining contemplated by the act. "In the present case the ultimate objective of the Board has been reached in having agreements with labor organizations," said the union's attorney. "[If] the Board is to take the stand that after an agreement has been arrived at that it is still the supreme body to settle things over a union, then there is no necessity for unions. We might just as well cut out the A F of L, the CIO, or the railroad brotherhoods, and call us adjuncts of the National Labor Relations Board, departments A, B, C, and the others, because the Board will then have the authority to step in and supersede any union, to supersede any settlement of its own grievances . . ."[107] In the same vein, AFL director of organization Frank Fenton told the Senate Committee on Education and Labor that "If [you heed] the urgings of the Board to leave it full power of discretion, it will indeed be but a short while before the act, labor unions, and collective bargaining are dead and buried."[108]

The Board did not decide *Taylor Milling Corporation* until August 1940.[109] Again Smith wished to establish that the mere existence of a valid closed shop contract would not justify an employer in taking action to enforce its terms at the request of the contracting labor organization if it were known that the majority of the employees in the bargaining unit had transferred their allegiance elsewhere. Again Leiserson refused to support his contention, and again no clear ruling was made on the issue by the Board. Not until September 1942, after repeated proddings from both employers and unions, did the Board clarify the position. Then Millis and the new member, Gerard Reilly, used a three-year-old case that the Board had originally tried to dismiss, *Rutland Court Owners,* to hold that closed shop contracts could not be allowed to nullify altogether the right of self-organization. "The fundamental policy of the Act, in the light of which all its provisions – including the proviso to section 8(3) – must be read, is to 'promote industrial peace,' thereby fostering commerce, through the protection of self-organization and the encouragement of collective bargaining by representatives of the employees' own choosing." If this fundamental policy were to be effected, the majority continued, it was necessary "as the life of the collective contract draws to a close, that the employees be able to advocate a change in their affiliation without fear of discharge by an employer for so doing."[110] Leiserson,

106. Ibid., 1313.   107. In ibid., 1314.   108. Ibid., 1314.
109. 26 NLRB 424.   110. 44 NLRB 587 (September 1942), at 596.

dissenting, would have held to the Board's original decision to dismiss the case, though not on the grounds that the Board had originally offered – that the case did not fall within the stream of commerce and was therefore outside federal jurisdiction – but on the grounds that the closed shop contract was perfectly valid. "If valid closed shop contracts, which are expressly permitted by the Act, have undesirable effects, it is for the Congress, and not for the Board, to make the modifications."[111]

By finally holding that closed shop contracts could not vitiate the reasonable exercise by employees of their right to self-organization, the Board showed that there were some limits to the extent to which it was prepared to see employee rights abdicated to contractual stability and order in collective bargaining relations. But by 1942 the Board was already well on the way to establishing that closed shop contracts or not, incumbent unions could normally count themselves safe from challenge for at least the first two years of any initial contract period or renewal thereof. In any case, the last word did not lie with the Board but with the courts, and here little hesitation was being shown in subordinating the right of self-organization to the asserted "public" interest in industrial stability. Here, as a result, incumbents enjoyed a second opportunity to use closed shop clauses to entrench themselves in collective bargaining relationships.

As we have seen, by the early 1930s courts commonly approached collective agreements as contracts negotiated between employers and unions for the benefit of the employee but to which he was not a party. This approach treated the union as the principal with which the employer dealt, legitimating the unions' claims to embody the interests of employees and at the same time providing unions with a contractual basis on which they might claim interests of their own.[112] By adopting the very different theory of principal and agent the Wagner Act had challenged this common law approach, creating a fundamental conflict between the common law of contract as administered by the courts, and federal and related state labor relations statutes. "The acts . . . deal with a choice of bargaining agencies by the employees. They do not deal, except incidentally, with protecting the interests of unions in agreements made with employers. If they mean what they say, the duty of the employer to bargain with his employees through an agency of their own choosing is a continuous one. Contract law, *per contra*, runs in terms of two parties who have bound themselves to deal with each other."[113]

111. Ibid., 603.   112. See above, Chapters Three and Four.
113. T. Richard Witmer, "Collective Labor Agreements in the Courts," *The Yale Law Journal*, 48 (1938), 221.

Observers predicted that these two sets of rules would have to be har-
monized in some way.[114]

The policies adopted by the Madden Board in order to overcome
what it perceived to be the danger of instability in bargaining relationships had already gone some way toward establishing a basis upon
which the harmonization of labor relations law and contract law could
take place. But at least in its early days the Board had attempted to
avoid positions which might imply that unions did, after all, have vested
interests in the contracts they negotiated. No such inhibitions were felt
in the courts where, as the Supreme Court put it in 1938, the "manifest
objective" of the Wagner Act's collective bargaining provisions was
interpreted to be "the making of contracts *with labor organizations.*"[115]
Here employees continued to be regarded as more or less passive benefi-
ciaries of contracts negotiated by unions on their behalf. Here the contract "would be strictly enforced as creating property rights in the
union."[116]

This refusal by the courts to vary their application of common law
contract rules to accommodate statutory innovations had far-reaching
implications for attempts by workers to change their bargaining representatives. Courts held, for example, that the simple transfer of majority
support from one union to another could not divest the original representative of interests it had acquired as a result of an agreement negotiated with the employer. Nor could the employees in question repudiate
the agreement where they had already accepted benefits arising from it.
Employees, in short, were saddled with both union and contract for the
full duration of the contract's term.[117] This was not all. If the contract
named the national union as the representative, which was not unusual,
or even a local union whose jurisdiction extended beyond the particular
unit in question, there was a real question whether it was not also
immune from repudiation by workers in the unit on the grounds that
the interests of the principal – the union – in maintaining the contract
stretched beyond the single unit which the contract covered to encompass the preservation of the union's strength for the benefit of its members everywhere. "As a source of strength in industry *as a whole,* the
contract is of vital importance to the union organization and *all* its
members."[118]

The effects of superimposing a position founded in the common law of

114. Ibid., 221.
115. *Consolidated Edison Company of New York, Inc. v. NLRB* (1938), 305 US 197,
      at 236 [emphasis supplied].
116. "Change of Bargaining Representative," 474.
117. Ibid., 472–4.   118. Ibid., 473 [emphasis supplied].

contract upon the approach embodied in the Wagner Act can be seen in cases like *Labarge v. Malone Aluminum Corporation* (1940),[119] where a New York state court enjoined performance of a contract negotiated by an employee with a union newly certified by the Board as a majority representative on the grounds that the life of the contract negotiated by the new union's defeated predecessor was not yet up. *NLRB v. Electric Vacuum Cleaner Company* (1941)[120] and *Triboro Coach Corporation v. New York State Labor Relations Board* (1941),[121] are also good illustrations. In both it was held that an incumbent union might effectively entrench itself against challenges by negotiating a renewal or extension to its contract even in the face of the hostility of a majority of its former supporters. Such decisions meant that by the early 1940s stringent limits on the right of employees to freedom of choice of representation were being set by both state and federal courts. According to one contemporary commentator, "if the present judicial attitude prevails, change of representative will be held ineffective during a valid agreement for whatever term."[122] The implications, indeed, were more severe even than this:

> It appears that a closed shop contract may be held by nature conclusive of representation for the purposes of negotiation even as to the future. In the absence of an officially proven shift, the authority of the existing formal representative may not be terminated by mere doubt as to its continuing majority status. Thus an outside union must, to prevent extension of an existing contract, establish a bargaining position during the term of the contract. Its difficulties in obtaining and proving a majority are increased by the employer resistance held permissible under the closed shop proviso. Since the union contract may be renewed . . . against the will of the particular employees, attractive possibilities are offered for self-perpetuation by an inside union.[123]

Judicial confinement of employee self-organization did not stop at the boundaries of the common law of contract. As Wagner himself had acknowledged in 1937, his act had done nothing "to repeal the multitudinous state and federal court decisions defining labor's rights," nor was it intended to "displace the numerous Federal, state and local laws directed against restraints of trade, improper picketing or violence by either party in the course of labor disputes."[124] The Supreme Court underlined Wagner's message early in 1939, when in *NLRB v. Fansteel Metallurgical Corporation* it held that the prior commission of unfair

119. 6 Labor Relations Reporter 887.   120. 120 F2 611.   121. 286 NY 314.
122. "Change of Bargaining Representative," 479.   123. Ibid., 479.
124. "Wagner Answers His Critics," *New York Times Magazine* (25 July 1937).

labor practices by employers did nothing to loosen the legal constraints on their employees' activities. Congress had never intended "to invest those who go on strike with an immunity from discharge for acts of trespass or violence against the employer's property," said the Court, and condemned all such behavior as completely contrary to the act's purposes. It took the opportunity to place a particularly wide range of employee activity beyond the act's protective pale:

> The fundamental policy of the Act is to safeguard the rights of self-organization and collective bargaining, and thus by the promotion of industrial peace to remove obstructions to the free flow of commerce as defined in the Act. There is not a line in the statute to warrant the conclusion that it is any part of the policies of the Act to encourage employees to resort to force and violence in defiance of the laws of the land. On the contrary the purpose of the Act is to promote peaceful settlements of disputes by providing legal remedies for the invasion of the employees' rights, to assure them self-organization and freedom in representation, not to license them to commit tortious acts or to protect them from the appropriate consequences of unlawful conduct. We are of the opinion that to provide for the reinstatement or the reemployment of employees guilty of the acts which the Board finds to have been committed in this instance would not only not effectuate any policy of the Act but would directly tend to make abortive its plan for peaceable procedure.[125]

The area of proscribed activity was further enlarged in subsequent decisions. In *C.G. Conn, Limited v. NLRB* (1939), for example, the Seventh Circuit Court of Appeals held that the use of "work-in" tactics in a collective bargaining dispute was not protected by the act.[126] Overturning the Board's decision to reinstate a group of employees discharged because they had refused to work compulsory overtime without being paid an overtime rate, the court held that their action in continuing to work a normal day but leaving at the end of the regular shift was not a strike, and therefore was not protected by the act. "We are unable to accept [the Board's] argument that an employee can be on strike and at work simultaneously," it stated. "We think he must be on the job subject to the authority and control of the employer, or off the job as a striker, in support of some grievance . . ." These were the only courses of action which workers were at liberty to pursue under the act. "When

125. 306 US 240, 1 CD 1346, at 1357. See also the Board's decision in *Republic Steel Corporation* (October 1938), 9 NLRB 219, where the Board accepted the corporation's contention that "acts of violence by individual strikers render . . . reinstatement inequitable in this case and would defeat rather than effectuate the purposes of the Act," the anterior commission of aggravating unfair labor practices by the corporation notwithstanding (387).

126. 108 F2 390 (1939).

[the employer] refused to comply with their request, there were two courses open. First, they could continue to work, and negotiate further with the petitioner, or, second, they could strike in protest." By doing neither the employees were behaving in a manner which challenged the legitimate sphere of employer authority recognized by the act:

> We are aware of no law or logic that gives the employee the right to work upon terms prescribed solely by him. That is plainly what was sought to be done in this instance. It is not a situation in which employees ceased work in protest against conditions imposed by the employer, but one in which the employees sought and intended to continue work upon their own notion of the terms which should prevail. If they had a right to fix the hours of their employment, it would follow that a similar right existed by which they could pre-scribe all conditions and regulations affecting their employment.[127]

The courts' circumscription of collective activity complemented their identification of common law contracts as the abiding purpose of the organization and representation of labor envisaged by the Wagner Act. Having defined that essentially limited goal as the act's "manifest objec-tive," the courts sought to ensure that the self-activity of workers re-mained focussed fully on the creation and maintenance of the institu-tions most likely to achieve its realization.[128] But this did not mean that the courts were pursuing policies at variance with those of the NLRB. To the contrary, the resolution of the Board's internal conflicts in 1940 had left it as committed as the courts to an ever-stronger emphasis on the achievement of stable collective bargaining relationships as the sole object of federal labor relations policy. Thus it is no surprise to find William Leiserson warmly approving a 1942 New York Court of Ap-peals decision which enjoined workers from engaging in picketing and boycotts to protest the certification of a rival union in a representation dispute. "If we are to have orderly labor relations," he wrote "it is obviously absurd to hold that a minority group may call a strike to force the employer to violate the law . . ."[129]

Nor did this thermidor in employee rights excite many protests from within the organized labor movement.[130] AFL union leaders, it is true,

---

127. Ibid., 397.
128. Klare, "Judicial Deradicalization of the Wagner Act," 265–339.
129. Leiserson to Paul M. Herzog (15 June 1942), in *Leiserson Papers*, Box 17, ("Her-zog"). Herzog at this time was chairman of the New York State Labor Relations Board. In 1945 he succeeded Harry A. Millis as chairman of the NLRB.
130. Indeed, the AFL was highly critical of the Board for its relaxation of closed shop restraints in the *Rutland Court* decision in favor of greater employee freedom to change bargaining representatives. By indicating their willingness to work under the original closed shop contract, the Federation argued, the employees in question

had been required to shrug off their jealous commitment to exclusive jurisdiction and private ordering – the heritage of voluntarism – in order properly to appreciate that benefits might accrue from federal intervention. But the act's promise of substantial increases in bargaining power had, in the long run, persuaded all but a tiny minority. As for the CIO, the majority of its affiliates had quickly learned to prefer the security which accompanied institutionalization and bureaucratic routine to the heady uncertainty of spontaneous rank-and-file action. As Nelson Lichtenstein has observed, "national trade union leaders recognized that, under the political conditions existing in the late Depression era, shop-floor bargaining . . . was incompatible with the establishment of a stable relationship with management."[131] Consequently, "Top leaders like Philip Murray and John L. Lewis declared collective bargaining contracts 'sacred,' and even younger militants like Walter Reuther and Harry Bridges sought to curb such unauthorized activity."[132]

The proliferation of administrative and judicial innovations safeguarding incumbents and circumscribing collective activity reflected the steadily growing influence of pluralistic industrial relations philosophies on the implementation of the New Deal collective bargaining policy. Seeing the collective agreement as the key to stability, pluralists increasingly stressed the importance of entrenching incumbents to the maintenance of that stability. On these premises, the courts and the Board between them created a new legal framework for stability and order in

---

had "contracted away . . . their rights not to remain a member of the AFL union and by contract made membership in that organization a condition of their employment." By refusing to acknowledge this the Board had "erroneously placed undue emphasis on the right of employees to choose bargaining agents as provided in the Act at the expense of the basic purpose of the Act to protect commerce by bringing about stable labor relations through collective bargaining contracts between employers and employees." See AFL general counsel Padway's "Petition for Rehearing" (3 October 1942), in *RG* 25, Informal File C-1639, *Rutland Court Owners*. The Supreme Court did not rule on the question until 1949. Then, in *Colgate-Palmolive-Peet Company v. NLRB*, 338 US 355, the Court held that "It is quite reasonable to suppose that Congress thought it conducive to stability of labor relations that parties be required to live up to a valid closed-shop contract made voluntarily with the recognized bargaining representative, regardless of internal disruptions growing out of agitation for a change in bargaining representative," and overturned a Board order reinstating certain employees expelled by the incumbent for activity on behalf of a rival and subsequently discharged by the employer in conformity with the contract (364).

131. Nelson N. Lichtenstein, "Industrial Democracy, Contract Unionism, and the National War Labor Board," *Labor Law Journal*, 33, 8 (August, 1982), 526. See also his *Labor's War at Home: The CIO in World War Two* (Cambridge, England, 1982), 20–66.

132. Lichtenstein, "Industrial Democracy, Contract Unionism, and the National War Labor Board," 526.

labor relations. In the process, however, it became apparent that where necessary the values of free choice and self-determination – the values which, it had been claimed, made the Wagner Act the symbol of a new age – would be allowed to fall by the wayside.

PART III

"Lie down like good dogs"

None of us — least of all yourself — thought that the Wagner Act could be the whole of a national labor policy. But we did know that no such policy could even begin to evolve until workingmen and women were protected in the right to form trade unions, as employers had long been at liberty to form corporations or band together in trade assocations. With that foundation now securely laid, we are free to move forward to deal with today's problems in the light of today's needs.

There are still some who would set the clock back and deprive labor of its hard-won rights. They fear American labor, forgetting that employees too are citizens, dedicated to our institutions and our way of life. There are others who would seek to use the progressive legislation of the past decade as an instrument or a justification for license to disregard the public welfare. Fortunately, neither group represents more than a small minority of the American people.

Paul M. Herzog, John M. Houston, and James J. Reynolds to
Senator Robert F. Wagner (21 April 1947), in *Wagner Papers*, 714
LA (Labor Files) 725, folder 150.

Introduction: responsible unionism

By the early 1940s, the right of workers to associate had clearly become subordinated in federal policy to the achievement of stability and industrial peace. Pursuit of these priorities had led both the Board and the courts to develop ever wider definitions of the unions' interests in collective bargaining agreements and simultaneously to narrow their definitions of legitimate collective activity among workers to what was in effect a search for contractual order, to be conducted for their benefit by their "designated" representative. The Board and the courts, in short, were functioning in such a way as to keep employees, as well as employers, within the parameters of the new model of industrial relations which they were establishing.

These trends were greatly reinforced by America's deepening involvement in World War II. By the end of 1941, as Nelson Lichtenstein has recently shown, union leaders had become increasingly concerned that the Roosevelt administration's pressure upon them to subordinate immediate trade union goals to the overall success of the defense effort would result in the growth of apathy and resentment amongst trade union members, causing increasing institutional instability and, ultimately, the decomposition of their organizations.[1] Judicial and administrative policies designed to suppress rank and file collective action and to entrench union authority even in the face of the hostility of a majority of those whom the union represented, helped to allay these fears.

Despite the clear conservative bias inherent in this growing stress upon institutional stabilization and responsible collective action, labor relations policy throughout the war and postwar periods was the object of growing hostility from conservative Congressional and entrepreneurial groups. Two reasons for their sustained opposition to unions and collective bargaining after 1940 can be offered. First, although union leaders might look to contractual relationships primarily as sources of

1. Nelson Lichtenstein, *Labor's War at Home: The CIO in World War Two* (Cambridge, England, 1982), 67–81.

247

institutional stability and security, they still embraced a rather more expansive view of the proper scope for union influence within those relationships than most managements were prepared to accept. This did not show up so much at plant level, for generally unions had exhibited no real desire "to usurp management's function of running the plant" and preferred instead to act as "intelligent critic[s] of management's policy."[2] At industry level, however, union leaders were quite successful in transcending some of the limitations of strictly bilateral negotiations with employers by entangling them in the complex web of tripartite political relationships between the government and the peak organizations of labor and capital which grew out of wartime compulsory dispute settlement and prevention procedures.[3]

Second, and just as important, both corporate management and Congressional conservatives were only too well aware of the political significance of mass union membership. Both had felt the impact of the CIO's campaigns on behalf of Roosevelt in 1936 and 1940, and both watched with increasing concern as the organized labor movement, led by the CIO, created structures to consolidate and sustain its capacity to intervene decisively in the nation's political life. "From the standpoint of the ultimate welfare of the people of the United States," wrote one Missouri business executive in May 1946 for the attention of presidential aide Clark M. Clifford, "I think there is no question but that if labor is permitted to consolidate its power and to use that power to elect more Claude Peppers and Henry Wallaces to positions of authority, we shall find ourselves in a position in which labor is stronger than the government of the United States and is able to dictate to it."[4]

On two occasions during 1945 there were signs that some elements within the business community and the organized labor movement might be able sufficiently to reconcile their conflicting perceptions of the proper role for unions and collective bargaining in industry to sustain the semi-institutionalized accommodation between leaders of both sides of industry which had developed out of necessity during the war.[5] In March, the

---

2. William M. Leiserson, "Union Labor Relations Policy and Government Policy" (draft) in *Leiserson Papers,* Box 50, ("Speeches and Articles"). See also Howell John Harris, *The Right to Manage: Industrial Relations Policies of American Business in the 1940s* (Madison, Wisconsin, 1982), 70–1.

3. Nelson Lichtenstein, "Industrial Democracy, Contract Unionism, and the National War Labor Board," *Labor Law Journal,* 33, 8 (August, 1982), 526.

4. Towner Phelan, vice-president, St. Louis Union Trust Company, to A.B. Lansing (31 May 1946), in *Papers of Clark M. Clifford,* Box 6, ("Case Bill Miscellaneous"). (Harry S Truman Presidential Library, Independence, Missouri). [Hereinafter cited as *Clifford Papers.*]

5. Harris, *The Right to Manage,* 105–18.

president of the U.S. Chamber of Commerce, Eric Johnston, joined Presidents Green of the AFL and Murray of the CIO in promulgating a "Charter" setting out principles by which postwar labor–management relations might be governed. Business would recognize labor's right to organize and bargain collectively and would refrain from its attempts to have current labor relations legislation repealed or amended; labor would recognize management's "right to manage" and agree to continuation of the no-strike pledge. Then in November, at Truman's Labor–Management Conference, business representatives again indicated their readiness to accept a permanent role for collective bargaining.[6]

Appearances, however, were deceptive. The "progressive" industrialists whom Johnson spoke for "were in fact a relatively uninfluential minority."[7] As for the Labor–Management Conference, although the employer delegates were prepared to acknowledge that they had a duty to bargain with the unions chosen by their employees, they underlined their determination to preserve management rights by restricting the scope of bargaining to "wages, hours and working conditions," by stressing the importance of rendering unions responsible for breach of collective agreements, and by insisting that unions be restrained from taking direct action on representation or bargaining questions in defiance of statutory procedures.

What the 1945 meetings demonstrated was that, on some issues, a degree of accord was possible amongst business and labor leaders. "Both had an interest in the orderly institutionalization of conflict."[8] But with the failure of the two sides to reach any agreement on a reconversion wage and price policy their fragile consensus was almost immediately placed under intolerable pressure by mounting industrial unrest. In any case, it could not accommodate those within and outside Congress who were committed to the destruction of the political power of the organized labor movement. Members of this group – men such as Sewell Avery of Montgomery Ward, Frederick Crawford of Thompson Products and a wide range of southern coal and textile interests – saw the unions not as a potential source of stability, but as the major obstacle to their attempts to eviscerate the domestic social welfare and planning policies of the 1930s. They denounced collective bargaining as "an assault on liberty . . . as an evil thing which is against the public interest," and demanded the repeal of all legislation "which conferred upon unions special privileges and immunities not enjoyed by any other citi-

6. Ibid., 110, 111–18.   7. Lichtenstein, *Labor's War at Home*, 219.
8. Harris, *The Right to Manage*, 118.

zen or entity" in order that labor might once more be subordinated to "the common good."[9]

The reconversion strikes of 1945 and 1946 and the results of the 1946 mid-term elections made it inevitable that legislation amending existing statutory labor relations policy would be passed in the new Congress. The elections also seemed to place conservatives of both parties in positions which they could use to ensure that the amendments would destroy the bargaining power and political influence of the organized labor movement, thus opening the way to legislation unmaking the New Deal. Certainly CIO president Philip Murray thought so. According to him, the Taft-Hartley bill to amend the National Labor Relations Act, passed by Congress in June 1947, was the "creature of the reactionary arm of big business." Having successfully destroyed price control and having just as successfully undermined the housing program, business reactionaries had now "deliberately created conditions leading to an industrial unrest" in order to justify the passage of legislation which would render the organized labor movement impotent "so that the march of profits, the growth of monopoly, the intensification of economic insecurity may proceed unhampered and unchallenged."[10]

Yet despite the indisputable accuracy of Murray's description of the legislation's sponsors and of their objectives, a close examination of Taft-Hartley provides evidence less of the manifold opportunities that existed after World War Two for those who wished to bring about a fundamental alteration in federal policy, than of the power of institutional forces constraining the proponents of the legislation to endorse basic continuity.[11] The strong and well-established institutional structures which populated the labor relations environment – the unions themselves, national and state labor relations bureaucracies, the center corporations and their industrial relations departments – had been unable to reach agreement in 1945, but virtually all still identified their interests as lying with the continuation of "realistic" industrial re-

9. John Scoville of the Chrysler Corporation, speech to the Detroit Kiwanis (8 August 1944) in Harris, *The Right to Manage*, 111; W. Edwin Moser to Clark M. Clifford (28 December 1946), in *Clifford Papers*, Box 7, ("Labor – 80th Congress"). See also Lichtenstein, *Labor's War at Home*, 219–221.

10. Philip Murray to Harry S. Truman (9 June 1947), in *Clifford Papers*, Box 8, ("Labor – HR 3020 – Publications"). Murray's view was shared by the first historians of postwar labor relations policy. See, for example, Joel Seidman, *American Labor from Defence to Reconversion* (Chicago, 1953), 264–9.

11. This essential continuity is reflected in the work of more recent historians. See, for example, Arthur F. McClure, *The Truman Administration and the Problems of Postwar Labor, 1945–48* (Rutherford, New Jersey, 1969); Philip Ross, *The Government as a Source of Union Power: The Role of Public Policy in Collective Bargaining* (Providence, Rhode Island, 1965).

lations.[12] While the act established beyond doubt Congress's determination to limit the influence of entrenched labor organizations, therefore, the ambitions of some of its proponents to go further than this and overthrow the model of labor relations established in the United States after 1940 remained unfulfilled.

The Taft-Hartley Act thus proved much less of a break with the past than has usually been assumed. Consequently, despite its objections to the sweeping character of many of the amendments, the NLRB did not find it difficult subsequently to accommodate them to the general thrust of federal policy. Indeed, as Clyde W. Summers pointed out long ago, "a careful study of the NLRB decisions suggests that . . . [b]y 1947, the Board itself had already adopted many of the 'changes' of Taft-Hartley."[13] Yet in thus confirming the institutional strength of the established pluralist model of labor relations the events of 1947 and their administrative aftermath also confirmed for all to see that the pluralist model had become as formidable a weapon against those elements within the organized labor movement which sought to live outside its considerable constraints as it was against delinquent employers. Nor were the unions unaware of this. "We may be at the threshold of an attitude of labor unions toward the Wagner Act which is reminiscent of an earlier stage in its evolution and which the Senator, I am sure, will remember," wrote Morton Stavis (legal advisor to Wagner's assistant, David Delman) in June 1944. "[I]n 1934, many of the trade unionists actively opposed the National Labor Relations Act because they feared the possibility that it could be turned as a weapon against them. Today there seems to be a resurgence of this feeling and a genuine fear that sinister developments are afoot which may make the Wagner Act the ball and chain of the labor movement."[14]

12. Harris, *The Right to Manage,* 120.
13. Clyde W. Summers, "Politics, Policy-Making and the NLRB," *Syracuse Law Review,* 6 (1954–55), 93–108. As the Princeton University economist, David A. McCabe, put it in 1949, "The Wagner Act lifted the unions out of the category of private clubs in which the Supreme Court found them in *Adair v. United States* and *Coppage v. Kansas.* They now perform a statutory function and they are therefore subject to regulation in the performance of it." Testimony of David A. McCabe, in *Hearings Before the Committee on Labor and Public Welfare, U.S. Senate, on S249, A Bill to Diminish the Causes of Labor Disputes,* 81st Congress, 1st Session (Washington, 1949), 1566. [Hereinafter cited as *Senate Hearings III*].
14. Morton Stavis to David Delman (5 June 1944), in *Wagner Papers* 700 LA 721, folder 104.

7

The road to Taft-Hartley

As labor organizations grew in strength and developed toward maturity, Congressional emphasis shifted from protection of the nascent labor movement to the encouragement of collective bargaining and to administrative techniques for the peaceful resolution of industrial disputes.

Boys Markets, Inc. v. Retail Clerks Local 770 (1970), 398 US 235, at 251.

The decade following the Supreme Court's validation of the Wagner Act in 1937 saw American unions sustain the remarkable rate of growth which had begun early in the 1930s. Having doubled their membership in the four years after 1933, the unions more than doubled it again, expanding from 5,780,100 in 1937 to 14,594,700 in 1947. This raised the fraction of the non-farm labor force organized into trade unions from 11.8 percent in 1933 to 17.9 percent in 1937 and 31.8 percent in 1947, a level which was sustained into the second half of the 1950s.[1]

The expansion of defense-related production and accompanying manpower shortages during the war accounted for much of the unions' success in the post–Wagner era. In manufacturing industries, affiliates of both federations grew more rapidly during the war than at any other time. Unions in durable goods industries, for example, tripled in size between 1940 and 1945. This pattern was repeated in the construction industry, where AFL unions underwent their most rapid expansion during the construction boom of the early 1940s.[2]

Alterations in union size were accompanied by noticeable changes in the labor movement's organizational structure. Already by the late 1930s, each federation had introduced innovations designed to enhance its authority over affiliated unions.[3] By the early 1940s, similar centralizing trends had become noticeable in many international unions, particularly

1. Leo Troy, *Trade Union Membership, 1897–1962* (New York, 1965), 1–2.
2. Christopher L. Tomlins, "AFL Unions in the 1930s: Their Performance in Historical Perspective," *Journal of American History*, 65, 4 (1979), 1021–42.
3. See, for example, AFL Executive Council *Minutes* (9 August 1939); CIO Executive Board *Minutes* (14 October 1939, and 4 June 1940).

the new industrial unions, leading to a further concentration of authority over the development of organizing and collective bargaining policy in the hands of top union executives. The constitution of the United Steelworkers of America, newly adopted in May 1942, is a useful example. It allowed the union's president complete authority "to appoint, direct, suspend or remove such organizers, representatives, agents and employees as he may deem necessary." This was by no means unusual.[4]

Organizational centralization and the location of authority in a hierarchy of national union executives complemented the massive shift toward an industrial relations system based on collective contracts which had begun in the late 1930s. This trend accelerated markedly as the American economy moved into the defense era, and as government policies intended to prevent labor disputes from disrupting the smooth expansion of defense production imposed upon unions a more and more explicitly disciplinary role vis-à-vis the employees they represented. The removal of power from the shop-floor and its monopolization by the upper levels of national union bureaucracies became essential if the unions were to avoid succumbing to rank and file opposition.[5]

Policy innovations pioneered by wartime agencies also offered unions some protection from rank and file protest. Both the National Defense Mediation Board and its successor, the more powerful War Labor Board, sponsored the inclusion of compulsory "maintenance of membership" clauses in union contracts, preventing the erosion of membership which would otherwise doubtless have resulted from wartime restrictions on free collective bargaining.[6] In addition, through the Office of Price Administration, the Roosevelt administration established first selective and then general price controls to prevent inflationary surges from overwhelming the War Labor Board's "Little Steel" wage restraint formula.[7] Finally, the NDMB and the WLB were instrumental in developing formal rule-bound grievance arbitration procedures, capped with independent adjudication by an impartial umpire, to facilitate settlement and prevention of disputes and prevent workers from resorting to direct action undermining the unions' no-strike pledge.[8]

4. William M. Leiserson, "An Inside View of Labor," *U.S. News* (February 19, 1943), 52–4. See also Nelson Lichtenstein, *Labor's War at Home: The CIO in World War Two* (Cambridge, England, 1982), 44–202.
5. Lichtenstein, *Labor's War at Home*, 178–202. 6. Ibid., 78–81.
7. Andrew H. Bartels, "The Politics of Price Control: The Office of Price Administration and the Dilemmas of Economic Stabilization, 1940–1946" (unpublished Ph.D dissertation, The Johns Hopkins University, 1980).
8. Lichtenstein, *Labor's War at Home*, 178–82. See also Howell John Harris, *The Right to Manage: Industrial Relations Policies of American Business in the 1940s* (Madison, Wisconsin, 1982), 49–50.

The result of these wartime developments was, on the one hand, considerable success in restraining inflation during the period of hostilities and, on the other, promotion on a national scale of the broad pluralist labor relations model toward which the NLRB had begun to work under the direction of Leiserson and Millis.[9] But while the routinization of the pluralist model confirmed the authority of central union bureaucracies over rank and file action, it did not translate into a similarly enhanced influence for unions over corporate management. To the contrary, the pivotal War Labor Board tended to treat the preservation of management's unrestricted authority over the formulation and implementation of enterprise policy as a necessary condition of granting unions a voice in the determination of the conditions of employment of their members.[10] What this meant in practice was that the grievance procedures sponsored by the Board "wrote into law the contract-policing role of unions in collective bargaining." Management retained "the right of initiative and a broad discretion," while unions seeking redress were to refrain from "damaging or unpredictable industrial conflict."[11] The creation of such institutional obstacles to effective action added to the frustrations of union activists already handicapped in their attempts to put pressure on management by the Board's lengthy procedures. Combined with the vast expansion of corporate management's influence over the formulation of all aspects of federal policy which took place during the war,[12] this meant that when the war ended and the status quo embodied in wartime prices and incomes policy began to break down, the unions, despite appearances, were not starting from a particularly strong position.[13]

Antipathy to the legacy of wartime labor policy did not all come from union activists, by any means. Amongst industrial management the entrenchment of "outside" unions through written contracts with maintenance of membership clauses, and the establishment of formalized grievance procedures to facilitate the orderly settlement of disputes occurring in the course of contract administration, were perceived as major threats to managerial control of the enterprise. As the postwar economic situa-

9. Ibid., 48–9. See also Joshua Freeman, "Delivering the Goods: Industrial Unionism During World War Two," *Labor History*, 19, 4 (Fall, 1978), 572–3.

10. Freeman, "Delivering the Goods," 574. See also Bruno Stein, "Labor's Role in Government Agencies During World War Two," *Journal of Economic History*, 17 (1957), 389–408.

11. Harris, *The Right to Manage*, 52; Lichtenstein, "Industrial Democracy, Contract Unionism, and the National War Labor Board," 527–31.

12. Harris, *The Right to Manage*, 52.

13. See Nelson Lichtenstein, "Ambiguous Legacy: The Union Security Problem During World War Two," *Labor History*, 18, 2 (Spring, 1977), 214–38.

tion deteriorated, and as an increasingly bitter debate erupted both within and outside Congress over the causes of that deterioration, this entrepreneurial antipathy toward unions and "pro-union" labor relations policies merged with renewed conservative condemnations of New Deal social and economic policy to become a widespread assault on "collectivism" and on the administrative state which had fostered it.[14]

At first, all eyes were focussed on price regulation. Even before the war had ended, the OPA's general price ceilings had been strongly criticized in Congress for preventing manufacturers from obtaining reasonable profits across their entire range of products, and thus inhibiting the production of some lines of goods. With reconversion imminent, Congressional critics feared that unless price ceilings were radically revised upward, production would simply stagnate. The pressure on price controls was further heightened by the rapid termination of wage and production controls after V-J Day, for this development was attended by demands for wage increases from workers fearful that the cessation of wartime production levels would mean loss of purchasing power and rising unemployment. With both employers and workers claiming hardship, the delicate wartime equilibrium deteriorated rapidly, culminating in the strikes of late 1945 and early 1946 and eventually in the abandonment of price regulation.[15]

The strikes helped shift the conflict over reconversion policy squarely onto the terrain of labor relations. The slow and erratic rate of growth of industrial production, particularly of consumer durables, helped keep it there throughout 1946 and 1947.[16] In fact, labor shortages, supply dislocations, depleted inventories, and speculation all played a part in holding down total output, while sustained consumer demand, belying the expectations of advocates of decontrol, created inflationary pressures sufficient to raise wholesale prices 50 percent and retail prices 30 percent between June 1946 and August 1948.[17] But Congressional conservatives and other critics preferred different explanations of what was happening to the economy. They attributed inflationary pressures to the wage claims and strikes which had signalled the final collapse of wartime restraint, and called for the destruction of the "labor monopolies" which were behind them. They blamed stagnant productivity on the

14. Richard N. Chapman, *Contours of Public Policy, 1939–1945* (New York, 1981), 241–77.
15. Lichtenstein, *Labor's War at Home*, 203–32.
16. The *Federal Reserve Bulletin's* Industrial Production Index stood at 255 in May 1945, and 210 in July, the last month of war production. By January 1946, the index stood at 160. Rising to 189 over the following twelve months, the index then slipped back to 182 in August 1947. In Bartels, "The Politics of Price Control," 518.
17. Bartels, "The Politics of Price Control," 492.

unions' restrictive practices and their obstruction of innovation, and sought relief from this imposition as well. Only through wage restraint and increased productivity, they declared, could production and price problems be solved.[18]

Attempts were made to embody these demands in legislation, first in 1945, in the form of the Ball-Burton-Hatch bill, and then in 1946, in the form of the Case bill. Both attracted considerable criticism from proponents of the pluralist labor relations model. William Leiserson, for example, denounced the Ball-Burton-Hatch bill as a bizarre mixture of voluntary adjustment and compulsion which tore the Wagner Act to bits by making participation in collective bargaining a matter of choice for the employer and by drastically weakening the legal rights of workers to self-organization and to protection from employer unfair practices, and which simultaneously rewrote the Norris-LaGuardia Act by making the lawsuit once again the principal means of adjusting labor disputes. "Great as is my admiration of the ability and public services of Senators Hatch, Burton and Ball," Leiserson concluded, "I think they are mistaken if they believe this bill can be the basis of a fair and sound labor policy to promote industrial peace."[19]

Leiserson's critique of the Ball-Burton-Hatch bill reflected his considerable reservations about the implications of some aspects of war labor policy for labor relations in the post-war period. He was particularly concerned by the encouragement which the War Labor Board experience seemed to be giving to those who advocated the use of compulsion in the settlement of labor disputes. "Precedents have been set by the government issuing orders which the labor people thought were all right because they had a friendly government" he stated in June 1944. "But . . . you never know how long a government or an administration is going to be in power, and if you set up precedents in one administration they can be used in the next administration." Governments should intervene only gingerly in disputes and then only to mediate or conciliate, not to force settlements. "The main reliance has to be on collective bargaining and on mediation without authority to issue orders."[20]

18. Congressman Fred Hartley, chairman of the House Committee on Education and Labor, described the Taft-Hartley Act as legislation in the service of higher productivity. The Act meant, he said, that "to get more for the dollars you spend, you must give more for the dollars you earn." In Papers of Robert A. Taft. 613–673, ("Labor Relations – Miscellaneous, 1947–50"). (Library of Congress, Washington D.C.). [Hereinafter cited as *Taft Papers*.]

19. "What's the Matter with the Hatch-Burton-Ball Bill?" (July 1945), in *Leiserson Papers* Box 50, ("Speeches and Articles").

20. William M. Leiserson, Address before a meeting of the International Association of the Brotherhood of Maintenance of Way Employees (17 June 1944), in *Leiserson Papers*, Box 50, ("Speeches and Articles").

Leiserson did not rule out compulsion in all forms. If "the processes of collective dealing by which mutual agreements are made and voluntary agreements reached" were to remain the basis of national policy, "certain positive duties and responsibilities must be assumed by workers and employers alike, and by their representatives and agents . . . Otherwise, the basic policy of depending upon cooperative contracting to fix and adjust the terms and conditions of employment cannot succeed, and peaceful labor relations cannot be maintained."[21] Leiserson's ideal postwar policy might reject compulsory *settlement* of disputes, that is, but he was ready to endorse legislation which would supplement the Wagner Act by imposing on each side the duty to negotiate and to make every effort to maintain collective agreements once concluded. In addition, Leiserson supported legislation requiring the parties to give adequate notice of decisions to terminate or renegotiate an established agreement and to avoid actions altering the status quo during the course of negotiations. The object was to arrive at a policy "firmly grounded in the methods and practices by which workers and managements organize themselves for their self-government, and for governing their relations with each other," while at the same time taking the Wagner Act to its logical conclusion by using it to compel negotiation.[22]

Leiserson developed this line of argument throughout 1945. Government intervention had initially occurred, despite the no-strike pledge, because of the failure of the two sides to develop their own voluntary machinery to facilitate the adjustment of disputes. The collapse of the National Defense Mediation Board in the captive mines dispute late in 1941 had pushed the government into increasing reliance on compulsion in designing the successor agency, the National War Labor Board. This in turn had encouraged each side in industry to shift the onus for achieving stability in industrial relations more and more onto government agencies. As a result "the primary purpose for which working people organize, namely, collective bargaining, has been to a large extent destroyed."[23] With the war over, the administration and the two sides could either press on to policies which would eventually see collective bargaining entirely replaced by compulsion, or, alternatively, they could return to the cooperation, mutuality and collective bargaining which lay at the heart of the pluralist model. Leiserson left no doubt

21. William M. Leiserson, "A Government Labor Relations Policy," Symposium on National Labor Policy (8 March 1945), in *Leiserson Papers*, Box 50, ("Speeches and Articles").
22. Ibid.
23. William M. Leiserson, draft article for *Labor* (September 1945), in *Leiserson Papers*, Box 20, ("K – General").

about the course he favored. "The growth of trade unionism," he stated, "is the American democratic ideal expressing itself in industry . . . Similarly, the growing liberalism of our general government is reflected in its encouragement of trade unionism and collective bargaining, as well as other legislation to promote labor welfare."[24] But renewed encouragement of trade unionism and collective bargaining depended on the willingness of both sides to accept responsibilities. Labor, in particular, had to offer a substitute for industrial warfare and reliance on beneficial government intervention. The unions should show some commitment to live up to their agreements and make "mediation and voluntary arbitration" a realistic alternative to compulsion.[25]

Whether the pluralist labor relations system which Leiserson defended would be vindicated in the postwar period was a question for the administration, and in particular the National Labor Relations Board. Upstaged during the period of hostilities by the War Labor Board, and plagued, particularly in the latter stages of the war, by internal disarray, the influence of the NLRB over the development of federal policy had diminished between 1943 and 1945.[26] The demise of wartime institutions at the end of 1945, however, meant that the major responsibility for shaping the contours of labor relations policy, and thus of the peacetime labor–management relationship, had returned to the NLRB.

Opportunity to organize and proper discipline

Although alone in the field, the Board lacked neither precedents nor advice upon which to draw in establishing the proper scope for collective bargaining and union activity in the postwar era. The courts, in particular, had always pressed upon it the importance of achieving an accommodation between unions and collective bargaining on the one

24. William M. Leiserson, "What's Ahead in Labor Relations," Address to the New England Council (16 November 1945), in *Leiserson Papers*, Box 50, ("Speeches and Articles").

25. William M. Leiserson, "Union Labor Relations Policy and Government Policy" (draft), in *Leiserson Papers*, Box 50, ("Speeches and Articles").

26. According to James A. Gross, "The National War Labor Board . . . replaced the NLRB as the administrative agency at the center of U.S. labor relations." See *The Reshaping of the National Labor Relations Board: National Labor Policy in Transition, 1937–1947* (Albany, New York, 1981), 243. See also Harris, *The Right to Manage*, 41–88. In July 1945, David C. Shaw wrote to the newly appointed NLRB chairman, Paul Herzog, that "the last couple of years have witnessed the disintegration of morale." Shaw to Herzog (23 July 1945), in *Papers of Paul M. Herzog*, Box 2, ("Personal Correspondence–S"). (Harry S Truman Presidential Library, Independence, Missouri). [Hereinafter cited as *Herzog Papers*.] See also Leiserson to Morse (21 December 1944), in *Leiserson Papers*, Box 27, ("Morse").

hand, and the prevailing political economy on the other; of recognizing, that is, that although the Wagner Act had created "new and important rights for labor," it had not "abrogate[d] the correlative rights of the employer."[27] Immediately after declaring the Wagner Act constitutional in *NLRB v. Jones and Laughlin,* for example, the Supreme Court had proceeded to delineate as clearly as possible the extent of the sphere of employer activity which remained untouched. The act, it emphasized, did not involve any curtailment of "the appropriate sphere of managerial freedom." It did not compel agreements between employers and employees. It did not prevent the employer from hiring individuals on whatever terms he might by unilateral action determine. It did nothing to impair the normal prerogative of an employer to manage his own business and to maintain discipline and control over his employees:

> The act does not compel the petitioner [employer] to employ anyone; it does not require that the petitioner retain in its employ an incompetent [employee] . . . The act permits a discharge for any reason other than union activity or agitation for collective bargaining with employees. The restoration of [the employee discriminatorily discharged in the instant case] to his former position in no sense guarantees his continuance in petitioner's employ. The petitioner is at liberty, whenever occasion may arise, to exercise its undoubted right to sever his relationship for any cause that seems to it proper, save only as punishment for, or discouragement of, such activities as the Act declares permissible.[28]

Collective activity by a union to compel an employer to do anything other than fulfill his obligation to bargain in good faith was thus unprotected.

27. *NLRB v. The Sands Manufacturing Company* (1938), 96 F2 721, 2 Labor Relations Reference Manual 712, at 715. In its report to the House Committee on Labor in 1939 the Board had acknowledged that while the act now protected employees in their exercise of the right to organize, "none of the other legal rights of employer were taken from him: the right to collective action by employers and the right to protection in his business through police regulation and injunction were unaffected by the Act." In National Labor Relations Board, *Report to the House Committee on Labor,* in *House Hearings,* 8 (83 pp.), 62.
28. *Associated Press v. National Labor Relations Board* (1937), 301 US 103, at 132. See also *NLRB v. Jones and Laughlin Steel Corporation* (1937), 301 US 1, 1CD [Court Decisions Relating to the National Labor Relations Act] 305, at 331. See also *Southern Steamship Company v. NLRB* (1942), 316 U.S. 31, 3CD 776, where the Supreme Court commented that in giving effect to the National Labor Relations Act the Board would do well to take into consideration "other and equally important Congressional objectives." The act, the Court indicated, was to be treated as one element in a general strategy which demanded "careful accommodation of one statutory scheme to another," and that it was "not too much to demand of an administrative body that it undertake this accommodation without excessive emphasis upon its immediate task" (785).

The courts also supplied narrow definitions of the area of union activity which *was* protected; activity, that is, in pursuit of collective bargaining and contracts. *Sands Manufacturing Company* (April 1936) is an early example. In this case, one of the first to arise under the Wagner Act, the Board had decided that it made no difference in determining whether an employer had refused to bargain with his employees that the employer was reacting to his employees' refusal to honor their contract.[29] The Sixth Circuit Court of Appeals disagreed, holding that the circumstances of the case rendered the union's activity illegitimate, and thus absolved the employer from having to comply with the act:

> Respondent was not bound for an indefinite time to negotiate with an organization which had broken its contract, nor to negotiate in order to secure its performance. The statute does not compel the employer to renounce reliance upon its rights under a valid agreement. It merely requires the employer to negotiate sincerely.

The court found that the employer had tried to persuade the union to honor its contract. "There was no refusal by respondent to bargain collectively until after two months of continuous effort on its part to secure performance of the contract." Under these circumstances, "Respondent was not obligated to prolong the impasse, and its refusal to bargain further did not constitute a violation of the statute." The union's breach of contract, although arising from "an honest difference of opinion" as to the contract's terms and committed in pursuit of collective bargaining, entitled the employer to abrogate the contract and to seek new employees.[30] The Supreme Court agreed. "If, as we have held, the respondent was confronted with a concerted refusal on the part of [the union] to permit its members to perform their contract," it argued, "there was nothing unlawful in the company's attempting to procure others to fill their places."[31]

Such decisions had early restricted the area of protected collective behavior. Unfair labor practice charges, it appeared, would not be sustained if the employer's refusal to bargain arose from a union's breach of contract, even where the breach developed out of "an honest difference of opinion" over the meaning of the contract. This was particularly important in light of the Supreme Court's decision in *NLRB v. Mackay Radio and Telegraph Company* (1938) that striking employees who were not engaged in a labor dispute arising from an employer's

29. 1 NLRB 546 (April 1936).
30. *NLRB v. The Sands Manufacturing Company* (1938), 96 F2 721, 2 LRRM 712, at 717.
31. *NLRB v. The Sands Manufacturing Company* (1939), 306 U.S. 332, 1 CD 1373, at 1380.

unfair labor practice did not enjoy the right of automatic reinstatement after the strike.[32]

Wartime court decisions also held that certain forms of strike action were inherently unlawful and thus beyond the act's protection. "In recognizing the right to strike," the Sixth Circuit Court of Appeals commented in 1943, "the act envisions a lawful strike . . ."[33] In *NLRB v. Condenser Corporation of America* (1942), for example, the Third Circuit Court of Appeals found that an employer could dismiss a group of wildcat strikers without being held to have committed an unfair labor practice. The court argued that employees could not "insist that their demands be met in the middle of a working day, when the employer has promised to deal with them as a group at the end of the day."[34] Two years later in *NLRB v. Draper Corporation* (1944), the Fourth Circuit Court of Appeals repeated this judgment at much greater length, explicitly addressing the question of the legality of wildcat strikes.[35] The strike in question, the court stated, was not protected activity, for even though it had broken no contract it had violated the purposes of the act. "The purpose of the Act was not to guarantee to employees the right to do as they please but to guarantee to them the right of collective bargaining for the purpose of industrial peace." Wildcat strikes were inherently damaging to that purpose:

> It is perfectly clear not only that the 'wild cat' strike is a particularly harmful and demoralizing form of industrial strife and unrest, the necessary effect of which is to burden and obstruct commerce, but also that it is necessarily destructive of that collective bargaining which it is the purpose of the Act to promote . . . [T]here can be no effective bargaining if small groups of employees are at liberty to ignore the bargaining agency thus set up, take particular matters into their own hands and deal independently with the employer.

As such, wildcat strikes were to be distinguished from other strikes because they were contrary to the purposes of the act and to the orderly procedures of collective bargaining which the act had chosen as the means to achieve those purposes:

32. 304 U.S. 333, 1 CD 637 (1938). This, however, had been established Board policy for some time. See Witt to Schlichter (21 May 1936), in *RG* 25 Box 338, ("Assistant General Counsel Witt's Records, 1935–36"), where Witt confirmed that "If the strike was not caused by an unfair labor practice, and if there is no unfair labor practice during the strike, the employer is not required to reinstate the strikers. (There has been no specific holding to this effect, but this is the drift of the Board's policy . . .)."

33. *NLRB v. Ohio Calcium Company* (1943), 133 F2 721, at 728.

34. 128 F2 67, at 77.   35.   145 F2 199.

Minorities who engage in 'wild cat' strikes, in violation of rights established by the collective bargaining statute, can find nothing in that statute which protects them from discharge. In the absence of the statute, there was nothing in the law which forbade the discharge of strikers. There is nothing in the statute, properly construed, which protects from discharge those who strike in defiance of its provisions. No surer way could be found to bring collective bargaining into general disrepute than to hold that 'wild cat' strikes are protected by the collective bargaining statute.[36]

Decisions taken by the Board indicated that it shared the courts' desire to discourage activities in breach of contract or otherwise disruptive of established bargaining relationships. According to James A. Gross, the Board did not embrace this restrictive position until after the ascendancy of Millis and Leiserson. "Millis and Leiserson," he writes, "moved . . . to establish union responsibility and to deny statutory protection to certain acts of unions and union employees under the Act . . ."[37] In fact, the Madden Board also accepted that the act empowered it to investigate employee and union behavior and the Board early made it plain that in some circumstances it would employ sanctions against actions which it considered inappropriate or a threat to the success of national policy. "Under the present act," the Board told the Senate Committee on Education and Labor in 1939, "employee misconduct is penalized whenever the policies and purposes of the Act demand it."[38] Thus, in a 1940 case, *Link-Belt Company,* the Board held that an employer could not be accused of unfair dismissal when his actions were based upon a "reasonable belief" that the employees in question were conspiring to do violence to his property.[39] But even if the trend did not originate with the Millis Board, certainly nothing was done to alter it, and the Board continued to restrict the realm of protected behavior. Thus, strikes to compel an employer to bargain with a minority union were considered unprotected activity, as were strikes to compel an employer to recognize or bargain with a union other than that certified by the Board, or strikes to compel an employer to violate a federal statute.[40] "The Act was addressed to employer, not employee misconduct," the Board held in 1944 in *American News Company,*

36. Ibid., 203.
37. Gross, *The Reshaping of the National Labor Relations Board,* 238.
38. Testimony of J. Warren Madden, *Senate Hearings,* 296.   39. 26 NLRB 227.
40. See, for example, *American News Company Inc.* (April 1944), 55 NLRB 1302; *Thompson Products, Inc.* (February 1947), 72 NLRB 886. See also *Hazel-Atlas Glass Company* (August 1941), 34 NLRB 346. See, in addition, Harry A. Millis and Emily C. Brown, *From the Wagner Act to Taft-Hartley: A Study of National Labor Policy and Labor Relations* (Chicago, 1950), 189–233. Gross, *The Reshaping of the National Labor Relations Board,* 297–8.

Inc., a case which involved an attempt by the International Typographical Union to force an employer to pay a wage increase vetoed
by the War Labor Board. "But this does not mean, and never has
meant, that employee misconduct is necessarily irrelevant to the determination of violations of Section 8."[41] The onus, in other words, was
on both sides – unions as well as employers – to conform themselves to
the pluralist model and to institutionalize the contract as the keystone
of their relations. In furtherance of this the Board joined the War
Labor Board in encouraging the parties to incorporate grievance
procedures culminating in voluntary binding arbitration in their contracts as a substitute for strikes. As the Board stated in *North American Aviation, Incorporated:*

> [A] collective contract is not complete as originally negotiated, nor
> is the process of collective bargaining complete upon the execution
> of the contract. After a contract has been negotiated and executed,
> it is continuously modified and supplemented by interpretations
> and precedents made by employer and employees from day to day
> in the course of their operations under the contract. This interpreta-
> tion of the contract, no less than its negotiation, constitutes an
> integral part of the collective bargaining procedures.[42]

Such decisions indicate that the Board was broadly in accord with the
courts' moves to restrain unions from using direct action to impose
settlements on employers in industrial disputes. As the Supreme Court
affirmed in 1945, it was always necessary to strike a balance between
the undisputed right of workers to organize in unions and to bargain
collectively and the "equally undisputed" right of employers to maintain discipline in their establishments. "Opportunity to organize and
proper discipline are both esssential elements in a balanced society."[43]
Like the War Labor Board, moreover, the NLRB also showed a tendency to combine restraints on unions with continued respect for a
broad right of management to preserve a sphere of enterprise affairs
free of bilateral negotiation. Thus, in *Peyton Packing Company* (May
1943) the Board found that "reasonable rules covering the conduct of
employees on company time" were "within the province of an employer
to promulgate and enforce,"[44] while in *Mahoning Mining Company*
(April 1945) the Board held that an employer could "change his business structure, sell or contract out of a portion of his operations, or
make any like change which might affect the constituency of the appropriate unit" without incurring any obligation to bargain with or even

41.   55 NLRB 1302, at 1311.   42.   44 NLRB 604, at 612.
43.   *Republic Aviation Corporation v. NLRB* (1945), 324 U.S. 793, 4 CD 958, at 961.
44.   49 NLRB 828, at 844.

consult "the bargaining representative of the employees affected by the proposed business change."[45]

One of the clearest statements of the Board's priorities in this regard was provoked by the controversy over whether supervisors – leading-men or foremen – should be given the protection of the National Labor Relations Act in their efforts to organize and bargain collectively. The Board had already answered this question affirmatively, if indirectly, in a number of early cases arising in industries, notably the maritime and printing trades, in which supervisory employees had traditionally orga-nized themselves on a craft basis. In mid-1942, however, the Board was required to rule on the rights of supervisors in mining and mass produc-tion industries where agitation for organization amongst foremen was much more recent, having been stimulated by the organizing activities of production workers and by the shop-floor pressures associated with the massive expansion of wartime production.[46]

The Board's initial response was to find that supervisors were covered by the act. "Section 2(2) of the Act is relied upon wherein an 'employer' is defined to include 'any person acting in the interest of an employer,' " it said in *Union Collieries Coal Company* (June 1942) describing the company's explanation of its refusal to acknowledge a representation claim lodged on behalf of its supervisory employees. "Section 2(3) of the Act is ignored. It provides that the term employee shall include any employee. There is no inconsistency in these provisions when facts are taken into consideration. A foreman, in his relation to his employer, is an employee, while in his relation to the laborers under him he is the representative of the employer within the definition of section 2(2) of the Act. Nothing in the Act excepts foremen from its benefits nor from protection against discrimination nor unfair labor practices of the master."[47]

The decision, which aroused considerable opposition among em-ployers, was not unanimous. Gerard D. Reilly, the former solicitor to the Department of Labor who had replaced Edwin Smith on the Board in October 1941, dissented on the grounds that the decision would encour-age blue collar unions to petition for the inclusion of supervisors in units of production workers and thus cause considerable disruption to man-agement. The Board majority sought to meet Reilly's objection in a sup-plementary decision issued in the same case three months later by reserv-ing judgment on the question of the precise form of the bargaining unit most appropriate to meet the needs of supervisors.[48] Reilly, however,

45. 61 NLRB 792, at 802.
46. Harris, *The Right to Manage*, 78–82.   47. 41 NLRB 961, at 966.
48. *Union Collieries Coal Company* (September 1942), 44 NLRB 165.

continued to argue that to endorse collective bargaining by supervisors would provoke conflicts of interest between their newly-recognized status as employees and their fiduciary obligations to management, and in May 1943, a year after the original *Union Collieries* decision, he succeeded in persuading former congressman John M. Houston, who had replaced Leiserson three months earlier, to join him in voting, over Millis's objections, that henceforth the Board should routinely dismiss petitions filed by, or on behalf of, supervisory personnel for the election and certification of collective bargaining representatives.

The Board's reversal came in *Maryland Drydock Corporation* (May 1943), a case which involved a petition from the International Union of Marine and Shipbuilding Workers-CIO that its established production worker unit should be widened to allow it to continue representing production workers temporarily promoted to lower-grade supervisory status.[49] The company held that to grant the petition would endanger "its right to control the management and affairs of the company."[50] The Board upheld the company's objection. Stating that it was no longer convinced that "from the mere determination that a supervisor is an employee it follows that supervisors may constitute appropriate bargaining units," the Board argued that Section 9(b) of the act required that it consider not only "whether the unit alleged to be appropriate in each case will ensure to employees the full benefit of their right to self-organization and to collective bargaining" but also whether it would *"otherwise effectuate the policies of the Act."* In exercising this discretion, the majority opinion continued,

> it is relevant for us to inquire . . . whether our determination in any particular case that supervisory employees constitute a unit appropriate for collective bargaining will . . . result in the disruption of the practice of collective bargaining rather than in industrial peace,

and concluded that:

> in the present stage of industrial administration and employee self-organization, the establishment of bargaining units composed of supervisors exercising substantial managerial authority will impede the processes of collective bargaining, disrupt established managerial and production techniques, and militate against effectuation of the policies of the Act.[51]

Significantly, Chairman Millis, although in dissent, did not disagree with the majority's major premise that the Board had the administrative

49. 49 NLRB 733.
50. "Brief on behalf of the Maryland Drydock Company," in *RG 25*, Informal File R-2511, *Maryland Drydock Company*.
51. 49 NLRB 733, at 738–9, 741 [emphasis in original].

authority to determine whether a certification of representatives would in any particular case expedite the achievement of the act's goals. The members of the Board, that is, were unanimous that the Board had the power to deny to any particular group of workers in any particular situation at any particular time the opportunity to exercise rights guaranteed by the Wagner Act, if the Board felt that such denial would help effect the act's underlying purposes. What Millis objected to was the majority's further assertion that, in the case of supervisory personnel, it was always going to deny the workers that opportunity, irrespective of the particular circumstances of the case. Rather than formulate a general rule denying all supervisors the Board's protection as a matter of policy, Millis argued, the decision should be made on a case-by-case basis:

> Manifestly to engraft upon the Act an amendment which denies to a substantial segment of employees as a class the protection vouchsafed therein to all "employees" is not within the permissible bounds of administrative discretion. It is administrative legislation.[52]

The trend toward relaxation of the Board's strictures on management and imposition of them upon employees and unions continued, even accelerated, after Paul M. Herzog succeeded Millis as chairman in July 1945 and began in earnest the job of shaping postwar labor relations policy. In *Diamond T Motor Car Company* (December 1945), for example, the Board narrowed the scope of its *Rutland Court* decision protecting employees from abuse of closed shop contracts by holding that an employer committed no unfair practice where his fulfillment of the obligations of a closed shop contract at the request of an incumbent

---

52. Ibid., 743. Matters did not rest here, however, and the Board reversed itself two years later in *Packard Motor Company* (March 1945), deciding that it would after all serve the preservation of order in labor relations to allow supervisors access to its procedures. The issue was extremely contentious on the Board, and Leiserson reported rising conflict between Reilly and Millis throughout 1944. See Leiserson to George O. Pratt (21 September 1944) in *Leiserson Papers*, Box 34, ("Pratt"); Leiserson to David Morse (21 December 1944), in *Leiserson Papers*, Box 27, ("Morse"). Following the decision in *Packard*, the Board continued to argue that industrial peace could best be served by allowing supervisors access to the act rather than forcing them to organize outside the act's protection. In *L.A. Young Spring and Wire Corporation* (January 1946), 65 NLRB 298, however, the Board went beyond *Packard* by holding that once it had decided that workers were "employees" within the meaning of the act, *it had no choice* but to allow them access to its procedures. This was confirmed in *Jones and Laughlin Steel Corporation* (March 1946) 66 NLRB 386, and *Waterfront Employers' Association of the Pacific Coast* (September 1946), 71 NLRB 80. The Board was divided in this attempt to solve the supervisor question, however, and in *Jones and Laughlin Steel Corporation* (December 1946), 71 NLRB 1261, it hinted broadly at the desirability of Congressional guidance. This was duly provided in the Taft-Hartley Act, as noted in Chapter 8.

resulted in the discriminatory discharge of employees active on behalf of a rival union, as long as it could be shown that the employer was not aware that the reasons for the discharge were discriminatory.[53] Shortly thereafter, in *Scullin Steel Company* (February 1946), the Board gave further indication that it was narrowing its unfair labor practice doctrine by voting that strikes would not be protected where they violated contractual commitments. "[I]n the absence of any showing that the [employer] had breached its contract, and in view of the admitted facts that the strike was not caused by any unfair labor practice and that the striking employees were not refused reinstatement because of their membership in either of the charging unions," it declared, "we shall dismiss the complaint . . ."[54] Subsequent decisions further restricted the sphere of legitimate collective activity by declaring that strikes to compel the modification of an existing contract or to compel an employer to agree to a contract provision determined unilaterally by a union were unprotected.[55]

The nature of the model for post-war collective bargaining being developed by the Herzog Board was most clearly revealed in *Thompson Products*.[56] This case, the subject of decisions by the Board in August 1946 and again in February 1947, established that strikes called to compel an employer to recognize one union in the face of the Board's certification of another were not merely unprotected but unlawful. It also graphically illustrated how far those responsible for the development of federal policy were prepared to go in order to accommodate its critics.

The *Thompson Products* case began with a representation petition filed by the UAW in April 1941. The Board eventually granted the petition and directed that an election be held in September of that year. In the interim, however, the company concluded a contract covering the employees in question with another union, the Society of Tool and Die Craftsmen. When the election was held the Society took part and won. The UAW contested the result on the grounds that the Society was a company union, but after hearings the Board dismissed the UAW's charges and certified the Society. The UAW then revived its claim to be the majority representative, filed another representation petition and, notwithstanding the Society's certification, accused the employer of vio-

53. 64 NLRB 1225. This case was taken up by the Board specifically to establish the employer's immunity from unfair labor practice proceedings in such circumstances as a point of law. See *RG 25*, Informal File 13-C-2414, *Diamond T Motor Car Company.*
54. 65 NLRB 1294, at 1317-18.
55. *Times Publishing Company* (February 1947), 72 NLRB 676.
56. 72 NLRB 886.

lating Section 8 of the act by refusing to bargain with it. In December 1942 the UAW called a strike to compel the company to begin bargaining. There followed a series of discharges of UAW members by the company.[57]

Following the discharge of its members the UAW filed new charges against the company, accusing it of discriminatory activity arising out of the strike. In the meantime, the Board found merit in the UAW's second representation petition and in March 1943 the UAW finally gained certification as the majority representative. The UAW then withdrew its discriminatory practice charges, but only because it wished to submit that matter, along with others arising out of disagreements in the process of negotiating a contract with the company, to the War Labor Board. That Board refused to take jurisdiction over the discrimination charges, however, so in June 1944 the UAW refiled the charges with the National Labor Relations Board. By this time only a few of the workers involved still sought reinstatement, and on the advice of the Board's Administrative Division (formerly the Field Division) the regional director dismissed the charges.[58] The union appealed and filed an amended charge. Yet another amended charge was filed in May 1945, and on 31 May the Board finally issued a complaint. Hearings were held in June before trial examiner Charles E. Persons.

Persons' intermediate report, released in August 1945, held that the evidence did not sustain the union's charges. According to the report the discharges had been occasioned by the strike called to compel the respondent company to bargain with the UAW even though that union had already been defeated in a representation election and another union certified as exclusive representative of the employer's employees. "The strike was therefore for an illegal purpose. UAW-CIO proposed to compel the respondent to violate the Act through use of the strike weapon." In this situation, Persons argued, the Board's decision was clearly controlled by the 1944 case, *American News Company*, in which the Board had decided that strikes to compel an employer to violate a federal statute were unprotected. "The strike was called and continued to compel immediate recognition of the UAW-CIO as exclusive bargaining agent. This was manifestly an illegal purpose. Further, it was in derogation of the provisions of the Act itself."[59]

Following the release of Persons' report the UAW sought leave to present oral argument. Simultaneously, representations were made by a

57. RG 25, Informal File 7-C-1266, *Thompson Products Inc.*
58. Smith to Bowen (5 February 1944), in Informal File 7-C-1266.
59. Charles E. Persons, Intermediate Report (25 August 1945), in Informal File 7-C-1266.

large number of CIO unions—the United Furniture Workers, the Oil Workers, the United Electrical Workers, the American Communications Association, the Federation of Architects, Engineers, Chemists and Technicians, the National Maritime Union—all protesting vehemently at the trial examiner's conclusions. Counsel for the American Communications Association, Victor Rabinowitz, stated that it was "extremely dangerous to have the Board indulge in findings that various types of strikes are 'illegal.' The right to strike is vital to the interests of the labor movement, and any limitation on that right must be resisted, especially by a government agency entrusted with the administration of the National Labor Relations Act. There is no justification under the Act for calling any kind of strike illegal."[60] William L. Standard, general counsel to the National Maritime Union, was even more concerned:

> If [the trial examiner's intermediate report is] adopted, union freedom of action will be confined within impossible limits. To declare that a strike called to compel recognition is in violation of the act and that striking employees will be denied statutory protection, is altogether foreign to the principles which the Board has heretofore expressed.
>
> The trial examiner has failed to apply the law correctly; he has, moreover, voiced a policy which, if permitted to stand, will go far to vitiate the functions of the Act. The Board cannot assume to inquire into the motives of union action, and to deny the protection of the law in those instances where it disapproves. It was not established to perform the work of a censor.[61]

The Board heard oral testimony in February 1946, and issued its decision in August. It was not unanimous. Indeed, each of the three separate opinions revealed a different perspective on how the postwar labor relations system should be constructed. Gerard Reilly, for example, thought that Persons was completely correct. The *American News* precedent was decisive and should be carried over into peacetime labor relations. The UAW had insisted on recognition despite the certification of the Society and despite the Society's contract. The discharges had been caused by its activity in support of its unlawful contention.[62] John M. Houston, in contrast, thought that the Board's more recent decision in *Columbia Pictures* (May and October 1945) had overruled *American News*. There the Board had stated that employees who chose

---

60. Rabinowitz to the Board (5 October 1945), in Informal File 7-C-1266. See also letters from Harry Weinstock, general counsel, United Furniture Workers; Lindsay Walden, general counsel, Oil Workers; and Julius Emspak, president, United Electrical Workers, in same.
61. Standard to the Board (9 October 1945), in Informal File 7-C-1266.
62. *Thompson Products Incorporated* (August 1946), 70 NLRB 13, at 19-23.

strike action to obtain a result which they might have achieved by invoking the procedures of the act "do not forfeit any of the rights which accrue to them as employees within the meaning of the statute." Thus, Houston argued, the Board should reinstate the employees discharged for activities in support of the UAW.[63]

Herzog tried to use what seemed to be a loophole in the case to fashion a workable compromise. By striking, the UAW had undoubtedly engaged in unlawful activity. The company, however, had not cited the strike as its reason for discharging the UAW supporters, and in fact the organizing activities for which they *had* been discharged were certainly protected by the statute. Herzog, therefore, sought to amend the trial examiner's report by ordering the workers' reinstatement while denying them back pay in order to "punish" the UAW for its illegal activity. "Even though the discharges here were not motivated by the complainant's action in striking to compel a violation of the company's obligation to bargain exclusively with the Society pursuant to our certification, it remains incumbent upon us to take such conduct into consideration in directing the remedy . . ."[64]

Herzog's purpose was clear. Like Reilly he wanted to keep *American News* alive in order to underline that the Board intended to respect and support its own certifications. There could be, he said, "neither moral, legal nor practical justification for our requiring employers to respect our certifications" if the Board were unwilling to respect them itself.[65] But Herzog also feared that the Board's chances of reestablishing a stable labor–management relationship in the post-war period would be seriously damaged if its decision carried on the wartime policy of penalizing men who struck to compel their employer to violate the law by depriving them of their status as "employees." Therefore he sought an alternative remedy. Herzog, nevertheless, concluded by stating that had the employer rested its case for discharging the employees in question upon the unlawfulness of the strike, he would have had no option but to join Reilly in refusing reinstatement altogether. Houston found this extraordinary. "I cannot subscribe to reasoning," he stated, "which would appear to adjudicate the legality of a strike solely upon the character of the excuse offered by the respondent to interfere with it."[66]

Notwithstanding the confusions in its decision, the Board proceeded to petition for enforcement. This provoked the company to file a mo-

---

63. Ibid., 23–5. In *Columbia Pictures* (May and October 1945), 61 NLRB 1030 and 64 NLRB 490, the Board had found that the employees in question retained the act's protection because although they had struck to compel recognition while another union's petition was pending the Board had not issued any conflicting certification.
64. *Thompson Products Incorporated*, 18.   65. Ibid., 18.   66. Ibid., 24.

tion calling for review of the decision in federal court. Five days later, however, the Board suddenly suspended enforcement proceedings, and after taking a month to consider the issues further it announced that it would review the decision itself. New hearings were held and on 21 February 1947 the Board issued a revised decision and order. This time Herzog joined James J. Reynolds, who had replaced Reilly on the Board two weeks after the original decision, in finding that Persons' intermediate report had been correct in all respects. The employees in question had not been treated discriminatorily because they had been engaged in a strike which had an illegal purpose.

The reasons for the Board's abrupt change of direction in *Thompson Products* are not difficult to discover. Throughout 1946, the Truman administration had been under growing pressure in Congress to accept labor law reform legislation. Those pressures increased further as a result of the 1946 mid-term elections and the November coal strike, precipitating the initiation of an intensive appraisal of the administration's policy options geared toward the announcement of specific proposals to the new Congress in the president's State of the Union Message early in the new year. On December 10 and 11, as part of this review, the Board submitted lengthy memoranda discussing the course of national labor policy.[67] These counselled change, for the Board agreed that in the current period the priority was to "lessen industrial strife at the point where it occurs most frequently, where strong labor, already recognized by strong management, thinks it necessary to call a strike to voice a grievance or enforce a demand."[68] But apart from recommending legislation to outlaw strikes against its certifications, the Board held that "no specific changes [in statutory policy] are necessary for the sole purpose of advancing the public interest." Responsibility for the course of national policy, it argued, should be left with the Board which, as in the past, could achieve an appropriate level of reform activity through its own administrative discretion:

> The Board and the courts have already restricted the right of persons who engage in certain forms of offensive conduct to secure the normal remedies under the Act. The Board does not order the re-instatement of men who engage in a sit-down strike, who strike in breach of a collective agreement, who engage in serious violence or who strike to compel violation of its certifications or certain Federal laws. Discretion is left to the Board; we believe it best to continue to permit the Board to distinguish between great and small

67. NLRB, Memoranda to the President on Labor Legislation (10 and 11 December 1946), in *Clifford Papers*, Box 7, ("Labor – 80th Congress").
68. Ibid. (11 December 1946).

offenses lest unions or employees find it no more costly to engage in the more serious forms of misconduct.[69]

Anxious to avoid identifying the administration with politically-compromising labor law reform proposals, Truman's advisors accepted the Board's advice, and the president's speech to Congress avoided endorsing sweeping alterations in the character of federal policy.[70] Meanwhile the Board reconsidered and revised its *Thompson Products* decision so as to demonstrate what could be done through administrative action. On the day the decision was released Herzog sent a copy to presidential aide John R. Steelman. His accompanying memorandum explained that the decision "implements one section of the President's program as announced in the Message. It denies reinstatement to men who strike to compel violation of the Board's certification."[71]

The Board's desire to retain the whip hand in the design and implementation of revisions in federal policy did not prevent it from realizing that some action at the statutory level might be politically appropriate. The administration, its December memoranda acknowledged, might well conclude "that certain changes would be so acceptable that, for reasons of equity or strategy, they should be advanced by the President without awaiting counter-suggestions from other sources."[72] In this category of policy developments the Board placed amendments allowing employers to petition for elections whenever confronted with unions seeking recognition as bargaining representatives, excluding foremen from the act's coverage, protecting employer free speech, and requiring unions to bargain in good faith. "We ... do not regard any of these changes as necessary in the public interest or as likely to lessen industrial strife. We say merely that they would not destroy the fabric of the Act if ultimately enacted in the law." It was opposed, however, to the proposals then current to write into law a further bifurcation of the Board's internal organization, to "equalize" the act by providing in the statute for unions to be made subject to unfair labor practice proceedings, to outlaw union security clauses, or to extend court review powers.[73] So far as it was concerned, significant steps to discipline both unions and employees had already been taken through administrative action. This, rather than legislative action, should remain at the core of whatever strategy the administration might choose to follow.

69. Ibid.
70. See Gross, *The Reshaping of the National Labor Relations Board*, 256–7.
71. Herzog to Steelman (21 February 1947), in *Papers of Harry S Truman*, Official File, Box 623, folder 145, ("NLRB 1947"). (Harry S Truman Presidential Library, Independence, Missouri). [Hereinafter cited as *Truman Papers*.]
72. "Memorandum to the President on Labor Legislation" (11 December 1946).
73. Ibid.

The Board continued to follow a strategy of reform through administrative discretion into 1947, suspending all petitions for unionization of foremen, restricting unions' access to its procedures, and excusing employers from their obligation to bargain where the union in question did not show good faith.[74] It also relaxed statutory protections of the right to organize by committing itself to respect an employer's freedom to address his employees directly rather than through their bargaining agent.[75] "[A]n employer is as free as anyone else to express his opinions on labor problems and policies," Herzog stated in September 1946. "We are mindful that there is reserved to employers an area of constitutional privilege within which statements, by reason of their freedom from coerciveness or other illegality, are protected."[76]

74. See *Times Publishing Company* (February 1947), 72 NLRB 676 (employer not obliged to bargain where union does not show good faith), and *Timken Roller Bearing Company* (August 1946), 70 NLRB 500 (initiation of arbitration proceedings vacates union's right to seek redress under the act). On 9 January 1947, the Board announced that it would suspend all action on foremen's cases until after the Supreme Court handed down a decision on the matter in *Packard Motor Company v. NLRB*. This case was decided in March. For other examples of the Board's moderation in 1946–7 see *Spicer Manufacturing Corporation* (August 1946), 70 NLRB 41 (employers not guilty of unfair practices in discharging workers in conformity with closed shop contracts even where they were aware that the reasons for employees' expulsion from union were discriminatory); *Reed Roller Bit Company* (February 1947), 72 NLRB 927 (a two-year contract is a bar even in the face of a contrary custom in the industry); *Detroit Edison* (June 1947), 74 NLRB 267 (a company union which has divested itself of employer influence can perform as an exclusive representative). In this case, Herzog wrote (279):

> Whatever reasons may once have existed for directing disestablishment in every case in which a violation of Section 8(2) was found, the Chairman doubts whether that remedy is invariably necessary today in order to effectuate the policies of the Act. This is 1947, not 1935; in the interim employees have learned much about protecting their own rights and making their own choices . . . There are situations in which, because of the passage of time, or the intervening attitude of an employer, it would appear unrealistic to assume that employees' free choice is inhibited solely because an unaffiliated organization to which many belong had an illicit beginning.

75. See *Bausch and Lomb Optical Company* (January 1947), 72 NLRB 132; *La Salle Steel Company* (February 1947), 72 NLRB 411; *United Welding Company* (February 1947), 72 NLRB 954. In *Fafnir Bearing Company* (May 1947), 73 NLRB 1008, the Board found that employer interference in a strike, in the shape of inducements to the strikers to return to work, was not unlawful where the strike was one in breach of contract.

76. Paul M. Herzog, "Words and Acts: Freedom of Speech and the NLRB," Address before the Annual Convention of Industrial Relations Sections of the Printing Industry of America (9 September 1946), Atlantic City, in *Herzog Papers*, Box 3, ("Speeches and Articles, 1946"). The tone of the NLRB's approach under Herzog is pithily summarized in an editorial which he wrote, confidentially, for the *Washington Post* which appeared on 14 January 1947:

> The working people of the country are as anxious as the rest of us to reduce the incidence of industrial warfare. We must cultivate this de-

By demonstrating the elasticity of doctrine in this way, the Board sought to commit the Truman administration to a gradualist strategy based on a combination of administrative reform with amendments strengthening the pluralist model. As we have seen, the administration accepted the Board's line. Consequently, Truman's message to Congress contented itself with endorsing a thoroughly pluralist bag of proposals. It called for legislation to outlaw the use of economic force in jurisdiction and demarcation (work assignment) disputes, in disputes over the interpretation of contracts, and in disputes over Board certifications. It also sought a ban on "unreasonable" secondary boycotts. All other questions were to be left to a bipartisan investigatory commission, a scheme of Herzog's devising. In the meantime, federal support for conciliation, mediation, and voluntary arbitration (Leiserson's proposals) would be increased.[77]

None of this impressed conservative critics of national labor policy. They responded with attacks on the president's weakness and on the Board's dismal record. Herzog answered such attacks by reiterating that "our decisions have been changing for over a year" and by pointing out that the Board was now being vilified as often by the unions for the eagerness with which it sought to appease its critics as by those critics themselves.[78] But the conservatives remained unmoved. "In recent weeks the Labor Board itself has made some decisions which are amendatory, or which at least change previous decisions," the columnist David Lawrence wrote in reply to Herzog. "The Board points rather proudly to those decisions and expects, I assume, conservatives to like the Board better because it is now changing its decisions to conform to the views which some of the conservatives have been expounding for many years. But to me this is a rather disappointing sign. It means that when pressure from public opinion grows great the Labor Board will change its decisions to conform to what it thinks is public opinion. I

sire for peace, not stimulate the desire for war, as we would by a program of strongly anti-labor legislation. Specifically we have in mind as "reforms" to reject the hard-won fundamental guarantees contained in the Norris-La Guardia and National Labor Relations Acts. This does not mean that some amendments of these statutes are not now desirable. They are. *Certainly we must increase union responsibility and give to employers the feeling that they have equal recourse to the agencies of government. America cannot afford to have either management or labor believe that it is not receiving fair treatment at the hands of the representatives of the people.*

in *Herzog Papers*, Box 6, ("Labor Legislation – 1947–56") [emphasis supplied].

77. See Susan M. Hartmann, *Truman and the 80th Congress* (Columbia, Missouri, 1971), 22.

78. Paul M. Herzog to David Lawrence (21 March 1947), in *Herzog Papers*, Box 1, ("Personal Correspondence – L").

don't believe any governmental agency ought to be given the power to change its views or its decisions to conform to public pressure." The Board should not be allowed discretion to cure defects in federal labor relations law. Rather, "legislative standards should be prescribed by Congress."[79]

Lawrence's strictures on the Herzog Board's performance underlines the persistence of conservative opposition to anything which smacked of discretionary regulation. But Lawrence's target was collective bargaining itself, not just administrative discretion, and he went on to attack contemporary labor relations policy for "delegat[ing] to private organizations of citizens the power to control jobs and work in America," and to denounce the National Labor Relations Act as "a vehicle of despotism [which] attacks the fundamental rights of the individual and extols collectivism as opposed to individualism."[80]

Lawrence was by no means alone in these opinions. Throughout the war, significant sections of Congress and the business community had nursed the same "anti-collectivist" fantasies of ridding America of unions altogether. In the wake of the 1946 elections, with a resurgent Republican Party supremely confident of regaining the White House in 1948 after fifteen years in the wilderness and eager to use every opportunity to hand to convince Americans that they had indeed "had enough" of the New Deal, the chances of punitive legislation had never been stronger. Informed opinion pointed to a crusade against the unions as "one of the greatest political opportunities in American history."[81] None was keener to seize the opportunity nor more suited to lead the crusade than "Mr. Republican" himself—presidential aspirant Robert Alphonso Taft.

Habits of orderly procedure

Robert A. Taft's political career began in Ohio, where he was born in 1889, and where, after graduating from Yale and from the Harvard Law School, he began his law practice. A stint as legal adviser to Herbert Hoover's Relief Administration took him away from his law firm during World War I, but Taft went back to Ohio after the war and in 1920 he was elected to the state legislature with the support of Cincinnati's Republican machine. He resigned after six years but remained

---

79. Lawrence to Herzog (4 April 1947), in *Herzog Papers.* 80. Ibid.
81. The Dunn Survey of Congressional Views (7 March 1947), in *Taft Papers,* 608–758, ("Labor Correspondence, 1947").

active in state Republican organizations, and in 1938 he was elected to the United States Senate at his first attempt.[82]

Taft entered the Senate eager to take a leading role in the developing conservative counter-attack against the New Deal's "collectivist" social and economic policies. Throughout the late 1930s, for example, he decried the growth of federal power over entrepreneurs and the resulting erosion of the marketplace freedoms valued by the small and medium-sized businesses for which he regarded himself the spokesman. "The businessman is willing to cooperate with government in reducing . . . risks in enterprise," he said. "When he has proof that he will share in the benefits of cooperation, rather than being made a pawn in the game of federal control, the American businessman will cooperate and will accept responsibilities as he always has in the past." But the president had shown no sign of trying to court the businessman. Instead, he had resorted to "punitive methods contrary to our democratic traditions." He had "surrounded himself with sixty new federal agencies" and had "boasted publicly about the 'new instruments of public power' which he has since used to curtail individual freedom in agriculture, industry, trade, and finance."[83]

During the war conservatives made their antipathy toward the administrative state the dominant theme of domestic politics. Taft was in the vanguard. "A Senator's life would be very haphazard and unsatisfactory if he did not deal with different subjects according to some underlying philosophy," he told an audience at the Tamiment Institute in June 1945. "I believe that the proper philosophy for dealing with American problems is the same as that which brought about the creation of the American Republic, namely the maintenance of a basic freedom for the individual, for his voluntary organizations, and for his local governments."[84] He allowed that "as a community becomes more complicated, more limitations must be imposed on freedom, because too much freedom for some interferes with the freedom of others." But "the purpose of regulations should be to preserve freedom and opportunity. We should not regulate for the sake of regulation. Too many do-gooders, and too many government officials want to run the lives of other people, because they consider themselves experts who know what is good for the average man better than that man can ever know him-

82. James T. Patterson, *Mr. Republican: A Biography of Robert A. Taft* (Boston, 1972), 69–179.

83. Robert A. Taft, "Centralized Control over Public Finance" (undated), in *Taft Papers*, 640; Patterson, *Mr. Republican*, 191.

84. Robert A. Taft, "Address at the Tamiment Institute" (6 June 1946), in *Taft Papers*, 1266–1376. See, generally, Chapman, *Contours of Public Policy*.

self." Like other conservatives, Taft singled out for particular condemnation the grave threat to due process posed by the spread of administrative procedure. "[M]any of the existing bureaus administer the law without any belief in the principle that the government should be fair to every individual according to a written law."[85]

In the increasingly partisan climate of domestic politics after 1940, conservative assaults on administrative government and economic planning hardened into a strident campaign to unmask a "collectivist conspiracy" in which the Democratic Party, aided by organized labor under the direction of the pro-Soviet CIO Political Action Committee, sought under cover of war and reconversion to centralize control of the economy in the government, guarantee full employment, invade states rights and subordinate the national interest to the particular interests of left-wing labor unions and their bosses.[86] By the mid-1940s, the language of politics treated contemporary domestic political battles in the same terms as the emerging international struggles of the Cold War. The choice in all policy debates was between "the advocates of a planned economy and those who believe that progress can only be achieved through the freedom of the individual and of economic activity."[87] Throughout the reconversion crisis, conservatives excoriated the administration's reluctance to shed wartime controls, condemning all who favored "a detailed control of American life and business by Washington bureaus" and who thought they could "direct the economy of the country to produce and maintain prosperity better than the ordinary laws of a free enterprise system."[88]

When in the postwar years conservative antipathy toward administrative government and New Deal "collectivism" became especially focussed on labor relations law, Taft was as usual at the forefront. The subject had first attracted his attention in 1939–40 when, as a freshman senator, he had followed closely the Smith Committee's investigation into the operations of the National Labor Relations Board. At that time, Taft had already declared his desire to see the passage of legislation providing a more precise statutory definition of the Board's duties and powers and limiting its administrative discretion, and the Smith Committee investigation simply confirmed his view that the Board had

85. "Address at the Tamiment Institute;" Robert A. Taft, "Equal Justice Under Law" (5 October 1946), Address at Kenyon College, Ohio, in *Taft Papers*, 1267–1377.
86. Robert A. Taft, Lincoln's Birthday Address before the Missouri Republican Club (12 February 1946), in *Taft Papers*, 1266–1376. See also Taft to R.I. Ingalls (2 January 1946), in *Taft Papers*, 776–952, ("CIO").
87. Robert A. Taft, Address before the National Industrial Board (16 May 1946), in *Taft Papers*, 1266–1376.
88. Ibid.

exhibited "bias and prejudice" in dealings with both employers and employees.[89] In 1947, when the opportunity to pass restrictive legislation finally arrived, Taft was not only chairman of the Senate Committee on Labor and Public Welfare, but also Senate majority leader. He was thus perfectly placed to exert a decisive influence on the outcome of the debate.

To its pluralist critics, the resulting legislation was an attack upon all of their attempts made over the previous seven years to achieve a labor relations system founded on an accommodation which treated organized labor and corporate capital as mutually indispensable and functionally comparable entities. Leiserson, for example, considered the Taft-Hartley Act to be biased toward employers. He feared that it would disrupt "the national collective bargaining policy [which] is based on the concept that labor and management are partners in production of goods and services for the good of the public including employers and workers."[90] George W. Taylor thought the act would "force labor relations more and more into the political arena and into the hands of lawyers and the courts." The act, he said, constituted "an assumption by the government of a new power to direct the affairs of labor and management. Instead of working out their own negotiating procedures to meet their particular needs and desires, labor and management would have to conform to rules as now prescribed and as later changed by Congress."[91] Similar criticisms were heard from many other leading industrial pluralists, such as Edwin Witte, Lloyd K. Garrison, E. Wight Bakke, and Sumner Slichter.[92]

Certainly, Taft had never concealed that his goal was to diminish the discretion of administrative agencies by establishing explicit rules of

89. Robert A. Taft, Address on CBS Radio (18 April 1939), in *Wagner Papers*, 706 LA 719, folder 68b.
90. Leiserson to Clifford (14 June 1947), in *Leiserson Papers*, Box 40, ("Truman").
91. Taylor to Clifford (13 June 1947), in *Clifford Papers*, Box 7, ("Labor–HR 3020").
92. See Witte to Clifford (11 June 1947) and Bakke to Clifford (14 June 1947), both in *Clifford Papers*, Box 7, ("Labor–HR 3020"). See also Slichter to Steelman (10 June 1947), in *Truman Papers*, Official File, Box 1114, folder 407, ("Taft-Hartley Bill, 1947–48"). Slichter's criticism was somewhat halfhearted:

> It is easy to find fault with the Taft-Hartley bill and it is unfortunate that so many matters were covered in one bill. Furthermore, the circumstances surrounding the passage of the bill are unfortunate and have generated an undue amount of emotion. The effect upon employer-union relations in many plants will be bad.

> At the same time, it is necessary to bear in mind that the bill attempts to deal with many matters which cry for action and that the trade unions have shown no inclination to put their own house in order and thus to make the bill unnecessary. Hence, merely vetoing the bill would be about as unfortunate as signing it – perhaps more so.

legal procedure.[93] But this at least was not qualitatively different from the recommendation of one of those leading pluralists that Congress ought to "make precise in a statute" the duties and obligations of both sides in collective bargaining "which have developed in practice," in order to encourage "habits of orderly procedure."[94] Nor had Taft ever publicly averred an intention to undermine collective bargaining. During the late 1930s, he had always tempered his attacks on federal labor relations policy with statements of support for the "fundamental principle that collective bargaining shall be guaranteed by law, unimpaired by any influence of the employer over his employees."[95] He stuck to this position after the war. During the fight for passage of the Case bill, for example, Taft claimed that the goal of those who sought the amendment of existing labor relations law was not fundamental changes to an industrial relations model based on collective bargaining, but rather restoration of the "reasonable" Wagner Act of 1935 which had been distorted by its pro-union administrators.[96] "The desired end of bargaining between management and labor is a contract, equally binding and enforceable on both parties with appropriate safeguards against resort on either side to wrongful and unlawful conduct."[97]

In subsequent years, Taft made the same claims for his own legislation, insisting that it shared the same theory and goals as Wagner's. "The real basic theory of the Taft-Hartley Act," he said in 1948, "is the same as the theory of the Wagner Act."[98] The whole purpose of the Taft-Hartley Act was "the strengthening of collective bargaining and the determination of wages, hours, and working conditions and other matters of interest to the workmen by a collective bargaining contract between the employer and the union which represented the majority of his employees."[99] The Taft-Hartley law was not a new law. It was "a revision of elaborate existing laws, such as the Wagner Act," which had been "written on sound principles,"[100] and incorporated nearly all of their provisions.[101]

93. "Address at the Tamiment Institute" (6 June 1946), in *Taft Papers*.
94. William M. Leiserson, draft article for *Labor and Nation* (November, 1945), in *Wagner Papers*, 710 LA 721, folder 105. And see William M. Leiserson, "A Government Labor Relations Policy" (8 March 1945), Symposium on National Labor Policy, in *Leiserson Papers*, Box 50, ("Speeches and Articles").
95. Address on CBS Radio (18 April 1939), in *Wagner Papers*.
96. Patterson, *Mr. Republican*, 305.
97. "Minority Views of the Senate Comittee on Education and Labor on HR 4908 – Labor Disputes Act of 1946," in *Taft Papers*, 604–754. ("Labor, 1946").
98. Robert A. Taft, Address at the Columbia University Club, Luncheon Forum (8 October 1948), in *Taft Papers*, 1273–1383.
99. *Taft Papers*, 606–756, ("Labor Bill, 1947").
100. Address (9 March 1948), in *Taft Papers*, 604–754, ("Labor, 1948").
101. Capitol Reports, No. 2 (19 May 1949), in *Taft Papers*, 1289–1399.

Such public endorsements of collective bargaining by one of their leading spokesmen angered many conservatives, and they expressed considerable disappointment that the sponsors of the legislation had not gone
further. Frank E. Gannett of the Gannett Newspaper chain, for example,
wrote Taft in March 1947 that the Wagner Act should be repealed in its
entirety. He condemned the "picayune amendments about giving the
employer freedom of speech and similar suggestions" which had been
occupying the Senate Hearings.[102] Henry Hazlitt agreed. "The Taft-Hartley Act is, after all, only an amendment to the Wagner Act," he wrote in
Newsweek the following year. "It retains what was centrally unsound in
the original law."[103]

As these examples illustrate, the proponents of amendatory legislation
in 1947 were bound by important constraints. Their language – the attacks on bureaucratic agencies and boss-dominated labor unions – was
genuine enough, and underlined their desire both to weaken organized
labor as a political force before the 1948 election and to roll back the
New Deal. But close analysis of the Taft-Hartley Act's substantive provisions suggests that in most respects the act did not far depart from the
pluralist road. The amendments imposed limitations on the discretionary aspects of the pluralist model, and by "writing rules of law governing certain limited phases of the labor situation" through resort to
"deliberate legislative processes" they imprisoned much of its accommodation of institutional "custom and practice" within a new and rigid
framework.[104] But even after the 1946 elections the Republican-South-
ern Democrat coalition lacked sufficient political power to mount a
sustained assault on the National Labor Relations Board and the organized labor movement.

Ludwig Teller, corporation attorney and an important proponent of
the Taft-Hartley Act, aptly summarized the situation which had faced
advocates of the amendments in the spring of 1947 during a speech to
the Labor Relations Section of the American Bar Association two years
later. The passage of the Wagner Act in 1935, Teller said, had been a
watershed in the development of American labor relations law. "The
period since 1935 has given birth to enormous developments in collec-

---

102. Gannett to Taft (19 March 1947), in *Taft Papers*, 608–758, ("Labor Correspon-
      dence, 1947"). See also Gannett to Taft (6 March 1947) and Taft to Gannett (11
      March 1947), both in *Taft Papers, 791–967*, ("Labor Legislation, 1947").
103. Henry Hazlitt, "To Improve the Taft-Hartley Act," *Newsweek* (12 April 1948).
      Some conservatives felt that Taft was going soft on the unions in order to improve
      his image in preparation for the fight for the 1948 Republican presidential nomina-
      tion. See John E. Galvin to Benjamin E. Tate (7 April 1947), in *Taft Papers, 608–
      758*, ("Labor Correspondence, 1947").
104. Robert A. Taft, "Address at the Tamiment Institute" (6 June 1946), in *Taft Papers.*

tive bargaining whose implications have been too deep and complex for complete understanding. There is little in the pre–Wagner situation which has survived. The private injunction in federal courts is virtually gone . . . The blacklist, the so-called 'Mohawk Valley formula,' the company-dominated union and the use of strikebreakers, are substantially remnants of the past."[105]

Because of this sea change, Teller indicated, the advocates of the 1947 amendments had had little alternative but to accept the Wagner Act's policy "of encouraging the growth of labor unions by outlawing interference with their formation and by compelling collective bargaining." The basic pattern of federal collective bargaining policy developed over the previous decade was not to be disturbed. Too much of the old system had gone for any other course to be possible.

105. Ludwig Teller, Address before the American Bar Association (6 September 1949), in *Taft Papers*, 610–760, ("Labor Legislation, New Amendments, 1950–51").

8

The Taft-Hartley Act

> The function of unions, broadly considered, is to maintain purchasing power at a high enough level to absorb the products of business competition. Business competition and national unions are the indispensable blades of our twin scissors of supply and demand.
>
> Robert F. Wagner, Address at the Institute of Social Order (7 May 1947), *Wagner Papers*, 105A SF (Speech Files), folder 62.

The Taft-Hartley Act had its immediate legislative origins amongst the large number of measures dealing with unions and collective bargaining introduced in both House and Senate in the first two weeks of the 80th Congress's first session. By 16 January 1947, twenty-one bills had been placed before the Senate and thirty-seven before the House. In addition, four resolutions were up for consideration in the Senate and seven in the House.

In the House, hearings on four bills – submitted by Representatives Smith of Virginia, Case of South Dakota, Hoffman of Michigan, and Landis of Indiana – began early in February before the Committee on Education and Labor under the chairmanship of Congressman Fred Hartley of New Jersey. Simultaneously, legislative asistants and other interested parties prepared a committee bill, HR3020, based on the 1946 Case bill and on the Smith bill to amend the Wagner Act passed by the House in 1940. Amongst its provisions were proposals which revised completely the structure of the NLRB, outlawed industry-wide bargaining, granted private employers direct access to injunctive relief, prescribed minutely the procedures to be followed in collective bargaining, and promulgated a "bill of rights" for employees which would require extensive government intervention in the internal affairs of unions. The procedures followed by the majority in writing the committee bill occasioned considerable protest from the committee's minority members, but despite this, and despite charges that the bill's real author was the National Association of Manufacturers, HR3020 passed the House on 17 April by a large majority.[1]

1. R. Alton Lee, *Truman and Taft-Hartley: A Question of Mandate* (Lexington, Kentucky, 1966), 49–79.

In the Senate, the Committee on Labor and Public Welfare began hearings late in January on two bills introduced by Joseph Ball of Minnesota, S55 and S360. The bill (S1126) reported by the majority at the conclusion of the hearings did not, however, incorporate all of Ball's key proposals. Consequently, Ball, committee chairman Taft, and two other committee members recommended amendments to the commitee bill, two of which were accepted during floor debate.² The Senate bill passed on 14 May.

Many contemporary observers considered that the Senate bill was much less severe than the House bill in its implications for prevailing collective bargaining policy, and during the House-Senate conference considerable publicity was devoted to calls to the House managers to retreat from some of the more extreme provisions of the House bill, inclusion of which might prevent the achievement of a consensus in Congress and thus "be fatal to the country's hopes for a comprehensive and constructive labor measure this year."³ Once the House managers showed they were ready to yield some of their ground, they were hailed for their responsibility and statesmanship. "Each concession . . . is a move toward the enactment of a fair and well-balanced measure which Congress can expect the President to sign and the country can expect the present Congress to pass over a Presidential veto if necessary."⁴

Critics of the amendments were less easily convinced. Board chairman Herzog argued that the conference bill was "*much* more stringent against labor than the bill passed by the Senate" and concluded that the total impact of the version which emerged from conference "is substantially to *weaken the protection now given employees* by the Wagner Act, and not merely to confer new rights upon employers." Moreover, the bill was "made increasingly unworkable, for employers' benefit as well as unions', due to the encouragement given to litigation." A week later he advised that Truman veto the bill.⁵ Truman of course did so, though not on Herzog's advice alone. The Taft-Hartley Act became law on June 23, when the Senate voted to override Truman's veto.

2. National Labor Relations Board, *Legislative History of the Labor Management Relations Act, 1947*, 2 vols. (Washington, 1948), 456–62.[Hereinafter cited as *Leg. Hist. LMRA*].

3. "Statesmanship on Labor," editorial (21 May 1947), *New York Times*.

4. Ibid. Susan M. Hartmann, *Truman and the 80th Congress* (Columbia, Missouri, 1971), asserts that "the House did make most of the concessions" in conference. 86. James A. Gross, *The Reshaping of the National Labor Relations Board: National Labor Policy in Transition* (Albany, New York, 1981), disagrees. 255.

5. "Supplemental Memorandum on HR 3020 (the Taft-Hartley Bill) as Reported out by the Conferees" (6 June 1947), in *Clifford Papers* Box 7, ("Labor – HR 3020). [emphasis in original]. And see Herzog to Truman (12 June 1947), in *Clifford Papers*, Box 8, ("Labor – HR 3020 – Publications").

The more things change . . .

Unlike the Wagner Act, the Taft-Hartley Act was an "omnibus" statute of four titles. Title I comprised amendments to the Wagner Act. It made changes in the administrative structure and the procedures of the Board as described and established in the Wagner Act, altered the act's definition of "employee" to exclude supervisors, and underlined the right of employees to refrain from participating in collective activity. It imposed restrictions on the behavior of employees and unions in pursuit of collective bargaining contracts, attempted to arrive at a definition of what was to be understood as "good faith" in collective bargaining, and required both parties to give notice of any intention to terminate or modify their contract. It added a proviso to Section 9 of the Wagner Act which declared that petitions for craft units should be assessed on their own merits, while in other amendments to this section it required unions to register with the secretary of labor and to file annual financial reports and non-Communist affidavits from their officers before they could be considered as certifiable bargaining agents. Title I also gave the Board formal authority to resolve jurisdiction and demarcation disputes, accorded solution of these disputes priority among the Board's duties, and attempted to ban "featherbedding" (forcing employers to pay for services not actually rendered). Finally, Title I restricted state jurisdiction over labor relations except in union security matters, banned the closed shop within the area of federal jurisdiction, and required the majority of employees in a unit to approve any attempt to negotiate a union shop contract.

In its remaining titles the act endorsed enhanced federal aid to conciliation, mediation and voluntary arbitration, encouraged parties to develop grievance procedures for the settlement of disputes and outlined procedures for the restraint of strikes considered to represent a threat to the national interest (Title II); declared certain categories of union and employer behavior unlawful, and set up procedures to regulate welfare funds, to facilitate private suits for damages arising from breach of contract and to restrict political expenditures by unions (Title III); and provided for a joint committee of Congress "to study and report on basic problems affecting friendly labor relations and productivity" (Title IV).

Each of the Taft-Hartley Act's provisions falls under one of two headings: either it modified or clarified existing policy and procedure as expressed in the Wagner Act or other state or federal statutes, or it introduced new policy. In neither case, however, did the amendments repudiate the established model. In many respects the Taft-Hartley Act simply formalized practices already current on the Board. In others, where the amendments did attempt more far-reaching alterations in prevailing federal policy, the Board was usually able, through subsequent reinterpretation, to modify the effects.

Perhaps the clearest break with the past instituted by the Taft-Hartley Act came in the provisions relating to the NLRB's administrative structure and procedures, for these conveyed the extreme antagonism felt by Congressional conservatives toward administrative agencies operating in spheres of social regulation outside common law structures and rules of procedure. The conference bill rejected the House provisions, which would have divided the agency in two by creating a separate office of "Administrator of the National Labor Relations Act" in the executive branch to be responsible for initiating all proceedings before the Board, but it still created an independent general counsel within the NLRB to have final authority over the investigation of unfair labor practice charges and the issuance and prosecution of complaints.[6] The Board assured the Senate Committee that such an internal bifurcation of functions had long been a feature of the NLRB's structure and had been rendered absolute in response to the Administrative Procedure Act of 1946.[7] Taft himself later agreed that the Board had always delegated control of prosecution to the general counsel to avoid any overlap of function.[8] Nevertheless, the Board's conformity with the uniform requirements of the Administrative Procedure Act was ignored, and the amendments instituted a separation between prosecuting and judicial functions more drastic than was required of any other federal agency. Hartley later asserted that the goal was to create a model which could eventually be applied to all other areas of government activity.[9]

The bifurcation of the Board was intended to obstruct the application of administrative as opposed to judicial solutions to labor relations problems. This, however, did not introduce a qualitatively new note into the Board's regulatory discourse. Rather, it ensured that the Board would become even more firmly committed to the legal models, procedures and

6. *Leg. Hist. LMRA*, 540–1.
7. *Hearings Before the Senate Committee on Labor and Public Welfare, U.S. Senate, on S55 and S.J.Res. 22, Having the Object of Reducing Industrial Strife in the United States*, 80th Congress, 1st Session (Washington, 1947), 1926. [Hereinafter cited as *Senate Hearings II.*]
8. Taft to John R. Murray (29 June 1950), in *Taft Papers* 817–993 ("Labor Legislation").
9. Fred Hartley, *Our New National Labor Policy: The Taft-Hartley Act and the Next Steps* (New York, 1948), 193. See also Harry A. Millis and Emily Clark Brown, *From the Wagner Act to Taft-Hartley: A Study of National Labor Policy and Labor Relations* (Chicago, 1950), 402–9.

tools of analysis which had been with it since its earliest days.[10] The result in the short term was a considerable increase in litigation and in the harrassment of respondents, particularly during the incumbency of the first independent general counsel, Robert N. Denham. As the Attorney-General's Committee on Administrative Procedure had stressed the year before in recommending *against* the creation of independent general counsel in federal agencies, the establishment of a special office or a special body with no function save to prosecute removed the restraining influence which "the added responsibility of deciding" placed on the activities of an undivided agency. "First, a body devoted solely to prosecuting often is intent upon 'making a record.' It has no responsibility for deciding and its express job is simply to prosecute as often and as successfully as possible. Second, it must guess what the deciding body will think. It can explore the periphery; it can try everything . . ."[11] The Board, however, found itself able to take steps to limit both litigation and harassment and eventually reestablished a degree of its former ascendancy over the general counsel in policy-making.[12]

10. A memorandum of 26 March 1947 from Thomas Shroyer and Gerard D. Reilly to the Senate Committee asserted that the creation of an independent general counsel would "leave the general structure of the Board intact." Reproduced in *Senate Hearings III*.

11. In Paul M. Herzog, "Comments on Title I of HR 3020 (13 June 1947), in *Clifford Papers*, Box 8 ("Labor – HR 3020 – Publications").

12. From 1947 until his resignation in September 1950, General Counsel Denham fought a long battle to concentrate policy-making power in the hands of the general counsel and to confine the Board to a purely judicial role. See, for example, Denham's address before the St. Louis Bar Association (3 November 1947), in *Clifford Papers*, Box 40 ("Miscellaneous Speech File – Robert N. Denham"). The conflict came to a head in 1949–50 over the Board's persistence in dismissing cases brought by the general counsel under a radically widened interpretation of the Board's jurisdiction (see, for example, *International Brotherhood of Teamsters* (December 1949), 87 NLRB 972, and resulted, eventually, in Denham's resignation. See Committee on Expenditures in the Executive Departments (House), 12th Intermediate Report, "Investigation to Ascertain Scope of Interpretation by General Counsel of the National Labor Relations Board of the Term 'Affecting Commerce,' as used in the Labor-Management Relations Act, 1947," *House Report 2050* (80th Congress, Second Session, 1948); Robert N. Denham, Speech Before the American Trucking Associations, Inc. (30 January 1950), and Paul M. Herzog, Statement before the House Committee on Expenditures in the Executive Departments (23 March 1950), both in *Truman Papers* Official File, Box 624, folder 145 ("NLRB, 1950"). Robert N. Denham, "And So I Was Purged," *Saturday Evening Post* (30 December 1950). The Board underlined its victory over the general counsel in *Hollow Tree Lumber Company* (October 1950), 91 NLRB 635, at 636:

> The Board has long been of the opinion that it would better effectuate the purposes of the Act, and promote the prompt handling of major cases, not to exercise its jurisdiction to the fullest extent possible under the authority delegated to it by Congress, but to limit that exercise to enterprises whose operations have, or at which labor disputes would have, a pronounced impact upon the flow of interstate commerce. This

Similar "inertial" effects can be seen at work in other procedural changes made in the Taft-Hartley Act, such as those requiring that proceedings be conducted in accordance with judicial rules of evidence ("so far as practicable"[13]) and that the Board's findings of fact in complaint cases be supported by "substantial evidence on the record considered as a whole" rather than simply by "evidence." Herzog pointed out that such changes promised to multiply the difficulties of administering labor relations policy. In particular, "provisions permitting excessive scope of judicial review may convert administrative tribunals into little more than conduits for the transmission of evidence to the courts . . . There is no value in having experts or specialists in their fields if no finality is to be given their determination and if judges with no special knowledge in the field are to be permitted to substitute their own decisions as final."[14] Yet in fact the words of the act did no more than repeat Section 10(e) of the Administrative Procedure Act, where it was provided that courts should set aside the findings of any administrative agency which were "unsupported by substantial evidence" and that in making this determination the court should "review the whole record."[15] Moreover, both the federal circuit courts of appeal and the Supreme Court had long since held in cases arising under the Wagner Act that the Board's "evidence" would have to be "substantial" if its findings were to be sustained.[16] After 1947, the federal courts considered the question anew and, admittedly with some exceptions, produced a considerable body of opinion which held that the Taft-Hartley law had had no effect on review procedures whatsoever.[17] Again, therefore, the impact of the act did not markedly disturb the labor relations model already in place.

These were not the only changes in the Board's procedures made by

policy should in our opinion be maintained. The time has come, we believe, when experience warrants the establishment and announcement of certain standards which will better clarify and define where the difficult line might best be drawn.

13. Taft stated on the floor of the Senate that this "really leaves it largely to the discretion of the Board and the [trial] examiners whether they shall apply the rules of evidence or not." *Leg. Hist. LMRA*, 1592.

14. "Comments on Title I of HR 3020," in *Clifford Papers*.

15. See *Pittsburgh Steamship Company v. NLRB* (1950), 180 F2 731, 7 CD (Court Decisions Relating to the National Labor Relations Act) 95, at 96.

16. See, for example, *Agwilines, Inc. v. NLRB* (1936), 87 F2 146; *NLRB v. Standard Lime and Stone Company* (1938), 97 F2 531; *Consolidated Edison Company of New York, Inc. v. NLRB* (1938), 305 U.S. 197, 1 CD 897, at 914.

17. See for example, *NLRB v. The Austin Company* (1947), 165 F2 674 (CA 7); *Eastern Coal Corporation v. NLRB* (1949), 176 F2 131 (CA 4); *NLRB v. Continental Oil Company* (1950) 179 F2 552 (CA 10); *NLRB v. Universal Camera Corporation* (1950), 179 F2 749 (CA 2).

the Taft-Hartley Act. The 1947 amendments required that unfair labor practice charges be filed within six months of the occurrence of the alleged unfair practice and allowed the Board to obtain injunctive relief pending a hearing instead of only after a hearing had been completed and a judgment entered. The Board, moreover, was required to give priority to the investigation of unfair labor practice charges arising from strikes and secondary boycotts and, if it issued a complaint, to obtain a temporary (five-day, non-renewable) injunction restraining such practices pending the entry of a judgment.

To some extent these amendments, like the others, formalized past practices.[18] Herzog complained that the six-month statute of limitations on unfair labor practice charges was far too short.[19] Nevertheless it actually doubled the three month limitation on the filing of charges in certain categories of complaint cases instituted by the "Frey" rider which had been attached to the Board's annual appropriation bill every year since 1943, and echoed the Board's own attempts to discourage dilatory filing of charges.[20] On the other hand, the amendments giving the Board the option of seeking temporary injunctive relief pending the resolution of unfair labor practice charges and mandating suits for relief in cases involving strikes and boycotts in pursuit of jurisdiction and representation disputes materially enhanced the Board's and particularly the general counsel's powers to regulate union and employer behavior. But the conference bill did not go so far as to meet the demands of business interests that it overturn the Norris-LaGuardia Act and allow private parties to obtain injunctive relief on their own behalf.[21]

Titles II and III of the Taft-Hartley Act introduced other important innovations in Board procedure by addressing areas with which the Wagner Act had not concerned itself. Drafted largely in response to the strike wave of 1946, Title II included provisions empowering the president to suspend for sixty days strikes considered to pose a threat to the nation's welfare while he made attempts to resolve the dispute. It also contained provisions encouraging parties to collective bargaining agreements to adopt their own procedures for the settlement of disputes arising from the construction and administration of agreements, holding that "final adjustment by a method agreed upon by the parties is the desirable method for settlement of grievance disputes arising over the application or interpretation of an existing collective bargaining agreement." In neither respect, however, did the provisions represent startlingly new ideas. As Attorney General Thomas Clark later contended,

18. See, generally, *Leg. Hist. LMRA*, 1592–7.
19. "Comments on Title I of HR 3020," in *Clifford Papers*.
20. *Leg. Hist. LMRA*, 432.   21. Ibid., 414, 1323.

the president had draconian powers in national emergencies, irrespective of whether he was granted them by statute or not.[22] As for Title II's dispute settlement procedures, these constituted simply an attempt to reestablish for the post-war period policies discouraging strikes developed during the war by the National War Labor Board.

Title III established procedures for suits in federal court by and against labor organizations in cases of contract violation. Opponents of the legislation did not question that unions should be subject to suit. Rather, they argued that the provisions were unnecessary because adequate procedures already existed.[23] As David J. Saposs had observed in 1938: "The decision in the *Coronado Coal Company* case and decisions and legislation to the same effect in the states, have established the liability of unions as associations. The *Danbury Hatters* [Loewe v. Lawlor] case established the liability of union members for suit as individuals . . . There is no well-defined body of law on the enforcement of collective agreements, but there has been an increasing tendency to recognize their enforceability by the courts, either by injunction, specific performance, or by an action for damages."[24] Curiously enough, this was also the position taken by Taft's law partner, J. Mack Swigert. According to Swigert, a great deal of nonsense had been talked "about the inability of an employer to sue a union or hold its members liable for damages . . ." The truth was, he said, "that in most states unions and their members have always been suable and liable for damages for breach of contract or unlawful acts." The non-suability of unions was thus "largely a myth." What the Taft-Hartley law did was open federal courts to all employers and protect individual union members from liability.[25] Title III, in short, offered a means to render uniform practices already in existence in a diversity of jurisdictions in order to encourage the development of a body of federal law governing the enforcement of collective bargaining contracts.[26]

22. *Senate Hearings III*, 261.   23.   *Senate Hearings II*, 1155.
24. David J. Saposs, "Union Responsibility and Incorporation of Labor Unions," National Labor Relations Board, Division of Economic Research (1938), in *Wagner Papers*, 703 LA 718, folder 57. See also "Responsibility of Labor Unions for Acts of Members," Note, *Columbia Law Review*, 38, 3 (March 1938), 454–73.
25. J. Mack Swigert, " 'Slave' Labor's Fourteen Freedoms," *Saturday Evening Post* (25 October 1947). AFL president Green also commented that the provisions "dealing with union liability for breach of collective labor agreements do not change existing substantive law. They are, however, calculated greatly to encourage litigation by removing the usual Federal jurisdiction requirements of diversity of citizenship and of an amount in controversy of not less than $3,000.00." Green to Gael Sullivan, Executive Director, Democratic National Committee (21 May 1947), in *Clifford Papers*, Box 7 ("Labor–HR 3020").
26. In 1953, William J. Barron, labor relations counsel for General Electric, would criticize the preemptive effect of federal law on the states' "traditional" authority to

In the area of procedure, then, the Taft-Hartley Act confined the New Deal model of collective bargaining within a framework of rational-legal rules limiting administrative discretion. This followed the trend of the previous decade toward conflation of common law and administrative approaches to labor relations regulation, particularly in the realm of contract enforcement, and further enhanced the NLRB's already pronounced dependence upon legal discourse. In some respects, as in the injunction clauses, it added to the Board's powers to regulate the behavior of the parties to labor relations disputes. But it did not alter the model itself.

Analysis of a second group of amendments, concerning employees and their rights to nominate bargaining representatives, leads to similar conclusions. Amongst these were amendments establishing that employees had a right to refrain from engaging in collective activity, redefining the statutory meaning of "employee" to deprive supervisors of the Board's protection, and limiting the Board's discretion in designating units.

Stating the right to refrain explicitly was of considerable symbolic importance. Wagner, however, had always claimed that it was adequately recognized in the 1935 legislation, and although Herzog warned that the new language might cause "confusion and difficulty,"[27] former Board chairman Harry A. Millis later confirmed that it "only made explicit what had been implicit and always so regarded by the NLRB ..."[28] House amendments which attempted to specify explicitly the structure and limits of collective activity by establishing an elaborate "bill of rights" minutely describing the relationship which was to pertain between individual union members and their unions were much more threatening to the pluralist model, but these were rejected in conference. As for supervisors, the Board, as we have seen, had been struggling with this question for the past five years. Its eventual decision, that the matter was not one for "administrative determination" at all but should be left to Congress to decide, was an open invitation for revision of the Wagner Act on this question.[29] Again, however, the conferees rejected the attempts of the House managers to

enjoin breaches of collective bargaining agreements and to grant damages in response to private suits. In *Hearings Before the Committee on Labor and Public Welfare, U.S. Senate, Proposed Revisions of the Labor-Management Relations Act of 1947,* 83rd Congress, 1st Session (Washington, 1953), 967. [Hereinafter cited as *Senate Hearings IV*].

27. "Comments on Title I of HR 3020, in *Clifford Papers.*
28. Millis and Brown, *From the Wagner Act to Taft-Hartley,* 421.
29. *Senate Hearings II,* 302. In September 1946 the Board had stated in *Waterfront Employers Association of the Pacific Coast,* 71 NLRB 80, that "although we are cognizant of the problems which exist ... we believe that the Act leaves us no alternative but to afford to all employees the opportunity freely to select representatives *of their own choosing.*" 92–3[emphasis in the original].

exploit this "gray area" by drawing into debate the status of other groups of employees, such as plant guards, concerning whom Board decision-making had been less hesitant.

Plant guards were not left entirely untouched by the Taft-Hartley Act, for their freedom to designate representatives was limited by changes made to Section 9 of the Wagner Act narrowing the Board's discretion in determining units. In particular, the Board was enjoined to segregate guards in separate units and to refrain from certifying organizations of production workers as their representatives. As a result of these amendments, the Board had to dismiss all pending petitions from unions of production and maintenance workers seeking to represent units of guards. Nevertheless, the Board qualified the effects of this limitation somewhat by holding that while the amendments prohibited the certification of any union as the representative of guards if it were affiliated, directly or indirectly, with another union which admitted production and maintenance workers, they did not bar the converse. "[C]ertification of a union as representative of a unit of production and maintenance employees" was not to be prohibited "just because that union happens to be affiliated directly or indirectly with a union already representing guards."[30]

The amendments to Section 9 ranged far wider than plant guards. As a result of changes instituted by the Taft-Hartley Act the Board could not (1) decline to designate a craft unit on the grounds that a prior Board certification had established a different unit, or (2) base a certification solely on the extent to which a union had organized workers. The amendments also required that a union be able to demonstrate that it had significant support among the workers in a unit before the Board could proceed with an investigation of its claim to represent them, prohibited the holding of elections within twelve months of a previous election, allowed employers to petition for an election if a union had demanded that the employer recognize it as the majority representative, and banned strikers not eligible for reinstatement from voting in bargaining unit elections.

Neither the twelve-month period between elections nor the requirement that a union be able to make a significant show of support was a departure from prevailing Board practice.[31] Nor, according to a March

---

30. *E.R. Squibb and Sons* (April 1948), 77 NLRB 84, at 86.
31. Herzog to Taft (18 June 1946), in *Taft Papers*, 781–957 ("National Labor Relations Board"); *Senate Hearings III*, 1326. See also Gerhard P. Van Arkel, general counsel of the National Labor Relations Board, "Speech at a Conference of Labor Attorneys" (7 and 8 November 1946), in *Leiserson Papers*, Box 28 ("NLRB"). Van Arkel emphasized the "impediments" which the Board had been concerned to place in the way of access to its election machinery over the previous eight years. "It was

1947 Senate Committee memorandum prepared by former regional director Thomas Shroyer and former Board member Gerard Reilly, were the proposals to limit the Board's discretion in respect of craft units particularly innovative, for they "[did] not change the current rules of decision of the Board." According to Shroyer and Reilly, the drafters of the Senate bill, the Board would be free to continue to reject craft units as long as bargaining history based on a prior determination was not the *sole* reason for rejection.[32] In practice, therefore, neither the craft proviso nor that which limited the Board's reliance on extent of organization in determining units, constituted a decisive alteration of federal policy governing bargaining units. "Although Congress carefully scrutinized the unit selection problem, and made some changes designed to encourage crafts, it apparently intended to restate then-existing law with regard to discretion in determining the 'appropriate' unit."[33] Resort to formal rules might limit the Board's freedom to solve problems as they arose in the light of experience, but the Board continued as in the past to enjoy considerable influence over bargaining structure. Indeed, it was able to state in its annual report for the year ending June 1948 that "most of the practices and principles of decision-making previously established by the Board in the administration of [Section 9 of the Wagner Act] remained unaltered."[34]

Other amendments to Section 9, were much more of a threat to the "uninterrupted and stable bargaining relations" which, the Board argued, had been established by the unrestricted operation of the New Deal model.[35] These comprised provisions allowing employers to file election petitions, disqualifying strikers ineligible for reinstatement (that is, anyone striking on any issue other than an employer's unfair labor practice) from voting in representation elections, permitting employees to petition the Board for the holding of decertification elections, and requiring unions to register with the secretary of labor before they could be considered eligible to represent workers.

Least serious was the employer petition proviso. For several years the Board had been permitting employers to petition for elections whenever they were confronted with competing demands from two or more

early discovered that some labor organizations were appearing on the ballot with little hope of winning elections; after making elaborate studies, the Board concluded that it would not hold elections unless evidence were produced showing at least a 30 percent representation by the petitioner among employees in the appropriate unit."

32. In *Senate Hearings III*, 1135.
33. *Mueller Brass Company v. NLRB* (1950), 180 F2 402.
34. National Labor Relations Board, *Thirteenth Annual Report* (Washington, 1949), 32.
35. "Comments on Title I of HR 3020," in *Clifford Papers*.

unions for recognition as majority representative, and in December 1946 it had informed the White House that an amendment permitting employer petitions in cases where only one union claimed bargaining rights could do little harm "provided proper safeguards [are] erected."[36] Once the amendment came into force, the Board moved quickly to put those safeguards in place by establishing that a union which had claimed majority status could subsequently choose to "disclaim" it if confronted with an employer petition. By so doing the union would bring to a halt whatever preparations the Board might have made for holding an election, without prejudice to renewal of those preparations if the union later decided that, after all, it did wish to seek certification. This effectively neutralized the considerable advantage in determining the timing of elections which the amendment threatened to give to the employer.[37]

The Board found the attempt to prevent participation by wage and hour strikers in Board elections a more serious threat to stability in collective bargaining. "The proposal would enable an employer to secure the rejection of an established bargaining agent at the very time that the public interest makes it particularly urgent that collective bargaining continue,"[38] for an election called during a strike would almost certainly result in a situation where the bulk of the incumbent's adherents having had their jobs legally filled by strikebreakers, could not vote. This would place the fate of the incumbent in the hands of the strikebreakers, virtually assuring its defeat. "Anti-union employers may thus be encouraged to refuse settlement of disputes *in order to bring about strikes* and thereby secure the defeat of the collective bargaining representative."[39] Wage and hour strikers had lost the right to vote in Board elections well prior to passage of the Taft-Hartley Act, however,[40] and in fact the Board continued to follow the same policy of only allowing such strikers to vote

36. "Memorandum to the President on Labor Legislation" (11 December 1946), in *Clifford Papers*, Box 7 ("Labor – 80th Congress").
37. *Ny-Lint Tool and Manufacturing Company* (May 1948), 77 NRLB 642. The Board was split on this question, as the majority opinion indicated (643):
> Our dissenting colleague maintains that the Board is required by the Act, as amended, to proceed to an election, and that failure to do so 'emasculates' the Employer's right to file a petition. To force the Union, under this theory, to an election in a unit which it does not claim to represent would result, not only in a futile act leading toward a purely negative result, but also in depriving the employees of any opportunity to select any bargaining representative for an entire year after the election. The right of the employer to seek an election is not a guarantee that it will secure one in every case . . ."
38. "Comments on Title I of HR 3020," in *Clifford Papers*. 39. Ibid.
40. See *Senate Hearings IV*, 43. Strikers protesting unfair labor practices were entitled to unconditional reinstatement, and therefore could not be declared ineligible to vote.

in cases where it was unclear whether or not they had been validly replaced.[41] While the attempt to prevent these strikers from protecting their bargaining agent was of considerable importance in regulating the uses to which a union could put its bargaining power, therefore, the Board had already begun to impose this restriction well before 1947.

Similar predictions of disruption of collective bargaining attended the Board's comments on the operation of the Taft-Hartley Act's decertification provisions. Unions had, of course, been deprived of certification under the Wagner Act through Board action. In *Cramp Shipbuilding Company* (August 1943), for example, the Board had indicated that whenever a certification "ceases to effectuate the policies of the Act, or when its continued existence would be contrary to settled principles adopted by the Board," the NLRB could, if it chose, revoke that certification, depriving the union in question of collective bargaining rights and the employees of the representative they had chosen.[42] But the Wagner Act had contained no provision allowing dissenters within the bargaining unit to question the incumbent's majority and bring collective bargaining to an end. Nor had the Board been willing to consider such petitions, fearing that they "could furnish employers with a useful device for undermining the position of the bargaining agent and for delaying collective bargaining."[43] In particular, the Board warned, employers might encourage dissident groups to file petitions repeatedly, placing the majority status of the bargaining representative permanently in doubt.[44] Consequently, once the amendment was adopted the Board moved to limit its operation by using its contract-bar rules and the one-year election provision to narrow considerably the opportunities which dissident groups might enjoy to file decertification petitions. It also routinely dismissed decertification petitions which could be shown to be the result of em-

41. See *Columbia Pictures Corporation* (May 1945), 61 NLRB 1030, and compare *Pipe Machinery Company* (February 1948), 76 NLRB 247.

42. 52 NLRB 309, at 311. See also *R.K.O. Radio Pictures, Inc., et al.* (March 1945), 61 NLRB 112, at 115–16, where the Board confirmed that a union's breach of its duty of fair representation would also be grounds for the revocation of a certification:
    It should be emphasized . . . that it is the duty of the exclusive representative of the employees in an appropriate bargaining unit to represent all employees therein without hostile discrimination and with a view to the promotion of their best interests. Should [either of the unions here certified in complementary units] engage in . . . restrictive practices, or otherwise circumvent the objectives of the Board inherent in this decision, the Board will not regard itself as precluded, upon consideration of the circumstances thus presented, from taking appropriate remedial action, including either a redetermination of the bargaining unit or revocation of the certification herein.

43. "Comments on Title I of HR 3020," in *Clifford Papers*.   44. Ibid.

ployer aid or inducement, and refused to consider petitions filed during unfair labor practice proceedings. Nor, finally, would the Board enquire into the reasons behind the withdrawal of petitions, leaving incumbents free to take disciplinary action against members who filed petitions in order to coerce them into withdrawal.[45]

The Board's safeguards resulted in the withdrawal or dismissal of many of the decertification petitions filed in the two years after the Taft-Hartley Act was passed. Nevertheless, 229 decertification elections were conducted, mostly in small units. Bargaining rights were lost in 144 of these.[46]

Unions not in compliance with Section 9(f), (g), and (h) of the Taft-Hartley Act proved particularly vulnerable to decertification proceedings, for such unions were not in a position to file charges against an employer who was abusing the decertification provisions. Compliance required that the union register with the secretary of labor, file annual reports updating its registration, and in particular furnish affidavits from its officers affirming that they were not communists. Taft argued that none of these requirements was a matter "which affected the basic principles of the Taft-Hartley Act" one way or the other.[47] But this was spurious. Their inclusion was of considerable significance, given in particular the well-publicized role of communists in a number of important CIO unions.

The Board had no objections to the principle that unions should furnish their members and the secretary of labor with organizational and financial data as required by 9(f) and (g), although it felt that provisions which imposed expensive burdens upon unions which wished to make use of "the orderly procedures of the Act" might encourage resort to self-help and thus recommended that fulfillment of the filing requirements not be made a condition of access to its machinery.[48] As for 9(h), the anti-communist affidavit, the Board was even more approving of the principle, for it "recognized the need for measures to remove the disruptive influence of Communists from the American trade union movement."[49] However, the Board foreshadowed a need for safeguards to prevent the penalties incurred by an organization's communist officers from damaging the interest of the organization as a whole.[50] These safeguards would take form in later years as the Board developed its "schism" doctrine, through which it sought to facilitate

45. Millis and Brown, *From the Wagner Act to Taft-Hartley*, 532–5.
46. Benjamin J. Taylor and Fred Witney, *Labor Relations Law* (Englewood Cliffs, New Jersey, 1979), 360.
47. Taft to P. Wineland (11 January 1950), in *Taft Papers*, 307.
48. "Comments on Title I of HR 3020," in *Clifford Papers*. 49. Ibid. 50. Ibid.

the speedy resolution of intra-union conflicts over "policy and management" by permitting dissident groups free rein to challenge the incumbent bargaining representative wherever the challenge was occasioned by the union's expulsion from a parent body on the grounds of communist domination.[51]

The amendments to Section 9 had the effect of entrenching the pluralist model while at the same time ensuring that the labor movement would be confined within it. The anti-communist affidavit, in particular, signified an intent to cripple by administrative process any union whose interpretation of its role was likely to be incompatible with pluralist values and assumptions. The same can be observed of the changes for which the Taft-Hartley Act is perhaps best known, namely the provisions dealing with unfair labor practices. Despite attempts in the House to dilute the prohibitions against employer domination of unions, the act left untouched the restrictions on employer behavior placed there by the Wagner Act. But it supplemented these with provisions restricting union and employee behavior. Henceforth it was to be an unfair labor practice for unions (1) to coerce employees exercising their right to self-organization or to refrain from self-organization; (2) to attempt to make an employer discriminate against employees who had been unfairly denied membership in a union; (3) to refuse to bargain; (4) to engage in secondary boycotts; (5) to engage in collective action intended to force an employer to recognize an uncertified union or to assign work to members of a particular organization; and (6) to require payment of wages for services not performed.[52]

These restrictions on union and employee behavior were significant statutory innovations. Some of the most important, however, had already been introduced administratively, without fanfare, under the Wagner Act. Union coercion of employees seeking to exercise their right of self-organization, for instance, had long since been dealt with by the

51. See, for example, *Boston Machine Works Company* (March 1950), 89 NLRB 59; *The Bassick Company* (May 1950), 89 NLRB 1143.
52. Taft-Hartley also added a Section 8(d) which outlined the duties of parties to collective bargaining. It required a party to give sixty days notice of its intention to terminate or modify the contract, offer to meet to negotiate a new contract, inform the Federal Mediation and Conciliation Service, and refrain from striking or locking-out during the sixty-day period. Harry Millis had suggested the wisdom of such a procedure in 1935, arguing that future legislators might want to require that parties give "due notice of changes in wages and working conditions and opportunity for conference and mediation before severance of [their] relationship by strike or lock-out." Millis also suggested that eventually "a rather full Federal code" governing industrial relations might well be needed. See *Leg. Hist.*, 1552. In 1950, the Board asserted that "Section 8(d) . . . substantially codifies the bargaining standards developed under the Wagner Act." *American National Insurance Company* (April 1950), 89 NLRB 185.

Board in the course of the evolution of its contract-bar doctrine.[53] Taft-Hartley strengthened and widened the prohibition, but the new law did not introduce it. Similarly, on a number of occasions the Board had reinstated employees whom it judged to have been unfairly denied membership in a union even though it had lacked power to take direct action against the union in question.[54] The Board and the courts had also found that strikes to force recognition in the face of a Board certification or to force an employer to bargain with an uncertified union were not protected by the Wagner Act.[55] Finally, under pressure from the courts, the Board had already decided that unions, no less than employers, were compelled to bargain by the Wagner Act.[56]

Except in three respects to be discussed below, then, the unfair labor practice provisions of the Taft-Hartley Act had been introduced in one form or another in the administration and enforcement of the New Deal model. They certainly tightened the restrictions on union behavior which had become an important part of that model, but they did not constitute a reversal of current policy.[57]

One final change introduced by Title I of the Taft-Hartley Act, that concerning union security, deserves major attention. The Wagner Act had permitted parties to include clauses in their contracts requiring membership in the majority's bargaining agent as a condition of employment. Under the Taft-Hartley Act, contracts could provide only that applicants for jobs had to join the union in question within thirty days of commencing employment. Such a provision, moreover, had to be approved by a majority of the employees in the unit in a "union shop" election organized by the Board. The Taft-Hartley Act also stated explicitly, in Section 14(b), that states were free to impose more stringent regulations than this on union security agreements if they wished to do so.

The explicit outlawing of the closed shop within the area of federal jurisdiction represented an important alteration in federal policy. In conjunction with 14(b), it formed a major barrier to the extension of American unionism beyond "the social and regional terrain that it had

---

53. As noted in Chapters 6 and 7.
54. Robert F. Wagner, "The Wagner Act: A Reappraisal," *Sign Magazine* (March 1947), in *Wagner Papers* SF 105a, folder 62. See also *James v. Marinship Corporation* (1944) 155 P2 329; *The Wallace Corporation v. NLRB* (1944), 323 U.S. 248. See also *Senate Hearings III*, 300–2 and cases cited.
55. As noted in Chapter 7.   56. Ibid.
57. Taft wrote in July 1947: "I don't think this Act does anything except correct injustices which have arisen in the laws and their administration . . . I don't think it will require a great many court decisions to interpret it, because our changes were based on existing decisions, and their purpose is clear." Taft to R.D. Stevens (15 July 1947), in *Taft Papers*, 791–967 ("Labor Legislation, 1947").

won in the previous decade."[58] It also placed important new limitations on the extent of union authority in those labor markets which had been thoroughly organized. The amendments' advocates were at some pains to point out, however, that the Wagner Act was itself empty of any declaration in favor of the closed shop and that it had actually limited the circumstances under which, within the federal jurisdiction, a closed shop might be obtained. Nor had that act in any sense pre-empted state union security laws. As Wagner had stated in introducing his bill in the Senate twelve years before, "[the bill] does not force any employer to make a closed-shop agreement. It does not even state that Congress favors the policy of the closed shop. It merely provides that employers and employees may voluntarily make closed shop agreements in any state where they are now legal. Far from suggesting a change, it merely preserves the status quo."[59] Indeed, advocates of the amendments insisted, most unions no longer sought the closed shop. Taft for example, claimed that the great majority of unions clearly preferred other forms of security, and stated that he simply wished to prevent "the absolute closed shop prohibiting the employment of anybody who was not already a member of the union." This would not have any effect on the approximately "90 percent of all so-called closed shops [which] are, in fact, union shops," because the union shop was, of course, perfectly legal under the Taft-Hartley Act.[60]

As in many other respects, therefore, the Taft-Hartley Act's union security provisions did not depart as far from current practice as seemed at first glance to be the case to contemporary observers. Unions did not find themselves appreciably hindered by the election requirements, winning 97 percent of the 46,000 union shop polls conducted by the Board between 1947 and 1951. So overwhelming was this evidence of support for the union shop that in October 1951 the election requirement was removed from the Act.[61] Moreover, while in formal terms the closed shop was banned from the realm of collective bargaining, in practice it tended to survive for some years in modified form in such industries as printing, construction and the maritime trades, where it had long been a

58. Nelson Lichtenstein, *Labor's War at Home: The CIO in World War Two* (Cambridge, England, 1982), 239.
59. *Leg. Hist.*, 1313. See also Wagner to New York *Times* (4 April 1936), in *Wagner Papers*, BB 120, book 2 (marked "not used").
60. Taft to Fulmer H. Latter (1 May 1947), in *Taft Papers*, 791–967 ("Labor Legislation, 1947"). Harvey W. Brown, president of the International Association of Machinists, told the Senate Committee in 1947 that "there are very few closed shops, if the term is meant to mean that none but union men can be hired." *Senate Hearings II*, 1609.
61. Taylor and Witney, *Labor Relations Law*, 361.

key institution in the labor market. It was even partially rehabilitated by the Board.[62]

Neither in theory nor in practice, one may conclude from this survey, did federal labor relations law undergo in 1947 the same sort of dramatic break that had come in 1935.[63] As Senator Paul Douglas of Illinois pointed out in 1949 during debates over revisions to the Taft-Hartley Act, an industrial common law dealing with many of the problems confronted in Taft-Hartley had begun to develop piecemeal under the aegis of the Wagner Act long before 1947.[64] His colleague, Wayne Morse, asserted in support of this contention that the Taft-Hartley Act had in fact been in large part simply an attempt to express this industrial common law in codified form, so as to reassure the public that the government was indeed involved in ensuring that the behavior of both parties to collective bargaining was being properly regulated.[65] This was also the view taken by the Supreme Court four years later: "Congress evidently considered that centralized administration of specially designed procedures was necessary to obtain uniform application of its substantive rules and to avoid [the] diversities and conflicts likely to result from a variety of local procedures and attitudes towards labor controversies." The Court added the observation that this was part of a wider and longer-term process of "federalizing" labor law. The government was "substituting federal statute law applied by administrative procedures in the public interest in the place of individual suits to enforce common law doctrines of private right."[66] The Taft-Hartley Act, seemingly, was at one with the Wagner Act and with the efflorescence of centralized, nonpartisan bureaucratic-administrative government, the ambitions of its more conservative sponsors notwithstanding.

While remaining in the mainstream of institutional development in labor relations law, however, the Taft-Hartley Act was not just an elaboration of past policy. Helping to entrench the pluralist model, the legislation simultaneously widened drastically the procedural and substantive limitations hindering the institution of collective bargaining

---

62. Ibid., 354; Millis and Brown, *From the Wagner Act to Taft-Hartley*, 635–6.
63. The Senate Committee's Minority Report commented on the "creditable rejection by the committee of many extreme proposals" and pointed to the majority's recognition of the "necessity for grudging inclusion in the bill of many presently applied rules." *Leg. Hist. LMRA*, 466. Millis and Brown, although highly critical of the Taft-Hartley amendments, confirm that "Much of the body of doctrine built up during the twelve years of the Wagner Act was left untouched by the amendments." *From the Wagner Act to Taft-Hartley*, 630.
64. *Senate Hearings III*, 298.   65. Ibid.
66. *Joseph Garnner v. Teamsters* (1953), 346 U.S. 485, 8 CD 1491, at 1494, 1497–8.

from penetrating and collectivizing facets of the employment relationship other than wages, hours and benefits. This process was most clearly revealed in the formulation and operation of those sections of the act giving the Board control of demarcation disputes, banning the closed shop and outlawing jurisdictional strikes and secondary boycotts. Together, these innovations imposed explicit limits on the sphere of labor–management relationships to be governed by collective bargaining. In so doing, they pointed up the existence of an intimate relationship between the postwar evolution of the pluralist model of labor relationships and the accelerating recovery and expansion of the corporate political economy.

The Taft-Hartley Act *is* a slave labor law

On 29 January 1947, the third day of the Senate Committee's hearings on labor law reform legislation, Theodore R. Iserman appeared before the committee to argue in favor of amending the Wagner Act. Iserman, a corporation labor lawyer, was the author of "Industrial Peace and the Wagner Act," a recent commentary on labor relations policy. Subsequently he would join Thomas Shroyer and Gerard Reilly in drafting S1126, the Senate Committee's bill.

Iserman's testimony covered a number of topics in considerable detail. But first he made a general opening statement which was to provide the context for all of his proposals. This hinged on the assertion that since 1935 those responsible for administering the Wagner Act had consistently been ignoring Congress's original purpose in passing it:

> Congress passed this Act for one purpose, "to eliminate the causes of certain substantial obstructions to the free flow of commerce, and mitigate and eliminate these obstructions when they have occurred." In simpler words, the purpose of the Act is to increase the output that moves in the stream of commerce, and thus to increase the flow of the stream of commerce. The Act seeks to accomplish this purpose through encouraging unionizing and collective bargaining . . . Congress has no power under the Constitution to deal with unionizing and collective bargaining as ends in themselves.

The purpose of the Wagner Act, Iserman insisted, had been "to increase output," not "to increase unionizing and collective bargaining at the expense of output."[67]

Iserman returned to this theme again and again. Though regrettable,

67. *Senate Hearings II*, 123–4, 125.

he said, strikes over wages and conditions were a normal accompaniment of collective bargaining. Congress should ensure that the right to strike was not so abused as to defeat the purpose of the act by holding up production, but should accept that strikes would always occur. Congress, however, should not hesitate to act against other practices arising from the organization of workers which tended to reduce output:

> One is that which calls on each member of the union to do no more than his fellows do. This tends to reduce the productivity of the whole group to that of the less productive members of the group. Another favors standardized pay, each man receiving what the others receive. Since this leaves unusual productivity unrewarded, it does not encourage people to excel. This attitude is reflected in widespread resistance by unions to incentive systems.

This was not at all:

> Unions frequently oppose new methods and machines that increase the productivity of workers. They not infrequently restrict output, limit the number of people who can learn a trade or work at it, and insist that two or more workers perform duties that one could do or require employers to pay for work that no one does, practices known as featherbedding.[68]

Iserman did not argue that restrictive practices had originated with the Wagner Act. They had been "evident and well-known for many years before the Wagner Act became law."[69] But the performance of the economy over the previous eighteen months had demonstrated that they posed an obstacle to productivity advances in American industry too great to be tolerated any longer. The need for Congressional action to stamp them out was overwhelming. "Many men with the closest and best knowledge of industry believe that if American industry had been more free of controls, both by Government and by the restrictive practices of unions, producing and output after the war would have jumped ahead with far greater speed; and instead of strikes, the smothering of output, and paralysis, there could have been the great activity that everybody hoped for, unheard-of productivity . . ."[70]

Like other witnesses who followed him, Iserman argued that Congress should take a number of steps to free production from the unions' restrictions. One was to safeguard management's "right to manage" by preventing foremen and supervisors from joining unions. Another was to encourage competition by prohibiting unions from imposing the

68. Ibid., 145.
69. This was clear, he said, because the utilitarian philosopher and political economist, John Stuart Mill, had been writing about them in 1869. In ibid., 146.
70. Ibid., 161.

same wage-bargain on all employers in an industry through "monopolistic" practices. A third was to reduce union authority over the labor supply by banning the closed shop and outlawing restrictive practices, jurisdictional strikes and demarcation disputes.[71]

As we have seen, the first of these, the ban on the organization of supervisors, was duly included in the Taft-Hartley Act. The second, however, was not. Employers were divided over the merits of giving regional cost differentials a central role in competition. Many, particularly those associated with the National Association of Manufacturers, emphasized the disadvantages to small and medium-sized businesses in meeting the wage levels paid by their larger competitors. According to C. Dickerman Williams, general counsel for the American Locomotive Company of New York, "monopolistic" industry-wide bargaining gave no recognition "to the widely varying economic and social factors applicable to the employers of the various union members, and of the localities in which they reside."[72] James D. Francis, president of the Island Creek Coal Company of Virginia, agreed. He argued that industry-wide agreements resulted in the maladjustment of competition between companies of different size in different places and using different methods.[73] The position of these employers was shared by senators like Ball and Taft who were sympathetic to small business, and they led the attempt to reintroduce strict regulation of industry-wide bargaining into the Senate bill in floor debate after it had been excluded during the committee stage.[74] But other employers from highly oligopolistic industries, or industries characterized by strong trade associations, stressed the great advantages of removing wage costs from competition. Earl F. Reed, counsel to the Weirton Steel Corporation, told the Senate committee that he was at a loss to explain why any employer should be opposed to industry-wide bargaining.[75] Almon E. Roth, president of the National Federation of American Shipping and Raymond H. Reis, of

71. The corporation labor lawyer, Ludwig Teller, told the Senate Committee that restrictive practices and jurisdiction disputes should no longer be tolerated because they obstructed the public interest in uninterrupted production. "Interference with maximum production, or with the introduction or use of mechanical invention in aid of maximum production," he advised, "should be declared illegal." In ibid., 248. On the question of labor productivity and its centrality to the political economy of postwar America, see David M. Gordon, et al., *Segmented Work, Divided Workers: The Historical Transformation of Labor in the United States* (New York, 1982), 165–227.
72. *Senate Hearings II*, 209.   73. Ibid., 245.
74. Taft to W.T. Holliday (11 March 1947), and Taft to Frank E. Gannett (11 March 1947), both in *Taft Papers*, 791–967 ("Labor Legislation, 1947"); Taft to Gerard D. Reilly (27 December 1949), in *Taft Papers*, 807–983, ("Labor"). See also Lichtenstein, *Labor's War at Home*, 37.
75. *Senate Hearings II*, 743–4.

the Clothing Manufacturers' Association, were also strongly opposed.[76] These employer representatives were joined by labor relations experts, who argued that in highly competitive industries industry-wide bargaining was in fact extremely beneficial to small firms. The overall problem arose not from distortions in the labor market caused by union "monopolies," but rather from the wage-leadership and pattern following which had been characteristic of oligopolistic industries dominated by multi-unit center corporations long before the emergence of mass industrial unions.[77] Most complaints, indeed, seemed to be coming from peripheral firms in oligopolistic industries, not from the center corporations or from firms in competitive industries where real industry-wide bargaining was taking place.

The lack of agreement among employers on the merits of a ban on industry-wide bargaining prevented its inclusion in the Taft-Hartley Act. As Raymond Smethurst, general counsel of the National Association of Manufacturers acknowledged, many employers had a vested interest in the competitive structures encouraged by the New Deal and had no wish to run the risk of undermining those structures for the sake of a questionable, short-term advantage.[78] Further, representatives of the NLRB confirmed that it was already Board policy to restrict its units to the employees of a single employer. Only if two or more companies operated as a single concern with centralized control of their labor relations, or if a group of companies had delegated bargaining to a single agent or trade organization, had done so in the past, and were committed to accepting the results, would the Board find for a more extensive unit.[79]

The absence of a ban on industry-wide bargaining from the Taft-Hartley bill reinforces the conclusion that the fundamental intent of the amendments was less to disrupt the collective bargaining structures which had developed over the previous decade than to ensure that unions were confined ever more strictly within those structures. This point is underlined by the bans and limitations – on secondary boycotts, restrictive practices, jurisdiction and demarcation disputes, and the closed shop – which the act *did* contain. All severely restricted the de-

---

76. *Senate Hearings II*, 623, 625; Esther Peterson, legislative representative of the Amalgamated Clothing Workers of America, to Taft (18 April 1947), in *Taft Papers*, 791–967 ("Labor Legislation, 1947"). See also *Hearings Before the Joint Committee on Labor-Management Relations on the Operation of the Labor-Management Relations Act of 1947*, 80th Congress, 2nd Session (Washington, 1948), 1078–81. [Hereinafter cited as *Ball Committee Hearings*]. See also *Senate Hearings IV*, 1331.
77. *Senate Hearings II*, 663–64, 1092–94; *Ball Committee Hearings*, 911–12; *Senate Hearings IV*, 1826.
78. *Senate Hearings II*, 1807.   79. Ibid., 3177.

gree of authority which unions could hope to assert at the point of production or through the bargaining process to counter corporate management's attempts to reshape the organization of production.[80]

Developments in a number of cases arising from provisions in the Taft-Hartley Act affecting demarcation disputes are particularly helpful in illustrating this tendency. Of these, perhaps the best documented is *International Longshoremen's and Warehousemen's Union* (April 1949), a case arising from a dispute over the allocation of work at a timber mill in Juneau, Alaska.[81]

In April 1948, the Juneau Spruce Corporation filed a charge with the National Labor Relations Board accusing International Longshoremen's and Warehousemen's Union Local 16 of violating Section 8(b)(4)(d) of the Taft-Hartley Act, which made it an unfair practice for a union to attempt to force an employer to assign work to its own members rather than to employees in another organization absent a determination from the Board that the first union was indeed the properly designated bargaining representative. The corporation's charge was duly investigated by an NLRB field examiner. He found that the charge arose from actions taken by Local 16 against the corporation to enforce its claim that all jobs involving the loading of barges at the corporation's recently-acquired subsidiary, J.L. Mills Incorporated, should be assigned to longshoremen. The union argued that these jobs had always been filled by ILWU members, and that in reassigning them to members of another union, the International Woodworkers of America-CIO, the corporation had acted beyond its authority. The field examiner established that the predecessor company had had a contract with the IWA under which its members performed milling operations, but that Local 16 had always been responsible for dispatching longshoremen for wharf work. The successor corporation, however, had refused to follow the predecessor's arrangement, insisting that the contract with the IWA be interpreted to assign all work in and around the mill to that union. Both unions disputed the corporation's interpretation of the IWA's contract, and in April 1948, Local 16 had begun a picket to force the corporation to assign the disputed work to its members in accordance with past practice. It was this picket which had precipitated the corporation's petition to the Board.[82]

In light of the corporation's attempt to redefine unilaterally the scope

80. See Joseph R. Dempsey, *The Operation of the Right-to-Work Laws* (Milwaukee, 1961), 2–9. See also Gordon et al., *Segmented Work, Divided Workers*, 185–215.
81. 82 NLRB 650.
82. *RG* 25 Informal Files 19-CD-2, 19-CD-4, 19-CD-5, *Pearson v. Graham*, Civil Action 2250 (International Longshoremen's and Warehousemen's Union).

of the IWA's bargaining unit so as to include the longshore work which had historically been performed by ILWU members, the field examiner concluded that the ILWU's actions were not in violation of the act and recommended that the charge be dismissed. In July 1948, however, the Juneau Spruce Corporation concluded a contract with the IWA which explicitly gave the IWA the work, in effect placing the ILWU in a position where its picketing was now unambiguously in violation of 8(b)(4)(d). Proceedings on the charge were suspended while the Board began an investigation of the merits of the dispute as required by section 10(k) of the act. Regional hearings took place in September, followed in January 1949 by oral argument before the Board.

The corporation's attorneys, led by former Board member Gerard Reilly, held that the only defense a union could offer to an 8(b)(4)(d) charge was proof "that the disputed work is covered by a prior Board order or certification."[83] In its decision, handed down four months later on April 1, 1949, the Board agreed with its former member:

> Inasmuch as we have found that the ILWU neither represented any of the company's employees nor had any certification, or contractual or other lawful basis upon which to predicate a right to the assignment of these particular work tasks, we find it unnecessary to consider the so-called tradition or custom alleged with respect to such work tasks . . . [W]here a union with no bargaining or any representative status makes demands on the company for the assignment of work to its members to the exclusion of the Company's own employees, the question of tradition or custom in the industry is irrelevant.[84]

Within the framework for collective bargaining created by the New Deal model, the Board's logic was irrefutable. Neither the Wagner Act nor the Taft-Hartley Act conveyed to any worker the right to be employed at a particular job, nor to any union the right to have its members employed on a particular job. These were matters for the employer alone to resolve, a point which the Taft-Hartley Act had underlined elsewhere by banning the closed shop. A union's rights flowed from the decision made by workers who were already employed to exercise their civil rights to choose it to represent them, and from the Board's approval of their choice. Such rights as a union enjoyed under the New Deal model, in other words, were strictly post facto.

One of the two new members of the Board, former congressman Abe Murdock, dissented from the majority opinion in the *ILWU* case. Mur-

83. Reilly to Murdock (6 January 1949), in Informal File 19-CD-4 and 5 (amalgamated).
84. 82 NLRB 650, at 660.

dock pointed out, correctly, that the majority had decided the question on the basis of whether or not the union represented the employees to whom the work in question had been assigned. Because the union obviously did not represent these workers, Murdock continued, the majority had concluded that it had no business intervening in the matter. But, said Murdock, this was not the point: "to arbitrate a jurisdiction dispute is to determine which of two or more trade or craft groups of workers, or their respective unions, *ought* to be assigned to perform certain disputed work. It is not to decide, as the majority has done here, the non-arbitrable question as to which of two or more unions is the chosen representative of the employees who *happen to be performing* the disputed work."[85]

The Board majority's rejection of Murdock's opinion was important for two reasons. First, it confirmed that, as under the Wagner Act, representation of the majority of the employees in a Board-determined "appropriate" unit was to be the sole basis upon which a union might legitimately seek to exercise influence in any workplace or industrial situation. This reinforced the tendency of labor relations law, particularly pronounced in the wake of Taft-Hartley, to bring about a separation between the union as an institution and the workplace, for as the Board stated in *National Union of Marine Cooks and Stewards* (April 1949) one week later, the question of whether an employer's work assignment was a violation of tradition or custom in an industry was irrelevant "where a union with no bargaining or representative status makes demands on an employer for the assignment of work to the exclusion of the employer's own employees who are performing the work . . ."[86] Second, it further underscored the exclusive right of the employer to make whatever assignments he pleased, in the absence of explicit and properly negotiated contractual limitations, by confirming that the Board has no business interfering with the actual allocation of work by employers.

The Board's position, particularly on the second issue, was further

---

85. Ibid., 662–3. See also *Lodge 68 of the IAM* (March 1949), 81 NLRB 1108.
86. 82 NLRB 916 (April 1949), at 922. The Marine Cooks, along with the Pacific Coast Firemen, Oilers, Water Tenders and Wipers Association and the International Longshoremen's and Warehousemen's Union claimed customary jurisdictions on vessels in the Pacific Coast coastal trade. The Board's field examiner reported that he had asked the representatives of the company involved in the dispute "whether or not they knew if the practice of the coast was to employ men from the three unions for the respective departments employing unlicensed personnel." He reported that the company's response was that "in their view it was immaterial under the statute as revised." In *RG* 25, Informal File 36-CD-2, *National Union of Marine Cooks and Stewards*.

clarified in *Los Angeles Building and Construction Trades Council* (May 1949). This case arose from a dispute between the trades council and a subcontractor over the assignment of work installing generators to members of a union not affiliated with the council – the International Association of Machinists – on a site covered by an exclusive agreement between the trades council and the primary contractor, Southern California Edison. The council demanded that the subcontractors, Westinghouse, replace the machinists with members of a millwrights' local which was a council affiliate. The council argued that the Board had neither the authority nor the competence to determine the dispute, and that in any event the work belonged to the millwrights because it fell within their jurisdiction as determined by the AFL's Building Trades Department in similar disputes. The Board, however, found that Westinghouse was not bound by the primary contractor's agreement or by union jurisdictional determinations, and was free to employ whomever it chose. The Board continued:

> We are not by this action to be regarded as 'assigning' the work in question to the Machinists. Because an affirmative award to either labor organization would be tantamount to allowing that organization to require Westinghouse to employ only its members and therefore to violate Section 8(a)3 of the Act, we believe we can make no such award. In reaching this conclusion we are aware that the employer in most cases will have resolved, by his own employment policy, the question as to which organization shall be awarded the work. Under the statute as now drawn, however, we can see no way in which we can, by Board reliance on such factors as tradition or custom in the industry, overrule his determination in a situation of this particular character.[87]

The employer was thus established in complete control of work assignments. As the Board stated several years later, "It is now well-settled that an employer has the right to make [work] assignments, free of strike pressure, unless the employer is failing to conform to an order or certification of the Board determining the bargaining representative for employees performing such work, or the claimant union has an immediate or derivative right under an existing contract upon which to predicate a lawful claim to the work in dispute."[88]

87. 83 NLRB 477 (May 1949), at 482.
88. *Local 173, Wood, Wire and Metal Lathers' International Union* (September 1958), 121 NLRB 1094, at 1108. See also *Teamsters' Local 175* (November 1953), 107 NLRB 223, and cases cited; *Local 16, International Longshoremen's and Warehousemen's Union* (June 1957), 118 NLRB 109; *United Brotherhood of Carpenters and Joiners* (November 1962), 139 NLRB 591.

The demarcation and jurisdiction dispute provisions of Taft-Hartley constituted affirmation that unions could not enjoy any authority in their relations with employers independent of statutory processes legitimating them as collective bargaining representatives. As the Board pointed out, however, the assertion was not new. "Apart from the restrictions contained in the provisions of the statute relating to employer unfair labor practices, neither the original act nor the amended act was intended to limit the employer's exercise of [the right to make work assignments]."[89] Ball had made the same point during the debates on the Senate bill:

> Every time the NLRB now handles a representation case, the Board must first decide what is an appropriate unit; and in deciding what is an appropriate unit, it assigns certain work tasks to the people within that unit. So that every time there is a representation case, the Board, in effect, now decides that kind of jurisdiction dispute. Of course, when it is a dispute between two unions as to who shall represent all the employees in a plant, we know that the Board determines those disputes.[90]

Unlike other elements of the Taft-Hartley Act, these provisions had attracted an important measure of bipartisan support. The program for labor law reform announced by Truman in his State of the Union Message in January 1947, for example, had envisaged the passage of legislation to outlaw strikes and secondary boycotts in furtherance of a jurisdiction dispute, and to give the Board oversight of demarcation disputes.[91] Wagner himself approved of legislative regulation of jurisdiction disputes, while the Senate committee minority report on S1126 welcomed the inclusion of Section 10(k), providing for compulsory arbitration of jurisdiction and demarcation disputes.[92] The Senate minority also supported legislation "to ban clearly unjustifiable forms of economic action by labor unions" such as strikes and boycotts in furtherance of jurisdiction disputes, although, like the House minority, it was critical of the majority for going too far. Two years later, when attempts were made to repeal the Taft-Hartley Act, even the legislation designed to fill the gap retained provisions giving the Board jurisdiction over demarcation disputes between unions and prohibiting strikes and secondary boycotts undertaken to undermine a Board certification.[93]

The existence of broad-based bipartisan support for measures of this

89. *Local 173*, 1109.   90. *Leg. Hist.*, LMRA, 1639.
91. Ibid., 356–58. See also Arthur F. McClure, *The Truman Administration and the Problems of Postwar Labor* (Rutherford, New Jersey, 1969), 242.
92. *Leg. Hist.* LMRA, 999, 480–1. See also 758, 1166.
93. Ibid., 481. *Senate Hearings III*, 1413–15.

kind is particularly significant in light of the concerted opposition to them within the ranks of the organized labor movement. Although the unions took exception to almost every facet of the Taft-Hartley Act, much of their attention was focussed on these particular sections of the new law. Thus, when the presidents of both the AFL and the CIO appeared before the House and Senate committees in opposition to the legislation, both singled out the provisions affecting jurisdiction disputes for particular attention. AFL President William Green told the Senate Committee that he deplored jurisdiction disputes, but that he was opposed to attempts to impose settlements on unions from outside the organized labor movement: "If our great movement took the position that it could do nothing . . . the situation would be different. But such is not the case. The whole influence of our 7,500,000 members is centered on finding a way to eliminate jurisdictional disputes." Philip Murray, president of the CIO, took the same position, arguing that the best thing the Senate Committee could do would be to leave the formulation of a solution in the hands of the organized labor movement. It should simply encourage "Willie Green" of the AFL to "sit down with Phil Murray of the CIO" and work out the whole program.[94]

Neither Green nor Murray, however, defended unions or workers who engaged in such disputes. Murray did not even attempt an explanation of why they came about.[95] Neither was able to offer any justification for their opposition to government intervention in jurisdiction disputes other than to say that it was unnecessary because the organized labor movement could better resolve such disputes within itself. Consequently, both were vulnerable to attack from Congressional critics who were able to point out that neither president had actually produced any real evidence to support this contention.[96]

Neither Green nor Murray could offer any defense of unions engaged in jurisdiction or demarcation disputes without challenging the New Deal model of representational unionism. This was something neither was willing to do. By 1939, as we have seen, virtually the entire trade union leadership, bar a tiny handful of AFL bureaucrats, had come to support fully the New Deal model. The sustained rapid growth in union membership and bargaining power which had continued during the succeeding years had confirmed the advantages of that model. While both presidents evinced a concern for the retention in unit adjudication and collective bargaining policy of that flexible recognition for estab-

---

94. *Senate Hearings II,* 985, 987, 1103.
95. Green's explanation was that the men really believed they were fighting for the jobs. Ibid., 985.
96. Ibid., 985.

lished institutional structures which had become associated with the phrase "custom and practice," neither could afford to haggle over the theory of union legitimacy on which the model was based. Consequently, each had to agree that union jurisdiction and the assignment of work was a matter of representation rather than vice versa, and that legitimacy could only be derived from certifiable majority status as a bargaining representative. Hence, they had also to agree that jurisdiction and demarcation disputes were an obstacle to the establishment of a union's legitimacy rather than a means of determining and defending it. Inevitably, this weakened the force of their argument against government intervention in such disputes.[97]

Coherent defenses of jurisdiction and demarcation disputes were, nevertheless, forthcoming. By far the most eloquent was that offered by the International Typographical Union. Unlike many other unions, the ITU still based its entire labor relations strategy upon the use of its economic strength to retain control of the work processes which comprised its jurisdiction. Taft-Hartley constituted an attempt to outlaw this strategy, according to the ITU, because it employed sanctions to prevent unions from ordering their members not to work with non-union men or on non-union products, from adopting and enforcing their own rules, and from protecting themselves by striking to preserve or extend their jurisdiction to cover related or competing processes or to dispute an employer's assignment of work. All of these aspects of Taft-Hartley undermined a union's ability to control the processes on which its members were employed, and hence threatened its survival.[98]

To the President of the ITU, J. Woodruff Randolph, the most disturbing aspect of these measures was their denial of the right to strike "whenever an object of a strike is to preserve the union."[99] The capacity to take action to preserve the union was of an importance "more fundamental even than the right to strike for better wages or hours,"[100] for, as he had put it the previous year, "the first and most

97. Ibid., 1263.
98. *Ball Committee Hearings*, 287–389. According to a pamphlet released by the union in 1949, "The Taft-Hartley Law was adopted for the purpose of depriving members of organized labor of many of their rights, and for the purpose of setting up a specified, limited number of rights which could not be enforced unless the unions accepted the status of slave labor organizations begging for their rights under the law and complying with stultifying requirements." Significantly, the union's argument continued "members of organized labor had always had those rights." But the proponents of the Taft-Hartley Act had "create[d] the legal fiction that since the Government granted rights to labor, labor was bound to accept the price exacted by the Government for those rights." See International Typographical Union, *The Taft-Hartley Act IS a Slave Labor Law* (February 1949).
99. *Senate Hearings III*, 1411.   100. Ibid.

important objective of any trade union is to stay alive."[101] Unions stayed alive, Randolph explained, by adjusting to changes in the work process which comprised their jurisdiction. "We have welcomed technological changes but we have insisted on their being a part of our trade. We have trained men to handle them . . . We are opposed to the destroying of the craft of the trade by splitting up that craft into numerous simple operations which may be done by a person partially trained in the craft."[102] The Taft-Hartley amendments hindered a union's ability to make such adjustments by their ban on jurisdiction and demarcation strikes and boycotts; and by thus placing the assignment of work more or less outside the realm of collective bargaining, they gave employers a means to undermine the union with impunity:

> A trade union which is prevented from using its economic strength to keep control over the job its members are trained to perform – or technical improvements of such jobs – will be destroyed by the employer giving that work to others whether union or non-union.
>
> The mistake of the Taft-Hartley law on this point is the assumption that all jurisdiction matters arise as between unions of already organized employees. Also that one group of organized employees is trying to force another group out of one union into another.
>
> The right of a trade union to contract only for all processes making its trade or craft is fundamental. Otherwise the union cannot live.[103]

The protests of ITU representatives were met with the advice that solutions would be forthcoming if only the union would conform itself to statutory processes. Thus, its critics advised the ITU that instead of pursuing the illegal strategy of attempting to maintain control of work processes, it should be seeking recognition as the representative of the men employed on those processes through a Board certification, as other unions did. As Gerard Reilly put it, "what Mr. Randolph stresses is the prohibition against a union striking because part of its jurisdiction is taken away. What he ignores . . . is that this prohibition does not apply when an employer violates a unit determination made by the Board . . . [A]ll that [the ITU] needs to do is to file petitions with the Labor Relations Board."[104] Reilly went on to point out that federal labor relations policy had in any case settled the whole question of the legality of jurisdictional strikes and secondary boycotts long before the passage of the Taft-Hartley amendments, "since the whole theory of [the Wagner Act] is to make the question of whether an employer

---

101. *Ball Committee Hearings*, 375.   102. Ibid., 378.
103. Ibid., 389. See also *Senate Hearings IV*, 2428–31.
104. *Ball Committee Hearings*, 578.

operates a union or a nonunion shop depend entirely upon the wishes of his own employees, not the wishes of the employees of another employer." Every objection that the ITU was raising to the Taft-Hartley Act, in other words, was actually an objection to the Wagner Act and to a model of labor relations long since accepted by the vast majority of unions comprising the organized labor movement in America.[105]

For the ITU, of course, it was no solution to be told that the only way to deal with its problems was to comply with the act and leave it up to the Board to determine its jurisdiction. Loss of control of its jurisdiction to the state was precisely what it was trying to avoid. Moreover, the union's reaction to Reilly's assertions that it was not the Taft-Hartley Act per se but the course of government policy in the long term which rendered its traditional policies illegal – that the methods which the union sought freedom to use were actually "repugnant to the spirit . . . of the Wagner Act"[106] – was not to abandon its criticism but rather to extend it until it encompassed the Wagner Act as well. Randolph gave full vent to these feelings in 1954 in his testimony during hearings of the Senate Committee on Labor and Public Welfare on proposals to amend the Taft-Hartley Act:

> Let me say that the only thing . . . that organized labor ever asked for to begin with was for the Government to remove the illegal interference of the big corporations with the American right to organize that we have always had in this country. The removal of the illegal restraints was all we ever asked for in the beginning. We did not get that even in the Wagner Act. We did not get the approach to the law that we asked for. All we asked for was a guarantee of our American rights. We got a law that said in Section 7 or 7(a), it is the right of workers to organize and bargain through representatives of their own choosing.
>
> It is a different approach. It supposedly grants somebody a right that they always had. All we asked for was an absolute effective prohibition and punishment of those big corporations that interfered with the already established right to organize in this country.
>
> I ask you to consider that fundamental in everything you do because you have now erected a mushroom of legal restraints, proposed rights alleged to be a magna carta of labor's rights, all of that is an invasion of an American right already existent . . .[107]

105. Ibid., 580–1.   106. Ibid., 576–7.
107. *Senate Hearings IV*, 3359. See also Freeman Champney, "Taft-Hartley and the Printers," *The Antioch Review*, 8 (1948–9): "They quite understandably look upon their traditional position as something they have won for themselves and are entitled to – not as something a New Deal government gave them and a Republican government can take away" (53).

By 1954, the ITU's was not the only voice calling for an end to state regulation. According to Taft, the building trades unions "would just as soon [have] never had" the Wagner Act.[108] Five years before, in 1949, John L. Lewis had also stated that the organized labor movement would have been better off if neither the Wagner nor the Taft-Hartley Acts had ever been passed. He repeated his opinion for the benefit of the Senate Committee in 1953.[109] By this time, however, the pluralist model was so widely established that few other labor spokesmen could be expected to share this position. Virtually all accepted the prevailing view that unions were now quasi-public "service organizations," the specific function of which was to supply administratively designated groups of workers with expert wage-bargaining services in a process studded with elaborate legislative checks conditioning the use of an ever-narrower range of economic sanctions.[110]

Nothing marks the entrenchment of the pluralist model better than a proposal brought to the House Committee on Education and Labor in 1954 by Congressman J. Edgar Chenoweth of Colorado. Chenoweth argued that Congress should exempt the few remaining "old-line craft unions" from the laws regulating union behavior in collective bargaining. These laws threatened the advantages that unions like the ITU had secured for their members, Chenoweth said, because the "old-line" unions had developed their bargaining and organizing strategies in the years before union behavior was regulated. "These few unions . . . should be permitted to continue the way of life they learned in America, and to retain the progress they have made, not without considerable hardship, sacrifice, and perseverance." It was only fair, after all, to allow them to enjoy the fruits of their labors.[111]

Chenoweth illustrated his argument with a telling analogy. These unions, he said, were like the major league baseball players, Burleigh Grimes and Red Faber. Grimes and Faber were two of that small fraternity of pitchers who had been allowed to continue throwing spitballs after organized baseball had outlawed the pitch from the modern game. "It was believed that practices indulged in by so-called spitball pitchers were improper and that organized baseball had progressed to a point where this type of pitching was no longer desirable," Chenoweth told his colleagues. But baseball had been wise. It had permitted those spit-

---

108. *Senate Hearings III*, 2574.   109. Ibid.; *Senate Hearings IV*, 1909.
110. See *Local 357, International Brotherhood of Teamsters v. NLRB* (1961), 365 US 667, at 675–6.
111. *Hearings Before the Committee on Education and Labor, House of Representatives, on H. Res. 115, Matters Relating to the Labor-Management Relations Act of 1947*, 83rd Congress, 1st Session (Washington, 1953), 165.

ball pitchers who were still active to continue to throw the pitch until the end of their careers.[112] In the same way, Chenoweth argued, Congress should exempt the old-line craft unions from regulatory legislation. They were, after all, the last of their kind.

Conclusion

On 7 April 1949, Melton Boyd, an attorney with the nineteenth region of the NLRB, arrived in Juneau, Alaska, to explain to members of Local 16 of the International Longshoremen's and Warehousemen's Union that the NLRB had ruled against their claim to the work assigned by the Juneau Spruce Corporation to members of the International Woodworkers of America. Boyd informed the ILWU members that, in light of the Board's decision, continued picketing of the corporation's mill in pursuit of the claim would render them liable to immediate unfair labor practice proceedings under 8(b)(4)(d) of the Taft-Hartley Act. He also told them that in such cases the Board's general counsel was empowered to apply for an injunction restraining unions from interfering with the employer's work assignment. The Federal District Court of Alaska ("which, incidentally," he commented parenthetically, "they derided") would undoubtedly grant his petition if it were filed because the Board's decision in the 10(k) proceeding had indicated that the union could have no hope of successfully defending itself against the complaint.

"To illustrate their position in terms that might appeal to their code of personal ethics and behavior," Boyd's report continued, "their situation was paraphrased as follows: they were in a game of three-handed poker. They had started the game. They held one hand, the IWA another, and the company a third. It was five card draw. The house—the Government in this case—was dealing. Four cards had been dealt to each player, face up. The company held four aces. Nothing else was showing and the chips were down. It would take more chips to see the fifth card. They had a right to call for it, if they wanted to do so and risk further loss. They could pull out of the game now if they chose to do so. We had come to Juneau to find out whether they wanted the Government to deal the fifth card."[113]

The metaphor which Boyd chose to convey his lesson is instructive. In

112. Ibid., 164.
113. Melton Boyd, regional attorney, to Thomas P. Graham, director of the nineteenth region of the NLRB (11 April 1949), in *RG 25*, Informal file 19-CD-4 and 5.

particular, the image of Local 16's members squandering large quantities of precious resources in a hopeless fight against a corporate employer assisted more and more vigorously by the federal government is an interesting comment on the state of American labor relations law in 1949. Just as interesting, however, is the response, also reported by Boyd, of the attorneys sent to Juneau by the ILWU's central office to safeguard the international union's position. Appreciating the dismay which Local 16's members felt at the erosion of their control over longshore work, the ILWU's lawyers nevertheless advised not only that it would be futile for the local's members further to pursue the fight against the company's work assignment, but that it would also prove highly dangerous to the international union. Members of Local 16 were therefore told that the International expected them to "accept the Board's determination as 'advice from the Government' and take it and 'lie down like good dogs.' "[114]

The images used by the protagonists on that day in Juneau, like those employed by Congressman Chenoweth five years later, convey much about the collective bargaining system that had grown up over the previous decade. First and most obviously, they convey the essentially limited role of union members in that system. By guaranteeing the union's security for as long as it was able to maintain stable collective bargaining relationships with employers, the Board's model encouraged the concentration of authority over the collective bargaining process in the hands of the international bureaucracy and limited the leverage of the local union member. The role of the members became reduced to the purely passive and often entirely formal signification of consent to be bound by the commitments made on their behalf by the union. Second, they also reinforce the impression, becoming increasingly clear during World War II but by no means absent before, that in the face of mounting sanctions unions really had little choice other than to conform themselves to the role assigned them in federal labor relations policy. Finally, they indicate that, even after having made that commitment, the degree of influence over the development of modern American industrial society which they could hope to gain in return was actually quite severely limited.

That unions and their members should "lie down like good dogs" or face the consequences from state agencies prepared to deal all the aces to their adversaries was the message which the Taft-Hartley Act sent the entire organized labor movement in 1947. In so doing, the act made

114. In Informal File 19-CD-4 and 5.

explicit the ambit of collective bargaining in the now firmly-established pluralist model of labor relations. Wages, hours, and working conditions were enthroned as legimate objects of industrial government. Activities which obstructed the further development, expansion and productivity of the corporate political economy, however, were to be avoided.

9

The state and the unions

Labor law doctrinal discourse ... is best understood as lies and errors.
Furthermore, the lies and errors have a bias in favor of the status quo.

Duncan Kennedy, "Critical Labor Law Theory: A Comment," *Industrial Relations Law Journal*, 4 (1981), 503.

By the mid-1950s, the organized labor movement was vastly larger than it had ever been in the years before the New Deal. Seventeen and a half million workers – one in every three persons in the non-farm labor force – were now enrolled in American unions. This was three million more than in 1947 and five times as many as had been members in 1934. Organized labor, it could not be doubted, had become a power in the land.[1]

For all their size, however, the unions' participation in the direction of the economy and the formulation of public policy was severely constrained. Identifying three levels of power in postwar America, the sociologist C. Wright Mills relegated organized labor to the second level where it jockeyed with medium-sized corporations and other organized interests in a competitive and pluralistic order situated between the mass of virtually powerless citizen-voters and the "power elite" of top corporate and state leaders who made the major decisions affecting national policy. "[L]abor," wrote Mills, "is without political, or for that matter economic, direction." The authority which the unions and their leaders appeared to wield was not "solidly bottomed." It did not have "the force of use and want and law." The unions' leaders were "government-made men, and they have feared – correctly, as it turns out – that they can be unmade by the government." As a result, Mills concluded, "Neither labor leaders nor labor unions are at the present juncture likely to be 'independent variables' in the national context."[2]

1. Leo Troy, *Trade Union Membership, 1897-1962* (New York, 1965), 1–2. See David Brody's acute analysis of the extent and limits of union power in post-war America in his *Workers in Industrial America: Essays on the Twentieth Century Struggle* (New York, 1980), 173–257.
2. C. Wright Mills, *The Power Elite* (New York, 1956), 263, 265.

One need not agree with Mills' analysis of the precise relationship between state and corporate power – his instrumental stress on the pivotal role of a power elite uniting state and economy – in order to share his opinion that, despite their considerable economic and political power, unions were "dependent variables." Even before the Taft-Hartley debates, it had become clear that such institutional legitimacy as unions could expect to enjoy in the post-war industrial relations system would be limited to activities which seemed to contribute to the well-being of the corporate political economy. A 1944 report of the Twentieth Century Fund's Committee on Labor early expressed this theme in criticizing unions for claiming that they were owed public protection under the Wagner Act while in the same breath denying the public's right to expect union practices, procedures and policies to serve the interests of all. To act in such a manner, the report stated, was to misunderstand "the reality of what unionism means today."[3] Unions should recognize that "*to serve themselves best they must serve the common prosperity most.*"[4] Their collective bargaining, in particular, should accept as a fundamental premise the necessity of "translat[ing] into action the economic philosophy that alone makes sense in an age of assembly lines and efficiency engineering," namely "high continuous production, high profits in return for genuinely venturesome capital, high wages at steady jobs, together with an unceasing stress upon ever-lowered unit cost." To produce "and produce and produce again," the report argued, was the only way to avoid "the decay of our capitalist system, and the decline of our political democracy."[5]

In fact, the legitimacy of collective activity putatively guaranteed by labor relations law had been conditional almost from the outset. During the debates of the 1930s, proponents of the Wagner Act had stressed, both before and after its passage, that collective bargaining was a means to an end, and that the end was industrial stability and labor peace. CIO general counsel·Lee Pressman was one of a few to offer an alternative justification, informing the Senate Committee on Education and Labor in 1939 that while he agreed that self-organization and the right of collective bargaining were indeed means to a desirable end, he also wished to suggest that the self-organization of workers was a desirable end in itself, "and should be protected as such."[6] But once the ascendancy of Leiserson and Millis on the NLRB was assured, conditional legitimacy became a foregone conclusion. By the end of the 1940s it was firmly established as the central pillar of the pluralist consensus

3. Twentieth Century Fund Labor Committee *Report* (November 1944), 33, in *Leiserson Papers*, Box 41 ("Twentieth Century Fund").
4. Ibid., 18.   5. Ibid., 18.   6. *Senate Hearings*, 4215.

which emerged during that decade and which set the terms of the postwar capital-labor-state relationship.

George W. Brooks of Cornell University described the substance of those terms to a meeting of the Industrial Relations Research Association in 1961, at the zenith of the postwar consensus:

> Industrial stability is a major public goal which has become urgent because of the international situation; it is the way we reconcile efficiency with democracy in labor-management relations. Responsible leadership on both the management and union side are essential, and leadership, in order to be responsible, must be relatively secure. Rival unionism is undesirable because it threatens this security, and also because it disturbs established relations and creates confusion in the plant. Labor and management work most effectively in the common interest when they hold similar ideologies. Communism must particularly be eliminated. Since anti-capitalistic views are unacceptable to management, their presence among union leaders is undesirable. While the right to strike should be preserved, the use of the strike should decline.[7]

Innovations in labor relations law during the 1950s and 1960s were instrumental in the construction and maintenance of these terms. The point of intersection between efficiency and democracy, for example, was precisely charted by the NLRB and by the Supreme Court in the two *Fibreboard Paper Products* cases of March 1961 and September 1962.[8] In the first case the Board affirmed that an employer who had decided unilaterally to contract out work previously done within a Board-certified unit was nevertheless innocent of an unfair labor practice because "basic management decisions, such as whether and to what extent to risk capital and managerial effort," were not within the ambit of the bargaining contemplated by the act. "The establishment by the Board of an appropriate bargaining unit does not preclude an employer acting in good faith from making changes in his business structure . . . without first consulting the representative of the affected employees."[9] The Board reopened examination of the issue eighteen months later and revised its decision to permit discussion of subcontracting. But it stressed that it did not contemplate a procedure which would in any way restrain an employer "from formulating or effectuating an economic decision to terminate a phase of his business operations."[10] Supreme Court justices Stewart, Douglas and Harlan subsequently sought

---

7. George W. Brooks, "The Relevance of Labor History to Industrial Relations," *Industrial Relations Research Association Publications,* 28, Proceedings of the Fourteenth Annual Meeting (Madison, Wisconsin, 1962), 211.
8. 130 NLRB 1558, and 138 NLRB 550. 9. 130 NLRB 1558, at 1560.
10. 138 NLRB 550, at 551.

to make certain that the Board's revised opinion would operate within narrow bounds. According to them the Board "most assuredly" did not mean "that every managerial decision which necessarily terminates an individual's employment is subject to the duty to bargain." In particular, the duty did not extend to decisions that lay "at the core of entrepreneurial control," decisions, that is, concerning "the commitment of investment capital and the basic scope of the enterprise."[11]

The intersection between efficiency and democracy to which Brooks referred in 1961 received further attention from the Board and the courts in the context of judicial and administrative innovations addressing the relationship between private grievance arbitration and the NLRB's unfair labor practice jurisdiction.[12] In its formative years the Board had been reluctant to make any jurisdictional concessions to dispute settlement procedures established by the parties (although this position was muddied somewhat following Leiserson's appointment). The rapid spread of no-strike grievance arbitration systems under the aegis of the War Labor Board softened this stance during and after World War II, however, and in a 1955 case, *Spielberg Manufacturing Company*, the Board moved to place the relationship between private and public dispute adjudication on a routine basis. It announced that where an unfair labor practice had already been the subject of arbitration it would henceforth defer to the results of the arbitration provided that "the proceedings appear to have been fair and regular, all parties had agreed to be bound, and the decision of the arbitration panel is not clearly repugnant to the purpose and policies of the act."[13] In 1962 the Board reaffirmed that position and advertised its firm intention to tailor its future activities to the results of agreements reached by the parties. "If complete effectuation of the Federal policy is to be achieved," it said, "we firmly believe that the Board, which is entrusted with the administration of one of the many facets of national labor policy, should give hospitable acceptance to the arbitral process as 'part and parcel of the collective bargaining process itself,' and voluntarily withhold its undoubted authority to adjudicate alleged unfair labor practice charges."[14] Only if the arbitration proceedings were clearly "tainted" or the award "repugnant" to the purposes and policies of the act would the Board take jurisdiction.

11. *Fibreboard Paper Products Corporation v. NLRB* (1964), 379 U.S. 203, at 218, 223.
12. For a full account see Katherine Stone, "The Post-War Paradigm in American Labor Law," *Yale Law Journal*, 90, 7 (1981), 1509–80.
13. 112 NLRB 1080 (June 1955), at 1082.
14. *International Harvester Company* (September 1962), 138 NLRB 923, at 927.

In thus delegating, in practical terms, a considerable portion of its unfair labor practice jurisdiction to private arbitration, the Board was following a lead given it by the Supreme Court. Acknowledging, in *Textile Workers' Union v. Lincoln Mills* (1957), that the Taft-Hartley Act disclosed a Congressional policy to prevent strikes by promoting no-strike agreements and by making federal courts available to resolve disputes instead, the Court nevertheless insisted that Congress had not intended the federal courts to become the primary forum for the resolution of labor contract disputes. Rather, Congress had wished to encourage the courts to develop a new body of substantive law promoting and enforcing grievance arbitration as the most appropriate mechanism for handling such disputes. "The agreement to arbitrate," the Court held, "is the *quid pro quo* for an agreement not to strike."[15] In the so-called *Steelworkers' Trilogy* three years later, the Court gave further "meaningful substance" to arbitration by holding that courts called upon to examine an arbitrator's decision should not review the substance of the hearing but confine themselves to the question whether the grievance was covered by the arbitration clause. The Court also held that doubts about the scope of the agreement to arbitrate should always be resolved in favor of coverage.[16]

Effectively, the Supreme Court's decisions placed grievance arbitration at the center of national labor relations policy. The consequences were two-fold. First, the NLRB confined its own statutory role in determining labor relations disputes to circumstances where arbitration was not available. By the end of the 1960s, the Board was declining to exercise jurisdiction not only in cases where arbitration had taken place, but also in cases where it was scheduled to take place and even in cases where no proceedings were scheduled but the issue was susceptible to arbitration. In other words, "the Board would withhold its processes and would dismiss unfair labor practice complaints for all disputes subject to an arbitration provision in a collective bargaining agreement. Whether the arbitration would actually occur, or whether it would cover the same issues and apply the same substantive rules as would NLRB review, were concerns that were disregarded."[17] Inevitably, this severely limited workers' access to the NLRB for enforcement of statutory rights. Second, workers found that their freedom to engage in

15. 353 U.S. 448, at 445.
16. See *United Steelworkers v. American Manufacturing Company* (1960), 363 U.S. 564; *United Steelworkers v. Warrior and Gulf Navigation Company* (1960), 363 U.S. 574; *United Steelworkers v. Enterprise Wheel and Car Corporation* (1960), 363 U.S. 593.
17. Stone, "The Post-War Paradigm in American Labor Law," 1533–4.

alternative forms of private dispute resolution outside the arbitration procedure was also severely curtailed, leaving them wholly reliant on the mechanisms created by the employer and the bargaining representative. This became clear in 1962 when the Supreme Court confirmed that the quid pro quo doctrine cut both ways – that an employer's agreement to arbitrate committed the union to an "implied" no-strike clause, whether or not it had actually agreed to one. Indeed, by 1969 the court was ready to allow lower courts to enjoin any strike over any employee grievance susceptible to arbitration.[18]

The institutionalization of grievance arbitration in the post-war period provided the essential institutional framework for an industrial relations "system" based on the bureaucratization and routinization of dispute management. By simultaneously rendering all other forms of collective action suspect, it also expressed perfectly the synchronicity of legitimation and confinement of collective activity inherent in the terms of the labor-capital relationship established by the all-encompassing post-war pluralist consensus. But grievance arbitration was by no means the only element in this process. Just as important were the steps taken during the 1950s to extend the Board's contract-bar doctrine. These were crucial to the entrenchment of "responsible" union leadership, to the discouragement of destabilizing rivalry, and to the elimination of ideologies "unacceptable" to management, all developments of considerable significance particularly at a time when what corporate managements in virtually all industrial sectors most wanted was to be able to engage in development planning and capital investment with their labor costs rendered stable and predictable through routinized contract negotiations and accommodating relationships with long-term incumbents.[19]

As we have seen, contract-bar expressed the NLRB's policy of guaranteeing the stability of bargaining relationships between employers and incumbent unions by refusing to entertain representation petitions from other organizations or from disaffected groups within the bargaining unit during the life of the incumbent's contract, or "reasonable proportion" thereof. By 1947, the Board had already established that a two year bar was presumptively reasonable, and in subsequent years it went much further, holding that where longer-term contracts were customary, "stability of labor relations" would be served, without unreasonably

18. *Boys Markets, Inc. v. Retail Clerks Local 770* (1970), 398 U.S. 235, at 251. See also, generally, Karl Klare, "Critical Theory and Labor Relations Law," in David Kairys, editor, *The Politics of Law: A Progressive Critique* (New York, 1982), 65–88.
19. Nelson Lichtenstein, *Labor's War at Home: The CIO in World War Two* (Cambridge, England, 1982), 241.

restricting the right of employees to change representatives, by holding that contracts "even for five years duration" could bar challenges for their entire term.[20] The considerable benefits which both employers and bargaining representatives could enjoy as a result of the doctrine were evident in cases such as *Hudson Transit Lines* (October 1949) and *William D. Gibson Company* (October 1954) where the Board protected the incumbent from displacement in favor of another by allowing a contract renewed in the face of a hostile majority within the unit to bar a representation proceeding.[21] "Where, as here, a labor organization has been representing an employer's employees," the Board stated in *Gibson*, "stability in industrial relations, *the primary objective of the Act,* requires that continuity in collective bargaining agreements be encouraged, even though a rival union is seeking to displace an incumbent." The contract having been renewed prior to the formal submission of a representation claim, the rival union's petition was not timely. "We conclude, therefore, that in the interest of industrial stability, which uninterrupted collective bargaining achieves, an employer should be permitted to continue recognition of an active, incumbent labor organization and to contract with it until such time as the union is displaced as the bargaining representative of the employer's employees in an appropriate Board proceeding . . ."[22]

Such guarantees, however, were not extended to ideologically unacceptable incumbents. Thus, in the years after the anti-communist purge within the CIO in 1948–9, which culminated in the expulsion of its eleven communist-influenced affiliates, the Board successfully manipulated its contract-bar rules to the disadvantage of the communist unions by developing a "schism" doctrine which effectively encouraged the raiding of Communist-led incumbents by AFL and CIO unions.[23] First

20. *General Motors Corporation, Detroit Transmission Division* (February 1953), 102 NLRB 1140; *Allis-Chalmers Manufacturing Company* (February 1953), 102 NLRB 1135.
21. *Hudson Transit Lines,* 86 NLRB 709; *William D. Gibson Company,* 110 NLRB 660.
22. 110 NLRB 660, at 662–3 [emphasis supplied]. Board member Rodgers, in dissent, argued that the majority's ruling "gives to every employer a complete and legal formula for destroying any organizing activity, by any outside union, for overriding the rights of the individual employee, for subverting any efforts at craft severance, and for perpetuating at his pleasure any union of his favor or choosing." Further, the Board was "serving notice that incumbency may be synonymous with perpetuity. Under such circumstances industrial stability, alone, would dominate the resolution of all representation problems before the Board." 664, 665.
23. See, for example, *Boston Machine Works Company* (March 1950), 89 NLRB 59, *The Bassick Company* (May 1950), 89 NLRB 1143, and *The Magnavox Company* (January 1955), 111 NLRB 379, and compare *Pacific Gamble-Robinson Company* (April 1950), 89 NLRB 293, and *The Budd Company* (November 1953), 107 NLRB 116.

articulated in *Boston Machine Works* in March 1950, a fully-developed statement of the schism doctrine appeared four years later in *A.C. Lawrence Leather Company* (April 1953), where the Board stated that "expulsion of a labor union by its parent organization, coupled with disaffiliation action at the local level for reasons related to the expulsion, disrupts *any* established bargaining relationship between an employer and that union and creates such confusion that the existing contract with such union no longer stabilizes industrial relations between the employer and its employees."[24] This initiative was warmly endorsed by the recently united AFL-CIO in 1958. The Federation applauded Board decisions which gave employees the chance to replace any union which it had expelled with "an honestly-led American union" and declared its complete support for "the policy considerations which unquestionably underlay [the Board's] decisions."[25]

Outside the anti-communist realm of the schism doctrine, unions were unanimous in seeking ever-tighter guarantees of incumbency. AFL-CIO general counsel J. Albert Woll, for example, used the occasion of a Board review of its contract-bar rules to petition the Board to treat all contracts as comprehensively barring employee activity on behalf of rivals for at least the first three years of their duration; this committed the Federation even more firmly to the "stability" pole of the "stability versus self-organization" dichotomy which had shaped pluralist debates over collective bargaining policy for the previous two decades.[26] So, too, did Arthur J. Goldberg, at the time general counsel of the United Steelworkers of America, in a companion brief submitted on behalf of that

24. 108 NLRB 546 (April 1953), at 549 [emphasis supplied]. The United Electrical Workers, one of the major victims of the schism doctrine, commented in 1958: We think that the entire doctrine of schism is a dangerous one. In the first place, it is impossible to administer without probing into internal affairs of unions, an objective which the Board has always disclaimed. Under what circumstances is a disaffiliation valid? How many members must remain in the Union? And how many individuals or what fraction of the union must give evidence that it seeks to replace the bargaining agent with a new one? The Board piously claims that a successful raid is not a schism. But when is a raid not a raid? How can the Board really determine whether the move to disaffiliate was instigated by external changes and when it is spontaneous? How is the Board to determine whether it is the result of the bribery of leaders of the incumbent union, by a rival union, or a genuine repudiation of the agency by the rank and file? How is the Board to determine whether the so-called schism is not merely a way of destroying or undermining a union for the purpose of obtaining an election which would not otherwise be available to a rival?
See *Consolidated Brief for United Electrical, Radio and Machine Workers of America (UE)* in RG 25, Informal File 6-RC-2062, *De Luxe Metal Furniture Company.*
25. *Memorandum on Behalf of the American Federation of Labor and Congress of Industrial Organizations*, in Informal File 6-RC-2062.
26. Ibid.

organization. Indeed, Goldberg went even further by suggesting that the Board's bar rules should not only underline the commitment of federal policy to the stability objective, but should also express a recognition on the part of the state that realistically unions were the only available mechanism for fulfilling that objective:

> From the start, it has been recognized that employees normally cannot, as a practical matter, effectuate the self-organizational rights granted them by the Act except through the framework of established unions. In selecting a bargaining representative in the first instance or in seeking to change bargaining representatives, workers normally are dependent on the aid and assistance of unions. For this reason, among others, unions as such are given protected status and certification and other rights under the Act, in addition to protection and rights accorded employees. Prominent among these union rights is the right of the union to be secure through negotiation of union security and checkoff arrangements and to have understandings reached with employers reduced to writing. Prominent among union responsibilities imposed by the Act is the obligation to adhere to the terms of contracts, including no-strike clauses, despite any contrary employee desires.
>
> When a union agrees to a contract for a period of years and the customary no-strike clause, the union waives one of the major protections – the right to engage in concerted activities – granted by the Act. In doing this, of course, the union implements the stability objective of the Act. The fact remains, however, that the union places itself at the mercy of rival unions if it must submit to an election during the contract term while it is powerless to resort to concerted activities to improve contract terms. Surely a union ought not to be penalized for waiving an important statutory right when the effect of such waiver is to encourage stable labor–management relations. It seems to us that such a practical penalty can only thwart stability by discouraging the consummation of contracts for durations consistent with the needs of changing industrial practice.
>
> We submit, therefore, that the doctrine of contract bar may be solidly grounded not only on the stability objective of the Act, but also on the important role of unions and the stress on union security under the Act. The waiver of a major statutory right involved in a fixed term contract of reasonable length is an added reason for according unions the protection of contracts for such terms. . . . We believe that these additional policy considerations, which complement the policy of stability, furnish added scope for striking the balance in favor of extending the scope of the contract bar doctrine.[27]

27. *Statement on Behalf of the United Steelworkers of America as Amicus Curiae*, in Informal File 6-RC-2062.

Goldberg's brief thus petitioned the Board to acknowledge explicitly that unions were the primary instruments of the state's interest in industrial stability, and that they should be granted security through the contract-bar doctrine commensurate with their fulfillment of that interest. "It is our view that when a union bargains on behalf of employees and, consistent with the stability objective, agrees to a contract for a reasonable fixed term and thereby foregoes its right for such term to engage in concerted activities for a new contract, the union is entitled to be secure in its bargaining status and the protections of the contract for its term."[28] As such, Goldberg's brief signalled just how complete the pluralist consensus had become. Historically, as we have seen, it was hardly unusual for unions to seek to restrict the collective activity of workers in order to achieve their own institutional interest in security. The state, furthermore, had shown an increasing tendency to impose restrictions on that collective activity in pursuit of *its* interests; specifically, its interst in industrial stability. The Steelworkers' brief now called upon the NLRB to marry the two concepts in law – to make a union's ability to demonstrate a capacity to restrain the collective activity of those whom it represented the criterion of its eligibility for the state's award of institutional security. Such a formulation expressed to perfection the deepest implications of the "conditional legitimacy" which comprised industrial pluralism's approach to collective activity. It also underlined the extent of the transformation in the relationship between the state and the unions which had taken place over the previous half-century. Unions in 1958 sought security where, after the turn of the century, they had seen only threats. The corollary, unfortunately, was that they were now required to address their ultimatums to their own members, and thus, ultimately, to themselves.

A counterfeit liberty

The influence of the pluralist consensus on American labor relations practice remains immense. During the 1970s, however, the accelerating decay of the consensus's material basis – the income security which was gained in exchange for guarantees of managerial authority – and the convincing evidence that this decay was merely one symptom of a more profound alteration of the terms of the labor-capital-state relationship which had prevailed for the previous forty-odd years, provoked many both within and outside the labor movement to begin to question the

28. Ibid.

real nature of that "astonishing degree of unanimity in our judgment of industrial relations" which George Brooks described in 1961.[29]

The position of the organized labor movement in this debate has so far been contradictory. On the one hand, unions have devoted considerable energy to attempts to win legislative and administrative reinforcement of the institutions which structure and maintain the pluralist consensus.[30] On the other, some prominent leaders have responded to rising corporate opposition to those efforts – itself a clear signal that the consensus is no more – by declaring their intent to "reforge the links with those who believe in struggle."[31] Whether this means the unions have now begun to appreciate that continued participation in institutions predicated on the confinement of workers' self-activity promises nothing so much as their own continued decline, or whether, more likely, it is simply an attempt to broaden the coalition behind their attempts to reconstitute those institutions – these are questions which cannot yet be answered with any degree of assurance. Indeed no answers will be forthcoming until and unless the unions at least acknowledge as a possibility that in building their future on industrial pluralism they have built their future on sand. This they are understandably reluctant to do.

Present circumstances nevertheless indicate that the organized labor movement would be well advised to examine closely its relationship with the state. What can this history of labor relations law contribute to such an exercise? "The principal difference between the working people and the courts," Samuel Gompers told members of both houses of Congress in 1914, "lies in the marked tendency of the courts to guarantee to the workman an academic and theoretic liberty which he does not want by denying him industrial rights to which he is ethically entitled."[32] Or in other words, what the state offered workers and their organizations was ultimately no more than the opportunity to participate in the construction of their own subordination. Whether Gompers would have agreed with Duncan Kennedy's recent terse restatement of this argument, quoted in the headnote to this chapter, is problematic. Probably, despite the rising incidence of government-led and court-sanctioned union bust-

---

29. On the impending dissolution and reconstitution of that relationship see David M. Gordon et al., *Segmented Work, Divided Workers: The Historical Transformation of Labor in the United States* (New York, 1982), 215–27.

30. See Brody, *Workers in Industrial America*, 245–55.

31. UAW president Douglas Fraser, quoted in Brody, *Workers in Industrial America*, 248.

32. Gompers was quoting from George W. Alger's *Moral Overstrain* (New York, 1906). See Samuel Gompers, "A Brief and Appeal to the Members of the United States Senate and the House of Representatives," (Washington, D.C., 1914).

ing, he would have thought it impolitic. But there is no gainsaying a conclusion that both Gompers and Kennedy could agree on, and which those labor leaders currently considering strategies to improve the present parlous state of their organizations might also wish to consider: a counterfeit liberty is the most that American workers and their organizations have been able to gain through the state. Its reality they must create for themselves.

Bibliographical essay

The organized labor movement

Manuscript sources

Study of the AFL during its first fifty years has become considerably easier than once it was thanks to the appearance of the magnificent microfilm edition of *The American Federation of Labor Records: The Samuel Gompers Era* (Microfilming Corporation of America, 1979). Among the records here reproduced are correspondence of the president's office, executive council vote books, speech files, an extremely useful circular and neostyle file, and voluminous miscellaneous materials gathered in "reference material" and "scrapbooks" files. Although most of the recorded material focusses on Gompers' presidency the circular and neostyle file also contains important materials from the later 1920s and 1930s. Major manuscript sources for the 1930s were *The William Green Papers,* held at the Ohio State Historical Society and also on microfilm at the AFL-CIO Library in Washington; *The John P. Frey Papers* at the Library of Congress; and, most important of all, the minute books of the AFL Executive Council held by the secretary-treasurer's office, AFL-CIO. The AFL-CIO library also holds the CIO Executive Board minutes on microfilm, but these proved to be fairly marginal to this study.

Secondary materials

Despite the large volume of secondary literature on the history of the organized labor movement published in recent years there are relatively few works which have yet attempted to offer the sort of synthesis of social, political and economic history by which a project like this can be guided. However, David Montgomery, *Workers' Control in America: Studies in the History of Work, Technology and Labor Struggles* (Cambridge, England, 1979) and David Brody, *Workers in Industrial America: Essays on the Twentieth Century Struggle* (New York, 1980) have

329

both offered persuasive though as yet somewhat skeletal sketches of what such a synthesis might look like. Unfortunately both are weakest on the developments of the 1930s. I have also been influenced by Richard C. Edwards, *Contested Terrain: The Transformation of the Workplace in the Twentieth Century* (New York, 1979) and particularly by David M. Gordon, Richard C. Edwards and Michael Reich, *Segmented Work, Divided Workers: The Historical Transformation of Labor in the United States* (New York, 1982).

Other than these I have profited most from the work of historians concentrating on particular periods and subjects. Thus, on the artisan trades and the emergence of a working class in the first half of the nineteenth century see Sean Wilentz's important essays "Artisan Origins of the American Working Class," *International Labor and Working Class History*, 19 (Spring 1981), 1–22, and "Artisan Republican Festivals and the Rise of Class Conflict in New York City, 1788–1837," in Michael H. Frisch and Daniel J. Walkowitz, editors, *Working Class America: Essays on Labor, Community and American Society* (Urbana, Illinois, 1983), 37–77; Howard Rock, *Artisans of the New Republic: The Tradesmen of New York City in the Age of Jefferson* (New York, 1979); Bruce Laurie, *Working People of Philadelphia, 1800–1850* (Philadelphia, 1980); and of course Alan Dawley, *Class and Community: The Industrial Revolution in Lynn* (Cambridge, 1976). On the development of labor organization after the Civil War and the origins of the AFL, see David Montgomery, *Beyond Equality: Labor and the Radical Republicans, 1862–1872* (New York, 1967); Lloyd Ulman, *The Rise of the National Trade Union: The Development and Significance of its Structure, Governing Institutions and Economic Policies* (Cambridge, 1955); and Robert Christie's unsurpassed *Empire in Wood: A History of the Carpenters' Union* (Ithaca, 1956). For insightful analyses of labor ideology at the time of the founding of the AFL see William Dick, *Labor and Socialism in America: The Gompers Era* (Port Washington, New York, 1972); Stuart B. Kaufman, *Samuel Gompers and the Origins of the American Federation of Labor, 1848–1896* (Westport, Connecticut, 1973); and the important article by Linda Schneider, "The Citizen Striker: Workers' Ideology in the Homestead Strike of 1892," *Labor History*, 23, 1 (Winter 1982), 47–66. Several non-American works have also influenced my perceptions of labor ideology. Of these the most important are Bryan Palmer, *A Culture in Conflict: Skilled Workers and Industrial Capitalism in Hamilton, Ontario, 1860–1914* (Montreal, 1979); Tim Rowse, *Australian Liberalism and National Character* (Melbourne, 1978); and William Sewell's magnificent *Work and Revolution in France: The Language of Labor from the Old Regime to 1848* (New York, 1980).

For the twentieth century I have relied predominantly on the manuscript sources listed above and elsewhere in this essay. Nevertheless, here too I have found a number of specialist works particularly useful. Thus, on early twentieth century labor relations see Bruno Ramirez, *When Workers Fight: The Politics of Industrial Relations in the Progressive Era* (Westport, Connecticut, 1978). On World War One and its consequences for the AFL see the important essays by Haggai Hurvitz, "Ideology and Industrial Conflict: President Wilson's First Industrial Conference of October 1919," *Labor History*, 18, 4 (Fall 1977), 509–24; Gary Dean Best, "President Wilson's Second Industrial Conference, 1919–1920," *Labor History*, 16, 4 (Fall 1975), 505–20; and Robert H. Zieger, "Herbert Hoover, the Wage-Earner, and the 'New Economic System,' 1919–1929," *Business History Review*, 51, 2 (Summer 1977), 161–89. Steve Fraser's fine essay "Dress Rehearsal for the New Deal: Shop-Floor Insurgents, Political Elites and Industrial Democracy in the Amalgamated Clothing Workers," in Frisch and Walkowitz, *Working Class America*, 212–55, is an excellent and perceptive analysis of developments in a key union during the 1920s. For the 1930s, Irving Bernstein's *Turbulent Years: A History of the American Worker* (Boston, 1971) remains the most complete account of the crisis in the AFL and the emergence of the CIO. However, Nelson Lichtenstein, *Labor's War at Home: The CIO in World War Two* (Cambridge, England, 1982) is superior in its analysis of the internal dynamics of that organization. In "AFL Unions in the 1930s: Their Performance in Historical Perspective," *Journal of American History*, 65, 4 (March 1979), 1021–42, I have tried to view some of the events of the New Deal decade, particularly the competition between the AFL and the CIO, from a perspective of the organized labor movement's long-term development.

Labor law, unfortunately, has attracted relatively little attention from historians. The essential work on the colonial and revolutionary era is, of course, Richard B. Morris, *Government and Labor in Early America* (New York, 1946), but no equivalent exists for later epochs. So far as the law of collective labor organization during the nineteenth century is concerned, therefore, one must rely on scattered monographs and articles. Marjorie Turner, *The Early American Labor Conspiracy Cases: Their Place in Labor Law: A Reinterpretation* (San Diego State College, 1967) is exceptionally useful both analytically and as a bibliographic guide. It deserves much wider circulation. See also the classic articles by Edwin E. Witte, "Early American Labor Cases," *Yale Law Journal*, 35

(1925–6), 825–37; Walter Nelles, "Commonwealth versus Hunt," *Columbia Law Journal*, 32 (1932), 1128–69, and "The First American Labor Case," *Yale Law Journal*, 41 (1931–2), 165–200; Francis B. Sayre, "Labor and the Courts," *Yale Law Journal*, 39 (1929–30), 682–705, and "Criminal Conspiracy," *Harvard Law Review*, 35 (1922), 393–427; Arthur Lenhoff, "A Century of American Unionism," *Boston Law Review*, 22 (1942), 357–74. Leonard W. Levy, *The Law of the Commonwealth and Chief Justice Shaw* (New York, 1967), also provides an important description and analysis of the case of *Commonwealth versus Hunt*. On developments in the early twentieth century see Barry F. Helfand's very useful piece "Labor and the Courts: The Common-Law Doctrine of Criminal Conspiracy and its Application in the Buck's Stove Case," *Labor History*, 18, 1 (Winter 1977), 91–114. The position improves when we come to historical analysis of the statute law of the 1930s and 1940s (see below), but historians pay almost no attention to the common law context within which collective bargaining developments occurred. For a basic guide see Charles O. Gregory and Harold A. Katz, *Labor and the Law* (third edition; New York, 1979), but see also the important articles by C. Lawrence Christenson "Legally Enforceable Interests in American Labor Union Working Agreements," *Indiana Law Journal*, 9 (1933), 69–108, and Ralph Fuchs, "Collective Labor Agreements in American Law," *St. Louis Law Review*, 10 (1925), 1–33.

Labor relations policy

Manuscript sources

Manuscript sources for the study of labor relations policy are voluminous. They fall into several categories: the papers of key participants in the policy-making process; the administrative records of government agencies; legislative hearings and published legislative histories; court and agency decisions and reports; and informal and formal case records.

In the first category we find collections such as *The Papers of William M. Leiserson*, held at the State Historical Society of Wisconsin, Madison. This collection represents a lifetime's activity in the field of labor relations as academic theorist, arbitrator, policy-maker, and administrator. Leiserson's correspondence is considerable and detailed, his involvements far-reaching, his contacts legion. Among the many treasures here are numerous documents relating to the legislative history of the Wagner and Taft-Hartley Acts, to the National Labor Relations Board, and to Leiserson's role in the Twentieth Century Fund Labor Committee. Not as rich as Leiserson's but just as important are the papers of the two major political figures in labor relations policy formation: Robert F. Wagner, held at Georgetown University, Washington, D.C., and Robert A. Taft, held at the Library of Congress. Both collections provide detailed insight into the political and legislative history of labor policy formulation.

Papers particular to J. Warren Madden, Edwin S. Smith, Charles Fahy, Nathan Witt, and other key NLRB personnel can all be found among the administrative records of the NLRB in the National Archives. These records are rich in sources for study of the internal politics and organization of the Board. Here too are the administrative records of the National Labor Board and the first National Labor Relations Board, among which are papers particular to some of *their* key personnel, such as Harry A. Millis. Also among the first NLRB's records are many materials relevant to the legislative history of the Wagner Act, particularly the very important Legal Division correspondence, while the second NLRB's records include the materials generated by the Special House (Smith) Committee which investigated the NLRB in 1940. So far as information on the later administrative history of the NLRB and the legislative history of the Taft-Hartley Act are concerned, see *The Papers of Paul M. Herzog, The Papers of Clark M. Clifford,* and *The Papers of Harry S. Truman* all in the Truman Presidential Library, Independence, Missouri.

Of considerable use in developing an understanding of the labor relations policy-making process are the published legislative histories of the National Labor Relations Act, 2 vols. (Washington, 1949) and of the Labor-Management Relations Act, 2 vols. (Washington, 1948). The former contains drafts of the legislation, transcripts of committee hearings, relevant House and Senate committee reports and details of floor debate for both the unsuccessful labor disputes bill of 1934 and the Wagner bill of 1935. The latter confines itself to drafts, reports and floor debate. As important are the numerous congressional hearings and reports on proposals to amend the legislation: *Hearings before the Committee on Education and Labor, U.S. Senate, National Labor Relations Act and proposed Amendments,* 76th Congress, 1st, 2nd and 3rd Sessions, 21 vols. (Washington, 1939–40); *Hearings before the Committee on Labor, House of Representatives, Proposed Amendments to the National Labor Relations Act,* 76th Congress, 1st, 2nd and 3rd Sessions, 9 v. (Washington, 1939–40); *Hearings before the Committee on Labor and Public Welfare, U.S. Senate, on S. 55 and S.J. Res. 22, Having the Object of Reducing Industrial Strife in the United States,*

70th Congress, 1st Session, 4 vols. (Washington, 1947); *Hearings be-fore the Committee on Education and Labor, House of Representatives, on Bills to Amend and Repeal the National Labor Relations Act,* 80th Congress, 1st Session, 6 vols. (Washington, 1947); *Hearings before the Committee on Labor and Public Welfare, U.S. Senate, on S. 249, A Bill to Diminish the Causes of Labor Disputes,* 81st Congress, 1st Session, 6 vols. (Washington, 1949), and that committee's *Report on S. 249,* Sen-ate Report 99, 81st Congress, 1st Session (Washington, 1949); *Hear-ings before a Special Subcommittee of the Committee on Education and Labor, House of Representatives, 81st Congress, 1st Session, on H.R. 2032, A Bill to Repeal the Labor-Management Relations Act of 1947,* 81st Congress, 1st Session, 11 vols. (Washington, 1949), and the full committee's *Report to Accompany H.R. 2032,* House Report 317, 81st Congress, 1st Session (Washington, 1949); *Hearings before the Com-mittee on Labor and Public Welfare, U.S. Senate, Proposed Revisions of the Labor-Management Relations Act of 1947,* 83rd Congress, 2nd Session (Washington, 1954); *Hearings before the Committee on Educa-tion and Labor, House of Representatives, on H. Res. 115, Matters Relating to the Labor-Management Relations Act of 1947,* 83rd Con-gress, 1st Session, 11 vols. (Washington, 1953); and of course the two major investigative hearings: *Hearings before the Special Committee to Investigate the National Labor Relations Board,* House of Representa-tives, 76th Congress, 2nd and 3rd Sessions, 30 vols. (Washington, 1940), and *Hearings before the Joint Committee on Labor-Manage-ment Relations on the Operation of the Labor-Management Relations Act of 1947,* 80th Congress, 2nd Session, 2 vols. (Washington, 1948).

The richest sources of information on the ideology and day-to-day development of labor relations law are the cases heard by the Board, and the circuit court and Supreme Court cases arising from appeals against Board decisions. The relevant Board cases are reported in the first 130 volumes of printed National Labor Relations Board *Decisions and Orders,* spanning the years 1935–1960. The relevant higher court decisions are gathered together in *Court Decisions Relating to the Na-tional Labor Relations Act,* a multivolume work published by the Na-tional Labor Relations Board from 1944 on. The NLRB's own *Annual Reports* (Washington, 1936–61) are a useful guide to points of legal and administrative policy arising from year to year.

More important than the printed case reports, however, are the for-mal and informal case files. These, particularly the informal files, con-tain the complete administrative record of a case and all documents relevant to its development. Well-organized files will contain chronolo-gies, correspondence, field reports, inter-office memoranda and recommendations, a copy of the decision, and details of the action taken. Where a case goes to a higher court on appeal its files will also contain discussions of legal strategy, legal correspondence, pleadings and occasionally court transcripts. These invaluable records can be found at the National Archives and Records Service Depository, Suitland, MD. A complete set of case records is available for cases heard prior to 1947. Thereafter, unfortunately, only a small sample, selected using qualitative criteria, has been saved.

Secondary Sources

James A. Gross's two volumes on the National Labor Relations Board, *The Making of the National Labor Relations Board: A Study in Economics, Politics and the Law* (Albany, New York, 1974), and *The Reshaping of the National Labor Relations Board: National Labor Policy in Transition* (Albany, New York, 1981) are an invaluable account of the legislative and administrative history of the Wagner Act and the NLRB. The former replaces Irving Bernstein's classic, *The New Deal Collective Bargaining Policy* (Berkeley, 1950), as the standard account of the Wagner Act's formulation. Peter Irons, *The New Deal Lawyers* (Princeton, 1982), also contains valuable material on the legislative history of the Wagner Act and complements Gross by paying much closer attention to the strategies developed by the Board's lawyers to secure the act's constitutionality. Irons is also more successful than Gross in placing the NLRB in the context of New Deal innovations in administrative law and government. Philip Ross, *The Government as a Source of Union Power: The Role of Public Policy in Collective Bargaining* (Providence, Rhode Island, 1965), is an important study of the evolution of federal policy, while Harry A. Millis and Emily Clark Brown, *From the Wagner Act to Taft-Hartley: A Study of National Labor Policy and Labor Relations* (Chicago, 1950), remains the most detailed account available of the similarities and differences of NLRB policy under the two statutes.

Material essential to an understanding of the general ideological provenance of the labor relations innovations of the 1930s can be found in Paul J. McNulty, *The Origins and Development of Labor Economics: A Chapter in the History of Social Thought* (Cambridge, 1980). See also Joseph Dorfman et al., *Institutional Economics: Veblen, Commons and Mitchell Reconsidered* (Berkeley, 1964), and Commons' own *Legal Foundations of Capitalism* (New York, 1924). On Wagner's political role see J. Joseph Huthmacher, *Senator Robert F. Wagner and the Rise of Urban Liberalism* (New York, 1968). Also useful is Cletus E. Daniel,

The ACLU and the Wagner Act: An Enquiry into the Depression-Era Crisis of American Liberalism (Ithaca, New York, 1980). On business's labor relations policies and policy preferences in the 1930s and 1940s see the fine study by Howell J. Harris, *The Right to Manage: Industrial Relations Policies of American Business in the 1940s* (Madison, Wisconsin, 1982). Like Harris, Richard N. Chapman, *Contours of Public Policy, 1939–1945* (New York, 1981), helps us approach the Taft-Hartley Act from the perspective of wartime developments in domestic policy. On Taft himself see James T. Patterson, *Mr. Republican: A Biography of Robert A. Taft* (Boston, 1972). On the Truman administration and the Taft-Hartley Act see R. Alton Lee, *Truman and Taft-Hartley: A Question of Mandate* (Lexington, Kentucky, 1966); Susan M. Hartmann, *Truman and the Eightieth Congress* (Columbia, Missouri, 1971); and Arthur F. McClure, *The Truman Administration and the Problems of Post-War Labor* (Rutherford, New Jersey, 1969).

A number of recent studies by legal scholars have had a major impact on perceptions of post–New Deal labor relations law. No labor historian can afford to ignore this work. The first of these studies was Karl E. Klare's "Judicial Deradicalization of the Wagner Act and the Origins of Modern Legal Consciousness," *Minnesota Law Review*, 62 (1978), 265–339. Subsequently there have appeared the following: Katherine Van Wezel Stone, "The Post-War Paradigm in American Labor Law," *Yale Law Journal*, 90 (1980–1), 1509–80; Karl E. Klare, "Labor Law as Ideology: Toward a New Historiography of Collective Bargaining Law," *Industrial Relations Law Journal*, 4 (1981), 450–82; Karl E. Klare, "Critical Theory and Labor Relations Law," in David Kairys, editor, *The Politics of Law: A Progressive Critique* (New York, 1982), 65–88; and, most recently, James B. Atleson, *Values and Assumptions in American Labor Law* (Amherst, Massachusetts, 1983).

Law and the state

The history of American law has become an area of great interest to scholars in recent years. No book has done more to sustain that interest, nor has any been more controversial in its conclusions, than Morton J. Horwitz's *The Transformation of American Law, 1780–1860* (Cambridge, 1977). Lawrence M. Friedman, *A History of American Law* (New York, 1973), remains a more penetrable survey for non-lawyers. The entire field owes much of its current buoyancy to the tireless labors of J. Willard Hurst, the author of such classics as *Law and the Conditions of Freedom in the Nineteenth Century United States*

(Madison, Wisconsin, 1956). The place of these texts in the historiography of American legal history, and the development of that historiography in the twentieth century, has been explored by Robert W. Gordon in a series of superb articles: "J. Willard Hurst and the Common Law Tradition in American Legal Historiography," *Law and Society Review*, 10 (1975), 9–55; "Historicism in Legal Scholarship," *Yale Law Journal*, 90 (1980–1), 1017–62; and most recently "Critical Legal Histories," *Stanford Law Review*, 36 (1984), 1101–69.

The place of law in the American political economy has been a subject central to the general growth of interest in legal history referred to above. Here the contribution of Harry Scheiber has been of considerable importance. See his *Ohio Canal Era: A Case Study of Government and the Economy, 1820–1861* (Athens, Ohio, 1969); "Public Economic Policy and the American Legal System: Historical Perspectives," *Wisconsin Law Review*, 6 (1980), 1159–89; and "Regulation, Property Rights and Definition of 'The Market': Law and the American Economy," *Journal of Economic History*, 41 (March, 1981), 103–09. On the subject specifically of law and the rise of the corporate economy see the extremely perceptive articles of Charles McCurdy, "Justice Field and the Jurisprudence of Government-Business Relations: Some Parameters of Laissez-faire Constitutionalism," *Journal of American History*, 61, 4 (March, 1975), 970–1005; "American Law and the Marketing Structure of the Large Corporation," *Journal of Economic History*, 38 (September, 1978), 631–49; and "The Knight Sugar Decision of 1895 and the Modernization of American Corporation Law, 1869–1903," *Business History Review*, 53 (1979), 304–43. Also useful in this regard in Jonathan Lurie, *The Chicago Board of Trade: The Dynamics of Self-Regulation* (Urbana, Illinois, 1979).

My understanding of the development of the modern American state has benefitted greatly from first reading Gianfranco Poggi's historical essay *The Development of the Modern State: A Sociological Introduction* (London, 1978). The leading American work is that of Stephen Skowronek, *Building a New American State: The Expansion of National Administrative Capacities* (New York, 1982). Students, however, should also be careful to consult Morton Keller, *Affairs of State: Public Life in Late Nineteenth Century America* (Cambridge, 1977). On the state during the progressive period and the New Era see Thomas K. McGraw, editor, *Regulation in Perspective: Historical Essays* (Cambridge, 1981), particularly the essays by Keller, Ellis Hawley, and McGraw himself. See also Hawley's valuable essay, "Herbert Hoover, the Commerce Secretariat, and the Vision of an 'Associative State'," *Journal of American History*, 61 (1974), 116–40, and the collection edited by Jerry Israel entitled *Building the Organizational Society: Essays on Associational Activities in Modern America* (New York, 1972). Theda Skocpol, "Political Responses to Capitalist Crisis: Neo-Marxist Theories of the State and the Case of the New Deal," *Politics and Society*, 10, 2 (1980), 155–201, offers a sophisticated guide to, and critique of, recent attempts by historians and others to theorize the state with particular reference to the experience of the New Deal. Fred Block, "The Ruling Class Does not Rule," *Socialist Revolution*, 33 (1977), 6–28, and Isaac Balbus, "Commodity Form and Legal Form: An Essay in the Relative Autonomy of the Law," *Law and Society Review*, 11 (Winter, 1977), 571–88, present very different but equally elegant and appealing discussions of the state's relative autonomy.

Index